DARK STAR

The Roy Orbison Story

Ellis Amburn

A LYLE STUART BOOK
Published by Carol Publishing Group

To Al Lowman, with love and gratitude

Copyright © 1990 by Ellis Amburn

A Lyle Stuart Book
Published by Carol Publishing Group

Editorial Offices
600 Madison Avenue
New York, NY 10022

Sales & Distribution Offices
120 Enterprise Avenue
Secaucus, NJ 07094

In Canada: Musson Book Company
A division of General Publishing Co. Limited
Don Mills, Ontario

Manufactured in the United States of America

10 9 8 7 6 5 4 3 2 1

Library of Congress Cataloging-in-Publication Data

Amburn, Ellis.
    Dark star : the Roy Orbison story / Ellis Amburn.
        p.   cm.
    "A Lyle Stuart book."
    Includes bibliographical references (p.   ).
    Discography: p.
    ISBN 0–8184–0518–X : $18.95
    1. Orbison, Roy.   2. Rock musicians—United States—Biography.
I. Title.
ML429.O78A8   1990
782.42166'092—dc20
    [B]   90–1740
                                                             CIP

Acknowledgments

I put 40,000 miles on my Thunderbird, tracking down Roy Orbison's family and friends throughout the American South, the Southwest and the West. Many of them graciously consented to be interviewed for *Dark Star*, and I am especially grateful for the cooperation of Roy's son, Wesley Orbison of Hendersonville, Tennessee. The entire family of Roy's first wife, the late Claudette Frady Orbison, were generous to me, both in terms of interviews and photographs. For two weeks in the winter of 1989, I virtually lived with Claudette's parents, Chester and Geraldine Frady of Crosby, Texas—friendly people with remarkable memories and loving hearts. Roy Orbison's brother-in-law, Bill Frady, and sister-in-law, Paulette Viator, dug deep into their past, much of it painful, for the sake of this book, as did Kadon Frady Mahan, Claudette's cousin and confidante. Patty Maddux, who befriended Claudette when Roy left her, was an interviewer's dream, both in Houston and later in Vernon, Texas.

In Memphis, Tennessee, Roy's producer Sam Phillips, founder of Sun Records, welcomed me into his home, and the transcripts of my marathon session with Sam and his son Knox would make a book in themselves. In Nashville and Hendersonville, Roy's collaborator Joe Melson talked with me off-and-on for a month, as did Paul Garrison, one of The Candymen. Other members of Roy's various bands, including The Wink Westerners and The Teen Kings, also generously contributed their memories of working and playing, and sometimes fighting, with Roy; they include Charles Evans, Billy Pat Ellis, James Morrow and Jack Kennelly (a.k.a. Jackson Kane). Bobby Blackburn, one of Roy's closest friends, talked with me for hours, delving deep into the past despite the pain it cost him. Ms. Braxton Dixon of Hendersonville filled in the missing parts of the Roy Orbison story as no one else ever has, or could; thank you Anna, for a valiant interview. In Texas City Roy's boyhood friend Orbie Lee Harris shared memories as well as photographs. Others I wish to thank for interviews and help of various kinds include:

In Wink, Texas, Roy's home town: Ron Slaughter, Barbara Wilson Slaughter, Anna Slaughter Taylor, Athenia Pierce, Dan Evans, J.L. Dodd, Buddy Gray, Susie Gray, Alisa Gray, Viola "Teach" Bayless, Mildred Howard, Lil Horner, Deputy Sheriff Mo Horton, Cathy Horton, Sandra Wilson. *Kermit, Texas:* Henry Morrow, Ruth Godwin, Bill Beckham, Margaret Beckham, Kathryn Crawford, Mary Mangrum, Bobby Dale Smith, John R. Lee, Patsy Bailey Dixon, G. Gilligan, Rev. Terry Anderson. *Odessa, Texas:* the late Floyd Frady, Annette Bailey Spiers, Frances Payne Long. *Pecos, Texas:* Faye Kingston, Clara Bolling Montgomery. *San Antonio, Texas:* Freddie Gonzales. *Crosby, Texas:* Percy Viator, Frances Gatlin. *Houston, Texas:* Joyce Diane Frady. *Deer Park, Texas:* Bill Mahan. *Elgin, Texas:* Ray Maddux. *Texas City, Texas:* Billie Rash Harris. *Vernon, Texas:* Sonia Evans, Jim Jerome, Deputy Sheriff Larry Lee, Edith Russell McKinney, Frances Russell, Robert Kennedy, Ricky Graf, Vicki Switzer, Mary Coleman, Horace Tabor, Tra Cardwell, Donna Karcher, Mary Jane Rudolph, Yvonna Fox, Sally Hester, Gary Hester, Brad Hester, Paul Jett, Doug Pharis, Jean and Shorty McNeely, Jim Brady, Jennifer Gerred, Krista Bishop, Ms. John Truelove, Guy Orbison, Delores "Dodie" Osden. *Memphis, Tennessee:* Barbara Pittman, Marion Keisker, Willie Gutt, Tim Goodwin, Michael Hanrahan, Roland Janes, Michael J. Carnahan. *Nashville, Hendersonville and Gallatin, Tennessee:* Boots Randolph, Aline Hampton, Joe Towe, Carrie Cash, Tommy Cash, Phylis Garrison, Jerry Harrison, Elizabeth Miller, Anita O'Brian, Tracey Leonard, Melinda Lee, Martha Highfill, Mary Putman, Dagmar Melson, Margaret Rose, Richard K. Rosenberg, Garland Briley, Steve Eng. *Akron, Ohio:* David Shoenfelt. *Los Angeles, California:* Priscilla Presley, Bill Swan, Jennifer McElwain, Peter Dixon, Claudia Turner. *San Francisco, California:* Burt Kaufman. *London, England:* Tony Sanchez.

Robert Burroughs of Staten Island, New York, an authority on Roy Orbison's recordings, contributed the discography which appears at the back of this book. Robert gave me access to his collection of clippings, records and rare video cassettes of Roy Orbison in performance and on TV talk shows. Paul Garrison of Nashville graciously shared his collection of memorabilia. I am also grateful to Ronnie Pugh and Jay Orr of the Country Music Foundation library; Florida Keys Community College library, Key West; the Margaret Herrick Library, Academy of Motion Picture Arts and Sciences, Beverly Hills, California; and to the staffs of the public libraries in Kermit, Texas;

Key West, Florida; Monterey and Carmel, California; Library of the Performing Arts, Lincoln Center, New York City; Memphis, Tennessee. I also wish to thank the staffs of Davis-Kidd Booksellers, Nashville; Tower Records, Nashville; The Keepsake, Baytown, Texas; and David Tibbals at Old Town Sounds, Key West.

Dark Star would not have been possible without the love and patience of my family. My sister Lu Bradbury and mother Belma Amburn of Fort Worth, Texas; my brother Bill Amburn of Lake City, Florida; and my sister-in-law Joyce Amburn and brother-in-law Bill Bradbury all helped me hold my life together during a strenuous year on the road. Thanks to the following friends, I always had a home away from home, as well as the spiritual and emotional support necessary to make it through one day at a time: Jean O'Neill, Wendy Tucker, Cy Egan, Jean Egan, Charles "Buddy" Rodriguez, Tom Taylor, Bill Manville and Michael Browning of Key West; Beverly B. Pemberton of Nashville; David Patrick Columbia, Bob Dolce, Shelley Winters, Michael Edwards and Steven West of Los Angeles; Eugenia Trinkle of Fort Worth; Odell Trammel of Houston; Allston James, Nell Crisante, Bob Malloy, Kim Novak, Pepper James, Martha Mosher and Scott Campbell of Carmel; Mireya Juarez and Rev. Terry and Ms. Anderson of Kermit; Dan Evans, Chris Evans, Amy Evans, Woody Evans and Zack Evans of Wink.

I have dedicated this book to my agent Al Lowman because of his belief in me and for his guidance as I made the transition in the last few years from editor to writer. I also appreciate the courtesy and constant help of his staff, Brian Moore, Laurie Liss, Doug Kirkpatrick and B.G. Dilworth III.

In Key West, where this book was written, Wendy Tucker and Cy Egan, both gifted writers, shared their knowledge and love with me. Steven Gaines of New York, a leading rock 'n' roll biographer, is another valued mentor.

My job as a biographer is to bring together different or varying perceptions of the same events. In telling the story of Roy Orbison, I have drawn from many interviews with the people who were involved in the key events of his life, as well as from his own statements to the press about those events.

I wish to acknowledge for Roy Orbison's own words, journalists, television personalities, broadcasters and authors who interviewed him over the years, especially Roy Trakin, Greg Mitchell, Steve Pond, Martin Ashton, Glenn A. Baker, Joe Smith, Jesse Nash, Kerry Doole,

Keith Briscoe, Solange De Santis, Bob Claypool, John Paul Pitts, David Hinckley, Bill Beckham, Jim Dickerson, Colin Escott, Peter Goddard, Michael Goldberg, Jeffery Ressner, Martin Hawkins, Robert Hillburn, James Hunter, Michael McCall, Jim Sullivan, Chris O'Neill, Simon Dee, Brian Matthew, John Dunn, Jay Leno, Joan Rivers, James Darren and Malcolm Boyes. All Orbison fans can be grateful to Jon Findley, executive in charge of production, and Linda Corradina, excutive producer MTV, for putting together the memorable *VH1: A Tribute to Roy Orbison,* and to Alan Clayson, author of *Only the Lonely,* for his portrait of Roy in Britain.

At Lyle Stuart, Carole Stuart commissioned this book and encouraged me; Bruce Shostak, a brilliant editor, pushed me to do my best; and Fern Edison, Ben Petrone and Jessica Black lent enthusiastic support. I am fortunate to have a publisher, Steven Schragis, of great energy and vision. To all of them, and to my British publishers Clare Bristow and Eric Major of New English Library, my heartfelt thanks.

Chapter 1

When Roy Orbison went on stage in England one night in the spring of 1966, he was nervous and frightened. Although he was one of the most popular male vocalists in the world and he had a string of hit records like "Running Scared" and "Oh, Pretty Woman" behind him, the audience had just gone wild over his warm-up act, The Walker Brothers, who had a current #1 hit called "The Sun Ain't Gonna Shine Anymore" and were younger and better-looking than Roy. On another British tour a few years before, The Beatles had demoted Roy from top billing and he was afraid of being upstaged again. But when Roy Orbison launched into "Only the Lonely" that night at Finsbury Park, the audience screamed and cheered and he realized his worries were groundless. Though Roy wasn't the sort anyone would look at twice, with his pale skin, double chin, eye glasses and frozen stance in front of the microphone, everyone fell in love with him the moment he started to sing. It wasn't just that he had what Elvis Presley described as the best voice in the world, it was that he sang with breath-catching conviction, taking his rapt audiences on an emotional joyride. Few other pop singers of the 20th century had the same vocal expressiveness and power to scream away the pain of heartbreak.

After this triumphant performance, Roy accepted an invitation to participate in a celebrity motorcycle race at Hawkstone Park. Roy said he'd loved motorcycles ever since he'd first seen Elvis Presley's parked outside Sun Records in Memphis a decade earlier. Though deceptively quiet and polite, Roy Orbison was hell on wheels, whether he was roaring around on a Harley or terrorizing motorists on the highway, challenging them to race his Ferrari. At the British celebrity motorcycle event, Roy took unnecessary chances and paid the price of his recklessness. After a gale blew up, he was advised not to participate in the race because his $750,000 insurance policy prohibited him from competing in bad weather. He had to content himself with conventional duties at the finish line, but it was clear to observers that Roy

1

was frustrated and disgruntled. He finally persuaded veteren biker Dave Bickers to let him take his 250 cc Czechoslovakian motorcycle around the track. Though Roy was wearing a cumbersome raincoat, he couldn't resist the opportunity to show off in front of the audience of 15,000. He even kept his dark glasses on under his helmet, hoping fans would recognize him by his trademark Ray Bans. He was right—a cheer went up the moment he appeared on the bike. He rode about 200 yards before he skidded and was violently thrown from his motorcycle. Though he heard bones cracking, his vanity compelled him to climb back on and complete the turn around the track. Later, scores of fans flocked to the pits, and though he was in agony, he signed their autograph books and souvenir programs. Roy limped from the pit and was loaded into his car. Gangs of mods and rockers escorted him to London's Thorpe Coombe General Hospital, where a doctor confirmed that Roy indeed had broken his ankle.

The incident is a symbol of the paradoxical life of rock 'n' roll's most mysterious and tragic figure, Roy Orbison. Though he seemed a gentle, soft-spoken person, he was as dangerous as a loose cannon, and within a few weeks of his motorcycle injury, his young wife Claudette was involved in a far worse motorcycle accident. No wonder Bruce Springsteen, an Orbison fan and also a motorcycle-accident victim, coined the term "suicide machines" in his song "Born to Run." Motorcycles were just one of the lethal addictions that helped destroy not only Roy's life but the lives of many of the people around him. Like his great peers Edith Piaf, Janis Joplin, Judy Garland, Elvis Presley, Sam Cooke, Jackie Wilson, Jimi Hendrix and Jim Morrison, Roy Orbison did not live out a full, normal life. He died at the age of fifty-two on December 6, 1988, driven by self-destructive forces that he never managed—or even seriously attempted—to control.

Roy came from Depression-torn West Texas, where he was born on April 23, 1936, in the small town of Vernon, located on the path of the Old Chisholm Trail. "If my story is ever to be really told," Roy once said, "it would include how my parents walked across Oklahoma in the Depression, walked all the way, and how they found a cigarette they shared most of the way." Roy's father, Orbie Lee Orbison, was an unemployed oil-field driller, and his mother, Nadine Schultz, was a sensitive, kindly girl who liked to paint and write poetry and who had been married and divorced before she'd met Orb. When Nadine and Orb met in the 1930s, they drifted from Oklahoma to Floydada, Texas, and then to Vernon, desperately searching for work. In their wanderings, they ran into another poor, proud family, the Harrises, with whom they became such close friends that they were really one big clan. When they hit a new town, the Orbisons and the Harrises settled in the same neighborhood, helped each other find jobs, usually ended up in the same oilfields and went fishing together. Their children were constant playmates and everyone who knew them thought they were first cousins. Roy's older brother Grady Lee, born in 1933, was exactly the same age as the older Harris boy, Melvin, and Roy's best friend was the younger Harris boy, Orbie Lee, who was named after Roy's father.

Roy wore glasses from a very early age, and Orbie Lee Harris remembers how and when it was discovered Roy needed them. One day they were sitting on the front porch of the Harrises' house in Vernon, playing with their crayons and coloring book, and Roy annoyed Orbie Lee by insisting on holding the book upside down. Though Roy didn't yet realize it, his vision was going haywire, and he was trying to bring the coloring book into focus by holding it at different angles. At the age of four he was fitted with thick bifocals, and when he peered from behind the lenses, his eyes looked like BB's. As Roy grew up he came to despise the way he looked, finally hiding his "beady eyes" behind dark glasses.

In Vernon, the Orbisons shared a duplex on Bowie Street with Frances and Clois Russell and their four children. "This was wide open country and we got the big dust storms," Frances recalls. "It was so dusty you could write your name on any surface in the house. We'd hang wet towels in the windows to act as filters." Orbie Lee Orbison and Clois Russell labored together in the oil patch, and after work they'd sit outside with their wives and kids and enjoy a big fish fry. Dinner over, Clois would get out his guitar and he and Orb would sing late into the evening. On hot summer nights Roy and the little Russell girl, Edith, would lie on pallets on the grass, and Roy would drift off to sleep to the soft, melodic sound of his father's voice. Another playmate was a little boy he knew in the first and second grades named Coyt Webb, and Roy exhibited the first sign of a whimsical sense of humor when he said, "You were flyin' around and got 'coyt' in a 'webb.'"

Edith Russell says it was her father who first put Roy's fingers on the strings of a guitar, but most likely it was Orb or his brother Charlie Orbison or Nadine's brother, Uncle Kenneth, all of whom played the guitar. Orb and Clois played and sang for country dances in the area, and Uncle Kenneth sang on the radio in Vernon. "He was real good," Frances Russell recalls, "and Kenneth Schultz could have gone far if he'd had anybody to help him." As Roy's sixth birthday approached, Orb asked him what he wanted for a present, and Roy replied, "I want a harmonica." "Wouldn't you rather have a guitar?" Orb asked.

Roy's Sears guitar had a picture of Gene Autry on it. Orb taught Roy the basic chords, following the fretboard symbols on the sheet music to "You Are My Sunshine." "From the very first moment," Roy said, "it was me *and* the guitar playing *and* singing." Though his left hand was still too small to shape a chord, he managed to play and sing "You Are My Sunshine," which was probably the one country song everyone in America knew by heart in the 1940s. Originally recorded in 1939 by Paul and Hoke Rice, it hit the charts in cover versions by both Gene Autry and Bing Crosby, but it was when Jimmie Davis adopted it as his campaign song in his successful bid for the governorship of Louisiana that "You Are My Sunshine" achieved unprecedented popularity and became one of the most played commercial songs in history. Country music, heretofore restricted to the hills of Appalachia, Nashville's Grand Ole Opry and the plains of Texas, made a quantum leap into the mainstream of American popular culture.

"My first music was country," Roy said. "I grew up with country music in Texas." The '30s and '40s were the heyday of live radio performances, with The Carter Family broadcasting from Del Rio, Texas, singing "Shall the Circle Be Unbroken" and "I'm Thinking Tonight of My Blue Eyes." And from Nashville's radio station WSM came the Grand Ole Opry's Roy Acuff singing "The Great Speckled Bird"; Minnie Pearl telling jokes about Brother, her boyfriend Hezzie, and her Uncle Nabob; and the Duke of Paducah signing off with his famous line, "I'm going to the wagon, boys, these shoes are killing me." Roy grew up listening to these beloved radio personalities, and the country ethos was so deeply embedded in him that years later, when he started making records, the great recording center he would be drawn to was not New York or Hollywood, but Nashville, Tennessee, home of *The Opry*. To anyone who grew up during these years in the South or Southwest, within earshot of WSM's 50,000-watt tower, Nashville was the musical mecca.

Stuart Hamblen, who would one day have a great hit record called "This Old House," had a brother, A.K., who taught school in Vernon when Roy was in the primary grades there. According to Frances

Russell, it was A.K. Hamblen who first encouraged Roy to sing. "A.K. Hamblen was a religious man," Francess Russell recalls, "and we liked to get him started on the Bible. He'd sing Stuart Hamblen songs and tell Bible stories and we'd miss the whole class. He got Roy to singin' when he was a little kid."

Roy's fascination with automobiles, another lifelong interest, also began in childhood. Orb went to work as a car mechanic when he lost his job in the oil field, and Grady Lee and Roy would come to the garage and stand watching their dad as he worked. Both boys learned how to take an engine apart and reassemble it, and Orb permitted them to drive the cars that were brought in for repair, as long as they stayed in low gear. Years before Roy ever took a car out on the highway, he had mastered the basic skills of driving.

By 1942, there wasn't enough work in Vernon for Orb to support his family, and they had to move on to Fort Worth, Texas, where jobs were available in the defense plants. The U.S. had entered World War II in 1941, and the big B-24 and B-32 bombers were being manufactured at the huge Consolidated Vultee aircraft plant adjacent to the Fort Worth Army Air Force Base. Here, both Orb and his friend "Double O" Harris were employed as sheet-metal workers, and their wives, Nadine and Opal, got jobs as riveters.

Roy said goodbye to his Vernon grade-school chums and made the day-long trip to Fort Worth with his family. Approaching the city, Roy saw skyscrapers rising from the prairie like the jeweled spires of Oz. Fort Worth was both modern metropolis and Old West cowtown, home of the famous Swift & Armour stockyards that were the final destination of the cattle shipped in from ranches all over Texas. The stockyards were located on the rough north side of town, and it was here that the Orbisons found an inexpensive apartment over a drug store. The Harrises settled in an apartment several blocks away.

For kids on the homefront, like Roy Orbison and Orbie Lee Harris, World War II was scary and exciting and suspenseful, especially the first year, when Wake, Manila, Bataan and Corregidor all fell to the Japanese. At school Roy and Orbie Lee Harris were the first to buy war stamps. They also started going to the movies together, and they especially liked the patriotic war films which played in the neighborhood second-run house, The New Isis. Roy became a lifelong movie addict, and when he grew up and could afford it, he often saw three films a day.

Orbie Lee Harris remembers the fun he and Roy had going on

adventures around Fort Worth. One day they found a Red Cross poster card with slots cut to hold donated coins. They used it for their own profit by holding it out to grownups on the street, and everyone, especially soldiers, obliged by patriotically fitting coins into the slots. They developed another money-making scheme when Orbie Lee's mother, Opal Harris, who worked at Renfro's Drug Store, brought home an entire case of Hershey bars. Due to wartime rationing, chocolate was scarce and always disappeared quickly from the stores. Appropriating Opal Harris's Hershey bars, Orbie Lee and Roy took them to the train station and sold them at huge profits to soldiers leaving on the troop trains. Opal Harris also let Roy and Orbie Lee come into the Renfro Drug Store where she worked and explore the contents of the huge magazine rack. They fell in love with comic books, and their favorites were DC Comics' Superman and Batman.

Roy acquired his obsession with airplanes from his father, who showed him how to identify Consolidated's big bombers, the B-24 and B-32, and Howard Hughes's spectacular P-38 twin-boom fighter plane as they soared over the stockyards. Roy's passion for building model airplanes began around this time, and he never outgrew it. But the childhood enthusiasm that had the strongest impact on Roy was the country music that poured from every jukebox in Fort Worth. "I was influenced by country ballads I heard in the early years during the war," Roy said, "songs like 'Born to Lose' and 'No Letter Today.'" Perfectly catching the loneliness and isolation of West Texas, Ted Daffan's "Born to Lose" was one of the key songs in the growth of country music in America, becoming a top jukebox smash of the war years, along with Ernest Tubb's "I'm Walkin' the Floor Over You" and Gene Sullivan's "When My Blue Moon Turns to Gold Again." "Ernest Tubb used to advertise milk in those days," Roy recalled, "singing off the back of a truck in Fort Worth when I was there."

In Fort Worth, Roy also heard plenty of Western swing, a genre of country music which started when Bob Wills and The Light Crust Doughboys sang "My Adobe Hacienda" and "Mexicali Rose" on local radio stations WBAP and KFJZ. "I used to sing Bob Wills's 'Dusty Skies,'" Roy recalled. "Dusty Skies" was composed by Cindy Walker, and when Roy became a recording star years later, Cindy gave Roy one of his greatest hits, "Dream Baby."

Using the cheap guitar his father had given him, Roy learned to pick out the hit songs of the day, including Bob Wills's "San Antonio Rose," which went to #7 on the '41 pop charts in a cover version by

Bing Crosby. Describing the difference between the pop and country charts, Roy once said, "A huge country can sell 60,000, whereas you have to sell 300-400,000 to get into the pop charts." He was beginning to dream of a career as a singer, and he had a vision that music would wrest him from poverty and take him to the heights of riches, glamour and fame. He described the prime catalytic experience of his life in an interview published posthumously in *Rolling Stone* magazine, telling reporter Steve Pond, "We lived in Fort Worth, Texas, and Mom and Dad were both working in a defense plant during WWII. It was a good place for relatives and everybody came by and played music. It was a time of intense emotion—the boys were going to one front or the other of the war, more than likely to be killed. And so when they were drinking, they'd drink with gusto, and when they were singing, they sang with all their hearts, and I got to stay up with these guys and sing.

"I guess that level of intensity made a big impression on me, because it's still there. That sense of 'do it for all it's worth and do it now and do it good.' Not to analyze it too much, but I think the verve and gusto that everybody felt and portrayed around me has stayed with me all this time."

The sense of urgency he retained from that experience would spark every performance Roy Orbison ever gave. He kept his delivery utterly fresh over the years. Even when "Only the Lonely" and "Crying" were decades old, he was still performing them with all the electricity and excitement of the very first time. But the most revealing comment in connection with his wartime epiphany was Roy's observation: "That's probably my life story as far as people and music is concerned—a great good time was had by all before possibly dying." That was Roy's own version of "Eat, drink and be merry, for tomorrow you may die," reflecting his attitude that it was okay to be reckless since there was little to lose during those years of poverty.

It's intriguing that Roy, a youngster not yet 10 years old, was permitted to stay up late and entertain drunken soldiers in the Orbison home. No wonder he grew up with a compulsive, obsessive and addictive nature. Within five years, he would be singing to drunks for money, working in the honky tonks of West Texas with his first band, The Wink Westerners. As had his father and mother, Roy would become a cigarette smoker, and he once tried a drink in childhood. Roy told a reporter from *New Musical Express* on December 20, 1980, "I had a big drink of whiskey once. I asked my father what it was. I said, 'Can I have some?' and he said, 'Sure.' So I slugged back a big shot of whiskey, and I think I was sick for days. So that turned me off drink forever. I still don't drink." Roy's claim of abstinence is at variance with other statements he made throughout his career, indicating that he did drink, and with his December 21, 1961, contract with Amicable Life Insurance Company of Waco, Texas, in which he wrote "Very slightly" after the question, "To what extent do you use alcoholic beverages?"

Though Roy's first musical influence was country, he was also exposed to the great 1940s flowering of popular music, which drew heavily on classical sources. The strains of Tchaikovsky were first heard across the Texas plains in the early '40s, when Freddy Martin's "Tonight We Love," adapted from Piano Concerto No. 1 in B-flat Minor, held on in the #1 spot on *Your Hit Parade* for eight weeks. The big Chopin craze of 1945 was stirred up by the film biography *A Song to Remember*, starring Cornel Wilde and Merle Oberon. The movie kicked off a year of Chopin hits by Jose Iturbi, Carmen Cavallaro and Perry Como, who called his vocal cover of the Polonaise "Till the End of Time." Many of the top hits of the '40s had Latin rhythms, such as Jimmy Dorsey's "Amopola" and "Maria Elena," and both these influences, classical and Latin, are to be found in Roy Orbison's unique contribution to rock 'n' roll, his great operatic ballads of the 1960s.

Around 1944, a polio epidemic hit Fort Worth so severely that Roy and his brother Grady Lee were sent back to Vernon to live with Nadine's mother. Grandmother Schultz had divorced her husband, an alcoholic, but he still lived in Vernon and the boys felt free to visit him whenever they wished. According to Orbie Lee Harris, despite the grandparents' divorce, the Orbison family was a big, loving, supportive group.

As the war wound down, workers began to be laid off in Fort Worth. Once again Nadine and Orb were on the move. They packed up their belongings and returned to Vernon, as did the Harrises, and were reunited with Roy and Grady Lee. In Vernon, there was a radio station, KVWC, which had a talent show, and Roy set his sights on crashing radio. All those nights that he sang for soldiers in Fort Worth now paid off. Roy bicycled to the studio, signed up to compete on an amateur show and sang "You Are My Sunshine." He was a truly peculiar sight, a cotton-headed, skinny kid who stood on a box to reach the microphone. But when he opened his mouth to sing, everyone in the studio stopped and stared, wondering how in the world such a big voice could emanate from such a small boy. He not only won his own spot on the show as featured vocalist but became its regular host. According to Roy, he received no pay, but he was happy to have the experience. Around this time, Roy wrote his first song, "A Vow of Love." "I wasn't mature enough to follow that through," Roy remembered. "I wrote it in front of my grandmother's house. I just hadn't been through enough to write a song. I started a radio show at about the same time—KVWC, Vernon, Texas, singing the same songs every Saturday."

In 1946, he received his first payment for singing. A traveling medicine show came to Vernon, a makeshift stage was set up, and colored lights were strung over rows of benches. A huckster advertised health potions, skits were performed, and the audience was invited to participate in a talent show. As a local radio star, Roy entered the contest, but as the time for his public debut neared, he was panic-stricken. Bravely, he launched into his first number, a hillbilly drinking song called "Good Ole Mountain Dew," by the Grand Ole Opry's "Grandpa" Louis Jones. The audience loved him and he then sang "Jole Blon," a Cajun tune that was one of his all-time favorites. "That was the song that did it for me," Roy said. He tied a fifteen-year-old for the fifteen-dollar prize. "My buddy went with me," Roy said, "and carried my guitar and rooted for me, so he figured he ought to have half. That was my first taste of a manager."

In 1946, the war over, soldiers started drifting back home, and no one caught their despair more poignantly than the honky-tonk singers of Texas. One of them, Lefty Frizzell, became Roy Orbison's first musical hero and role model. Both Hank Williams and Lefty Frizzell played in dives throughout the South and Southwest, and Roy caught one of Lefty's stage shows when he was ten years old. The impact of honky-tonk music on Roy was profound and can be heard in most of the lyrics he would later write. Before the advent of the Texas honky-tonk style, country music was about a soft kind of love, all about sweethearts. Now it was about fornication, betrayal, shattered dreams and booze; it mirrored reality. In the same way American acting was about to receive a shot of honesty from Montgomery Clift, Marlon Brando and The Actors Studio, country music was transformed by the realism of postwar honky-tonk music. Disillusioned, drunken WWII veterans at last found a music they could relate to, and bar owners were quick to notice that customers drank more when there was a band around. Accompanied by drums, steel guitar, electric guitars and bass, honky-tonk singers soon dominated the entire country scene. Their nasal moan became the most familiar sound in country & western. The big hits of the late 1940s were Tex Williams' "Smoke! Smoke! Smoke!," the Sons of the Pioneers' "Cigareets, Whusky and Wild, Wild Women," Lefty Frizzell's "How Far Down Can I Go" and Kitty Wells's "It Wasn't God Who Made Honky Tonk Angels."

But it was Hank Williams, with hits like "Honky Tonk Blues" and "Lovesick Blues," who emerged as the all-time king of country & western. Roy Orbison loved to hear his dad sing Hank's classics like "Jambalaya" and "Your Cheatin' Heart," and Hank was one of only two songwriters Roy Orbison would devote an entire LP to (the other one was Don Gibson). Born in Mount Olive, Alabama, in 1923, Hank was a sad youth who started drinking at 14 and was an alcoholic by fifteen. His meteoric career in Nashville ended when he overdosed on morphine and alcohol, dying in the back seat of his Cadillac at the age of twenty-nine.

In the mid-1940s, Orb was again out of work, and so was his friend Double O Harris. Double O said he'd heard there was work way down in the middle of the Permian Basin, in a remote shanty town called Wink, Texas. Both families set out across the barren prairie, where the only signs of life were lazy pumpjacks nodding up and down on well heads and tumbleweeds rolling crazily across the highway, coming to rest against barbed wire fences. As they approached Wink they saw a sprawling tank farm, and then, around a curve, a ragtag collection of shotgun shacks. They seemed to have landed in the middle of nowhere, but if it was any comfort, they were just fifty miles from larger towns like Odessa and Pecos. The people who founded Wink in the 1920s figured if they named their town after the local Civil War hero, Col. C.M. Winkler, they'd become the county seat. But that honor went to nearby Kermit, and Wink was stuck forever with its quirky name. Like Seminole, Borger and Burkburnett, Texas, Wink started as an oil-boom town, with a population that mushroomed to 30,000 overnight. By the time Roy Orbison got there the population, devastated by the Depression, was about 1,800.

Roy spoke of Wink with cool disdain to the reporters who interviewed him after he became famous. When Keith Briscoe of *The Odessa American* asked him why he didn't come back to his home area more often, Roy chillingly replied, "I always thought of West Texas as a little out of the way. I especially thought that when I lived there. You know, I wrote 'Only the Lonely' in West Texas." Roy's little brother Sammy Keith, born in the late '40s, still refers to Wink with icy contempt, and Billy Pat Ellis, who would be in Roy's first band, felt that he had escaped to paradise when he shook the dust of Wink from his boots and headed for Oregon. In 1988, Roy told *Rolling Stone*: "It's really hard to describe, but I'll give you a few things: it was macho guys working in the oil field, and football, and oil and grease and sand and being a stud and being cool. I got out of there as quick as I could, and I resented having to be there, but it was a great education. It was tough as could be, but no illusions. No mysteries in Wink.

"If you saw the film *Giant*, it was filmed 80 miles out of Wink. There's nothing. No trees, no lakes, no creeks, a few bushes. Between Wink and Odessa, where I used to drive all the time, one of the towns is called Notrees, Texas. And it has trees. But Wink was an oil-boom town, there was one movie theatre, two drug stores, one pool hall and one hardware store, and that was about it. In fact, the Sears, what you did was go to this little office and look at the catalog."

Roy's bitterness about Wink stems from the ridicule he was subjected to there as a shy, sensitive, standoffish child. Roy despised Wink so much that he disclaimed it when he became famous, telling interviewers that he came from Odessa. But in some deep place in his consciousness he also harbored a love for Wink, for this is where his dark star began to rise.

When the Orbisons arrived in Wink, followed shortly by the Harris family, they immediately discovered that housing was hard to come by. Many of the residents lived out at the camps in company-owned shacks, but the Orbisons and the Harrises didn't yet have jobs, so they had to search for quarters in the town itself. Both families finally settled in the run-down Townsend Apartments, famous for having the only shade tree in Wink. The Orbisons had an indoor toilet but the Harrises had to use a two-seater outhouse. The Townsend Apartments faced what was left of Wink's red-light district—a pool hall, still in use, and some abandoned saloons and whorehouses.

Oil-field workers like Orbie Lee Orbison, who was a driller and tool pusher, were paid only $1.36 an hour, so Nadine had to go to work as well—usually menial jobs like waitressing in cafes, but later she would become a licensed vocational nurse in Wink and nearby Kermit. Roy was once again left to fend for himself, and to make some pocket money he and Orbie Lee Harris opened up a bicycle-repair shop. With a keen sense for the value of advertising, they plastered signs all over Wink to promote their garage operation. "We didn't know a thing about bikes," Orbie Lee confessed, "and they were often in better shape when they came in than when they went out."

Unlike Vernon, Wink was too little to have a radio station, and Roy missed singing on radio shows. "Roy did his first singing in Wink at The Derrick Hotel," said Bobby Blackburn, whose enterprising parents, Jim and Violet, not only ran The Derrick but also, at various times, the local hardware store and The Day Drug Store. Violet Blackburn also taught English at the local school. "Daddy let Roy sing for Mother's parties," Bobby recalls. "Mother was a social climber but the Orbisons couldn't help her up the social ladder, so she didn't like Roy. He would sing bawdy party songs he'd learned from soldiers in WWII, like my-girl's-a-corker-she's-a-New-Yorker, that kind of thing. Roy was so little he couldn't carry his guitar by himself, so I'd help him and he'd share his tips with me. There was a pretty girl named Susie Newbert and we'd get Susie and all walk over Wink and out to the Humble camp and Roy was singing the whole way. When Roy first got to Wink, he liked to sleep under the stars, so we'd pitch a bed roll between two houses and sleep outside, laugh all night, listen to country music, smoke cigarettes and watch people coming home from The Rig Theatre. A kid named Joe Ray Hammer had given us smokin' lessons at the tennis courts at the school. We'd lay there and smoke and Roy would tell me how I ought to marry Susie Newbert when I grew up."

The town's main drag had a wooden sidewalk and a row of stores. There was an overhang the length of the sidewalk, and shingles dangled from it at regular intervals, identifying the electric company (today the city hall), The Rig Theatre, Haynes Barber Shop, Blackburn Hardware, The Sports Den and Central Drug. Roy and Bobby would get on their bicycles and race down the sidewalk, hitting every shingle and trying to get to the last one before they stopped swinging. Merchants found this a nuisance and drove nails into the shingles, filing the heads off so that both ends were sharp. "It was a shredder," Bobby says. "You only had to hit that once. Both of us got bloody nubs."

Across the street was the intersection they called "The Crotch," and that was where Ms. Blackburn ran The Day Drug. Just as Ms. Harris had done in Fort Worth, Ms. Blackburn permitted Roy and Bobby to read the store's inventory of comic books free of charge. "Mother liked to see kids read," Bobby said. "She was gonna have to teach them English pretty soon and it was easier if they could read."

Old men sat on the benches in front of the stores in Wink, talking, whittling wood and chewing tobacco. It looked like a pretty good life to Bobby and Roy, except, as Bobby said, "Their 'thangs' didn't work any more." Roy and Bobby started referring to the old men as "deadpeckers." "They always seemed to be having a good time," Bobby recalls, "so Roy and I laid out our retirement plan. We were going to be deadpeckers together some day."

"I used to pitch Roy quarters over there at Day Drug on Main Street," said Charles Ogle, a neighbor who still lives in Wink. "He used to play the guitar there when he was a little-bitty twerp. The roughnecks would come in after they got off work, and Roy would sit up on a stool and sing every day after school. And them roughnecks and us, we'd pitch quarters at him." Ogle described Roy as "a pale, scrawny kid who couldn't make the football team and sometimes got picked on by bullies." Another neighbor, Ken Brodnax, who today lives in Odessa, added, "Tell you the truth, listening to him was better than looking at him."

People laughed at this strange looking kid whose dishwater-blond hair, frizzed by the West Texas wind, stood up like a frayed boll of cotton. But one person who didn't laugh was Viola "Teach" Bayless, a young teacher severely crippled by polio. "Roy had a real nice smile," Ms. Bayless recalls. Many people called Roy an albino, but Ms. Bayless said he couldn't have been. "Albinos have pink eyes," she said, "and Roy's eyes definitely were not pink."

The center of life in Wink was the school, a handsome art-deco red brick building, the only solid architectural entity in this jerry-built town. Roy had been in and out of schools since the first grade, but the Wink school was different. It was a proud and splendid place with an ample budget, thanks to the big tank farm that sat on the edge of town. The Houston drillers had to pay tax on all the oil stored in those tanks, creating a multi-million-dollar tax base for the school. The Wink school was outstanding, then and even today, because it offered good salaries and attracted top teachers. In the '40s and '50s, the school was known throughout West Texas for its music department, marching band and virtually unbeatable football team, The Wink Wildcats. In this down-and-out town, the Wink school was as paradoxical a presence as a feudal castle rising from the squalor of a medieval village.

Roy and Orbie Lee Harris entered the Wink school in the fourth grade. Orbie Lee fit in right away, as did Grady Lee Orbison, Roy's brother, who played football on the junior high football team, The Wink Kittens. Orbie Lee and Grady Lee were both little ruffians, but withdrawn, skinny Roy was in for trouble. Classmate John Paul Pitts said that Roy had "a perpetual grin, loved to tease, tell jokes and come up with catch phrases like 'mercy...mercy.'" When it was learned he could play the guitar, Roy made his debut at school with "a few strums during intermission of the high school's performance of *Corn's a Poppin'*." But it was a tough school and when the kids made fun of Roy's "four eyes," he started clamming up, his short-lived joie de vivre dampened for life. Under attack, bewildered and confused, Roy drew further into himself, and, as classmate Helen Morton put it, "He didn't play like other kids. During recess, the rest of us would be roller-skating, playing jacks, jumping rope and stuff, but not Roy. He played his guitar. He was a quiet type. He had those thick glasses. Kids picked on him. It took a lot to push him. He wasn't scared, though. When he had had enough, he would fight."

After school each day, a congenial trio of playmates—Roy, Orbie Lee Harris and Bobby Blackburn—convened at The Townsend Apartments. Sometimes their big brothers Grady Lee Orbison and Melvin Harris joined them, teaching them how to handle a football. Grady Lee was already a gridiron star, and Roy looked forward to the day when he too could join the football team. In Texas, football players were idolized even above movie stars and troubadors, and Wink High had sent two champs, the Ezell brothers, to Texas Christian University in Fort Worth, home of Hall of Famers Davey O'Brien and Sammy Baugh.

Though Roy would never excel in sports, his other gifts were beginning to be noticed. Besides singing, he could draw pictures amazingly well. When he was in the fourth grade, around Christmastime, he brought to school a greeting card with a painting of Santa Claus and his reindeer on it and recreated a gigantic version of the scene on the blackboard. The teacher was so impressed that she told principal R.A. Lipscomb and, one by one, every class in school trooped through the fourth grade home room, admiring Roy's spectacular creation.

The school-wide attention Roy attracted with his singing and drawing proved a mixed blessing, earning him a measure of fame but also making him a target for even more ridicule and scorn. "Roy wanted to be accepted," classmate Ronnie Slaughter said. "In Wink, you had to fight your way in. Roy took all the needling and the barbs. Finally, he blew up and took a stand and had his first fight, with Pooky Blakeney. Roy had small eyes and poor vision and wore thick glasses and when he took off those glasses and stood toe-to-toe with Pooky, he couldn't see anything." A crowd gathered around as Pooky tore into Roy. Roy handed his glasses to a classmate and said, "Point me at him." "The fight lasted the whole noon period," Ronnie says, "but only two blows were struck. Roy couldn't see anything and started windmilling. The only time he hit Pooky was when Pooky was close enough for him to smell."

Football star Bobby Gann once told Roy, "*Your face looks like my ass.*" The guys who overheard him say it started calling Roy "Facetus," and the loathesome nickname stuck, spreading like wildfire through school and town. By the end of the term, when the yearbook came out, Roy was so used to being called Facetus that he used the name in autographing his friends' copies. "Roy tried so hard to be one of the boys," Ronnie Slaughter remembers. "A bunch of us were swimming one day and he took a dive off the high board and broke his neck. His eyesight was so bad he couldn't even see where he was diving, and he hit a big airplane inner tube we used as a float. He would do anything to prove himself. He was in a neck brace all year."

By junior high school, Roy had recovered sufficiently to go out for The Wink Kitten football team. The Kittens were the feeder team to the famous Wildcats, and under coach Glen Frazier, The Wildcats were the champs of the Permian Basin. Grady Lee Orbison was now on the high-school varsity team, and everywhere the Wildcats played, The Wink Kittens always played the night before. In September 1950, on the eve of the first home game at Wildcat Field, Roy posed for a photo in his uniform, in back of the bleachers, with Orbie Lee Harris and classmate Barna Richards. Barna was already lanky and tall, and Orbie Lee was crouched and ready, looking ferocious. As for Roy, despite the helmet and shoulder pads, he looked fragile, posing no threat with his matchstick legs, vulnerable, open-mouthed smile and thick eyeglasses.

"He didn't know how to walk and chew gum at the same time," said Ronnie Slaughter, who made the varsity team. "When Roy went out for junior-high football, it was a total disaster. They knocked his head off." There were no face guards in those days, and Roy had difficulty keeping his glasses on during a play. After a few games, and many cuts, bruises and bone-jarring jolts, he realized he would never survive a season on the football field. His disappointment cut to the quick. Now he had to stand on the sidelines and watch his classmates and his own brother, Grady Lee, make the grade. A boy who didn't play football in Texas wasn't exactly a sissy, but he had no status. It seemed like Roy had to settle for second-class citizenship in Wink, and he would never forget or forgive this town for what it denied him.

Years of mockery left Roy's self-esteem in shreds. Referring to his adolescence in Wink, he said "the intensity of your emotions is something awe-inspiring, no matter how painful it might sometimes seem. I believe that none of us ever really grows out of that." Throughout his life he suffered from insecurity and chronic shyness. Although shyness is thought to be a minor problem by everyone except those who suffer from it, the shy know that it is a tortuous mental and emotional disorder, a degree of insanity that holds them back from experiencing life fully. Without the intervention of blind circumstance, it is virtually impossible for shy people to break through their reserve and initiate relationships with other people. Fate deals a double whammy to those who are both shy and unattractive, and tragically the two conditions often come in the same package, as they did in Roy Orbison.

Genetics had not been kind to Roy. Though Roy and Grady Lee bore a strong family resemblance—Grady Lee even had the same comical big ears—a slight but crucial genetic variation was turning Grady Lee Orbison into a good-looking kid. A shock of light brown hair tumbled over a broad, masculine forehead. Electric eyes, lighter than his skin, glinted with fun and deviltry, and a button nose set his face off perfectly. When Grady smiled, enviable creases appeared in his cheeks. Even as a child he had a thick, muscular neck, and though he would never be large, he had an athletic build, with broad shoulders and narrow hips and a springy, nimble stance.

Roy on the other hand was flabby and bottom-heavy, with unattractive, unruly hair. Though nature had given him a voice that one day would be hailed as the greatest instrument in rock 'n' roll, in the looks department he definitely got short-changed. To escape people's jeers he often retreated to the darkness of The Rig movie theatre. Classmate Charles "Slob" Evans and his mother ran The Rig, and Slob befriended Roy. Though a football player and a class favorite, Slob was kind and sympathetic and didn't tease Roy. Unlike Ronnie Slaughter, Slob remembers Roy as being "tough as a boot, someone you wouldn't mess with." Billy Pat Ellis was another varsity athlete who became a close friend of Roy's. Billy Pat was a basketball star, but he says today that he didn't take the same condescending attitude toward Roy as the other Wink jocks did "because I was just as funny-looking as Roy. I was tall and skinny and had pimples."

There was something else drawing these young men together, and it was their mutual love of music. Roy, Bobby Blackburn, Charles and Billy Pat all joined the Wink marching band, which was the pride of Wink, second only to the Wildcat football team. Roy fell under the influence of the band's talented baritone-horn player, a musical prodigy named Joe Ray Hammer, and Roy too took up the baritone horn. It had been Joe Ray who taught Roy to smoke cigarettes, which would prove to be one of his most tenacious and damaging addictions. "Roy was straight," Bobby said, "but Joe was Roy's first love. Joe had everything—he inherited money and he was good looking."

In band practice, no one could play the tone poems but Roy. They were intricate, challenging pieces of baroque music, and Roy loved them. Music filled most of his waking hours, since he was still playing the guitar and singing every chance he got. In order to memorize the lyrics of popular songs he'd slow down records with his finger. One of the great hits of the day was Patti Page's cover of "The Tennessee Waltz," which sold six million copies. To aspiring young singers like Roy, music suddenly offered access to fame and wealth. "I always wanted to be a millionaire," he said, "even when I was thirteen."

Roy began singing "Sixteen Tons" and "Old Shep" on West Texas radio stations by the time he was twelve. In nearby Lubbock, Buddy Holly was also beginning to sing over the radio. Like Roy, Buddy had won a talent contest as a child and had been performing ever since. Roy attracted so many fans on local radio that, before long, he had a show with Charline Arthur on KERB radio in Kermit every Saturday afternoon. A young woman in her twenties, Charline was a Western singer and played the guitar around Odessa clubs.

Roy and his family lived in Kermit for a while, as well as any other town in the area where Orb could find a job. For a while they lived in Andrews, and once again they shared a duplex with Frances and Clois Russell. "Roy used to drive me crazy singin'," Frances remembers. "His voice was changin' at the time." The Orbisons always moved back to Wink as soon as Orb could find work there. Back at the Wink school, drum majorette Patsy Bailey remembers that everyone gathered around Roy on the playground when he got out his guitar and started singing his rendition of current hit songs. Principal R.A. Lipscomb often asked him to sing at assembly. A man known as "Eight Ball," who'd bought The Day Drug from Bobby Blackburn's mother, invited Roy to come inside the store and sing, and he liked Roy's songs so much that he locked the door at closing time and enjoyed a private show as people gathered outside and peered through the glass. After all the ridicule, Facetus was beginning to be appreciated at last.

The Korean War started just as Roy was entering Wink High in 1950. Some of the upperclassmen, like popular Denton Wood, went into the service right away, and soon Denton was brought home in his coffin. Roy and the boys' quartet sang hymns at the memorial service for Denton in the school auditorium. To Roy and so many others born in the 1930s, Korea seemed like a continuation of World War II, over less than five years earlier. The so-called silent generation had known nothing but depression and war.

In the boys' quartet, Ronnie Slaughter sang lead, Joe Ray Hammer sang bass, and Richard West sang baritone. Surprisingly, Roy Orbison sang *second* tenor. Ms. Violet "Jake" Claiborn, who organized the boys' quartet, felt that Roy sang through his nose. "Roy didn't always have that voice," Ronnie said. "He used to have to strain for the high notes, and he would flatten out. Ms. Claiborn was always trying to get him to open his mouth, but he wouldn't do it. Finally she cured him of it by making him stick two fingers in his mouth every time he opened it to sing."

While girls liked Roy, they took no account of him as a male. Annette Bailey, who was in the glee club with Roy, said, "I thought of him as my best girlfriend," explaining that she could confide in Roy and count on him to protect her. And when Lettie Mangrum heard that Roy wanted to ask her to a dance, she said, "I hope he doesn't," and avoided him thereafter. "Every relationship I'd ever been in," Roy once said, "the girl already had one going when we first met—even as far back as kindergarten." According to Bobby Blackburn, Roy's habitual preference for younger girls started in his school years. "In Wink he was looking at girls two or three years younger—that's a big difference in school, where it can mean the difference between, say, the fifth grade and the third grade." Conversely, Bobby recalls that in the sixth or seventh grade Roy had had a crush on an upperclasswoman named Joan Franklin, who was the school's drum majorette. "We were all in love with her," Bobby says. "To us she was a pretty old lady. Then, between our junior and senior years in high school, my cousin Adelle Heasley, who was tall, brunette and real good looking, came to visit from Houston and Roy fell in love with her. But she had to go home, and it was always that way—we fell in love with unreachables. We wouldn't get rejected that way."

Roy was part of Wink High's tight little clique of musical prodigies, which met at Annette Bailey's house to socialize. They'd roll back the rug and dance until the morning hours to pop hits like Frankie Laine's "High Noon" or The Mills Brothers' "Glow Worm." Jackie Brenston's #1 R&B hit, "Rocket '88," was the first sign of the coming era of rock 'n' roll, and it was the first time any of them had seen Sam Phillips' Memphis label, Sun Records. Then, in 1951, a white man from Highland Park, Michigan, named William John Clifton Haley covered "Rocket '88." This was the first the world had heard of Bill Haley, and the advent of rock 'n' roll as a national craze was not far away. According to Bobby Blackburn, Roy learned how to sing ballads from listening to Frankie Laine. "Roy also loved Mitch Miller arrangements, especially the French horns," Bobby said. "But what really caught his attention was later in the '50s, when The Four Lads sang 'Standin' on the Corner,' and their tenor went about three octaves higher than the rest. He also liked Guy Mitchell and Rosemary Clooney."

Ronnie Slaughter remembers Roy's loneliness and yearning for someone to love. In a few years, Roy would make a record of a plangent ballad called "Love Star," which is about a man who is so shy that he fears that life—and love—are going to pass him by. "There are so many ways to be lonesome in West Texas," Roy once said, and apparently he was doomed to learn them all. "More than anything else," Ronnie recalled, "Roy wanted someone to love and cling to." Though Roy had a crush on Barbara Wilson, Barbara chose handsome Ronnie when she was old enough to date. Soon, almost all his friends had paired off as couples, and Roy was one of the few left alone.

"All the rest of us were talking about getting married and having families," Barbara Wilson remembered, "but Roy was dreaming of stardom." Soon, Roy's dreams turned into unwholesome obsessions. While the other boys and girls were discovering the sweetness of life in each other's arms, Roy was lost in a secret world of grandiosity and delusion. Throughout his life he would write and sing of dreams, seeming to prefer them to reality. In a sense, he had lost his mind, but it is equally true that without recourse to fantasy and dreams, he probably would have never survived the deprivations of his adolescence.

There may have been girls in Wink who were willing to date him, but they weren't up to his high standards of beauty. In his pride, he chose isolation rather than settling for second best. A misguided sense of values made him hold out for pretty girls he had no chance of attracting, and soon he sank even deeper into alienation, dreaming his life away. Meanwhile, his friend Joe Ray Hammer was dating pretty Annette Bailey, who'd previously gone with Billy Pat Ellis. Annette and Billy Pat hatched a scheme to fix up Roy with Helen Morton. Like Roy, Helen wore glasses, and so Roy decided to continue holding out for a beauty. Billy Pat wrote in Annette's yearbook, "I've about given up on getting Roy to date Helen because he won't settle for anything less than a movie star."

In the 1950s, girls were expected to remain chaste until marriage, and impatient Texas boys found a sexual outlet in the Mexican border-town brothels. One day in 1952, Roy, Bobby Dale Smith, Slob Evans and Billy Pat Ellis decided to surrender their virginity to the whores of Ojinaga. "We went to Big Bend National Park one day and got a wild hair," Smith said. "We got the girls in Mexico to show us the ropes."

Orbie Lee Harris remembered a trip to Ojinaga with Roy and John Pitts. "Ojinaga was our hot spot. We were in the tenth grade, about fifteen years old. We went in the middle of the night. The soldiers in El Paso were paid on the first and the fifteenth of the month, so we'd schedule our trips in between, when the price went down. The girls in Ojinaga knew when the payroll was in and inflated the price to as high as three dollars. We schoolboys negotiated down to a dollar. We made sure we didn't go on the first or the fifteenth of the month. I know Roy went down there with John and Freako Gonzales."

Pitts said Roy was grinning from ear to ear after his first trip. It must have been a relief to discover that love could be bought, if only for a moment. Maybe other dreams could be purchased as well, like living in a penthouse in a great city, where he could look down on the rest of the world. One day, he'd return to Texas in a Cadillac Eldorado with a beautiful girl sitting next to him. "I don't know who I'll marry," he confided to Annette Bailey, "but she'll be beautiful."

The music crowd at Wink High liked Roy, and his happiest moments growing up came when he was with them. "Everyone thought we were crazy," Charles Evans remembers. "We'd jump into someone's car and roar around singing at the top of our voices." Roy, Charles, Annette Bailey, Joe Ray Hammer, Bobby Blackburn and Ronnie Slaughter were all in the band, the chorus, the glee club and the boys' quartet or the mixed octet. They loved to harmonize as they "cruised the drag," the highway between Wink and Kermit, singing Hank Williams' "Cold, Cold Heart," Dean Martin's "Amore," and anything by The Mills Brothers. "We all wanted to go into music professionally," Annette said. "Roy is the only one who made it, fortunately or unfortunately." Susie Newbert said that people could see and hear them coming for blocks—teenage songsters roaring down the road with smoke billowing from every window.

In high school, Roy could be feisty. He ran afoul of tough J.L. Dodd, coach, history and government teacher, and, in 1989, the principal of Wink High. "I got the board and busted him a couple of licks for getting smart," Dodd said. "I was only ten years older than Roy. He came into my class late, and I said, 'Roy, you're tardy.'

"'I'm not tardy,' he replied.

"'Look at your watch,' I said. 'What does it say?'

"'Tick tock,' Roy said. He was gonna be cute, so I busted him in front of the class. It's hard to be a big man in front of your friends with tears in your eyes. He took it okay."

Roy liked to shoot snooker at the pool hall with Joe Ray, Charlie Evans, Bobby Dale Smith and Orbie Lee Harris. Both Roy and Joe Ray were expert snooker players. One day, Roy got into a poolroom brawl with Charles and Orbie Lee. Roy was shooting snooker when they came in and demanded that he pay Charlie back some money he owed him.

"No deal," Roy said, returning to his game.

"Orbie Lee Harris could whip anybody," Charles remembered, "but he couldn't whip Roy. It got heated and Orbie Lee told Roy he couldn't hit me because I had my arm in a sling. But Roy hit Orbie Lee and whipped me."

Charles Evans said he and Roy often fought but held no grudges. When Roy inscribed Charlie's yearbook, he referred to their many disagreements and slugfests, but insisted "Slobby" was his very best buddy. He acknowledged Slob's enormous popularity in school, and he signed his message, Roy (Lefty Frizzell) Orbison.

That Roy Orbison signed himself as Lefty Frizzell shows how deeply he identified with Texas's great honky-tonk singer. At the end of Roy's life, in 1988, his identification with Lefty was just as strong, for the name Roy took as one of the fictional Traveling Wilburys was Lefty. Roy had been a fan ever since Lefty Frizzell first started singing in beer joints around Big Spring, Texas, in the late '40s. Lefty's recording career took off in 1950 in Dallas, and in hit records like "If You Got the Money Honey I Got the Time," Lefty introduced the intimate, sexy sound that has dominated country music ever since. Roy liked Lefty's honky-tonk songs of hopelessness and despair like "This Just Ain't No Good Day for Leavin'." Roy's father often sang these country standards around the house, and Roy learned to style a song by listening to Orb. "I'll never forget my father singing for me when I was a teenager," he said. "His voice still sounded very, very young. That's what struck me. He must've been forty, which I considered to be very old. I was blessed with his voice."

Roy was an average student in everything but music, but even there, Wink denied him honors. When competition for all-state music honors were held, Joe Ray Hammer and Priscilla Vinson won. The band director, Martin Epps, had always remained unimpressed by Roy's guitar playing and fledgling songwriting efforts. According to Annette Bailey, he told Roy, "Put down that banjo and stick to your baritone horn. If I can't get my music published, you certainly can't." Years later, Roy ran into Annette and told her, "I got even with him. After 'Only the Lonely' hit, I went back to a football game one time in Andrews. At halftime I walked over and talked to Martin Epps. After we chatted, I walked away and heard a kid say, 'Mr. Epps, do you know *Roy Orbison*? That just made it for me. I feel like I got even that night."

When he was thirteen years old, Roy organized his first band, using Billy Pat "Spider" Ellis on drums, Slob Evans on bass fiddle, Richard "Head" West at the piano, and James Morrow on electric mandolin. One day Principal Lipscomb asked the boys to play at assembly, and afterwards a bio-chemistry teacher named Eva June Harbin dubbed the band The Wink Westerners. Ms. Harbin believed in school spirit and never missed a Wink Wildcat football game, yelling, *"Talk it over, big team! Talk it over!"* when the boys went into a huddle.

Lipscomb enlisted The Wink Westerners to help him campaign for district governor of the Lion's Club. Though he lost the election, Roy and his band enjoyed a free trip to Chicago. "We were the only kid band in West Texas," Billy Pat said, "so it wasn't any problem getting plenty of dance dates." Eager for experience, they played for free. Roy opened their sets by announcing, "Okay, folks, you've heard of Guy Lombardo and the sweetest music this side of heaven. Now you're about to hear the *other* side!"

The band's theme song was "Under the Double Eagle." "The first songs we played were 'Kaw-Liga' and 'Mexican Joe,'" Charles noted. "Then we started singing all kinds of music, and 'In the Mood' was a favorite." The band competed at the regular jamborees in Jal, New Mexico, often taking first prize. Roy went up to the mike and assumed the posture he'd seen Hank Williams, Lefty Frizzell, Hank Snow and Webb Pierce use—knees slightly bent and shoulders slightly hunched.

When Slim Whitman played The Rig Theatre in Wink, Roy and his band were asked to back him up. Slim Whitman was the leading exponent of yodeling and falsetto singing in country music, and by the time he played Wink, he'd scored a Top 10 hit with "Keep It a Secret," and other hits soon followed, such as "North Wind," "Secret Love" and "Rose Marie." Slim rehearsed with The Wink Westerners for about ten minutes before showtime. "He told us what key to play in," Slob said. "We knew all the tunes already."

During summer vacation Roy shoveled tar for the county, receiving $80 for two weeks' labor. Sweating in the hot Texas sun, he vowed he'd never work this hard again. Soon, The Wink Westerners started earning money for playing dances. Between sets one night a man approached Roy and said, "We'd like for you to come and play a dance for us."

"We only know ten songs," Roy said.

"We'll give you $400."

Roy recalled, "We showed up and made eighty dollars a piece for doing what we had been doing for nothing. It was amazing. I didn't know what the stumbling blocks were or how likely you were to succeed at singing, but it didn't matter." Nothing mattered to Roy, really, but somehow getting out of Wink.

Chapter 2

The Wink Westerners played most of the honky tonks in West Texas. One of them, The Archway in Monahans, was a tough joint, and every time Roy sang there, a man who was a convicted murderer and ex-convict came up to the bandstand and commanded The Wink Westerners to play "In the Mood." "We never turned him down," said Slob Evans. It sometimes got rowdy at The Archway, and one night a woman settled an argument with her boyfriend by blowing him away with her .45 pistol. Tough as it was, this apprenticeship before barroom crowds turned Roy into a compelling singer and a terrific guitarist. He also studied guitar with one of the professionals in the area, Troy Parker, who played a guitar in a well-known West Texas dance band called The Kingsmen. "One day we were broadcasting at KERB in Kermit," Parker recalled, "and Roy was standing there watching us. I was making some chords that he didn't know, and later he asked me if I would show them to him. I didn't know his parents, and I had never seen him before. But then he started coming out to the house whenever he felt like it, and he would just make himself at home . . . He was kind of a pest at times. He was very determined. If he wanted something, he really worked at it . . . I don't think he ever had a date . . . Sometimes he would get in and sing with us. Roy's voice could reach from the basement to the sky, and just as true as a bird, always."

West Texas was one of the cradles of rock 'n' roll and Roy was one of its earliest pioneers. In Wink, where everyone else his age seemed to be dating and necking, Roy sat with his guitar in the car in front of the house and wrote songs. Classmate Kathryn Crawford remembers driving by with a bunch of kids having a good time and seeing Roy, always alone and absorbed in his work. "He was out in the car because his dad was on morning towers [tour of duty in the oil field], and he didn't want to wake him up," Ms. Crawford explained. Roy wrote one of his earliest songs with Ronnie Slaughter, who remembered, "I was out working on an oil rig when Roy brought my girl friend, LaNell

24

Gray, out to see me and we started writing a song. We called it 'I Am Just a Dreamer,' and we made a record of it on a home recording machine rigged up by Richard West, who was an electronics wizard. There were no acoustics and it sounded flat, but it was Roy's first record."

Roy, Ronnie and Joe Ray Hammer began to experiment with sound, trying for acoustical pyrotechnics. "We were at a midnight preview in Kermit," Ronnie said. "The movie was boring that night, so we went to the restroom and began singing and discovered how great the acoustics were in there. When we came back out, about 45 people were standing in the lobby, clapping."

Slob Evans remembers Roy's moviegoing as a less joyous, more solitary activity. Slob let him slip into The Rig Theatre for free any time he wanted to, and he usually showed up alone. When Slob wasn't there, Bobby Dale Smith, who was janitor and assistant manager, admitted him. "There was a door where you could go directly to the balcony," Bobby recalled. In the darkness of The Rig, Roy lost himself in lurid '50s fantasies of salvation through sex—Burt Lancaster and Deborah Kerr wallowing on the beach in *From Here to Eternity* and Jennifer Jones and Charlton Heston writhing in the swamp in *Ruby Gentry*. Life was beginning to seem like something that happened to everyone but Roy Orbison.

He was not the only boy growing up unhappily in Wink. His classmate Harvey Russell killed himself while still in high school, and the gifted Joe Ray Hammer was also suicidal. Neither Roy nor Joe Ray was being brought up in a way that would prepare them for adult life. Both were so pampered at home that they would forever have trouble making decisions for themselves. "Roy was spoiled," says his drummer in The Wink Westerners, Billy Pat Ellis. "When we were in high school we went camping once. Roy was supposed to wash the pans but he put it off until it was time for us to leave and then he said, 'Oh shit! I'll take 'em home and have Mother clean 'em."

The jocks continued to harrass Roy and his musical friends, and even Ronnie Slaughter, who was on the football team, was discriminated against because of his singing. "My teammates thought it was kind of sissy to be in the school choir," Ronnie said. "I was very shy about singing, because I knew I was going to take it on the chin. I was going to get a lot of kidding from my teammates. Boy, some of those guys were unmerciful. We'd be in the shower after practice, and they'd say, 'Oh, Ronnie, won't you please sing something for us?'

"And at the Christmas cantata, Roy was in the chorus and I was positioned up in the balcony. All my football buddies started swooning and acting silly over my singing, and I really got embarrassed."

Wink's football team was at its most victorious in 1952, when the Wildcats went to Houston and beat Deer Park for the state championship. That a hamlet of less than 2,000 could whip mighty Houston was nothing short of miraculous. All of Eva Harbin's exhortations to *"Talk it over, big team!"* had paid off. Swallowing their resentment of their redneck tormentors, Roy and his friends in the marching band proudly paraded down the highway that served as Wink's main street, Patsy Bailey prancing in front as drum majorette. Though Roy may have been a star later on, it was his brother, Grady Lee, who stole the limelight in '52. As a guard on the championship team, Grady was an authentic high school football hero. In the Orbison household, however, Roy remained the favorite son. Grady had a wild streak, but Roy caused so little trouble that, as he put it, "I was totally anonymous, even at home."

In the early 1950s a singer with a voice not unlike Roy's, Johnny Ray, was stunning the nation. Ray's "Cry" was the #1 hit for eleven straight weeks in '50-'51. Americans were beginning to buy more and more records in the '50s, and Roy dreamed of having a monster smash some day like "Cry" or Gordon Jenkins and The Weavers' "Good Night, Irene," which held the #1 position for an unbelievable 13 weeks, the longest run any record had ever had. Roy thrilled to Frankie Laine's big, soaring renditions of "Cry of the Wild Goose" and "That Lucky Old Sun," but the voice Roy loved most of all was his own. "It was sort of a wonder," he said. "It was a great feeling, and it didn't hurt anybody, and it made me feel good, and some people even said, 'Roy, that's nice.' I've always been in love with my voice. It was fascinating, I liked the sound of it, I liked making it sing, making a voice ring, and I just kept doing it."

Though he had perfected some great guitar licks, Roy realized his major gift was as a singer rather than instrumentalist. "When I was 15, I went in the back of the house to play my guitar and sing a little bit. And I could only play what I knew. I couldn't think of any innovations, or any other chords. I made the decision then not to be a guitar player, but to use the instrument as an accompaniment to my singing." For Roy Orbison, the instrument he played was an essential part of the

creative act, just as it is with many other rock singers, including Ray
Charles, Carole King, Janis Ian and Elton John.

According to Orbie Lee Harris, Buddy Holly played a crucial role in
Roy's eventual decision to become a performer. Roy had serious doubts
that anyone who looked the way he did could ever make it on the stage.
"But Buddy Holly wore glasses, too," Orbie Lee noted, "and I think
that gave Roy courage, made him think, If this guy is going to try to
make it big, maybe I can too."

Roy and Buddy lived only ninety miles from each other in West
Texas. "I would go see Buddy Holly's shows," Roy said, "and he would
see mine, and back and forth there, until he made the super big time.
Buddy was a very bright boy, very dedicated. He wasn't uppity, or as
we'd say in the business, 'flashy.' He could tell jokes. We had a
relationship that developed."

Buddy lived in Lubbock, the biggest city in West Texas. In 1949,
when he was thirteen and attending Hutchinson Junior High, Buddy
and his friend Bob Montgomery formed the duo Buddy & Bob and
played around Lubbock, calling their music "Western Bop." Like Roy,
Buddy loved Hank Williams, and his favorite song was "Lovesick
Blues." By 1954, Buddy had a show on Lubbock's KDAV, one of the
first all-country stations in the U.S. KDAV started airing the new rock
music in 1955. In the beginning, rock was dismissed by the media as
vulgar and faddish. But on KDAV, local entertainers such as Buddy
Holly and Waylon Jennings were showcased on the "Sunday Dance
Party." Waylon was born in Littlefield, Texas, June 15, 1937, and by
the age of twelve he was already hosting his own disk-jockey show. "I
met Buddy Holly in Lubbock in 1954," Waylon said. "We worked a lot
of shows together. I remember one time we all were together: me,
Buddy Holly, Roy Orbison, and Weldon Myrick, who was a great steel
guitar player in Nashville, and Sonny Curtis, who everybody knows,
and at the bus station in Lubbock, Texas, and we had a quarter and
Sonny put it in the juke box and played Chet Atkins, and that's about
all we had was a quarter and we snuck into a Sonny James, Jim Reeves
Show."

While Buddy Holly was getting a foothold on radio and TV in
Lubbock, Roy was busily staking out his own turf in the Midland-
Odessa area. "I didn't see a TV set at all until 1953," Roy said. "At that
time there was a contest in Odessa which I won. The prize was a
thirty-minute spot on TV." The sponsor was Pioneer Furniture, and

after the show Roy asked the Pioneer owner, "Why don't you sponsor us every week?"

"How much would it cost me?" the man asked.

"Sixty dollars," Roy said.

"Apiece?"

"No, for the whole group."

Roy then suggested to the furniture-store owner that he sponsor *two* shows a week, and he agreed. "The guy was so successful that he opened the biggest furniture store in West Texas," Roy said. Roy took advantage of every opportunity to perform, sharpening and perfecting his skills.

The Wink Westerners did a Friday night show on KMID-TV, Midland, and a Saturday night show for KOSA-TV, Odessa. "The best thing about being on TV," Roy said, "was that we could tell the people where we would be playing during the week." Through their TV exposure The Wink Westerners achieved local fame as West Texas's first kid band.

With so many public appearances on the horizon Roy decided at last to do something about his looks. Over the years his white hair had turned to dishwater gray, and he asked Susie Newbert if she would help him dye it jet black. Ruth Johnson, the local beautician, gave them a bottle of dye and Susie left the mixture on Roy's hair for twenty minutes. "At first everybody giggled and laughed at him," Susie noted. "But he liked being black-headed, and after a while everybody got used to it." Next, Roy persuaded Annette Bailey's mother to give him a permanent wave. "He was real curly after that," Annette said. "It was really funny until it settled down."

Roy still hadn't had a date, but when the junior prom came around, he took a girl named Dorice Hammond. In his senior year, he finally acceded to the efforts of Billy Pat Ellis and Annette Bailey and went with Helen Morton to the prom. Helen's yearbook photo reveals a sensitive-looking girl with pretty blond hair and unbecoming spectacles. Roy had known her for years. "When The Wink Westerners started playing on TV over in Odessa," Helen recalled, "we mustered up all the money we could to buy a tank of gas and get over there to see them, because none of us had TV's. We thought we had gone to the end of the world, getting that far away from home."

Roy became aware of the man who would become the single most important force in his life during his senior year. Elvis Presley was playing the Sportatorium in Dallas as part of a country & western jamboree on April 16, 1954. Roy said he could never "overemphasize how shocking he looked and seemed to me that night." Elvis spat out his chewing gum, dropped to his knees and humped and hunched his way to the edge of the stage, singing Chuck Berry's "Maybelline." Girls started screaming and fainting. "What came out of him was not a show," Roy said. "Elvis lives it altogether." Until Elvis, Roy said, his generation had never had the type of music in which they could get passionately involved. "After that," Roy said, "I wanted to put on a show like Elvis."

The spring of '54 was graduation time, and the senior prom was held in the school cafeteria. That night, the band from Texas Western played pop music for dancing. Roy's date, Helen, wore a pink-and-silver strapless, and he presented her with a pink-carnation corsage. "Roy probably wore a hand-me-down suit," Billy Pat Ellis remembered, "like the rest of us." Helen gave Roy a white carnation boutonniere. "He wasn't a very good dancer," she said. "He was like most musicians. He played, he didn't dance."

Orbie Lee Harris remembers that everyone but Roy got loaded on purple passion, and Roy ended up having to help Orbie Lee sober up enough to make it home. After graduation he got out of Wink as fast as he could. He would always have a love-hate relationship with his home town, diplomatically telling local papers, "I always felt at home in Wink," while expressing his true hatred to *Rolling Stone* and other national publications.

In the fall of 1954, Roy, Billy Pat Ellis and Joe Ray Hammer headed for college in Denton, Texas. Roy's first group, The Wink Westerners, disbanded. At North Texas State College, Roy declared a major in geology, explaining, "My father had worked in the oil fields, and knew there'd always be a demand for geologists." Geology was the key to Texas's hidden oil. Having spent his first 18 years sitting on top of millions of dollars worth of oil, Roy was about to join the ranks of Texas boys determined to strike it rich, scientifically.

As it turned out, he had little interest in his freshman geology course, a Darwinian explanation of the origin of the earth that seemed to have very little to do with finding oil in the Permian Basin. In the second semester, students were expected to memorize the names of hundreds of rocks and identify them on sight. Roy would much rather play his guitar and have jam sessions with Billy Pat and their fellow NTSC students Dick Penner and Wade Moore, who'd written a song called "Ooby Dooby." According to Billy Pat Ellis, "Wade was in our fraternity. Roy was playing a jam session in the frat house, just playing around on the guitar. Dick Penner gave him 'Ooby Dooby' and a couple of other songs. We liked 'Ooby Dooby,' thought it was just great." Roy's own account differs slightly; he said he first heard the song when Wade and Dick performed it at a concert in the Main Hall. "It knocked me flat," Roy said. "I was astounded because they made more music than the whole orchestra."

Like many early rock 'n' roll classics, notably "The Twist" and "The Locomotion," "Ooby Dooby" had lyrics that both described and promoted a dance, the idea being not only to have a hit record but to create a dance craze as well. In "Ooby Dooby," a boy tells his girl to join him in a dance and tells her how to do it—start wiggling with all she's got, act like a rattlesnake and just let go and have a good time. Many nonsensical do-wah's were mixed in with the lyrics. It was a snappy, catchy rockabilly song.

"It was a good year, but it was a lonely year," Roy said. "I guess it was an attempt at being legitimate, or not being a free spirit. I think the reason it was really lonely was that I wasn't where I needed to be."

Roy was in fact *exactly* where he needed to be—his first hit had just dropped into his lap. He began to make inquiries about how to cut a recording of "Ooby Dooby." Meanwhile, his classwork suffered, especially geology. Roy was learning what every college student soon realizes—science majors have to give it all if they expect to pass. Roy was washed out fairly quickly. "I stayed up late one night to study, fell asleep and missed my eight o'clock final," he said. "Then I turned to the idea of secondary education and studied history and English."

Roy knew he had little aptitude for teaching and that his true love was singing. But the chances of making it big in show business were slight, and he knew he needed something to fall back on. "I wanted to get a diploma in case I didn't make it in the music business," Roy said. One of his NTSC classmates, Pat Boone, was already hitting it big as a recording star. Pat was a clean-cut, pious young man, an atypical rock 'n' roll star, but he was to score thirty-eight hit singles in the next ten years. Pat's specialty was taking black music and repackaging it for white record buyers, and his first #1 hit was a cover of Fats Domino's "Ain't It a Shame."

Though Roy Orbison did not find Pat Boone inspiring, he was impressed with Pat's phenomenal success. In rapid succession, Pat had four Top 20 hits, "Two Hearts," "At My Front Door (Crazy Little Mama)," "No Other Arms (Can Ever Hold You)" and "Gee Whittakers." "I was at North Texas the same time he was," Roy said. "I was playing guitar but had to leave school to go to work with my daddy for a while. Pat used school to help his career. They even let him out of college to tour. So, in that respect, he inspired me to get off my duff and get to work."

Roy returned to Wink for the 1954 Christmas holidays. "I had a TV show in Odessa," he said, "and we played mainly country music. But after Elvis Presley came through town in late 1954 I began to notice the rhythm of music. I had heard groups like The Clovers and their hits like 'One Mint Julep' all based on seventh chords. And I really didn't like them. But at a New Year's Eve dance in 1954, we had to play through the actual time of midnight and when someone suggested 'Shake, Rattle and Roll,' we struck up on it. But we had nearly ten minutes to go to the hour, so we kept playing the same song. By the time we were finished, I was fully converted. I think it's a matter of instruments that defined whether you were playing country or rock. We had a drummer."

The drummer, Billy Pat Ellis, explained the evolution of the band from country to rock 'n' roll: "When we played Western, we also played songs like 'Once in a While,' 'Dreams' and 'In the Mood.' With our instrumentation it was still country and western. Then we started playing 'Ooby Dooby' and then Chuck Berry's 'Roll Over, Beethoven.' We just evolved into rock 'n' roll."

Roy was emphatic about the impact Elvis Presley's first record had on him. "What convinced me that I was in the wrong place at the wrong time was I heard a record by a young fellow on the jukebox called 'That's All Right.'" Roy was moved to start writing rock 'n' roll songs himself. Billy Pat Ellis said, "Roy and I wrote 'Go Go Go' at North Texas. Elvis came out with his record 'That's All Right' and we really liked it. We were in the room playing the guitar, just playing around. We decided to write a rockabilly song. We used to play 'Kaw-Liga' in The Wink Westerners. 'Let's just jazz up "Kaw-Liga" a little bit,' I said. 'Yeah,' Roy said. 'Just jazz up the melody and change the lyrics.' It was fun to do, and we didn't think we'd ever record it." Under the title "Down the Line," "Go Go Go" was destined to become a well-known song as well as a source of conflict between Roy and Billy Pat.

Roy finally made his commitment to a career on the stage. Despite the vast difference in their looks and style, Elvis remained his model. But as rock's ugly duckling, Roy was going to have the longest and most torturous road to stardom of any of his contemporaries. "Elvis was doing the things I wanted to do," he said, "and I was in the wrong place at the wrong time. If you have something to fall back on, you probably will." At the end of the semester, Roy dropped out of college. "I jumped into the music business," Roy said. "I moved to Odessa to attend junior college, got my band together with different guys and started in doing what I wanted to do."

Slob Evans didn't want to be in the band anymore. "I grew up in the Palace Inn beer joint in Wink," he said. "Mother was a waitress there during the war. Now I wanted a life I could handle." He told Roy that he'd be going to Texas Tech in Lubbock in the fall but would continue to play with the band, mostly at The Archway in Monahans, over the summer. They were all short of money and needed every penny they could earn.

A long, hot summer stretched before Roy, and he was broke. "I still had my band," Roy said, "and we played for dances in the evening. I was working for El Paso Natural Gas in the daytime, cutting up steel and loading it onto trucks and chopping weeds and painting water towers. That's where I came up with the idea for 'Working for the Man.' Our straw boss was Mr. Rose, and he wouldn't cut me any slack. I worked in the blazing heat, hard, hard labor, and then I'd play at night, came home and some nights be too tired to eat or even to undress. I'd lay down, and I wouldn't even turn over. I'd wake up in the same spot and hit the oil patch again."

Billy Pat Ellis, who was with Roy all that summer, claims that Roy managed to avoid most of the hard labor. Slob Evans agreed, saying, "Mostly what he did was chop weeds in the parking lot and around the office building." In the fall, Roy formed his new band, The Teen Kings, using Billy Pat and James Morrow again and adding "Little Johnny" Wilson, also known as "Peanuts," and Jack Kennelly. Jack recalled, "When Richard West left the band, I joined. 'You play bass?' Roy asked me.

"'I don't know,' I said.

"'Hell, we'll find out. Come on.' He took me to the Armstrong Music Store, gave me a bass fiddle and said, 'Can you go boom-ta-ta?' It was a slap rhythm, and when I tried it he said, 'Yeah. You play bass.' It took a week to learn it and one Friday afternoon we rehearsed from 5:45 till 6:00 in the duplex we all lived in and played on Channel 2 TV that night. It was the scariest thing I ever did."

The Teen Kings shared living expenses in their duplex apartment in Odessa, and Slob Evans moved in with them after a semester at Texas Tech, though he did not rejoin the band. "We flipped to see who had to sleep with Roy," Slob remembered. "I lost. Roy was dying his hair and his pillow would be solid black. We didn't wash a lot, and Roy figured out a way to tell when it was time to launder his Levi's. He'd throw them against the wall, and when they stuck, it was time for the laundry." They let dirty dishes collect in the sink, and when the sink was full, they stacked them, still dirty, in the cabinet. Finally, Billy Pat or Slob would have a girlfriend come over and clean up the kitchen for them.

They all enrolled at Odessa Junior College, and The Teen Kings started playing at local dances and on Midland and Odessa radio stations. "We were a 'commonwealth' group with no leader," Jack Kennelly recalled. "We had three vocalists, me, Little Johnny and Roy. The load was equal, and it was the overall group, not any one individual, that drove the kids crazy. We had a frantic show. I danced 'The Bop' and Billy Pat Ellis did a drum solo. We did 'The Bug Dance'—Little Johnny, James Morrow and me—throwing a bug on each other while Ellis did a wild Bo Diddley beat. We'd throw the bug from one to the other and you had to dance when it hit you—the kids loved that. I also remember singing Ray Charles's 'Unchain My Heart' and 'Hallelujah I Just Love Her So,' a Chicago blues number by Lou Rawls, and a song called 'Little Bit' from Little Milton's album *Grits Ain't Groceries*."

Soon, The Teen Kings were a very popular local group. Their social life centered around The Kingston Apartments, where their friend James Blackburn, Bobby's brother, let them use the swimming pool. "We'd party there every weekend," Slob said. Roy was still having a hard time getting girls to go with him. Billy Pat finally asked his girl to fix Roy up, and they went out on a double date with Slob Evans. "Roy bought her a beer or two and was trying to make out with her," Slob admitted, "but she stuck her head out the car window and said, 'I love Billy Pat!'"

One night, Jack Kennelly brought his date, Claudette Frady, to one of the dances The Teen Kings were playing, and she was the prettiest girl Roy had ever seen. "Roy fell in love with her the first time he saw her," Jack said. "We'd met in a movie theater in Odessa and had gone together for three or four months. I was eighteen at the time and I thought she was older than I, in her early twenties. The I found out she was fourteen and broke it off—in those days fourteen was considered jail bait. She drove my folks nuts for a month. Her parents thought I was a rock 'n' roll star and were all for Claudette and I hooking up. She was not real bright and I had a string of girls." It was after he'd broken off with Claudette that Jack took her to the The Teen Kings dance. Though Roy was smitten with her, Little Johnny Wilson moved in on her before Roy did and, according to Jack, "over the next several months she went with one or two guys in the band."

Though only fourteen, Claudette Frady was already a fully developed woman and her sweaters looked like they were sprayed on. The shape of her breasts was clearly visible and they looked like the fantasy bosoms on the highly idealized Vargas pin-ups in *Esquire* magazine. Roy wondered how a short guy like Little Johnny, who was only five-foot-two, could rate this stately beauty, when Roy couldn't even get a date. As he told Ronnie Slaughter, "If I had any money, I couldn't even *hire* someone to go out with me."

Soon all that changed. "The whole group was red hot," Jack says, and when Roy went on the road with The Teen Kings, as Billy Pat puts it, "Gals threw themselves at everyone in the band." Roy was besieged by the first generation of rock 'n' roll groupies, teen-age girls whose main ambition was to sleep with members of a rock band. According to Ronnie Hawkins, later famous as founder of The Band, one of the great rock groups of the 1960s, Roy by this time was drinking and enjoying girls. As Ronnie said when he hired guitarist Robbie Robertson, "You won't get much money, but you'll get more pussy than Frank Sinatra." Ronnie's drummer Levon Helm agreed: "Women on the road—I love them. That's why we're on the road."

Ronnie hired Roy to perform at The Rockwood Club in Arkansas and they became friendly. Recalling their first meeting, Roy said, "There were some strange happenings. Some people at the University of Arkansas told me they had a young man who wanted to sing with me, so I said that he should come up. But he played all my numbers—before me. I couldn't believe it. So I went ahead and sang them all over again anyway. It was Ronnie Hawkins. Later, I sang him the song 'Mary Lou' that he went off and recorded. He made a big hit before I ever made it."

Ronnie's cut of "Mary Lou" hit the charts at #26 a couple of years later. Ronnie drifted up to Canada, where he put together the group that became the legendary Band, Bob Dylan's backup group. In addition to Robbie Robertson, Richard Manuel, Garth Hudson, Rick Danko and Levon Helm, at one time or another Duane Allman, Roy Buchanan and Dominic Troiano all worked for the eccentric Ronnie Hawkins.

"Roy hadn't even recorded yet," Ronnie remembered, "but he'd come, stay overnight and play his new songs. He'd just sit down with an acoustic guitar and pick all night long. He was really good on that finger-pickin' stuff on the geetar—that's him doing leads on 'Ooby Dooby' and 'Go Go Go.' Rockabilly was a form Roy did real well, and he invented a lot of licks. With that octave range of his, you'd think Roy would be ripping out his vocal chords, but he could hit those notes sitting next to you in the car. It was scary! Roy was always quiet, almost shy-acting. He never hardly raised his voice, always spoke low and quiet. He wasn't one to do all that rowdy stuff, but he liked the girls, just like any normal rock 'n' roller, and he'd take a few drinks."

But the drug of choice for the first wave of rock 'n' rollers was speed, and Roy's use of "diet pills" as well as cocaine and barbiturates is confirmed by some members of his family, by at least one close friend and by some of the musicians he worked with. Eventually, he was addicted to both speed and sleeping pills. As Robbie Robertson put it, "The road has taken a lot of the great ones—Hank Williams, Buddy Holly, Otis Redding, Janis Joplin, Jimi Hendrix, and Elvis Presley." Though the road was still fun for Roy in 1955, the combination of drugs, sex and rock 'n' roll would prove to be as dangerous as it was potent.

Roy kept in touch with Dick Penner and Wade Moore in Denton and still had the inside track on recording "Ooby Dooby." "I took this song back to West Texas," Roy said. "I was on TV with it and it was a huge local success—the song and the show." Roy knew of a man named Norman Petty who had a recording studio in Clovis, New Mexico. Petty had started NorVaJak in the mid-'50s with royalties from a record he'd cut with The Norman Petty Trio. The term "record producer" was not yet in usage, but when Roy and later Buddy Holly and Buddy Knox began recording, that's roughly the function Norman Petty performed.

"The boys and I went down to Norman Petty's studio in Clovis," Roy said. "I was the first to use it other than Norman who used it to record his own trio. He built it for them. We hired the studio to make 'Ooby Dooby.'"

Roy was penniless, but James Morrow, his mandolin player, raised the funds to get a cut of "Ooby Dooby." "James was a dirty bopper on stage," laughed his father, Henry Morrow. "He could hook it. Johnny Horton called him 'the boy with the loose ass.'" According to drummer Billy Pat Ellis, James Morrow met a cute accordionist and singer named Jeanne Oliver when The Teen Kings played a jamboree in Jal, New Mexico. Jeanne's father, who worked for Phillips Petroleum, formed a company with a friend named Weldon Rogers for the purpose of producing Roy's recording of "Ooby Dooby," and they called the company Je-Wel, deriving the name from *Jeannie* and *Wel*don. Roy's own version of how "Ooby Dooby" came about differs somewhat from Billy Pat Ellis's account. "There were some people in Seminole, Texas, who wanted me to make a record for them," Roy said. "They paid for the time and were going to start a record company. One of the fellows was Weldon Rogers. The fellow who was putting up the money for Weldon Rogers' venture had a daughter named Jeanne—so Weldon and Jeanne were Je-Wel. They paid for the session. It was the first custom session that Norman Petty ever did. He and his wife Vi or Di and somebody else had this huge truck with a thing that brought the organ down hydraulically. From that, he and I recorded 'Ooby Dooby' and 'Trying to Get to You.'"

"Ooby Dooby" was issued as Je-Wel 101, and the flip side, "Tryin' to Get to You," was a song Roy had heard Elvis Presley sing. "When I first heard my voice recorded," Roy said, "I thought, If I hear that voice again, I'll know I've heard it before. I wasn't thinking, "That's beautiful, or Do I sing wonderfully well? I thought, There might be something there, because if I'm trying to get something across and you hear it one time or twice maybe you'll recognize it the next time you hear it. I thought that was a good quality to have."

When "Ooby Dooby" was released in West Texas and New Mexico, Roy became something of a local celebrity. Feeling bold and successful, he decided to make a play for Claudette Frady, the girl who had been dating several of The Teen Kings. If Claudette would date a guy like Little Johnny Wilson, who was at least five inches shorter than she, perhaps she'd go with Roy, despite his BB eyes. "She showed up at The Archway one night in Monahans," Bobby Blackburn recalls. Roy took her out, and on their first date the magic of romance began to happen at last for Roy. She was the first pretty girl he'd ever known who seemed to be crazy about him.

Claudette was born when her parents, Chester and Geraldine Frady, were very young and she'd been farmed out to live with friends when she was six years old. She was reunited with her parents after the first grade but she spent a lonely childhood as a latchkey child, since both Chester and Geraldine had to hold down fulltime jobs to make ends meet. While other kids were out playing, Claudette had to stay at home and help raise her younger brother and sister, Bill and Paulette, whose nickname was Dinky. "She was always on duty," Dinky said, "keeping the house together, protecting me from my big brother. She never got to play, never got to go out or have many friends. She always smiled, but it was only to cover up the sadness inside. She was alone so much, it made her a sad and lonely person."

Claudette and Roy could certainly relate on that level, but physically they were miles apart, Roy plain and Claudette a raving beauty. She was a cheerleader in junior high and, according to her cousin and best friend Ms. Kadon Frady Mahan, she dated from the time she was twelve. "She matured early and always looked older than her age," Kadon felt. "She was a big girl and had a terrific body."

"Roy was crazy about her," Charlie Evans said. "He'd never gone with many girls, and she was the first who really paid attention to him, and he just ate that up. And of course she was a beautiful girl—I mean, *gorgeous*." When Roy arrived for their nightly dates, Claudette would come out of the Fradys' modest dwelling at 2104 North Muskingum looking like a cover girl. She was an anomaly—a working-class, small-town girl with the flair of a *Vogue* model.

Claudette's parents were in the catering business with her uncle, Floyd Frady, and one day Claudette took Roy to Frady Brothers Barbecue restaurant in Odessa for lunch. When they pulled up for curb service, Claudette's mother, a car hop, took their order. Geraldine Frady was an attractive, well-built woman with lustrous brown hair, and in her slacks, tight leather belt and sleeveless top, she was getting wolf whistles from the cowpokes and roustabouts who regularly ate there.

Before they left, Claudette took Roy inside the cafe to meet her father. A rugged man who claims descent from Frank and Jesse James, Chester Frady had been a motorcycle cop, butcher, fireman and construction worker before going into the cafe business. He was also a kind and gentle man, and he and Roy took to each other right away. Recalling their first meeting, Chester said, "Roy was just an old strugglin' hunker whenever we met, but Claudette worshipped him."

Claudette's mother, known as "Gerry," at first was less enthusiastic about Claudette's new boyfriend. She didn't find Roy attractive and Claudette was already engaged to one boy and had another in love with her. Geraldine was concerned that Claudette would follow her own pattern; she too had been in junior high when she'd met Chester Frady, and she too had been engaged to another man. Falling in love with Chester, she'd returned her fiancé's ring, lost interest in school and dropped out after the ninth grade, marrying Chester when she was eighteen. Gerry was proud that Claudette had always been a good student, and she told her daughter she didn't want her to get so involved with boys and dating that she'd neglect her homework. She recalls Claudette saying, with successful results, "Calm down, Mother. Just get yourself a beer and sit down."

Gerry's fears, however, proved well-founded. As soon as Roy and Claudette started going steady, Claudette's grades began to suffer. And when Claudette wasn't with Roy, she was playing his record. "All we heard around the house, day and night," Gerry remembered, "was 'Trying to Get to You.'" Everyone else was listening to "Ooby Dooby" but Claudette loved the flip side, a haunting ballad about a boy longing for his girlfriend, who is very far away. When he receives a letter from her, he knows that he must get back to her, though the journey will be long and arduous. But he has faith that God will light his way. Claudette loved the contrast between the song's spirituality and the earthiness of the rinky-dink piano and bluesy sax, and she was moved by Roy's voice—so low-key in this song, but relentless.

When Gerry tried to discipline Claudette, she met immediate and strong resistance. Claudette slipped out of the house for a date with Roy after Gerry had restricted her to her room, and when Claudette returned, Gerry gave her a whipping. After that, Claudette defiantly started smoking cigarettes and spending time with a thirty-year-old woman who lived in the house across the street. "She was one of these kind of women you could talk to about anything," Gerry said. Claudette soon became a heavy smoker, and every time she lit up, her father left the room, unable to stand seeing Claudette smoke. Gerry noted, "She'd smoke one right after the other. Roy was a heavy smoker too."

Claudette and her little brother Bill had knock-down-drag-out fights every time Claudette caught him bullying Dinky, but Bill and Claudette never held grudges. "I got mad at her for fightin' my fights," Bill admitted. "I had fights just about every day at school. I was always for the underdog. If a big guy was pickin' on a little guy, I fought the big guy. Mom never asked me how I did in school, just how many fights I had that day. Claudette always tried to take up for me."

One day, Bill and Claudette were talking out in the back yard when

Claudette told him that she was going to run away. "I'm going to be with Roy," she said. "Whatever you do, don't tell Mother or Dad where I'm goin'." That night, Bill could hear Claudette sneaking out of the house. "It took her a good while. Mother was a light sleeper—slept with one eye open, ear too. Roy and the band had moved to a little place that was just down the street from us. When mother found out she was gone, she wanted to know where Claudette went and finally I broke down and told her, 'Over to Roy's.' Dad stood up and said, 'Well, let's go down and git her.'"

When they pulled up at Roy's house, Chester told Bill, "You go on up to the house and tell her to come home." Bill stood on the porch for a moment, peering through the open door. "There were only two chairs," he recalled, "and she was in one of them. She saw me and got up and let me in. Then she sat back down and asked me if I wanted a Coke or anything. I noticed that there wasn't all that much furniture around. Roy and them didn't have any money left. At that time, the band was busted."

Claudette said, "Roy's in the kitchen making us some sandwiches. Do you want one?"

"Dad's out there," Bill responded.

"Dad? You told them?"

"Yes. You know how Mom is. Wangled it out of me. Gave me the guilt trip. Anyway, Dad wants you to come home."

Bill started out to the car and Claudette followed him in a few minutes.

They drove the short distance home in silence. Gerry had no choice but to accept the situation with her daughter. "After that," Bill said, "Roy started coming over to the house. I always got a big kick out of that. Roy was one of the greatest fellows I ever met. I was about 10 or 11 years old, yet he treated me and talked to me like I was an equal. Not like talkin' to a kid at all. I had a problem with math homework and I asked him to explain it. He sat down there and explained it until I had the grasp of it."

Dinky did not share her brother's affection for Roy. She preferred Claudette's previous suitor, Billy Jack, a tall, good-looking guy who had taken her for rides in his Ford and let her sit in his lap and guide the steering wheel. Perhaps sensing Dinky's resentment, Roy seemed to keep his distance from Dinky.

One night, the Fradys gave Roy a birthday party. Recalling the scene, Gerry said it was Roy's twentieth birthday, and during dinner she found herself chatting about ages. "I said to Roy, 'Well, Claudette's daddy is seven years older than I am. And you're five years older than Claudette.'

"'I'm *what*?' Roy asked.

"'I said you're five years older than Claudette.'

"'You mean that I've robbed the cradle?'

"'You sure have.'

"'She told me she was eighteen years old.'

"Claudette just looked at me and said 'Mother!'"

Soon, Roy was a regular in the Frady household, but Gerry and Chester agreed that he was lazy. "He wanted everybody to wait on him," Chester said, "and he thought everybody should. Claudette waited on him hand and foot."

Though Roy once said his fascination with motorcycles was sparked by Elvis Presley, it actually started much earlier, when he began associating with the Frady family. It was an addiction that would bring Roy Orbison and Claudette Frady both joy and sadness. Chester and Geraldine lived and breathed motorcycles. Chester participated in dirt-road races and loved to bound and fly around the obstacle course. "Hell, Claudette was raised on one of them blame things," Chester said. "When she was two weeks old I held her in my arms on a motorcycle. She rode between me and Gerry when she was a little girl. Claudette learned how to ride a motorcycle by herself." Gerry agreed, saying, "She loved it. Whenever she started riding, she was doing something she wanted to do."

But from the beginning, there was something ominous about the Fradys' weakness for motorcycles. When Claudette was an infant, a man selling Chester a used bike said, "I tell you what I'll do. I'll give you this check back if you'll leave me that baby."

"You gotta be kidding," Chester told him. He refused the trade, but Gerry named the bike *Claudette*, and the incident marked the beginning of a sinister relationship between Claudette and motorcycles. Both Chester and Gerry Frady had a series of near-fatal accidents, Gerry sustaining a concussion and broken ribs and Chester a punctured lung and four broken ribs, as well as two compound leg fractures that almost resulted in amputation. There were plenty of signs that these machines were going to bring calamity into Roy and Claudette's life, but neither heeded them.

As the Frady family got to know Roy better, Claudette's mother sensed that there were problems between Roy and the members of his band, The Teen Kings. One day, Roy brought the boys into the restaurant for lunch, and Gerry overheard one of the musicians saying to Roy, "If I was out on the desert starving for water, you'd bring me a peanut butter sandwich." In addition to trouble with the band, Roy was also having legal problems with his record producer, Norman Petty, just as Buddy Holly would a short time later. "When I signed the contract," Roy said, "Norman Petty had his name on it. He got half the writer's share and all of the publishing." Thus began Roy's lifelong battle with record producers and song publishers. Roy was convinced that a bigger record company could sell more copies of "Ooby Dooby," and he decided to break the contract. After talking it over with his father, he and Orbie Lee Orbison went to see lawyer John R. Lee of Kermit, Texas.

"Don't worry about it," John Lee told Roy. "You're minors. You're not old enough to contract legally. I'll file a case on your behalf with the Odessa District Clerk's office. This will all be over in no time."

An injunction was granted to prevent Je-Wel from putting "Ooby Dooby" on jukeboxes, selling it, or disseminating it. "We ended up settling with Je-Wel," John Lee reported. "We paid them the cost they spent in recording it and cutting the copies and they delivered all their inventory of that record to us."

Before Roy could seek another label for "Ooby Dooby," John R. Lee needed to clear up some remaining matters with Je-Wel. Busy in court, John decided to turn Roy's case over to his partner, George Finley. Je-Wel wanted to continue the deal and make a contract for a new partnership agreement, but since Roy and The Teen Kings were still minors and couldn't contract, John Lee instructed his partner George to arrange for the boys' parents to sign. A month or so later, according to Lee, George Finley called and said, "I sent Roy and his dad a bill for our legal work. They're in receipt of that, but they don't have the money. They'll give us ten percent of the profit they make off Roy's performances. What do you think? Want to gamble on it?"

"Why hell no!" John told him. "Nobody's going to listen to that little ugly son-of-a-bitch."

John R. Lee was annoyed with The Teen Kings anyway. He lived right across from their duplex. "Every damn Saturday morning on my one day off that's what woke me up. They were out there in the garage practicing."

"Well," George said, "Roy doesn't have the money."

"Tell them to go over there at that damn Wink bank and borrow it.

Hell, it was $454. If they won't loan it to him, I'll go over there and sign the note, but I want our money." He got it, but he would live to regret not taking ten percent of Roy Orbison's profits.

Roy's headaches over "Ooby Dooby" were not over. After he dissociated himself from Norman Petty, he went to Dallas and recut the demo for Columbia Records. Columbia turned it down but quickly had one of their own contract artists, Sid King, cut a cover of "Ooby Dooby," which they released before Roy could offer his tape to another record company. The B-side of Roy's Je-Wel record, 'Trying to Get to You,' was bought by Imperial at this time and released as the flip side of a Weldon Rogers record. It was also credited to Rogers.

It's rather miraculous, after all this treachery, that Roy persisted in his determination to become a recording artist. There are several versions of how Roy and Sam Phillips of Sun Records got together. Roy credited Sun recording star Johnny Cash, who once appeared on Roy's Odessa-Midland TV show and suggested that Roy call Sam. Roy said that Sam told him that Johnny Cash did not run his company and hung up on him.

Sam Phillips denied this flatly, as did Billy Pat Ellis. "We never met Johnny Cash," Billy Pat recalled. "He never came on our show. I don't know where that story comes from but it's not true." Jack Kennelly remembers seeing Cash and Presley at the Odessa High School gym but insists The Teen Kings didn't meet Cash until they played on the same bill in Norfolk, Virginia, after they already had their deal with Sam.

Cash himself confirms Roy's version, saying, "In late '55 or early '56, I was touring with Elvis when I met Roy in Texas. He was planning a sock hop in Odessa and we went to Midland to appear on TV. On the way back to Odessa we were listening to the radio and talking about all the clichés in rock songs, like 'go-go-go' and 'real gone' and I suggested he write a song incorporating all these phrases. This became 'Go Go Go,' later known as 'Down the Line.' I told him to get in touch with Sun Records if he wanted to be a recording artist." In Roy's version, it was Cecil Hallifield who got through to Sam and arranged for the Sun recording of "Ooby Dooby."

Billy Pat confirmed one part of Roy's account, saying, "A record store owner in Odessa liked us and played the Je-Wel recording of 'Ooby Dooby' to Sam Phillips on the phone. Then he put us in touch with Sam, and we made arrangements to recut the record. Sam

Phillips got 'Ooby Dooby' because of a man at a record shop in Odessa. This is the end of April 1956. We were in Odessa College." Teen King James Morrow agreed, saying, "It was 'Pop' Hollifield, owner of a record shop in Odessa, who played the record 'Ooby Dooby' to Sam Phillips on the phone." Jack Kennelly also confirms this version and adds that they were all sitting in a record-listening booth in Pop's store.

In an interview on March 21, 1989, Sam Phillips gave his recollection of the affair. "I got a call from Roy. Not this bit you hear about Johnny Cash. I made up my own mind about who I wanted to audition. I didn't want to take on too many artists and not do them justice. I looked for stylists more than good basic rudimentary singers as such or musicians. I wanted to see if there was anything I heard that I thought might break the mold a little bit, you know.

"Now what happened was that when Johnny and Carl and even later Jerry Lee were on the road, somebody always wanted to know how they could get on records. The first thing they ask you when you run into ambitious young people was, 'How in the world can I get a record made?' or 'Reckon I could get an audition?' A lot of them didn't even know what the word audition was—most of them just asked, 'How can I make a record?' Cash was a nice guy; you talk about really bending over to help people. He's just a kindhearted type of guy. I'm sure he told Roy, 'Well, hey, call Mr. Phillips.' They all called me Mr. Phillips. Roy said, 'Johnny Cash told me that you might listen to me if I called.'

"I told Roy, 'If y'all are comin' this way some time,' and I asked him the usual questions: 'Do you have your own band?' 'Do you feel like you have some material?'

"He said, 'Yeah.' They'd recorded 'Ooby Dooby.' 'I've got a couple of things,' he said. 'We've just put it on tape.'

"I said, 'Well, send me your tape and let me listen to it, and, Roy, if I hear anything that I think is a little different, I'll get back with you. Now if I don't call you, in a couple of weeks after you send me the tape, you call me back, because that could slip my mind.'

"He sent the tape in and called me in a couple of weeks and I told him, 'Man, I like this 'Ooby Dooby.' When can you get it together and come in here—'

"'Man, we can get over there—!'"

"We didn't even bother to withdraw from school," Billy Pat said.

"Didn't bother to take our finals. We got F's as a result, and we could have officially withdrawn and got Incompletes." But Roy Orbison didn't care. He saw this as the chance of a lifetime. He was going to be a Sun recording star, like Elvis Presley and Johnny Cash. "Just to be on a label almost meant you were a star to me," Roy said. "You didn't have to have a hit record, just be a recording star of stage, screen and radio." But Roy's days at Sun Records were to prove a mixed blessing at best.

Chapter 3

After Sam Phillips heard "Ooby Dooby" early in 1956, events moved swiftly. Jack Kennelly recalls, "Pop [Hollifield] played it on the phone to Sam on Friday and Monday we were in Memphis recutting 'Ooby Dooby' and then the following Thursday we went to Norfolk, Virginia, to play with Johnny Cash."

Roy said goodby to his folks and then went over to Odessa to bid farewell to his girl. He and Claudette were so much in love it couldn't have been easy for them to face this separation, and Roy may well have been describing his feelings in the recording he was soon to make at Sun Records entitled "A True Love Goodbye," a simple and elegant tune about the heartbreak of two young lovers parting for the first time.

The vast, lonely stretches of West Texas were now behind him. Memphis was an exotic new world, the gateway to the Southland, rich in myth and music. The city is situated on a bluff over the wide Mississippi River, which sometimes creates its own weather, spreading a thick fog from bank to bank. Everything about the Mississippi is overwhelming—it inspired Mark Twain's greatest stories, George Gershwin's "Summertime" and Jerome Kern's "Old Man River." It was the home of sugar plantations, levees and catfish, and its myriad tributaries included the blue bayou Roy would immortalize on a hit record. Memphis, the queen of Mississippi cities, was the birthplace of the blues and rock 'n' roll, "St. Louis Woman" and "That's All Right, Mama," Beale Street and Sun Records, W.C. Handy and Elvis Presley.

Sun Recording Studio was a few minutes' drive from the river, situated on Automobile Row at 706 Union Avenue. Formerly a radiator repair shop, Sun sat on a corner, an unimposing but neat two-story brick structure. Roy and The Teen Kings went inside, and Roy saw a small, unimposing room with an angular ceiling and walls covered with white acoustic tiles. There is something touchingly humble and modest about this room where Elvis Presley ignited the fuse that

45

produced the rock era. The studio has remained unchanged over the years, and today it is open to the public, who are permitted to stroll around and touch the original drums, piano and the same big microphones Roy and Elvis used.

Sam Phillips was a compact, handsome man with blue eyes and a full head of brown, wavy hair. Although he was a decade or more Roy's senior, he looked like a contemporary. There was something reserved about him that Roy could immediately relate to. Despite Sam's hearty greeting—"Hell! Get on in here, boys"—Roy recognized under Sam Phillips' bluster a shy, fragile person like himself.

"When they came in here," Sam recalled, "I was impressed with their appearance and manner. They were a clean-cut-looking bunch of kids."

Just before their audition, Sam chatted with Roy and the boys man-to-man. "Just do it like you did it in the garage," he said. "Be yourselves. Give it all the soul you've got. And relax. I've heard your tape and I like it or I wouldn't have asked you to come to Memphis."

Later, Sam remembered, "I left them with a feeling that if I couldn't get it out of them maybe they might have it down the road, so that they didn't feel like, hell, if they 'failed' an audition at Sun Records, that that was the end of the world."

Carl Perkins was in the studio that day, celebrating the success of "Blue Suede Shoes," which had just gone into the Top 100. As Sam entered the control room, he invited Perkins to join him. They stood behind the window looking out at Roy and The Teen Kings as they began their audition. "This is a boy from Wink, Texas," Sam said to Carl. "What do you think about him?" As he listened to "Ooby Dooby," Carl sensed the country roots in Roy's voice. "It's different," he responded. "He's got that high voice like Bill Monroe. I like it." Bill Monroe was the Kentucky bluegrass singer who'd written one of Elvis's first records, "Blue Moon of Kentucky."

Malcolm Yelvington, one of Sun's rockabilly luminaries, was also in the studio that day. "'Ooby Dooby' was the silliest thing I ever heard," he said, "but it went over. It was going to be a hit." Indeed, "Ooby Dooby" was exactly the kind of music—rockabilly, which is basically taking a country song and rocking it—that Sun Records specialized in.

"We got in there and wheeled around with 'Ooby Dooby,'" Sam recalled. "The band wasn't great and Roy wasn't great particularly on that song, but he was one of the most unusual guitar players I'd ever heard. That impressed me as much as his voice. Nobody played a guitar like Roy Orbison. He played a lot of bass strings on his stuff, then he would go down and, man, he'd get a goddamned E string and A string and he played it coming up more than he did going down." After the audition, Sam invited them into his office and spread out a contract on his desk. "If you got anything hangin' over your head that's going to give you problems," he said, "let's air 'em out now and see if we can't get them in the arrears, because we're going to be bustin' our ass and we want to have fun doin' it. You can't do it if you're all uptight about personal things. That's no way to create in a studio.

"I signed them to a contract for a year or two. Everybody's always sayin' Elvis Presley was a fuckin' overnight hit. I got news for them. It took a little while. [I told Roy] 'Just don't expect too god-danged much too soon and don't let anything break you down before you have gutted yourself inside, spiritually, trying to do the thing that you think that you can do. If you want to go on over to Nashville and sing country or something, fine. But we're looking for music for the younger people here. Young white people are beginning to like the black artists, because the blacks are vital, have effervescence. Their music has a real vitality. The white fathers and mothers and preachers, number one, they don't like the damn music, number two, the artists used to be all black and they thought these young people were falling in love with blacks, with niggers so to speak.'"

Roy had sprung from white country music, with some Tex-Mex thrown in, and he was shocked to hear Sam Phillips tell him that he should try to sing like a black man. Roy knew nothing about rhythm and blues. In the 1950s, many Texas towns still had signs saying "Negroes—don't let the sun go down on you in this town." And in a big city like Fort Worth, the only store stocking rhythm and blues, then called "race records," was a little shop way up on the wrong end of Houston Street, where thirty-five or forty rhythm and blues records were stacked on the counter. If anyone in The Teen Kings was rhythm and blues oriented it was Jack Kennelly, who says, "I was the only white boy in Wink who sounded black."

While Roy and Sam Phillips had in common a background of poverty, musically they were worlds apart. As an underprivileged white boy, Sam had always felt a kinship with the poor blacks of the South and loved their music and dreamed of finding a way to get it to the white market. A visionary, he knew how to draw what he wanted out of rockers like Elvis Presley. Starting as a disk jockey, Sam had put a studio together in 1950 by wiring up a radio board and recording weddings and funerals. He was an innovator from the start, and at Sun, even in the era of monaural recording, he created great sound through angular ceilings and walls and he invented the slapback echo, balancing what was coming out of the microphone and what was coming out of a tape machine. He was also a great promoter who knew how to hawk his artists to DJs and distribute his product to retailers.

Roy arrived at Sun a few months after Sam sold Elvis's contract to RCA for $40,000. Elvis had never hit the national charts at Sun, but now he was on his way to #1 with his first RCA cut, "Heartbreak Hotel." Roy was relieved that Elvis was no longer at Sun and that Sam Phillips was looking for someone to replace his star. Though Roy and Sam weren't really on the same wave length musically, Roy felt he had a chance to become Sam's new fair-haired boy. Perhaps at last Roy Orbison was at the right place at the right time.

They recut "Ooby Dooby" that first day. Roy said, "This version is a little more intense, has a little more drive. At Sun we all played our own instruments. It was unusual for people to go into a studio to record popular records without backup musicians and orchestras. You couldn't go back and overdub. All the records were done on the spot. Another thing was that the studio was a tiny place. When heavy drumming came on the scene, you had to sing over everything. Recording was a process of cancellation. Whatever was loudest came through. Presley, Cash, Jerry Lee Lewis, we all developed strong voices through this."

The B-side of "Ooby Dooby" was "Go Go Go," the song Roy and Billy Pat wrote at North Texas State College, basing it on "Kaw-Liga." "We were standing there trying to figure out what to record," Billy Pat said. "We did 'Go Go Go' warming up and Sam Phillips liked it and put it on the back of 'Ooby Dooby.'" Billy Pat was shocked when the record was issued in May 1956 with Roy claiming sole authorship. "That teed me off," Billy Pat said. "We were all put out with him." The only assistance on "Go Go Go" Roy acknowledged was Johnny Cash's, saying Johnny helped him turn this rocker into a parody of other rock 'n' roll songs. Billy Pat would continue to fume as this song, retitled "Down the Line," became a rock standard, recorded by both Jerry Lee Lewis and Ricky Nelson. Billy Pat says that although Roy fought to get him a money settlement from Sam, the billing matter was never set right.

The night after that first session at Sun, The Teen Kings checked into The Claridge Hotel in Memphis. "We had a big suite on the eighth floor," Jack recalled. "Sam paid for the first two or three days, and by Thursday we were in Norfolk to play with Cash."

As Roy waited for "Ooby Dooby" to be released, he dreamed of becoming Sun's next big star. "We all went to Beale Street to shop," Roy said. "We went into the stores and bought chartreuse coats and lace shirts and pointed shoes and pink-and-black shirts."

One day, Roy told Sam Phillips he had some ballads he'd written and would like Sam to hear them. "*Ballads*?" Sam said. "We're at the wrong stage of rock 'n' roll to come out and start croonin' like Dean Martin. Look at Pat Boone. Even he's not doing all that much croonin'. 'Tutti Frutti'! If I put you out singin' some damn ballad, the world will never hear of Roy Orbison again. That's not the tenor of what is going on in the United States of America as far as music and rock 'n' roll are concerned."

Crestfallen, Roy saw his chances of stardom quickly fading. As a veteran honky-tonk entertainer, he could rock with the best of them, but his heart and soul were in softer emotions than Sun's spitfire rockabillies were howling about. Instead of blue suede shoes and hound dogs and alligators and flying saucers, he wanted to express the joy and ecstasy he was feeling in his love affair with Claudette. In fact, he was working on a song called "Claudette."

The Sun Records Roy was joining was a hectic center of creativity run by a few devoted, overworked staffers, one of whom was Sam's secretary, Marion Keisker. "I was working late," Marion remembered, "and I saw Roy and his musicians go to sleep on the studio floor." According to Jack Kennelly, they were probably taking a break during a late recording session. "My son David came in a little later," Marion continued. "He knew if he wanted to see his mommy, he had to come to the studio. I had been there seven chaotic years. When I began, Sam was still doing local radio. He needed money to keep the studio running. Sun hours were around the clock. I was sitting on the studio floor painting baseboards one night and was shocked to hear a voice saying, 'What are you doing here this time of night, Miss Marion?' I looked up and saw the biggest blackest giant I'd ever seen. It was three a.m. and it was Howlin' Wolf. 'Oh,' I thought, 'if my mother could see me now!' Mother was terrified of blacks."

Howlin' Wolf was Chester Arthur Burnett, a blues singer from the

Delta, and one of the original shapers of rock 'n' roll. "Blacks like Howlin' Wolf drifted into Sun whenever they felt like it," Marion said, "regardless of appointments missed, and Sam would say, 'Come on in, guys, let's see what you've got.' Sun records was in a very dark area of Memphis, and there was an auto repair service across the street. I was the gofer. Though it was the segregationist 1950s, I would go to a hamburger joint on Madison Avenue and bring food back to the studio for the black artists. I also did janitor work in the studio—anything that needed doing."

Roy soon discovered that getting a record contract at Sun didn't automatically make him rich. There was no advance payment. An artist cut a record, was paid maybe thirty-five dollars for the session, and waited for royalties, if any, to come in. A singer couldn't survive that way, and it was necessary to play some gigs just to put together enough cash to rent an apartment. Fortunately, Sam Phillips had established a booking agency that enabled his artists to make some pocket money touring and singing before live audiences until their records hit. The Teen Kings performed under the auspices of Stars, Inc., which Bob Neal was running for Sam. Jack Kennelly recalls, "Air fare was too expensive so we had to pitch in and buy a car. There were seven or eight acts in these shows and it was a spectacular caravan. We put so many miles on the cars that the only thing that would hold up was something big like a Cadillac, so that's what we got. Carl Perkins always had a Lincoln or a Chrysler Imperial. Johnny Horton drove the '55 Olds he was eventually killed in. I ended up taking over the payments on that first Cadillac. I was back in class in Wink for a while and looked out the window one day and saw it being 'repo'd.'"

When Roy went back into the studio with The Teen Kings in the spring of 1956, they cut "You're My Baby," "Rockhouse" and "Domino." The first was a Johnny Cash song, and "Rockhouse" was a collaboration between Roy and Conway Twitty, then known as Harold Jenkins. When Roy and Twitty met and realized they were both writing songs called "Rockhouse," they simply put them together into one song. Roy's half had been written when he was in Chester and Gerry Frady's house in Odessa. According to Gerry, "He went to the bathroom and stayed there two hours. When he came out I said, 'What in the world is the matter with you, Roy? Are you okay?' He just laughed and said, 'I've just written a song called 'Rockhouse.'

Remember that when it becomes a hit.'" It would never be a hit but it was a fine little rocker, especially with Billy Pat on drums. In the lyrics, the rockhouse is a place where there's no trouble, no blues, and it's going twenty-four hours a day—an early vision of the rock paradise that would materialize in the disco palaces of the '60s and '70s.

"The first artist Sam gave me to record was Roy Orbison," Sun engineer and producer Jack Clement remembered. "I recorded 'Rockhouse' with Roy, and it was good. But Roy was not into what the Sun Studio was capable of back then." From Roy's viewpoint, it was Sun that was not capable of handling him. "I was writing more ballads then but I didn't bother to ask Sam to release them. He was the boss and there was no arguing. I made some demos of things like 'Claudette' but that was about it. I would never have made it big with Sun. They just did not have the ways to get into the audience I wanted to go for." Roy recorded a number of first-rate rockabilly songs that Sun didn't bother to release. Sam held on to "Domino" for years, and when he finally issued it, he received the composer's credit. The lyrics reflected Roy's idealized self-image—a cool cat who wore diamond rings and white shoes, had coal-black hair with long sideburns and drove a blue sports car: girls threw themselves at him.

Unfortunately for Roy, Sam Phillips had already lined up Elvis' successor at Sun and his name wasn't Roy Orbison. Sam sized Roy up as a gawky teenager with a pear-shaped face and thick glasses. "I knew his voice was pure gold," Sam said. "I also knew that if anyone got a look at him, he'd be dead inside of a week." The man Sam saw filling Elvis's shoes was Carl Perkins. Carl was not only a born rocker, very much to Sam's taste, but he was presentable as well, and in the spring of 1956 it looked as if "Blue Suede Shoes" could dethrone Elvis Presley as the king of rock. By the time Roy reached Memphis in March '56, "Blue Suede Shoes" was going to the top of all three charts—pop, country and rhythm and blues. Elvis Presley had failed to score a single Top 10 record at Sun, so Carl Perkins was not only Elvis's successor but Sun's biggest star ever. Over at RCA, Elvis was also hitting nationally for the first time with "Heartbreak Hotel," and the first big race for king of rock 'n' roll was on. Carl's career was tragically derailed when he was injured in a car wreck while driving to New York to appear on network television. Bedridden for weeks, Carl watched helplessly as Elvis Presley acquired the rights to make a recording of "Blue Suede Shoes" (which any singer can do by applying to the copyright holder of any song) and proceeded to cover

Carl's song with a version that split the market, prevented Carl's version from ever reaching #1 and forever identified "Blue Suede Shoes" as an Elvis Presley song in the public's mind.

With Carl Perkins out of the running, Roy got yet another shot at becoming Sun's big star. On May 1, 1956, Sun 242, "Ooby Dooby"/"Go Go Go" was issued. *Billboard's* review was a rave: "Orbison's spectacular, untamed quality spells big action for both sides of this new disking. The top side is already getting healthy initial reaction and regardless of competition, figures to cash in for plenty of loot in the rural sectors. The flip is a wild, swingin' country blues with an impressive primitive flavor. Either one here." A few weeks later, *Billboard* wrote, "Orbison is one of the few of the numerous group of country blues singers to have sprung up recently who is succeeding. It has taken several weeks for this disk to make its full impact felt, but by now it is well established in most key Southern and Northern markets. For the past two weeks it has been on the Memphis territorial chart. Flip is 'Go Go Go.' A previous *Billboard* 'Spotlight' pick."

At 706 Union Avenue there was a heady air of victory throughout May '56. With or without Elvis Presley, Sun Records dominated the Memphis chart. The Top 8 looked like this:

1. "I Walk the Line," J. Cash, Sun
2. "Blue Suede Shoes," C. Perkins, Sun
3. "Boppin' the Blues," C. Perkins, Sun
4. "Heartbreak Hotel," E. Presley, Vic.
5. "Ooby Dooby," R. Orbison, Sun
6. "Rock 'n' Ruby," Warren Smith, Sun
7. "Yes, I Know Why," W. Pierce, Dee
8. "Come Back to Me," J. Newman, Dot

Roy and The Teen Kings were to be featured at the birthplace of rock 'n' roll, Memphis' Overton Park Shell, where Elvis had made his debut. It was rumored that Elvis was going to show up at the Overton that night, to take a look at Roy Orbison, Sun Records' latest singing sensation. On the eve of the Overton concert, Sam Phillips told Roy that, other than Elvis', Carl's and Johnny's records, "Ooby Dooby" was Sun's most successful rockabilly release. It had sold over 250,000 copies and reached #59 on the national pop charts—a minor hit but a hit nonetheless.

The Overton Park Shell is one of America's acoustical gems. A person can stand on the stage and whisper and be heard with crystal clarity in the back row. The bill on June 1, 1956, when Roy played the Overton, included, in descending order, Carl Perkins, "Mr. Blue Suede Shoes in Person"; Johnny Cash, "Cry Cry Cry"; Warren Smith, "Rock & Roll Ruby"; "Ooby Dooby" Roy Orbison and Eddie Bond, "Rockin' Daddy." The price of admission for this bill was one dollar for adults and fifty cents for children.

Elvis was in the audience that night, and the crowd treated him like a favorite son. No longer a local Southern phenomenon, Elvis was a national hero, having sold ten million records in the past twelve months, sixty percent of RCA's entire output. After the show, Elvis came back stage to greet the performers. As Roy recalled in a 1974 interview, "Elvis told me he would never work the same show I worked—meaning it in the nicest form. Which was marvelous, whether he meant it or not. That would stand out to a young fellow just starting in the business as the greatest compliment that could be paid. It's not that I'm looking for compliments, but I'm very sensitive, and if an artist says this, that or the other, I listen."

Billy Pat was listening that night, too, but he heard something different. Interviewed in 1989, Billy Pat recalled, "Elvis told Jack Kennelly, 'You're a damn good bass player.' I don't remember him saying anything to Roy." "Roy had a personal hit on the record 'Ooby Dooby,'" Jack Kennelly said. "Before that we'd had no leader but now we had to do just the tunes that were on the records. Roy's dream was to be a star, and once Sam inflated his ego he couldn't be a part of a unit. Roy became egomaniacal." Roy's relations with The Teen Kings were rapidly deteriorating.

When Roy received his first royalty check from "Ooby Dooby," he made the down payment on a new white 1957 Cadillac. His next purchase, the dream of many Depression babies, was a diamond ring. When Elvis invited Roy to Graceland, he was able to pull up to the Music Gates in style. "One night," Roy said, "we went to pick up Elvis's girlfriend in his purple Cadillac—I think he was making twenty million dollars a year at the time. When he knocked on the door, the girl said, 'I'm sorry. You're too late,' and walked back in. We all went on to his house and had Pepsi Colas and potato chips. I couldn't believe that some woman would turn down a date with Elvis Presley."

"It was Elvis who, without knowing it, made me a motorcycle fan," Roy said. "I saw a motorcycle outside Sun Records Studio and somebody told me it belonged to Elvis Presley. I finally managed to get to take a motorcycle ride with the guy who bought that machine from Elvis and that was the start of it."

Roy returned to Texas to tour with The Teen Kings and to visit Claudette and his own family. Claudette was now living with her folks in Lubbock, and Roy picked her up in the white Cadillac and drove down to Wink. He saw old high-school friends like football hero Buddy Gray and Susie Newberg, who were going together. Susie recalled, "What really shocked us was that Claudette was going with Roy. 'She's so good-looking,' everyone was whispering. 'How did he get her?'"

Roy told Susie and others in Wink, "I'd prefer you didn't call me Facetus." Susie said someone whispered, "I guess he thinks he's too good to be called Facetus now."

"I remember him pulling into the filling station there on Main Street," former classmate Bill Beckham observed. "Claudette was really a good-looking girl, and that car...well, it was quite a sensation. But he was still the same old Roy. He spent thirty or forty minutes there, just laughing about the old days."

The Teen Kings followed Roy home, and one night they played a dance at Odessa's Eagle Club. Chester Frady was a member there, and the whole Frady family came to hear Roy sing. Sitting at a big table up front were Claudette, Bill, Chester, Gerry, and Kadon, who had a date with James Morrow. "James didn't make much of an impression on me," Kadon said. "He was very quiet and very tall. Our first date was accidental. I was going to that dance with Roy and Claudette and James came along because they were playing and we just kind of wound up together. We saw each other a couple of times after that." Discussing that night many years later, Kadon said, "Claudette knew right away she wanted to marry Roy. She was not hard to get. They were going around in Roy's car, though they could barely afford gas. I liked Roy. He was definitely his own person, quiet, witty, a dry sense of humor. He did something weird when he received a royalty check. It was for $500 and he got it all in $1 bills and carefully ironed every one of them. He said he felt like he would never be any more than lead singer with The Teen Kings."

Roy began to tour all over West Texas with The Teen Kings, and Susie Newberg, who was now attending TCU, caught their act at The North Side Coliseum in Fort Worth. During a break, Susie and the band sat outside talking. "I asked them how everything was going," Susie recalled, "and they said, 'This isn't all it's cracked up to be. You ride all night to get some place, and you try to clean up a little bit, you have a show, and then it's back in the car and you're driving some place else. It's expensive, too.'

" 'How much are they paying you?' I asked.

" 'Aw, they're paying us thirty dollars a night, each one. You can't buy the gas and get your clothes cleaned and afford a room every night. When we get through, we're sleeping in the cars.'"

Roy seemed unaware that the band was demoralized. "Roy was okay with touring," Susie remembered. "It was what he wanted. But the band was disillusioned." According to Jack Kennelly, "Roy was on an ego trip. He carried himself aloof from us and we started getting shoved aside. We were being treated as hired hands instead of the group that had got us to where we were."

Roy met his future songwriting collaborator Bill Dees at an Odessa radio station one night when Roy was substituting for an ailing DJ. Bill was part of a group called The Five Boys and they did five songs on the air, with Roy in the control room. Formed as a student group at West Texas State College, The Five Boys took their style from The Gladiolas' "Little Darlin'" and The Chords' "Sh-boom," and their first single, "Jitterbugging," was released on a Dot Records subsidiary. The B-side was Bill's composition "Unforgotten Love." The Five Boys changed their name to The Whirlwinds and backed up Roy during one of his Texas gigs. Bill remembered that when his guitar strap snapped, Roy had an extra one and immediately handed it over to him.

Like Roy, Bill and his group recorded at Norman Petty's studio in Clovis. In fact, during his Sun years, Roy continued to drive "back and forth, on and off" to Clovis to work with Norman Petty, who was more receptive to Roy's songs than Sam Phillips, and Peanuts Wilson usually made the trip to Clovis with Roy. Norman Petty helped Roy develop many of his early songs.

As 1956, rock's first great year, drew to a close, Roy regretted that he hadn't been able to follow up "Ooby Dooby" with another hit. His second Sun single, number 251, "You're My Baby," was a commercial failure when it was released in September. The flip side, "Rock-house," didn't do any better. Elvis Presley held the #1 position in America from mid-August through October with "Don't Be Cruel" / "Hound Dog" and then, without interruption, stayed in #1 through November and the first week of December with "Love Me Tender." No wonder people in the record business were calling 1956 Elvis Presley's year. Some of the other records that soared to the top in '56 as Roy hovered at the bottom of the rock heap were The Platters' "My Prayer," Guy Mitchell's "Singing the Blues" and Fats Domino's "Blueberry Hill." *Billboard's* Disk Jockey Poll revealed the Most Played Record of 1956 to be Kay Starr's "Rock and Roll Waltz" and the DJs' own favorite record was Morris Stoloff's "Moonglow and Theme From *Picnic*." Though Elvis was the Most Played, the DJ's preferred Frank Sinatra and his *Songs for Swinging Lovers*.

While still touring the Southwest, Roy played the campus of West Texas State College, and Buddy Holly was also on the bill. After the show, a student on athletic scholarship sought Roy and Buddy out and asked them how to make a record. His name was Buddy Wayne Knox, and he had formed a band with some glee club friends called The Four Orchids. Roy remembered starting The Wink Westerners virtually the same way, and both he and Buddy Holly became friendly with Buddy Knox, suggesting that he go to nearby Clovis, New Mexico, and cut his record at Norman Petty's studio.

Following their counsel, Buddy Knox managed to get a three-day session in Clovis, arriving with sixty dollars in his pocket and a song he'd written when he was fifteen called "Party Doll." Norman Petty's drummer David Alldred didn't have a complete set of drums, so they used a cardboard box stuffed with cotton and a microphone. Backup vocals were provided by girls recruited from the Clovis High School marching band.

Both Roy and Buddy Holly were shocked when they looked at the *Billboard* charts a few months later, in early 1957, and saw that Buddy Knox had beat them both to the #1 position. Buddy Knox was the first singer of the rock era to write his own chart-topping song, and "Party Doll" marked the recording debut of the Southwestern brand of rockabilly known as Tex-Mex music. "I really don't remember writing 'Party Doll,'" Buddy Knox said, "but I did, out on the farm, behind a haystack. When I got into college, we started hearing about Elvis

Presley and Jerry Lee Lewis and Chuck Berry, and found out we were doing the same kind of music they were doing."

Buddy Holly began to record in Clovis in 1956, and he taped an unreleased version of Roy and Billy Pat's "Go Go Go." Buddy also recorded two of Roy's songs, "You've Got Love," co-written with Peanuts Wilson, and "An Empty Cup (and a Broken Date)." But Roy's relationship with Buddy Holly developed overtones of bitter rivalry. Roy said that Holly's first single, "Blue Days and Black Nights," "sounded just like Elvis. Buddy followed Elvis and they were tied up in my thinking." Roy was in for a terrible jolt when Buddy Holly became a star before he did.

Buddy Holly cut "That'll Be the Day" in Clovis at about the same time Buddy Knox was recording "Party Doll," but Buddy Holly's record, perhaps the most acclaimed and influential of the early rock period, did not hit #1 until later in 1957—September in the U.S. and November in the U.K. Buddy Knox was drafted into the Army, and 1957 would belong to Buddy Holly, just as 1956 had been Elvis' year. Roy Orbison must have wondered when it was going to be his turn. Dejected, he said "Buddy Holly became a big Number One star, and that was way out of my league. But I continued to record for Sun at the time."

Roy was beginning to learn about the business end of being a recording artist. He was touring in New Mexico with Carl Perkins when he learned about BMI and realized he wasn't getting paid when his records were played on the radio. "I was still in New Mexico when I was with Sun Records," Roy said, "and I met a guy named Slim Willet who wrote 'Don't Let the Stars Get in Your Eyes.' He said, 'How's your BMI running?' I thought he was talking about a foul note. I didn't know what he meant. So he says, 'When they play your song on the air, they pay you.'

"I said, 'Bull.' Then he told me how much he made on 'Don't Let the Stars Get in Your Eyes.' I told Carl Perkins, 'They pay you to play those songs.'

"Carl said, 'Roy, you're not telling me the truth.' So we floor-boarded the car all the way to Memphis to talk to Sam about it. When you're young and enthusiastic, contracts are not the main thing in your life. I don't think I was manipulated back then. Maybe a little constricted."

Roy came through Lubbock to say goodbye to Claudette and her family. Chester Frady recalled, "Those two kids went out and had Cokes and hamburgers and then Roy didn't have any money to get back to Memphis on. We gave him what we could, and somehow he made it back there."

In Memphis, Roy never succeeded in making ends meet. At the same time, over in Nashville, Patsy Cline, with whom Roy would soon be touring, complained to her friend Brenda Lee that she wasn't making a dime off her hit record "Walkin' After Midnight." Patsy had signed with an independent producer, Bill McCall, who owned a small label called Four-Star. According to country star Faron Young, "Patsy signed a two percent deal with Four-Star and McCall was probably leasing her to Decca for eight percent. Slim Willet, the boy who wrote and cut 'Don't Let the Stars Get in Your Eyes,' was owed over $100,000 in 1953 and received only $1,500. If you got in McCall's office past his ten secretaries, he was such a smoothie he could talk you out of killing him. God knows, enough of us tried! But Slim just walked in there, reached over McCall's desk, grabbed him by the neck, and like to beat the shit out of him. He left with a check for $60,000 in his pocket."

Later in his career, Roy Orbison would go to court to fight Wesley Rose, his manager, for what he deemed to be his fair share of his song-publishing income. The business practices of recording companies were summed up by a Nashville disk jockey named Ralph Emery, who broadcast over WSM and was married to country singer Skeeter Davis: "When you're a singer and you're not making records and you want to be so badly, you'll do damn near anything to get it. Then if you have a few hits and become successful, you get pissed about the deal you made. But it's a two-way street. It's hard if not impossible to have it both ways.

"A lot of the big shots took publishing, writing, everything they could get their hands on in those days. And they could justify it by saying that if it wasn't for them putting up the money for the sessions and the costs, no one would have been making records. It was their way of getting back their money, in some cases, which is the purpose of business. Exxon does that every day."

When Roy and The Teen Kings returned to Sun to record on December 14, 1956, Jerry Lee Lewis, a blond kid from Ferriday, Louisiana, was all over the place. He'd sold thirty-three dozen eggs to finance a trip to Memphis to audition for Sam, who had been away in Nashville. Jerry had staged a sit-down strike until Jack Clement agreed to record him. Now Sam was about to release Jerry's first single, "Whole Lotta Shakin' Goin' On."

That day in December, Roy cut "Sweet and Easy to Love," "Devil Doll" and "The Cause of It All." Other than "Ooby Dooby," "Sweet and Easy to Love" was the most engaging of Roy's Sun records, and Roy felt certain that this would be the hit that would take him to the top. On this record, Roy sounded touchingly adolescent, with a high, childish voice, the same "midget" sound that would take Paul Anka to #1 in a few months with "Diana." Brenda Lee would also succeed with this almost bizarre sound, which struck some listeners as appealingly innocent but sounded peculiar and androgynous to others. It was a sound that didn't work for Roy Orbison commercially, though it would still be a few years before he realized what was wrong and lowered his voice. On this record, Roy used some backup singers doing catchy do-wadda-wah's, and variations on these pioneering rock riffs would emerge in the songs of his major period later on.

"Sweet and Easy to Love" was backed by the very hot and infectious "Devil Doll." With two strong sides, this recording was Roy's big bid for the 1957 charts. Sam Phillips' gifted recording engineer Jack Clement supervised the session, and the recording had everything going for it. Its commercial failure must have been daunting. As Martin Hawkins and Colin Escott pointed out in their astute liner notes for one of Roy's U.K. albums years later, "'Sweet and Easy to Love' deserved to be a hit but came at a time when most of Sun's resources were being channelled toward Jerry Lee Lewis and Johnny Cash."

The flipside, "Devil Doll," also deserved better, and the record marked the first time Roy used a vocal chorus. He found the group, called The Roses, in West Texas and brought them to Memphis to back him up, perhaps emulating Elvis Presley's successful association with The Jordanaires. The Roses added a wistful quality to "Devil Doll," and later, Norman Petty lured the group to Clovis to work with Buddy Holly. The Teen Kings probably resented Roy's brief fling with The Roses and added it to their growing list of grievances. Little Johnny Wilson was sure that he could be as big a rockabilly star as Roy, and Norman Petty was encouraging him to cut a single without The Teen Kings. The band was headed for an imminent breakup.

Roy's cut of "The Cause of It All" was not deemed up to Sun standards and was held back for more than a decade. "Jack Clement did do some sessions with me where we got into a different style of music," Roy said, "but I remember him also telling me not to be a ballad singer. He told me I'd never make it, saying, 'Stay away from those ballads, Orby.'" Jack Clement was an ex-Marine who returned to Memphis in 1954, working in a dance band at The Eagle's Nest. Jack brought Billy Lee Riley's "Flying Saucers Rock 'n' Roll" to Sun, and Sam Phillips hired Jack as his first engineer-producer, paying him nineteen dollars a week.

"From the beginning it was a heady experience," Jack noted, "cutting Roy Orbison on the first day, getting Jerry Lee's 'Whole Lotta Shakin'" down on tape almost as an afterthought at the end of a session, writing 'Ballad of a Teenage Queen' and 'Guess Things Happen That Way,' pop hits for Johnny Cash."

Billy Lee Riley sometimes jammed with Roy at Sun. A gifted multi-instrumentalist from Pocahontas, Arkansas, he played harmonica, guitar, drums and piano. With the success of his Sun singles "Red Hot" and "Flying Saucer," Billy Lee became one of the key figures in the brief but boisterous heyday of rockabilly.

Warren Smith was another popular rockabilly singer, and Roy placed one of his compositions, "So Long I'm Gone," with Warren, who recorded it in January 1957. Though Roy's favorite composition, "Claudette," was ignored by everyone around the studio, he loved being a part of the rock repertory company at 706 Union. He did not consider Sun a good studio and criticized its tiny size and meagre facilities, but Roy valued his associations with the great pop musicians of rock's first flowering. "Being there with everybody working actually made it seem like a workshop," Roy said. "The technology of what made those records sound great was that they were two-track recordings. Everything would be on one track, and then you'd put echo on the second track. One track for me and the band, the other for echo. Sam was pretty much full of himself. He seemed to know what he was doing. As it turned out, I don't think he did. But he may have lived his life the way he wanted."

Sam Phillips appreciated everything about Roy but his voice. "Roy had probably the best ear for a beat of anybody I recorded outside of Jerry Lee Lewis. Roy would take his guitar by himself and if we had a session going, he would come in early and pick an awful lot, warming up and getting his fingers working. His timing would amaze me, with him playing lead and filling in with some rhythm licks. I would kid him about it. I said, 'Roy what you're trying to do is to get rid of everybody else and do it all yourself.'

"Roy just hated to lay his guitar down. He was always either writing or developing a beat or an approach to what he was doing. He was totally preoccupied with making records at that time."

Sam Phillips was probably closer to the truth than he thought when he said Roy Orbison was trying to get rid of everybody else and do it all himself. The Teen Kings were sensing the same thing, because in 1957 they walked out on Roy in the middle of a recording session. The issue was Sam Phillips' intention to change the name of the act from The Teen Kings to Roy Orbison and The Teen Kings. Roy had said, "Okay, but what about the cut?" That did not set well with The Teen Kings. According to Jack Kennelly, "Sam no longer wanted to promote the group. He wanted one name up front and as Roy was doing the vocal he decided to push Roy. We agreed reluctantly as long as there was no pay cut." On the day Roy and The Teen Kings broke up, according to Sam Phillips, they were arguing over money, but the basic problem Roy always had in keeping a band together was that he was too much of a loner and a driven egotist for anyone close to him to flourish or even survive. In other rock groups such as The Beatles, Rolling Stones or The Beach Boys, everyone became famous, even an ordinary drummer like Ringo Starr. But Roy was too insecure and too intent on hogging the limelight to foster careers other than his own, and sometimes, as at Sun Records that day, the price was high. Suddenly he was a lead singer without a group. That was a serious matter at Sun, where there were no studio musicians. If a singer didn't have a band backing him up, he was finished.

Chapter 4

"Roy was lazy," Billy Pat Ellis said. "Never would help loading and unloading. That aggravated us, and I was annoyed about a song we wrote together, and when it was recorded, his name was the only one listed as writer. The way we did it, leaving Roy at Sun, was bad. Sam Phillips and Roy went next door and we just loaded up and left, which is pretty rotten. I'll regret it all my life. Roy held a grudge against me for leaving him high and dry. He liked revenge."

Sam Phillips recalled the incident in detail. "I didn't know anything about it until the damn people were racking up their drums and walkin' out. I was back in my office and they were rehearsin' in the studio a little bit, and the next thing I knew, Roy came back there and he looked like death had set in on him. He felt that he had been totally deserted. I never really knew what the dispute was, but I'm one of these son-of-a-bitches who feels if you can't take it, get out, and I said to Roy, 'Tell them bastards to go! Shit! What's your problem, Roy?'

"'Well,' he said, 'we just had a misunderstanding about what percentage everybody—'

"'Let's wait until we make some goddamned money,' I told him. I think I built a little backbone in him. Roy was—well, he had a song called 'Chicken Hearted' he wrote. Roy wasn't chicken-hearted but he was very soft-hearted. That was just his nature.

"You've got a bunch of kids there, they're all contemporaries. Unless you can be the take-charge guy...believe me, the rest of his musicians, they didn't have enough to offer me, in my opinion, without Roy Orbison. Where were they without Roy? There wasn't a goddamned one of them could sing. I don't think any one of them could even carry harmony, as far as I knew. Of course, I didn't go for all that damned harmony bullshit then. I liked for somebody to get out in front and tell me about it.

"Roy said, 'We've been splittin' up our money, what little we've made. Basically, I don't really have anything. I'd just love to stay in town.'

"'Roy,' I said. 'No problem! Nobody around here's goin' to bed hungry. I don't usually invite my artists out to my house. I want to get away from you damn fools!' That's exactly what I told him. But I said, 'I love you.' This is when he brought Claudette in. I said, 'We can make room for her too.'

"Claudette was his inspiration when all of this happened. He called her up and she came in town. They came out here and stayed a long time. I said, 'Look, you're not company in my house. You get up and do, you cook and here's where the eggs are and there's where this is, you know, and feel at home.' They weren't married at the time and they didn't sleep together when they stayed with us."

Sam's son Knox, who was twelve at the time, recalled, "We had a pinball machine and a pool table in the den and a big dining table in the kitchen. We all sat around the table and talked for hours, and Roy played pinball with me and let me win some games. All the kids in the neighborhood were in awe of Claudette. She was the most beautiful thing that had ever walked around this vicinity, especially when she wore her green and gold dress.

"One night, Elvis Presley showed up unannounced, and Mother [Becky Phillips] and Claudette fixed a big meal, despite the hour." Elvis still called Sam Mr. Phillips, mindful that Sam had taken a chance on him and guys like Carl Perkins and Roy Orbison when no one else would. "You got us to play what we thought you didn't want to hear," Elvis said, "what we played on the front porch or in the garage." After dinner they sat around the big table and talked about cars. Roy loved driving Sam's purple four-door Cadillac Eldorado with a white interior.

Roy and Claudette remained for weeks in the protective environment of the Phillips home, cared for by Sam, Becky and young Knox. Claudette was able to make Roy strong and confident again, with her warm, loving nature. But they were broke, and Roy, getting no royalty payments from his string of flop records, had to go back to work. It was painfully clear he couldn't survive as a recording artist. He had to hit the road again.

Nineteen fifty-seven was a vintage rock 'n' roll year, and Roy toured with the most exciting singers of the rockabilly era. One of the classics of the rockabilly genre was Sonny Burgess' "We Wanna Boogie." Roy loved to tell of working a show with Sonny in Albuquerque. "Sonny was traveling with Johnny Cash because his car had broken down," Roy said. "We had to leave a lot of gear behind and the show was a complete disaster because the band did not know what we were doing. Sonny at least created a diversion with his appearance. He had dyed his hair red, had a Fender guitar with red shoes, along with a red suit. But even that didn't save him. He came to the car afterward and said, 'Man, they'll always remember us in Albuquerque as the Wink Wildcat and the Red Clown.'"

Eddie Cochran and Gene Vincent were among the other rockabilly innovators Roy toured with at this time. Eddie had a #18 hit with John D. Loudermilk's "Sittin' in the Balcony," and Gene Vincent, famous for his stutter-and-hiccup style, contributed one of the most delightful of all rockers, the #7 hit "Be-Bop-A-Lula." Gene was another rock 'n' roll motorcycle victim, and he wore a metal leg brace for life.

"When I was on tour in 1956, '57, with Eddie Cochran and Gene Vincent, in Scranton, Pennsylvania," Roy said, "all around on these big packaged shows, there would be acts with only one song. Maybe the song would be 'Bad Days,' and the next act had 'Good Days,' then 'Lonely Days,' and then 'Happy Days,' and then oblivion. I never wanted to be in the position where the only thing I could do was something I had already done. So I started writing songs.

"When I first started touring with guys like Eddie and Gene, I wondered where the material would come from to sustain their success. I just figured I'd write my own. On the road to becoming a true and deserving professional, my songwriting ability came along to go with my singing. It was a blessing and a gift." Roy would be a long time getting his songwriting career off the ground. Though both Jerry Lee Lewis and Ricky Nelson had recorded "Down the Line," it had charted for neither. And although Roy loved the song he wrote about Claudette, he still couldn't sell it to anyone.

"I toured in the Sun days with just one hit record," Roy said. "I'd go onstage, and I'd play everybody else's stuff—Chuck Berry's stuff, Little Richard's stuff—then I'd sing my one hit record and get off. And I really did want to have a few to play. And when I got the few, I cared for them enough that I never minded performing them."

Barbara Pittman, who would come to be known as The Queen of Rockabilly, was one of the Sun recording artists who regularly toured in Sam and Bob Neal's shows. She recalled meeting and performing with Roy in 1956-57: "Roy looked like Alfred E. Newman in *Mad* Magazine. I swear to God. He had ears out to here. Sweet, nice, quiet boy, Roy Orbison, with thick glasses. Dumbo ears. Very private. I kind of thought he was a snob. He really didn't have anything to do with us. He had an attitude. I thought he'd been a schoolteacher and looked on the rest of us as uneducated teenagers. He seemed like a little bitty guy. He was not very tall, and at that time he was really small, or that was my impression."

One night on tour there was a violent incident backstage, and Roy came close to getting beaten up. It occurred in Memphis when Barbara, Roy, Warren Smith and Carl Perkins were playing The Malco Theatre (now called The Orpheum), and suddenly Dorsey and Johnny Burnette came storming in, drunk, rowdy, belligerent and looking for a fight. Johnny Burnette was a Memphis boy who'd gone to Humes High with Elvis and worked as a Mississippi bargeman and boxer before forming a trio with his older brother Dorsey and a friend named Paul Burlison. At the time of the incident at The Malco, they were angry because Sam Phillips had rejected them as being too similar to Elvis. Later, Johnny scored hit singles with "You're Sixteen," "Dreamin'" and "God, Country and My Baby," and Dorsey had a hit in "Tall Oak Tree" and a song he wrote for Ricky Nelson, "Waiting in School." But that night at The Malco, they were mad and loaded and vengeful.

"They burst in and wanted to go on stage," Barbara related. "We wouldn't let them because they were drunk and they'd been fighting and were all torn up and bleeding. They'd been brawling with sailors, and they got mad because the manager wouldn't have them on the show. They decided to beat up Roy Orbison, not because he was doing anything, or would. He was a lot smaller than the Burnette brothers and he was scared to death. They had him backed up on the stairway when Carl Perkins and his brother and cousins came by. Carl took one look at what was happening and then beat up both Johnny and Dorsey, drawing some blood, and threw them out of the theatre." After that, Roy Orbison and Carl Perkins were friends for life.

Roy often went on tours that included Barbara, Carl, Warren Smith, and now Jerry Lee Lewis. At this time, Jerry Lee and Elvis were fighting over Barbara, and Barbara was proudly wearing the red vest Jerry Lee had worn during the "Great Balls of Fire" recording session at Sun. Later, when Jerry married his adolescent cousin Myra, Barbara put Jerry's vest in a frame and hung it on her wall.

"Roy was strange," Barbara said. "We toured with Jerry Lee on his bus *Great Balls of Fire*. Jud Phillips, Sam's brother, was Jerry Lee's agent and he was usually with us. It was a great looking bus with a big flame running down the side and a bar inside. We'd tour the Memphis area, Alabama, Mississippi, and Arkansas in the bus with Jerry Lee, Roy, Warren Smith, Carl Perkins and myself.

"They'd all get together with their guitars. Me, I just sat quiet, because I was a kid and scared to death. The guys would raise cane, but the girl artist, me, was always just sort of there. Roy was like me. He sat back in a corner and said nothing. This guy just absolutely did not associate. He didn't socialize with anybody. He'd sit back there and play his guitar. He loved to play flamenco."

Jerry Lee Lewis said, "I remember Roy minded his own business, stayed in his place. He always kept to himself, pretty much. He might come by just to say hello, hug your neck real nice and get out of your hair. He was that kind of person. He was a pretty nice guy, wasn't he. And he sang his butt off."

In April of '57, Jerry Lee would have "Whole Lot of Shakin' Goin' On" in the Top 40 for twenty weeks, peaking at #3. His concert price jumped in one year from fifty dollars to $10,000 a performance. Warren Smith was hitting it big, too, with "Ubangi Stomp."

"Warren Smith was 'Mr. Organizer,'" Roy said, "one of those guys who used to appoint himself boss. Well, we were all touring on a Sun package show and one night Smith came into the dressing room and said, 'Roy, go warm 'em up for me!' I said, 'To hell with you. You go open the show.' He gave me a mean look and said, 'Well, then I'll go get Jerry Lee to open the show!' I figured, I gotta see this, so I followed him into the next room.

"Warren said, 'Jerry Lee, how about you going out and opening the show for me?' There was a pause, and then Jerry Lee said, 'You're out of your bleepin' mind, you bleep-bleep-bleeper!' Smith got real mad at that and he reached down and picked up a chair to hit Jerry Lee with. He lifted it up, just barely got it above his head, when we all heard this real loud CLICK! Warren looked down...and saw Jerry Lee holding this open switchblade! Must've been at least a foot long!

"He never said another word. Just real slowly lowered the chair all the way back down to the floor. Then he kinda coughed and said, 'Ah, Roy, I think I'll, ah, go on out and do six or eight numbers for the folks. Then you can come out afterwards. And then Jerry Lee can, ah, follow you. Okay?'"

Roy Orbison and Jerry Lee Lewis had in common a penchant for pubescent girls. Roy was going with fourteen-year-old Claudette and

Jerry was falling in love with his cousin Myra, thirteen. Elvis Presley was about to begin a long, tumultuous relationship with a fourteen-year-old, Priscilla Beaulieu. Chuck Berry would soon face two years in prison, found guilty of transporting a minor across state lines for immoral purposes. In fact, most of the first-generation rockers were on the verge of serious trouble in their personal lives. Buddy Holly was drinking so much that Phil Everly had to take him home from a party in Eddie Cochran's room at The Park Sheraton in New York. At one rock show, Buddy had sex backstage with Little Richard's stripper-fiancée, Lee Angel, while Little Richard looked on. "Once in a while you'd go out and tie one on," Phil Everly said. Don Everly was addicted to speed. "Ritalin made you feel energized," he said. "You could stay up for days. It just got me strung out. I got so far out there, I didn't know what I was doing." The Everlys thought nothing of driving their blue Olds 98 at suicidal 100-mph speeds. The irrepressible Eddie Cochran bragged of making love to a stewardess during a flight to Australia. Carl Perkins and Gene Vincent were alcoholic, Elvis Presley discovered speed in the Army, and Johnny Cash was beginning to have problems with the same drug. Roy, who toured with Johnny Cash in a rented pink Cadillac they shared with Carl Perkins and Jerry Lee Lewis, was also devoted to speed and sleeping pills. On speed, according to Johnny Cash, "Energy multiplied, timing was superb, and I could perform with a driving, relentless intensity." Soon, however, Johnny began to notice that his eyes were dilated, he was twitching, popping his neck bones, he couldn't stand still, and he was "torturing nerves to the breaking point, twisting muscle and bone, stretching my nerves." Wide awake, he wrecked his car. At last, Johnny Cash had to ask, "What am I doing to myself?" Later generations of rockers discovered marijuana, LSD, heroin and cocaine, but Roy and the founding fathers got hooked on ups.

Meanwhile, Buddy Knox, Buddy Holly, The Everly Brothers, Jerry Lee Lewis and other new acts kept hitting it big, but nothing was happening for Roy Orbison. By 1957, he had to face the fact that he probably wasn't going to make it as a singer. He'd burned his bridges in college, and now he had nothing to fall back on. He'd gambled everything and apparently lost everything. His band had deserted him, Sam Phillips was preoccupied with Jerry Lee Lewis, and the bright hope that Sun Records represented now began to vanish. He continued to pitch his song "Claudette" to singers he met on tour, but it was hard work. Some of them looked at him skeptically, as if thinking, How could anyone who looks the way you do have anything I'd want?

In August of 1957, for the first time without his band behind him, Roy cut a series of records at Sun Recording Studio. Roy said he accompanied himself on acoustic guitar, but Sun added a backup band when they released the records after he got famous. There are no hidden masterpieces among these early cuts, but they demonstrate that Roy was just as good as his more successful contemporaries at that time. In "Mean Little Mama," for instance, Roy delivers a terrific, low-down rocker just as exciting as Elvis Presley's "Hound Dog." Sun, however, let this one sit in the can until 1961, when Roy had become a star at Monument Records. In another song, "Fool's Hall of Fame," Roy's voice is startling in its richness, clarity and youthful vitality, but Sun let it sit around for fifteen years. Another cut, "Chicken Hearted," enumerates the character defects of a born loser who is shy, lacks nerve, wants to be a great lover but can't even attract a girl, yearns to perform heroics but has no guts, and dreams of being a wicked rebel but fears he'll get hurt. As a portrait of the adolescent as jerk, it's surprisingly touching, and the parallels with Roy's own experience growing up are obvious. Sam Phillips released "Chicken Hearted" in December 1957 but it failed to register with the public. Nor did another cut, "I Like Love," despite good trade reviews.

Another recording from this period, "Problem Child," is about a girl who is running wild. Roy wrote it himself, perhaps thinking of Claudette when she ran away from home to his hovel in Odessa. Another song, "This Kind of Love," was Roy's finest cut at Sun. With a driving beat and a steady, relentless progression, this is the only Sun song that foreshadows the grandeur of "Running Scared" and other great Orbison performances of the early 1960s. Sun didn't know what to do with it in the 1950s but shrewdly included it on Roy's *Rockhouse* LP in 1961, a year after he signed with Monument.

Roy was washed up in Memphis. There didn't seem to be any point in staying there, though he had allowed Sam Phillips to sign him up for another stint at Sun. "He was staying out here at the house again," Sam recalled, "and Roy was going into the studio and just writing and playing by himself when we didn't have a session."

In fact, Roy had given up the idea of becoming a recording artist.

"I'd sort of quit recording," Roy said. "Sam had released a couple of songs that I didn't think he should have, so I sort of retired." He was beginning to feel like a one-hit wonder, and he suspected he should get a regular job in West Texas and settle down with Claudette. "I lost all interest and quit," Roy said. "For seven months I just ambled around. No, I didn't do a thing, except to think."

Claudette had gone home to Texas, and Roy knew he couldn't leave a pretty girl like Claudette alone indefinitely and expect to keep her. Dreaming of his girl, he left Memphis and headed for Texas once again. As soon as he and Claudette were reunited, they began to talk about getting married. Though she was only fourteen, a junior high dropout and a very insecure young woman, she was so pretty and composed that everyone assumed she was a sophisticated grownup. In actuality, she was a child in a woman's body, and she was confused and frightened when people talked to her as though she were an adult. In order to survive, Claudette learned to pretend that all was well; she became an actress. Perhaps, one day, she'd be able to catch up with herself. Years later, after they'd experienced marital problems, Roy put all these aspects of Claudette in a song, appropriately entitled "The Actress." But in their first years together, Claudette was exactly what Roy wanted in a woman—someone who idolized him, someone he could absolutely control. As Wesley Orbison, Roy and Claudette's son, would say years later, "Dad was just like me—all a woman had to do was be there for him, all the time, and he'd give her everything he had." As Roy and Claudette began to talk about a wedding date, what they didn't realize was that although Claudette could accept his absences on rock tours now, it would be very different once they started having children and needed to establish some kind of family life.

There was an important development in Roy's career soon after his return to West Texas. He met a young singer from Bonham, Texas, named Joe Melson, and they began collaborating on songs in 1957. "Our singing voices were completely different," Joe said. "His was driving and piercing and mine was soft and mellow. We used mine to do the soft backups to contrast with his hard driving instrument—the soft against the piercing made for lovely contrast. I'm on every one of the major records, from the dum-dum-dum-dum-be-do-wah's on 'Only the Lonely' to the sha-la-la's in 'Blue Angel.' All the backups were created by my sound, and everybody who covers these songs now duplicates it. I wanted to sing like that because Roy sang real loud and strong. My softness against his voice would, I thought, give the songs the flair they needed.

"The backups were integrally incorporated into the writing from the start. We kept adding things to plain songs until it began to be a complex creation. That was my style—one voice singing and one voice doing parts with it to give it that flair. This influenced his whole career. There has never been a time that he recorded without backups.

"Roy Orbison and I contributed exactly fifty-fifty to the great songs of his major period in the early 1960s. We each had our own style and we put those styles together and it became greater than both of us. The world bought more than we ever dreamed would come out of our writing. But in the beginning, the dust of West Texas was in our eyes and mouths, and music seemed as far away as China."

Joe had a group called The Cavaliers, and they did shows all over the area, playing in the same dives Roy had for years. Joe had often seen and heard Roy and thought, "Man! I like that voice!" Joe's manager, Ray Rush, encouraged him to show Roy his song "Raindrops," which would soon be included on Roy's first Monument LP *Lonely and Blue*. When they met, Joe recalls that Roy said to him, "I hear you're playing around. I remember your band. Ray Rush says you've got a song." They were standing in Roy's small apartment in Odessa, and Joe Melson remembers seeing a girl sitting on the bed who looked like Elizabeth Taylor. "Claudette was just watching us and smiling. She was a beautiful thing, a big-bodied lovely, though when Roy later described her in a song she was his pretty little girl Claudette. She was very quiet but she watched everything and held her head high. Roy said, 'Let me hear your song, Joe.'"

Joe began to sing in his soft, angelic voice, which sounds much like the Everly Brothers. When he finished, according to Joe, Claudette said, "I love that song! I want you to get a dub of that song for me, Roy. Will you?"

"I like it, too," Roy said. "It's really good, Joe."

"Man," Joe admitted, "I sure love your voice."

Months passed and they lost touch, but Roy hadn't forgotten Joe. He was preoccupied with Claudette and their plans to get married. She had inspired him to write what he considered his best song, "Claudette," and he was pinning all his hopes on getting a major artist to record it. Finally he found an opportunity to offer it to The Everly

Brothers. The Everlys were now a national craze, having created an ecstatic new sound that broadened the definition of rock 'n' roll. Singing in close, celestial harmony over acoustic guitar, the Everly sound combined the sweetness of Kentucky bluegrass with the manic urgency of rock. "Bye Bye Love" went to #2 in May 1957, and in September, "Wake Up Little Susie" shot to #1, holding the top position for a month. Roy knew that if the boys chose to place "Claudette" on one of their sides, he'd not only make a small fortune, he'd be instantly established as a songwriter. He had to borrow money to get to Indiana, where he performed one night as the warm-up act for the Everlys. Backstage with the other acts before the show, Roy hoped Don or Phil would notice him and speak to him. He sat on a window ledge, smoking a cigarette as the others vied for the Everlys' attention. Everyone was talking about what song Don and Phil should put on the B-side of their new recording by Felice and Boudleaux Bryant, "All I Have to Do Is Dream." Roy knew he should speak up about "Claudette," but he was shy and angry with himself for having forgotten to bring along the demos he'd made especially for the Everlys.

Finally, Phil Everly turned to Roy and said, "Didn't you write 'Ooby Dooby'?" Roy nodded nervously, but then they got into a discussion of recording companies and royalties. The Everlys were recording with Cadence, and Roy was surprised when they told him that they got five percent of sales. "I'm only getting three percent at Sun," Roy said, realizing that he was probably going to have to leave Sun if he couldn't get his contract rewritten. But with no hit records, who else would want him? He turned and started to leave the room.

"Say, Roy," Don told him, "hold on. Stick around for a while. You wouldn't happen to have any material, would you?"

"I have one song I've written," Roy said, brightening up. Using Don's guitar he played and sang "Claudette." The boys listened attentively and when Roy finished, Phil said, "Well, write the words down, Roy." Roy didn't have anything to write on, but he spotted a cardboard box on the dressing table, tore off the top and carefully wrote down the lyrics. He handed it to Don, the boys passed it back and forth, looked at each other, nodded, and Don said, "We'd like to record it. We'll take it back to Nashville with us."

"The next thing I knew," Roy later recalled, "Wesley Rose from Nashville's calling me in Memphis at Sun Records, telling me to sign this contract for the song 'Claudette' that the Everly Brothers were going to record—they actually had already recorded it."

Roy was still under contract to Sam Phillips, and he had cut a demo of "Claudette" at Sun, so he needed to get a release in order for the Everlys to use "Claudette." Sam Phillips remembers Roy coming in to his office and saying, "Mr. Phillips, I know you've got the publishing on 'Claudette.' I've got a chance to get the Everlys to record this, but they are under contract to a Nashville publishing company, and if they do it, they'll have to have the publishing rights or otherwise they won't do it. The Everlys are hot now, see? Okay? But the Nashville publishing company has to have the publishing rights."

"No, I won't do that," Sam told him. "Now, goddammit, I've spent too much time over here and everything." According to Roy, Sam wanted a share of the "Claudette" proceeds. "We had a three-way conversation," Roy said. "Wesley said, 'Why do you want Roy's money?' So Wesley sounded great and Sam sounded like he was a...wanted a little too much, so I left then. I left Sun."

Sam Phillips has a different recollection of his parting with Roy. "'Okay,' I told Roy, 'we'll work a deal here and you go ahead. I don't want to knock you out of getting this recording. I hate to give up a song, but you go ahead and do that.' Then the next thing I know Roy came to me like a gentleman and said that he had an opportunity to record for somebody else if it was all right with me. Well, we had to sit down and have a little prayer meeting. I considered everything in my interests and hopefully in his, and we worked out a deal on the songs which gave him the opportunity to do it. I thought a lot before I let Roy go. It wasn't that I didn't believe in Roy Orbison and what he could do and eventually got around to doing—his forte was ballads—but I didn't feel it was fair necessarily to keep Roy. I told him, 'Roy, if you go and it doesn't work out...don't sign a long-term damned contract. A year ought to be the maximum, and see what they're going to do for you. Hell, if that were me...I tried to give him the advice I would my son or younger brother."

Roy's own recollection of his departure from Sun was tinged with bitterness. He said that Sun's royalty rate was below industry standard, and he was still angry that he had never been informed that he was entitled to composer's royalties from BMI. "Sam taught me a lot about business and contracts, afterwards," Roy said. Those were the paramount reasons for his leaving Sun after two years, Roy asserted.

He found Sam Phillips likable and charming enough, but he felt restricted.

Besides recording "Claudette," The Everly Brothers opened up an important new Nashville contact for Roy, the powerful music publishing and management firm of Acuff-Rose. Roy became a staff songwriter in Acuff-Rose's Nashville offices, though he was more often in Texas than Tennessee. It was around this time when he became aware of the rock scene beginning to form in England. "I was in a restaurant in Nashville one time with the Everlys having lunch," Roy said. "Buddy Holly came in and said he'd just been to England and it was magnificent. So the Everlys said they'd go, and it was magnificent. At the same time, other people had gone and it was a disaster. (I won't say who.) So I didn't really want to go."

Roy wanted to revive his own recording career, and in order to do so, made strenuous efforts to get his musicians, The Teen Kings, back together. He lent money to Jack Kennelly and Little Johnny Wilson to start an exterminating business in Odessa, trying to induce them to go back to work for him. He met with James Morrow and his wife Wanda at a hotel in Ruidosa, New Mexico, hoping to make up. Claudette was along on this trip, and the two couples were supposed to go to dinner together, but the Morrows shunned Roy and Claudette and nothing came of Roy's plans to reunite The Teen Kings. Eventually most of The Teen Kings went into the armed services, but Little Johnny Wilson, following his stint as an exterminator, became a rockabilly star. With Norman Petty's help, Little Johnny cut a song he had written with Roy, "Cast Iron Arms," and then went on to a career in the recording business in Nashville.

Although Roy's formal association with Sun Records was now at an end, he often returned to the studio to record and to produce other artists' sessions. He retained an affection for Sun and its volatile owner. As Roy's future was anything but certain, he also continued to ask Sam for advice. "I owe Sam so much," he said. He returned to West Texas in 1957 broke but elated that he had at last placed one of his songs with the great recording duo, Don and Phil Everly.

According to Claudette's father, Chester Frady, Roy approached him in Odessa around this time and asked for his daughter's hand in marriage. Chester looked at Roy and said, "If you think you can take care of her, okay." Chester then told his wife of Roy's intentions, and

Gerry recalls taking Claudette aside and saying, "You can do better than that."

"Mother," Claudette replied, "It's not what's outside but what's inside people that counts." In a few days, according to Gerry, Claudette called them from Wink and said that she and Roy were getting married. The ceremony took place in the Church of Christ in Kermit, which did not permit music, and then they went to live with Roy's parents in Wink. They remained there waiting for the Everlys' "Claudette" to come out and hoping it would bring in some money.

The newlyweds enjoyed a robust love life. Claudette had been dating boys for years, and Roy loved to crow in "Mean Little Mama" about what a great lover he was. In his song "Claudette," Roy praised his wife's amorous nature. Barbara Pittman said many women seemed to be attracted to Roy, though certainly *she* wasn't. Sam Phillips noted, "I never saw Roy with a bad-looking broad," and Slob Evans said Roy told him, even after marriage, "I've got more than I can handle." It must have come as a shock to Roy when he discovered that, even with a warm, pretty woman in his life and all the affection he wanted, happiness still eluded him. Only a few years earlier he was saying he couldn't get a date even if he paid a girl to go with him. Now he had one of the prettiest girls in West Texas, but he was chewing his fingernails to the quick, a habit noted by his mother-in-law Gerry, and worrying himself into a duodenal ulcer, an illness documented on his insurance policy.

Without a recording contract, Roy felt lost. He was still welcome at Sun, but it was a far cry from being a Sun recording star. Sam admitted, "It is my regret that I did not do the promotion on Roy—I still had Carl, Johnny and Jerry Lee at that time—and I didn't get into him in the way I could have done if his band had not broken up when it did. I have to take the blame for not bringing Roy into full fruition. Roy continued to work with us after the band split, but it wasn't the same."

Sam certainly had his hands full these days with his headstrong and sometimes violent star Jerry Lee Lewis. On December 30, 1957, "Great Balls of Fire" climbed to #2 and remained there for a month. Jerry Lee was being talked about on both sides of the Atlantic as the successor to Elvis Presley, and once again, Roy had to watch a lesser talent go for Elvis' crown, something he desperately wanted. Jerry Lee came close but stumbled, and the consequences were catastrophic for his career, his personal life, and for Sun. Jerry Lee's troubles started when, like Roy, he married his teen queen. At thirteen, Jerry's little cousin Myra Brown was an even younger bride than Claudette, and Jerry Lee kept her carefully under wraps. However, he made the mistake of taking Myra to London with him on a Sun promotional tour in May 1958. Jerry Lee lied to the British press, adding two years to Myra's age, saying she was fifteen, but London reporters flew into a fit of righteous outrage anyway. Sitting in America with his own teenage bride, Roy must have gagged on his coffee when he saw the British headlines:

> JERRY BRINGS WIFE NO. 3, FAIR AND 15,
> LIKE A WELL-SCRUBBED FOURTH-FORMER

and

> MEET MYRA FROM MEMPHIS—WIFE AT 15!

Editorials cried "Clear out this gang," calling for deportation. Jerry Lee's audiences heckled and booed, calling him "baby snatcher" and "kiddy thief." Police inspected Myra's passport and filed a report with the Home Office Secretary, who had the power to expel questionable foreigners. Jerry Lee and his child bride were driven from England in disgrace. He tumbled from the top of the hit parade on both sides of the Atlantic.

Though Roy was not yet so known that his marriage to a teenage girl would be of any interest to the press—in fact, Roy would be of minor interest to the U.S. press until his death—he may have decided to keep Claudette as far back in the shadows as he could. Compared with Yoko Ono, Bianca Jagger, Jerry Hall and Linda Eastman, who became instant celebrities when they married rockers, Claudette Orbison remained the most obscure wife of the rock 'n' roll era—this, despite the fact that she was the only rock wife celebrated in a song bearing her name.

Like Roy, Elvis Presley also concealed his fourteen-year-old girlfriend. In time, Elvis introduced Priscella to drugs, and on one occasion she passed out for two days on two 500 mg. of Placidyls. Priscilla urged Elvis to go all the way with her, but he declined, putting her through years of tantalizing foreplay. As for Jerry Lee and Myra's sex life, she passively submitted to his lovemaking but was uncomfortable during intercourse, pretending to be asleep. Of the three rock 'n' roll child concubines, Claudette Orbison was the most fulfilled. Writing about her in "Claudette," Roy extolled her erotic expertise, praising her for the best lovemaking he'd ever had.

All her relatives say that Claudette was thrilled over being immortalized in an Everly brothers hit record, and both she and Roy eagerly awaited its release on Cadence Records in 1958. The Everlys' first two records were monster hits in 1957, and in the new year, "This Little Girl of Mine" charted in the Top 40. "Claudette" was to be the flip side of their fourth record, "All I Have to Do Is Dream," which was scheduled for release in April.

With Jerry Lee Lewis blacklisted from radio and in decline as a recording star and Private Elvis Presley temporarily out of the running, the rock throne again was empty. The timing could not have been worse for Roy, who didn't even have a record label. Again, this would not be his year to make it as a singer. But with the release of "Claudette," Roy was finally in the right place at the right time—on the B side of an Everly Brothers smash. On April 28, "All I Have to Do Is Dream" went to #1 and stuck at the top of the charts for five weeks. It was the Everlys' biggest hit ever, and 1958 was their most successful year, with *seven* straight hit singles, including two #1's. On the flip side of "All I Have to Do Is Dream," how could "Claudette" miss? Two weeks after "Dream" went to #1, "Claudette" entered the Top 40 for two weeks, reaching #30. It meant a neat pile of cash for Roy, and this windfall came just in time, because Claudette gave birth to a son, Roy DeWayne, in 1958. He was a healthy baby and grew into a bright-eyed, intelligent little boy. Fortunately, Roy DeWayne inherited all of his mother's good looks and none of Roy's homely features.

Songwriting royalties from "Claudette" poured in, and Roy bought himself the most expensive new Cadillac in stock in Odessa. "It was classy," Joe Melson said, "long and thin and elegant, with sweeping green tailfins." Roy and Claudette spent every minute they could running around in it. The young couple were blessed with two sets of indulgent grandparents to do their babysitting. With Chester and Gerry in Odessa and Nadine and Orb just forty-four miles away in Wink, there was always someone to take care of Roy DeWayne, or "R.D.," when the young parents felt like taking in a movie or when Claudette accompanied Roy to whatever bar he was singing in.

Orbie Lee Harris spent an evening with Claudette and Roy around this time. Roy and Claudette were staying at the Zia Motel in

Farmington, New Mexico, where Roy was doing a one-nighter. Orbie Lee and Billie Harris were living in Farmington, and had just returned from a visit to Las Vegas. Roy was the headliner at the show that night, and his opening act was Donnie Brooks, a young man from Dallas who sang "Mission Bell." Soon Donnie would score a #7 hit record singing the same song.

After the show, they all climbed into a car with Bobby Blackburn and started looking for a place to eat. Billie Harris distinctly remembered that Roy had performed that night in dark glasses, because in the car he took his shades off and put on his regular glasses. "Everyone's seen me tonight," he said, "so I guess I'll put my other glasses on so I can see everybody." Billie explained that Roy wore dark glasses because the clear ones distorted his eyes and made him look strange. Orbie Lee elaborated on the point, adding, "Roy had a fetish about his little beady eyes. That's the way he described them himself. The shades covered them up. He was always worried about how he would appear to others with his 'small beady eyes.' They were small because he had to squint."

A restaurant called Everybody's was the only place in town open, so they went there and ate catfish. Over dinner, Roy quizzed Orbie Lee and Billie about Las Vegas, urging them to tell him about all the shows in detail, including the lighting and the staging. "I'm going to play there one of these days," Roy said.

With a hit single on the charts, Roy was again in a writing mood, and he sought out Joe Melson, whose song "Raindrops" he and Claudette had heard a few months ago and liked. "I was sitting in a drive-in in Odessa, drinking a Coke with someone," Joe recalled. "I'd been going to Odessa Junior College a few years. Suddenly, I glanced up and saw Roy Orbison driving by in a green Cadillac. He'd seen me and was pulling up to the drive-in. I went over to the car and stuck my hand out. 'You want to ride around?' Roy said. 'Maybe we can talk.' We drove across town and Roy told me about his hit record. 'Made a little bit of loot there,' he said. 'First thing I did was run out and get me this green Cadillac.'

"Roy and I compared notes on the gigs we were doing. Roy was playing in Hobbs, New Mexico, and I said, 'I've been playing, too, doing some TV, some [record] hops around Midland.' After a while, Roy said, 'Claudette still wants that dub of "Raindrops."' I knew that what he meant, but was too shy to say, was that he wanted to write songs with me, wanted us to make music together. Finally he said, 'You know, you write a pretty good song, and I write a pretty good song. If we got together, we'd write some great ones.'

"You *know* it,' I said. 'I bet we'd make it, too, make it really big.' Roy grinned and puffed on his cigarette. 'Great,' he said. 'When do you want to start?'

"'Any time!' We both knew it—two forces had joined, creating an unstoppable drive. A sand storm was coming up and we were both biting West Texas sand. We hadn't started a single song, but I knew we were going to make it because I knew Roy had the potential to move that fantastic voice in any direction."

A few days later, Joe stood on his porch and watched Roy and Claudette move into the house next to him in Midland. Deliverymen lugged in a huge brand-new TV console and an expensive record player. Joe recalled Roy saying, "I rented me a big TV. I couldn't afford the one I wanted to buy but I had to have it. Couldn't live without it. So I rented one just like it. You know, I got about twenty-five thousand dollars out of 'Claudette.'"

New purchases continued arriving daily and expensive bracelets appeared on Roy's wrist. Joe was concerned. Though they were writing every day, they were turning out nothing but cute ditties, mediocre, typical '50s songs. When they sent them in to Roy's Nashville publisher-manager Wesley Rose, he wrote back, "You're doing good."

Joe recalled that Roy said, "Yeah, but ain't nobody cutting them."

"And no money's coming in," Joe added. "If we're as good as he says, why ain't we rich?"

Roy and Claudette kept spending lavishly month after month, and finally Joe said, "Roy, how much of that loot have you got left, anyway?"

"I've got enough to get through this month, Joe. Then I don't have any. I've spent it. That's all right, though—I'm enjoying myself." At the end of the month, Roy and Claudette were broke and had to pack up everything and return to Roy's parents in Wink. Roy gloried in tooling around town in his green Cadillac, flaunting it in front of his former classmates, even though he didn't know where the next payment was coming from. "Orb ended up making the payments on that Cadillac," Chester Frady said, just as he had on its white predecessor. "Then that ended, and it was repossessed." Roy bought an old used car but was so ashamed to be seen in it that he would hide it several blocks from his destination and walk the rest of the way. One day Roy showed up at Joe's house on foot and when Joe asked him why he didn't have his car, Roy said, "I ain't gonna be seen *dead* in that old clunker. I parked it up the hill."

Roy started singing in beer joints again for fifty-dollars a night. Joe knew he was hard up but it wasn't until Roy stuck him with a restaurant check that he realized how utterly destitute Roy was. Roy ordered the most expensive entree on the menu, a pepper steak, wolfed it up and then hid in the men's room until Joe settled the check. Years later, Joe smiled as he reminisced about the contretemps. "He knew I'd always help him. He never paid me back. He wanted that big old pepper steak, and he didn't have any money. So, it was a gift, I guess. We were great friends. I loved him. Even later, when he was getting all his money and I hadn't gotten any yet, he'd call me long distance collect. It wasn't that Roy was stingy. He was very free with his money. It was just a quirk he had. When he wanted to do something he did it. When he wanted to eat he didn't think about it costing anyone. Didn't matter if he was a pauper with a pepper steak appetite."

Hard times were upon Roy and Claudette. They had run through the "Claudette" royalties, the Sun disks were producing no income, and none of the new songs Joe and Roy wrote were acceptable to Nashville. Before long, Roy and Claudette were so broke they couldn't afford to buy groceries. Roy's parents had their own financial problems and could no longer contribute, and Joe Melson recalled that Roy and Claudette resorted to some extreme measures to keep from starving. "They rolled up cornmeal and water just to get some bulk in their stomachs," Joe said. "They didn't even cook it. That stuff *wouldn't* cook." According to Jack Kennelly, who had now married, "When they were down and out, Roy and Claudette stayed with us in Odessa."

Later in 1958, Roy's fortunes improved somewhat. He earned a few dollars working at Pure Oil, and then he began to make occasional trips to Memphis to cut more rockabilly records with his old friends at Sun. Roland Janes said, "After The Teen Kings left him, Roy cut some records with me and Jimmy Van Eaton." One of them was "I Was a Fool," recorded September 4, 1958, with, in addition to Roland and Jimmy, Ken Cook, Jack Clement and Billy Riley. Ken Cook was a singer Roy met in Texas and brought to Sun. Their voices were similar, uncannily so. According to Martin Hawkins and Colin Escott, "It is not clear what Sam Phillips was aiming for unless he sought to continue his plans for Roy through Ken Cook. On this song, it may be that the successful harmonies of The Everly Brothers were a guiding factor. It is interesting that tapes exist of Ken Cook's vocals recorded over backing tracks used on Roy's records. Possibly other duets were planned had this one been a hit."

Roy also tried his luck in Nashville, both as a songwriter and recording artist. He finally managed to land a contract with RCA Records, where, according to *Rolling Stone*, "he floundered under the misdirection of Chet Atkins." Boudleaux Bryant, who'd written "All I Have to Do Is Dream" for the Everlys, said, "I remember Roy Orbison when he used to hang around the studio showing his songs to record artists. I remember him as a timid, shy kid who seemed to be rather befuddled by the whole music scene. I remember the way he sang then—softly, prettily, but almost bashfully, as if afraid someone might be disturbed by his efforts and reprimand him. He got a contract with a record company—and sang the same way. I remember well because he cut one of my songs, 'Seems to Me,' and it was the turkey of the season. He was dropped by the record company.

RCA must have sized Roy up as another Paul Anka type, because they gave him teeny-bopper bubble-gum tunes to record. In the history of rock 'n' roll, 1958-59 was the teen-queen period, and Paul Anka's "Diana," Connie Francis' "Lipstick on Your Collar," Ritchie Valens' "Donna" and Buddy Holly's "Peggy Sue" were all Top 5 hits. These childish, sentimental tunes followed the demise of rockabilly and the 1958 induction of Elvis Presley in the U.S. Army, and rock 'n' roll would not have lasted if someone hadn't come along to save it from pubescent inanity. That someone was Roy Orbison, whose operatic rock songs like "Only the Lonely" provided a bridge in the early 1960s between Elvis and The Beatles, thus insuring the survival of rock. As Roy himself once put it, his main contribution in the overall picture was that he "helped hold some things together." But in 1958, Roy too was stuck in bubble-gum pop-rock. At RCA, he was "too much in awe" of Chet Atkins to object to the material he was given. Atkins at the time was still riding high on the strength of his association with Elvis Presley, whose move to RCA from Sun had resulted in unprecedented record sales.

Roy was convinced that Chet Atkins lacked the clout at RCA to implement his vision for Roy's career. Though Atkins would later attain great power at the studio, at the time he handled Roy he was unable to determine which of Roy's cuts would be released or to set promotional strategies.

Though all of Roy's efforts at RCA failed commercially, they were not without charm, especially a touching rendition of his own song "Paper Boy." Unlike most of Roy's songs about unrequited love, which offered no cures for the broken-hearted, this one contained a kernel of wisdom, saying that anyone could feel better by simply sharing his pain with someone. It was a welcome alternative to wallowing in self-pity, the usual nostrum of '50s love songs.

Roy also recorded John Loudermilk's "I'll Never Tell" for RCA, and on it he sounded much like the Everlys and Buddy Holly. In the lyrics, filled with euphemisms for sexual intercourse, the boy tries to persuade his girl to comply by promising not to kiss and tell. "Sweet and Innocent," also recorded at RCA, displays Roy's voice at its most seductive and appealing, as he assures his girl that her naïveté and inexperience make her all the more desirable. "With the Bug" was Roy's attempt at RCA to duplicate the success of "Ooby Dooby" and to start a dance craze called The Bug, as Chubby Checker would the following year with The Twist. It didn't work out that way—RCA didn't even release the tune. On another RCA cut, "Almost 18," Roy sings with a glottal twitch as accomplished as Buddy Holly's, and his two RCA ditties by Boudleaux and Felice Bryant, "Jolie" and "Seems to Me," benefit from Roy's stylish performances.

So why was Roy bombing as a singer in Nashville, just as he'd struck out in Memphis? By now he had been exposed artistically to all the musical sages of the South and Southwest—Norman Petty, Sam Phillips, Chet Atkins, Wesley Rose, the Bryants, Bill Justis and Jack Clement—and the act still wasn't working. In Nashville, he was once again in the wrong place at the wrong time. Nashville was a country-music town, so conservative that drums were not allowed on the stage of the Grand Ole Opry—hardly a condusive atmosphere for an aspiring rock 'n' roller.

By 1958-59, New York and Los Angeles had taken over as the new creative centers of rock, and the hits began to emanate from both coasts. Buddy Holly had moved to New York and was charting hit after hit, including "That'll Be the Day" and "Rave On." While Roy languished in Nashville, Phil Spector was in Los Angeles recording one of the best rock ballads ever written, "To Know Him Is to Love

Him," which went to #1 for three weeks. And on the East Coast, Neil Sedaka and Howard Greenfield's #14 hit, "The Diary," set the stage for the takeover of Tin Pan Alley by rock 'n' roll writers. Carole King and Gerry Goffin wrote The Shirelles #1 hit "Will You Love Me Tomorrow." Barry Mann and Cynthia Weil gave The Righteous Brothers "You've Lost That Lovin' Feeling" and Jeff Barry and Ellie Greenwich were writing "little symphonies for kids" like "Da Doo Ron Ron" and "River Deep—Mountain High." Jerry Lieber and Mike Stoller, Neil Diamond, Bobby Darin, Gene Pitney, and Burt Bach-arach and Hal David were some of the other dynamic and innovative talents who were making the Brill Building on Broadway the capital of rock.

Behind it all was Phil Spector, who brought his Wall of Sound to New York in 1959 and completely redefined rock 'n' roll. The Sound was big, echoey and mysterious, powerful, pounding, dramatic, lush with strings and vocals, totally unlike anything ever heard before in popular music. This was still the age of mono, and people simply couldn't believe the sounds coming out of their radios, such as the *baion*-inflected *boom-ba-boom* in The Drifters' #2 hit "There Goes My Baby," reverberating like thunder. Also in New York, the doo-wop groups that had formed on Bronx streetcorners were now in the studios making great music, like Dion and The Belmonts' "I Wonder Why" and "A Teenager in Love." The hit records that Roy Orbison and Joe Melson were about to spring on the world were a result of their taking the fusion of pop and rhythm and blues that was occurring at this time and turning it into their original contribution to rock 'n' roll—the operatic rock ballad.

For the first year of their collaboration, Roy and Joe were mired in rockabilly (which was passe) because Joe was afraid to show Roy the rhythm-and-bluesy songs Joe had been writing on his own. If he introduced something so radically new into their partnership, Roy might end it, or so Joe thought. At this time all the new sounds coming from the East were lush with strings, tympani, echoes and especially with black rhythm and blues, and Joe and Roy were out of step with the new beat of pop music. According to Joe Melson, "At last I said to Roy, 'Why aren't we getting something cut? We're not getting anywhere sending songs to Nashville.'"

"'Don't worry about it. Things will happen.'

"'Roy, I want to change styles. We've been writing over a year and though the songs are beautiful and I love the way you sing, we don't have the types of songs that're gonna make it. I want to start showing you some other things—if you'd like to hear them.'

"'Sure, man!'"

Joe was surprised. "I'd expected Roy to say, 'Well, maybe if you don't like writing with me, let's just drop it.' Instead, Roy said, 'Okay, what kind of thing are you hearing?'

"'Let me work on some stuff and I'll give you a call.'"

What Joe had in mind was a song he'd written called "Blue Avenue," but he lacked the nerve to perform it for Roy face to face. Instead, just as he'd promised, he called Roy and sang it to him over the telephone. It was a simple ballad about loneliness but in singing it, Joe added some falsettos, breaking the word "blue" in the middle and doing the second half in falsetto. "When I finished I said, 'How do you like that?'

"'Aw, man, I love it. It's beautiful. Let's write it.'" According to Joe, that was the first time Roy took falsetto really seriously, and his voice began its flowering as they worked on "Blue Avenue."

Roy was depressed when RCA lost interest in him after releasing only two singles from all the songs he'd cut there. In Nashville, Wesley Rose was equally concerned. One day, he called a former record distributor named Fred Foster, who had established his own label, Monument Records, in Nashville in 1958. Fred Foster gave this version of how his association with Roy began:

"'Have you ever heard of Roy Orbison?' Wesley asked. 'Yes,' I said. 'I heard "Ooby Dooby" and "Rock House."'

"'Roy's been on RCA, but the last session we did, it went to the New York office for approval and it's been rejected. I just don't want him on RCA if they don't believe in him. Would you like to have him?'

'Well, yes, I would, as a matter of fact.'

"'There's one condition. I want you to duplicate the session they turned down. I think it's good. After that, you can do as you please.'"

In 1987, interviewer Roy Trakin said to Roy, "You haven't had much luck with record labels over the years," and Roy replied, "That's right." His first release with Monument, "Paper Boy"/"With the Bug," was disappointing. His next release, "Uptown"/"Pretty One," managed to touch the charts at #72. Roy said, "I never embarrassed Fred by bringing it up, but I got the feeling he thought he was signing Warren Smith. Wesley told him that I'd cut 'Ooby Dooby' and Fred may have thought he said 'Rock 'n' Roll Ruby.' We all have genius after the fact." As a Texan, Roy would not have had automatic entry into Nashville music circles. Many producers in the country-music capital were unfriendly to Texas artists. As R. Serge Denisoff wrote in his biography of Waylon Jennings, "The relationship of Texas and Nashville has always been volatile. The Lone Star State did not mirror the mores or values of the old Confederacy. Nearly all of the crossover and rockabilly artists had come from the Southwest or had made their reputation in these parts. The idea of an 'alternative Nashville' did not sit well with producers, session men, or union engineers in Music City."

Another Texan, Willie Nelson, was sitting idle in Nashville at this time. His whispering style went unrecorded in Nashville for years. "I always thought I could sing pretty good," Willie said, "and I guess it kinda bothered me that nobody else thought so." In trying to fathom Nashville's baffling resistance to the genius of Willie Nelson, *The Encyclopedia of Folk, Country, and Western Music* refers to "the inability of the country-music establishment of the 1950s and 1960s to understand the groundbreaking features of his material, grittier and more probing than much of the country music fare of those days." Roy was one of the many artists who would record Willie's songs before Willie finally gave up in Nashville, went to Austin, Texas, and at last achieved the stardom he had long deserved.

Joe Melson remembered when he first heard the news of Roy's new association with Monument Records. He was sitting on a couch in the motel where he worked in Odessa, and Roy walked in puffing his cigarette, looking pleased. "'I'm going to Nashville,' Roy said."

When Roy left for Nashville, he dumped his wife and baby with his parents in Wink. Claudette had to face the fact of being left behind in the oil patch with a year-old baby to care for by herself. Though full of friendly people, physically the town was a depressing, junk-littered eyesore. Roy's child bride was smart enough to realize that her husband had to go out and earn a living for them, and, for the moment at least, she accepted this reality. Periodic separation from their wives is an occupational hazard all married male rock stars contend with. Some wives follow their husbands, like Linda McCartney, who learned to play keyboards and joined Paul's band. Claudette's Aunt Patty said that Claudette's first mistake was to let Roy out of her sight. Perhaps Roy couldn't afford to take Claudette along, perhaps she didn't want to travel with the baby, but whatever the reason, this separation was the beginning of a pattern that would dissolve their marriage. Claudette was ill-equipped to fend alone for herself and the baby. If she had resentments, she became adept at hiding them behind her smile, and Roy probably wouldn't have sensed them anyway, caught up as he was in dreams of big houses, fine cars, boats, jewelry and expensive clothes. He thought these possessions would bring them happiness, and now that they were once again within reach, his ambition was fired all the more.

"I flew to Nashville and took a taxi to Acuff-Rose to see Wes Rose," Roy told Glenn A. Baker. "Someone said, 'Roy, you're late for your session.'

"'What are you talking about?'

"'You have a session going on. Jump in the car.' We drove over to RCA and the session was in progress. Only I wasn't there. Now that I was there they just run me straight into the studio and we started recording the same two songs that I'd done for RCA—'Sweet and Innocent' and 'Almost Eighteen.' There was more that we redid with Monument that wasn't released because things were happening so fast. Fred Foster had signed me, thinking I was Warren Smith, and we made this record before I met Fred Foster. We went to dinner afterwards, after the session was over, and I said, 'If I had known, we've written a couple of songs [including "Uptown"]...If I had known we were going to have a session I could have brought them. We could have finished them and polished them up.' He said, 'When you get them together come on back up and we'll do another.'"

Fred Foster's account does not jibe with Roy's at all. According to Foster, "Roy walked into the studio here in Nashville. I came from Washington and Roy came from Texas, and we met for the very first time. I thought he was a very shy, sensitive soul, sort of timid, even, in a way. It was very difficult to get his voice above the band. In order to get his voice above the band, I had to put him in a corner of the studio, pull a coat rack in front of him, and we covered the rack with coats and blankets. I couldn't see him, because he was hidden behind all that. Out of that came the isolation booth. They claim here in Nashville that was the first time that was done. I don't know."

Closer to Roy's account, a 1976 publicity release from Monument Records states that Fred didn't even meet Roy at this session. "Fred Foster, head of Monument Records, hadn't even met Orbison when he agreed to record him. There was a mix-up in flight schedules when he arrived for his recording session with Foster. He didn't get to meet him until after the session. 'Paper Boy,' 'With the Bug,' and 'Double Date' (the latter recording was never released) were cut at this session." "Double Date" was in fact released three decades later in *Rare Orbison Vol. II*, 1989.

After the session, thrilled and confident, Roy told both Fred Foster and Wesley Rose all about his partner Joe Melson. "Joe would like a contract, too," Roy said. "He's got it," Fred Foster told him, and Wesley Rose said he was also interested in handling Joe.

When Roy returned to Texas, he and Joe went back to work on "Uptown" at the Odessa motel where Joe was employed. "We gave it a kind of 8th driving beat," Joe recalled. "I put a rocking beat to it, sliding something like a Kansas City beat underneath it, and that transformed the song, moved it along." When Roy sang "Uptown" for the first time, it had magic. According to Joe, "Roy said, 'That's a hit! It's a hit!'

"'Yeah," I said. 'But I want you to do something.'" Roy still hadn't got used to the idea that he had a *different* voice. He was still singing low key, even in "Uptown." "'I want you to do some falsetto,' I said, 'like we did in "Blue Avenue."'"

"'How about this, Joe?'" Roy started singing "Uptown," and as he ticked off all the things he lusted after—penthouses, cars, clothes, girls, the materialistic paraphernalia that stood for happiness to him— his voice sailed into falsetto notes, suddenly giving the song the punch it needed.

Joe told him it was perfect, and then they went to work finishing up "Blue Avenue" and "Raindrops." Roy told Glenn A. Baker, "We called Fred Foster in about two weeks and said, 'We got it.' It was 'Uptown' and the other side. He said, 'Okay,' and he met us in Nashville."

Chapter 5

When Roy and Joe arrived in Nashville in 1959 they ran into saxophonist Boots Randolph on Music Row, and in an interview thirty years later he recalled, "Roy and Melson came in town on a watermelon truck. They'd had some little bit of success but they were ready to get with it. Roy and Joe were pretty close at the time, but how well Joe worked in with Roy I don't know." Boots would score a hit record in a few years with "Yakety Sax."

On September 18, 1959, Roy and Joe went into RCA Victor studios in Nashville, which Monument was using, and recorded "Raindrops." The technician was Tommy Strong and the engineer was Bill Porter, a team Roy would later work with often. In Joe Melson's recollection of the session, when Fred Foster joined them, "Roy said, 'Fred, we were wonderin' if we might have some strings?'

"'Yeah,' Fred said. 'Why not? It might be good. We'll use three.'

"'Boy, wait till Claudette hears this!'" Roy said to Joe "'Wait till they hear them strings back there in Texas!'"

They met their arranger, a man named Jim Hall, worked up the song, and went into the session. Roy sang "Raindrops" with the three strings in the background. It's a fragile little tune about lost love, and the raindrops stand for tears, which are heard dropping one at a time on a glockenspiel. Joe Melson recalls, "Roy asked me, 'How'd it sound?'

"'It's coming out beautiful,' I said.

"'Cool! My voice is good, huh?'

"'Yes, just keep putting your feelings into it and thinking of the story. It's coming.' Roy ran back out of the control room, saying, 'I'll do another cut.'"

Afterwards, they stood listening to the tape. When the strings came in, blending with Roy's voice, Joe almost cried. So did Roy, looking at Joe and whispering, according to Joe, "'Isn't that beautiful? Just listen to that.'" Joe recalled years later, "Wesley Rose and the rest were laughing, watching us fall in love with the tender and delicate

87

way 'Raindrops' sounded with our small string section. Wesley said, 'You're like two big kids in a candy store.'"

Next, they cut "Uptown," with Anita Kerr as the arranger and the Anita Kerr Singers providing backup vocals. Roy rehearsed the singers and told Joe to go out in the studio and show the musicians the licks. Harold Bradley was on bass guitar and Sugar Ray was on lead guitar, and Joe recalls, "I told them, 'The licks go like this,' humming them, and Harold said, 'I know exactly what you want.' It was a shuffle beat, and they picked up on it, and Buddy Harman on drums also picked it up."

After Roy finished rehearsing the Anita Kerr Singers, Joe worked with them until they were singing A-Hup-Town, A-Ho-Yeah exactly the way he wanted them to. When everyone had the beat and the feel of the music, Roy went to the mike and sang "Uptown." Afterwards, according to Joe, "He came into the control room and asked, 'How's the beat?'

"'It's not *fast* enough, Roy. They don't have the dance *feel* yet. Remember, we want kids to dance to this. They're really bopping these days. Move it up enough to get the kids interested. There's a certain beat they like, and it's faster.' Roy went back out into the studio and said, 'All right, everybody! Speed it up. It's not fast enough.' Afterwards Roy returned to the control room, and this time I said, 'Okay, but you're not doing your falsetto.'

"'Aw, well, right! I'll get it this time. You listen!'" They cut "Uptown," and it was upbeat, fresh and catchy.

Before they left Nashville, Joe Melson was signed up by Wesley Rose and had his own solo session, cutting a song called "Oh Yeah." It was a cute rocker, but it wasn't in the same league with "Uptown." Perhaps it would have been if Roy had put the same effort into Joe's session that Joe had put into Roy's. Years later Joe said, "I feel like if he'd helped me with 'Oh Yeah,' it would have been a lot better."

Returning to Texas, Roy spent some time with his wife and infant son. Evidently Claudette was adjusting to the unusual rigors of a marriage that involved chronic separations, or perhaps she was just concealing her loneliness and confusion. In the ardent days of courtship, she had been given to understand that she came before everything else in Roy's life and always would. But it was growing clearer that his real priority was ambition, that he was as driven as any workaholic, and that she and Roy DeWayne were there to fill in during career lulls.

Roy Orbison's parents, Orbie and Nadine Orbison, in Wink, Texas. (Courtesy Orbie Lee Harris)

The Orbisons and their close friends, the Harrises. Left to right are Roy, his father, his brother Grady, his mother holding baby brother Sammy Keith, Orbie Lee Harris, Melvin Harris and Opal Harris. (Courtesy Orbie Lee Harris)

Wink, Texas, 1948: Roy and his pal Orbie Lee Harris cavort for the camera. (Courtesy Orbie Lee Harris)

Roy showing off the Christmas mural he drew on the blackboard of his fifth-grade homeroom. His creation drew the attention of the entire school. (Courtesy Orbie Lee Harris)

Members of the Wildcat Marching Band: David Lipscomb (the principal's son), Roy and Freddie "Freako" Gonzales. (Courtesy Fred Gonzales)

Grady Lee Orbison, Roy's older brother. Although Grady inherited the "Orbison ears," he was blessed with handsomer looks than Roy. (Courtesy Orbie Lee Harris)

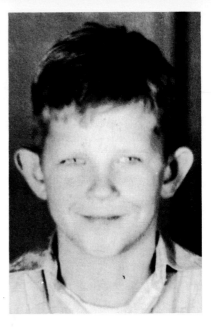

September, 1950: Roy wearing glasses under his Wink Kitten football helmet. Roy's attempt at football during junior high was doomed. (Courtesy Orbie Lee Harris)

Roy Orbison
To lead a Western Band
Is his after school wish
And of course to marry
A beautiful dish;

Roy's 1954 senior photo and its prophetic inscription (Courtesy Wink High School)

Roy formed his first band, The Wink Westerners, in high school.
Pictured here, left to right, are James Morrow, Billy Pat Ellis, Roy,
Charles Evans and Richard West. (Courtesy Charles Evans)

The Teen Kings while they were recording at Sun Records. Left to
right are Billy Pat Ellis, Roy, James Morrow, Little Johnny "Peanuts"
Wilson and Jack Kennelly. (Courtesy Chester and Geraldine Frady)

Sam Phillips, who signed up Roy and The Teen Kings at Sun Records in 1956, embracing Barbara Pittman, the "Queen of Rockabilly." (Courtesy Barbara Pittman)

The bill for Roy's 1956 debut at the Overton Park Shell in Memphis. (Courtesy Michael Hanrahan)

Roy's first wife, Claudette Frady, as a child in Odessa, Texas. Her mother, Geraldine poses her (left) with a neighbor's child. (Courtesy Chester and Geraldine Frady)

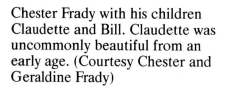

Chester Frady with his children Claudette and Bill. Claudette was uncommonly beautiful from an early age. (Courtesy Chester and Geraldine Frady)

Roy holding onto his own teen queen, Claudette Frady. She was fourteen when they married. (Courtesy Chester and Geraldine Frady)

The young husband and his mother-in-law: Roy Orbison and Geraldine Frady. Geraldine was not at first pleased by the idea of her daughter marrying a man with Roy's looks. (Courtesy Chester and Geraldine Frady)

1958: Roy's first Cadillac, the dream car he bought with royalties from his first record. (Courtesy Chester and Geraldine Frady)

Claudette Orbison in the late 1950s. (Courtesy Chester and Geraldine Frady)

Roy Orbison on British television in 1963. (David Redfern/Retna Ltd.)

One day, Roy played Claudette a dub of "Uptown." "She flipped over it," Joe said. "Claudette just flipped when she heard those strings. Roy didn't say a word, just sat there, smiling."

When "Uptown" was released in January of 1960 it became a modest hit. It took six months to a year for royalties and BMI earnings to reach an artist; Joe said he didn't receive a penny on "Uptown" for at least a year. But with "Uptown," Roy and Joe had their first Top 100 song together. Though it only sold about 100,000 copies, it was nice for Roy to be back on the charts for the first time since "Ooby Dooby."

"It was the first record out of Nashville with strings as opposed to fiddles," Roy told Glenn A. Baker. "'Uptown' was so good as compared with 'Paper Boy,' the record we'd just released, that Fred Foster covered it up with 'Uptown.' So 'Paper Boy' wasn't really even an official release; it was just put out to the disk jockeys, withdrawn and then 'Uptown' was put out and it did well enough to set up 'Only the Lonely.'"

In a few days, according to Joe, Roy said, "We better write some more songs. Let's get ready for our next session." "Only the Lonely" was about to be born. As Roy put it, "Joe wrote a good bit of ['Only the Lonely'] and he had some of it when we started even. I remember [rehearsing] one day and it was sort of heading up and I just went with it... for a baritone to sing as high as I do is ridiculous. It only comes from the fact that I didn't know what I was doing." Joe Melson was there to guide him, and they were creating not only a song but the vehicle that helped them discover the full range and richness of Roy's voice.

"When we started working on 'Only the Lonely,'" Joe recalls, "I asked Roy, 'Do you remember the phrasing in "Raindrops"? It doesn't stay on straight notes, Roy. It *curls*. You've got to wind around inside them. It has flair to it. It has curlicues. That's the kind of phrasing we're going to do now. I want you to twist these notes. Don't do them straight any more.'"

Rhythm and blues had never been a part of Roy's background, which was country, pop and Tex-Mex, but now, according to Joe, he taught Roy to sing the blues. "Roy began to understand blues phrasing, how to curl and weave in and around the octave, up and down, playing around." Joe sang "Cry" and demonstrated what he wanted out of Roy, and then said, "If we're really going to make it big we're going to have to get into better songs even than 'Uptown.' Let's get into ballads, let's get into the pop blues market with 'Cry.'"

Roy assimilated Joe's suggestions into his own style and delivered a sound that was distinctly his own. When he sang a few phrases it was clear that he was reinventing the blues. Joe knew that the Roy Orbison act was now complete: the falsetto, the crescendo style and the blues. "It was The Voice," critic Chet Flippo said, and the era of the rock ballad and the singer-songwriter had begun.

Discussing their collaboration, Roy said, "We both compose music and we both write lyrics. As a result, we can switch jobs on any song if we should hit a snag. A song starts with an idea, a conception, a theme. Usually it's about love and the object of that love.

"I develop my songs in different ways. I have thought of a good idea, then worked until early hours of the morning trying to match the right tune to it. Either words or music can come first...I do know that my inspiration comes from somewhere else and I help it...A lot of people when they want to be involved with music, turn on the radio to listen and they're fulfilled. When I get that way, I write what I feel—I go create what I want to hear...I can be turned on by a good group or a good sound...The good things that turned out to be good were no struggle—came out easy. The things that didn't make it—were a struggle. If it's not a successful feeling, you might as well not write."

Though Roy was not generous in crediting collaborators and other colleagues in the music business, he acknowledged Joe Melson's contribution as co-writer on many of his songs, saying that he enjoyed using collaborators because it gave him better perspective and made songwriting a more enjoyable task. Roy believed that there were only three proper subjects for a song, and he listed them as "boy-girl relationships, fellow-man, and relationship with God. All the rest anyone writes about doesn't mean anything."

Explaining the genesis of "Only the Lonely," Roy said, "I wrote 'Only the Lonely' in a car outside the house because we didn't have enough room in the house. So I wrote it in the car, and that was a lonely situation to write in. But writing is an alone kind of thing...I sensed what people needed was to be together. People are all we have in the world. I didn't consciously think this, but I realized that only the lonely know the way I feel. That's an exclusive statement, but the club is very big. I felt the need, as a young man, to share my loneliness, so everybody could share theirs. And maybe cause a few of them to get together...or remember they were once together.... With "Only the Lonely" being the first, I guess they said, 'Well, he's a lonely singer'.... When I wrote, let's say, a sad song, a melancholy song, I was feeling good at the time. Because I have to feel good and at peace with myself before I can think creatively. I've heard guys say, 'Well, I got my heart ripped out and got wasted for three weeks and wrote this song.' I couldn't do that. I'd be crying. I couldn't eat and all that. Of course, I knew what 'Only the Lonely' was about when I wrote that. I had been alone and lonely. I wasn't at the time, though."

Joe Melson calls "Only the Lonely" "an audience-participation song, addressed to a specific group. The song specifies who we wanted to react to this song. They felt like there was nobody as lonely as they were, and the lonely would understand. But everyone's lonely." It turned out to be a far larger crowd than either he or Roy had ever expected. When they put the finishing touches on the song, Roy refused to send it to Nashville. He knew how good it was, and he was afraid someone would hear it and steal it. According to Joe, Roy said, "There are certain writers in Nashville . . . well, if they heard that great theme, it would be written when we got to town."

As Roy told Glenn A. Baker, " 'Only the Lonely' wasn't the original title on the song. We called Fred and said we're ready to record again. He said, 'What is it called?' When I told him he said, 'That was a hit about a year ago.' I called him again and said, 'Here's what it's called,' and he said, 'Pat Boone just recorded that.' It was getting real frustrating, so I come to Joe's house and said, 'Here's what we're going to call the song: "Only the Lonely." ' We went right through it and had it finished in ten minutes. We'd already worked on the song for months. I called Fred and said, 'Here's the title of the song. I don't care if it's out now, yesterday or if it's a smash right now, it don't make any difference, this is what it's called.' Fred said, 'Okay, come on.' "

Accompanied by Roy's drummer, Roy and Joe headed for Nashville and when they got as far as Memphis, Joe recalled, "Roy said, 'Look, we need some loot. Let's stop by Elvis's here in Memphis.' I said, 'Roy, I've had my heart set on *you* recording "Only the Lonely." ' "

" 'I hate to give it up, Joe, but if Elvis cut it, we'd have so much money, we'd still have time to work some more, and we can write another one.' "

In fact, Roy decided to give a whole batch of songs to Elvis, not just "Only the Lonely." They pulled up at 6 a.m. in front of the Music Gates at Graceland. As Roy said in the Baker interview, "I handed the guard a note telling him I was at the gate. I was going to hang around if it was too early until everybody got awake and eventually sing him 'Only the Lonely' . . . he was just out of the Army and due to record.

Elvis sent a note back saying, 'Everybody's all over the place. Everybody's sleeping everywhere there is a place. See you in Nashville. We're leaving today. See you then.' It was sort of a slight. That's the way creative people are. We get our feelings hurt. He should have at least found out I've got a smash here. If he's going to record he needs it."

According to Joe Melson, Roy looked at him and said, "I guess Elvis isn't made up yet."

They drove on to Nashville and went to the Acuff-Rose dub studio, and Don and Phil Everly happened to be there. "They loved our writing," Joe said, "and they loved Roy." The Everlys were on the threshold of another fantastic year in 1960. They charted six Top 40 hit singles, including "Let It Be Me" and "Cathy's Clown," which remained #1 for five weeks. Roy sang "Only the Lonely" for Phil Everly, who responded by singing one of his own songs. More interested in pitching "Only the Lonely" than having a jam session with Phil Everly, Roy was frustrated. As he told Glenn A. Baker, Fred Foster saved the day by suggesting that Roy put the vocal figure from his song "Come Back to Me, My Love"—dum-dum-dum-dum-bedo-wah—in "Only the Lonely" and he'd have a hit. Roy was so excited with the results that he wanted to go into the studio immediately to record the refashioned "Only the Lonely," but it was impossible because Elvis Presley had the RCA facility booked around the clock.

On March 25, 1960, they finally got into the studio to cut it, and Roy later told an interviewer "Only the Lonely (Know How I Feel)" took only 20-30 minutes to record. Tommy Strong was the technician, Bill Porter the engineer, and, according to Joe, Anita Kerr was the arranger. "Anita was an excellent arranger," he said. "She had the knack of doing just enough and not too much."

Joe was preoccupied these days with his own solo career as a singer, and he wasn't expecting to participate significantly in the session that day. Once rehearsals started, however, he realized he needed to show the Anita Kerr Singers how to render the important vocal, the "dum-dum-dum-dum-bedo-wah," that is the first sound heard in "Only the Lonely." They were doing it wrong, singing on the notes, pronouncing each "dum." Joe recalls instructing the singers, "These sounds have to be *rounded*. Make them *flow*. They have to be full of feeling if we're going to be on-the-nose commercial." He rehearsed the singers on his sound and phrasing until they had it exactly right. Joe remembers that Anita, after watching him work with her singers, turned to Roy and said, "'*Joe* should sing that vocal figure with you, Roy. There's something in his voice that's just what it needs.' Fred Foster looked at Roy, Roy thought a second and then said, 'Hey, fine. Use Joe.'"

In the Baker interview, Roy said, "Bob Moore, who'd been the bass player on the session, said, 'I don't see how you could advance to that. It's not in meter.' I didn't know what he was talking about 'in meter.' He said, 'You'd be dancing along and you'd have one foot off the floor.'

"I said, 'I don't care if people dance or don't dance.'

"Bob said, 'You've got to dance to a record.' I didn't know what he was trying to do but Fred Foster said, 'No, we're going to leave it like it is.' Out-of-meter means in musicians' terms there's supposed to be a four-bar here and a two-bar here and all that and this one didn't have a pattern. All musicians every time they record for me say, 'Okay, how long is it going to take for us to learn this one?'"

In 1989, Fred Foster offered his own version of the session that produced "Only the Lonely." "He had a song that was about a teenage girl dying on her sixteenth birthday. It was a song called 'Come Back to Me, My Love.' A beautiful song, but 'Teen Angel' had been a hit just a couple of years previously and I told him that I thought it was too quick to come up with another one of those topical songs like that. But that song had a beautiful vocal figure in it. Then had another song that had a thirty-two-bar rubatto verse, which means it was out of tempo and just sort of took about two and a half minutes to get through this verse and then he went into the main body of the song which was 'Only the Lonely.' It was of course quite short, having such a long verse. So I suggested we drop the verse, take the vocal figure out of 'Come Back to Me, My Love,' and insert it between the lines of 'Only the Lonely.' So that's where the dum-dum-dum-dum-bedo-wah came from that went into 'Only the Lonely.'" Joe Melson, by the way, also takes credit for the vocal figure, saying that the opening of "Only the Lonely" came from a song he'd written earlier called "Cry."

In 1986, Robert K. Oermann interviewed Roy for *The Tennessean*, and in discussing the sound produced that day at Monument, and the roles of Fred Foster, Anita Kerr, Joe Melson and everyone else involved, Roy said: "I have to say *I* was the one who was really responsible for that sound. The sessions weren't the first, but they were among the first to use orchestras on Music Row. We hired violinists from the Nashville Symphony. We still didn't have enough, so we got one violin teacher to bring in his students. There were 30 people crowded into that little studio room. I was backed up against a coat rack singing."

In 1988, Roy told David Hinckley of the *New York Daily News*: "Monument was not all that much more sophisticated than Sun. It was a matter of 'Write your song, then come in and sing it.' Pretty soon, it was clear you knew as much as the people who were supposed to be teaching you.'"

In one of Roy's concert program booklets, he said, "Fred had been a promo man, and he was fairly new to producing. His first hit had been 'Gotta Travel On' with Billy Grammer, and, together . . . well, I don't know what you'd call it, but it was like a flowering of talent, an outpouring of pent-up creativity. I was just a kid, really, from Wink, Texas, and I'd always been fairly inhibited and shy, and Fred gave me my chance to do it all—and I did it! I wrote and arranged songs, even produced some of the sessions, in a sense. I'd been frustrated for three or four years, and now it just came pouring out."

When they finished recording "Only the Lonely," Joe assumed they would return to Texas. He had a family to feed, he was going to college and working at Standard Oil and needed to resume his job. "Roy got the boogies about going home," Joe said. "Roy told me Fred Foster had said, 'Don't go out on the highways and get killed. The weekends are really rough.' Roy told me, 'Man, I don't want to go home. We're fixin' to make it.' I said, 'Well, I've got to get back home,' and Roy said, 'Man, here I am fixin' to make it and then go out on the highway and get killed.'"

Roy may have been reluctant because of the spate of recent deaths of friends of his in violent crashes—Buddy Holly and Ritchie Valens had died in an airplane crash, and Eddie Cochran was killed in a car wreck on his way to Heathrow Airport in London. Gene Vincent, who'd been touring with Eddie, was also in the car, and his already damaged leg was further crippled.

Finally Roy shook off his fears and told Joe, "Okay, okay, I promise you. We'll leave in a day or so." Eventually, Joe went back to work and Roy returned to Claudette. They were living in Wink in a house with corrugated metal walls, and Roy was lucky to get twenty dollars a night as an opening act on one-nighters or forty dollars to work an entire dance. Roy had gone through every penny he'd ever earned, and without a band backing him up, it wasn't easy getting work in the beer joints anymore. Joe recalls, "Roy said, 'I don't know what to do, but I have to go back to work. I don't want to but I have to. I've got a wife and baby.' Joe cut him in on his gigs at the VFW and The Gateway, agreeing to split the $100-200 fees. They had an argument when Roy tried to charge Joe for use of Roy's PA system. "I'm givin' you half my money," Joe pointed out, "and you're not chargin' me nothin'."

Joe and Roy had another disagreement at this time, and this one concerned the title of "Only the Lonely." As Joe recalls, Roy started the argument by saying, "'I came up with that title.'

"'I did,' I said.

"'Bull!'

"'It doesn't matter,' I said. 'It's a great song, right?'

"'Yeah,' Roy said, 'but I gave you the title.'"

Then they tried to laugh it off, and, according to Joe, Roy finally said, "Let's just say we wrote it."

"Okay," Joe said. "Fine."

Years later, Joe noted, "I let him think he came up with it." But arguments like this made it clear that their egos were on a collision course, and their collaborating days were numbered.

Just before the record was released, Roy and Joe started singing "Only the Lonely" during their act in dance halls and bars around Odessa and Monahans. At the end of the song, the crowd remained completely silent. Thinking they didn't like it, Joe looked at Roy and said, "Well, they didn't go wild." Roy remarked, "Don't worry. It's soaking in." They decided there was so much in the song that people would have to hear it two or three times before it began to get to them. "It goes so many different directions that they couldn't grasp it all," Joe recalled. "People came to like it a little at a time."

It was released on April 15. Feeling lucky because it was his birthday month, Roy was convinced "Only the Lonely" would make the Top 20, and he headed for New York with Fred Foster on a promotion tour. They were in a Manhattan movie house when Fred suddenly decided to make a telephone call to see if the record had charted yet. It had—"Only the Lonely" was #71 in one trade paper and #88 in the other. "We've got it made," Roy said.

Joe Melson, back in Texas, was at work one day when someone said to him, "That song you've been telling us about, 'Only the Lonely,' you know, I think you've got a hit. I was walking down the road and a guy was out watering his lawn and he was humming your song. I heard him going 'dum-dum-dum-dum-bedo-wah.' When they do that, Joe, it means a hit. Hell, they're singing your song all over town!"

Joe recalled, "I thought, Yeah, it'll probably sell a quarter of a million records, and then next time we'll get a really big one. But then Roy called me and said, 'The record broke into the Top 100.' It broke

first in Boston. That's where the big orders came from first." When
Roy was in Philadelphia for his first national television appearance,
Joe Melson remembered, "He called and said, 'I'm going on The Dick
Clark Show, *American Bandstand.* Fred set me up with Dick Clark!'

"'You're calling collect?'

"'Yeah, because—'

"'Because you're charging it to me is the reason!'

"'No, Joe, I'm sorry, but I'm not near a phone where I could charge
it to myself. I don't have any change on me, either.'

"'I can't believe you're calling me collect.'

"'Joe, I'm fixin' to go on The Dick Clark Show!'

"'Fantastic! When is it? I'll be watching!'

"'The record is going to be a monster!'"

Roy went over great on Dick Clark. Unfortunately, Claudette was
not there to share this triumph. "She was still back in Texas," Joe
said. "Although the career had started, money was not real prevalent.
It takes about a year to get your money. I didn't realize any big money
until about '61–62. Back then, we didn't have today's wide range of
market. Today you can put songs everywhere—restaurants, movies,
videos, television, radio, every grocery store, discount store. The
market is huge. If we'd had that market then, 'Only the Lonely' would
have sold ten million."

"Only the Lonely" finally crested at #2 in the U.S. Then, on June
20, 1960, it went all the way and hit #1 in the U.K. It held the #1 spot
on the British chart for two weeks—October 22 and October 29. It
began to come out in other countries and go to the top. Though "Only
the Lonely" never reached #1 in the U.S., it was a magnificent global
smash.

Just as important as its commercial triumph, "Only the Lonely"
represented something new in rock 'n' roll. A dramatic, operatic,
beautifully melodic ballad, it came as a stunning contrast to the pile-
driving sound of early rock. It was the flipside of the cockiness of
rock. On careful inspection, however, the hope its lyrics offered the
lonely was a deluded one. Its compassion and tenderness were
authentic, and the song would always be treasured by millions of
people. Like most love songs of the time, however, it suggested that the
cure for heartbreak was falling in love again. Tomorrow someone else
would come along with the magic elixir and, presto, no more pain.
While romantic love is one of life's great joys, it never yet brought an
end to sorrow, as Roy would soon discover in his own marriage. "Only

the Lonely," like most love songs, mistakenly suggests that happiness is only for lovers.

People in Nashville were stunned. Along with Brenda Lee's "I'm Sorry" and "I Want to Be Wanted," both 1960 releases and both #1 hits, "Only the Lonely" was among the first big pop records to come out of the hillbilly capital. Critics christened Roy "the Caruso of Rock" and raved about his "three-octave range." Years later, they were still trying to define the eerie power of "Only the Lonely," which was somehow inseparable from Roy's unique voice. Rock writer Robert Hilburn referred to its "surreal aura...a purity and passion that conveyed the delicateness and ache of romantic disappointment and doubt." BAM praised "Only the Lonely" as the first of Roy's "dissolute, doomed, heartbreaking melodramas that cast Orbison as the perennial loner, born loser and rejected lover...the emotional honesty of country music, the doo-wop sound he lived with in the '50s and the more mainstream ballads of older singers. The mixture married to that beautiful voice perfectly suited the angst-ridden insecurities and frustrations of the blossoming teenage culture."

Other artists could scarcely believe their ears. When had a voice like Roy's ever been heard in popular music? It was a miracle, but there was also something inexplicably mysterious and touching about it. Untrained, raw, quavery, it seemed to exist on a fine line between amateurism and genius, and listeners held their breath as they waited to see if Roy was going to hit that note or not. The hint of strain somehow made his voice all the more appealing and poignant; the difficulty he had in reaching a note somehow made his inevitable realization of it seem both triumphant and courageous, adding an unexpected power to any song he sang. Like Edith Piaf and Jimmy Durante, Roy Orbison was a phenomenon who escaped being made into a joke—as were Mrs. Miller and Tiny Tim—by a hair's breadth.

Duane Eddy, the Phoenix, Arizona, rocker famous for his twangy guitar and hit record "Rebel-'Rouser," said, "As a musician-singer-artist Roy was without parallel. He was just the greatest. You know, of course, that he was Elvis Presley's favorite singer. He certainly was one of mine. The thing about Roy was that while he influenced so many people through the years nobody could ever do what he did exactly. Very few singers have the range that he had and even if they did and could sing the songs that he sang they still didn't have that raw power and that same sound that he could create, and I thought that that was marvelous. The thing about him was that when he'd sung as high as you thought he could possibly sing he would effortlessly go even higher and finish up with a big finish and it was wonderful."

Bruce Springsteen, an adolescent at the time, would later recall, "He made a little town in New Jersey feel as big as the sound of his records. I'll always remember what he means to me and what he meant to me when I was young and afraid to love."

At Graceland, Elvis listened to "Only the Lonely" and then sent someone out for a whole carton of records, distributing them to all his friends. Roy had offered "Only the Lonely" to Elvis in March, and in April, Elvis had cut a startingly similar record, "It's Now or Never," which was adapted from "O Sole Mio" and marked an enormous change in Elvis' style. Elvis's big booming ballad had the same adult, operatic sound as Roy's hit.

The week of July 18, 1960, the Top 5 consisted of "Only the Lonely" in #4, Brenda Lee's "I'm Sorry" in #1, The Hollywood Argyles' "Alley-Oop" in #2, Connie Francis' "Everybody's Somebody's Fool" in #3 and Duane Eddy's "Because They're Young" in #5. "Only the Lonely" held fast in the Top 5 for a few weeks and would have started moving up again on August 8 if it hadn't been for a wild novelty tune, Bryan Hyland's "Itsy Bitsy Teenie Weenie Yellow Polka Dot Bikini," which slipped into the #1 spot. Bryan, sixteen, was a student at Franklin K. Lane High School in Brooklyn. Elvis' "It's Now or Never" was in the slot just over Roy that week, #3, but on August 15, Roy stayed in #4 and Elvis went to #1, displacing the itsy bitsy bikini. "Only the Lonely" had lost its chance to reach #1.

"It's Now or Never" went on to become the biggest-selling single of Elvis's career, holding the #1 spot for five weeks. In England, it topped the charts for nine weeks and was the fastest-selling single in U.K. history. This was the recording that opened a whole new audience for Elvis, whose songs could now, for the first time, receive air play on easy-listening stations. Suddenly, Frank Sinatra fans found Elvis palatable. Together, Roy and Elvis established the genre of the rock ballad, redefining the parameters of rock and expanding its audience to listeners beyond the teenage fans.

"Only the Lonely" remained in the U.S. Top 40 for fifteen weeks and sold over three million copies. It was #1 in most of the countries of Europe and in the U.K., automatically making Roy an international recording star. Right before stardom, according to Orbie Lee Harris,

Roy had worked for Pure Oil in Wink to support Claudette and the baby. Claudette had stuck with him through the leanest of times, and now she could see easier days ahead of them. She looked forward to some family time, when Roy could be with her and R.D., as they now called Roy DeWayne, and she hoped their life would be less stressful, with Roy keeping more regular hours. But this was not to be. Roy had attained the success that he'd always yearned for, but he wasn't about to stop and relax. Instead, he saw greater vistas ahead. "There is no limit and I would ride it all the way," he said. "The door is open, I walk through. I don't want to sit around and wait for it very long. I always take things too seriously."

Though Roy and Claudette were still living in Wink, Roy came to Joe's house in Midland, where they wrote new songs. "He would come down and we'd write at night," Joe said. "After 'Lonely' I'd talk to him on the phone but he got so busy. He started booking in Dallas, and we went down to The Guthrie Club there. Roy was the star and I did the backup for him and the crowds went wild."

According to Joe, Fred Foster advised Roy to move to Nashville. "Roy called me," Joe remembered, "and said, 'Are you going to move to Nashville with me?'

"'Yeah, but I think we're going to have to wait until we get some of the money in from "Only the Lonely."'

"'Fred wants us both to move out.'

"'I can't until I get some loot.'" Roy assured Joe that money would be coming in soon, and as they said goodbye, Joe told him he'd just become a father for the second time. He already had a son named Michael, and now his daughter Michelle Deanne was born. When Joe went to the hospital in Midland to see Michelle, he was cruising down the street thinking, "Wow! A new daughter!" Just then a cop stopped him and started to give him a ticket. "My wife just had a baby," Joe pleaded, "and I guess I just wasn't thinking, officer. Was I speedin'?"

"You won't be a father very long speedin' like that," the cop responded. "I'm gonna write you out a ticket anyway, Big Daddy."

Driving away, Joe calmed down and thought again about his new kid. He knew there had to be a great title connected with the blessed event, and then "Blue Angel" came to him. "I started working on the song," Joe said, "and some beautiful things came together. There's a nice break, some transition parts and verses to get into another bridge, great instrumentation—I couldn't wait to tell Roy about it. When Roy called me on the phone, I ended up singing 'Blue Angel' to him." Roy thought it sounded like a hit and wanted to take it to Nashville where they would get together and finish it up.

Joe made a dub of "Blue Angel," and Roy said he'd drive by and pick it up on his way to Nashville. After that, Roy packed up everything he owned and started out for Lubbock, where Claudette and R.D. were staying with the Fradys. But first he decided to visit his old friend Ronnie Slaughter, with whom he remained close ever since high school. Roy yearned to have a sidekick go to Nashville with him; he'd never liked traveling without a buddy or two along. Things hadn't worked out well for Ronnie and Roy felt there was a good chance he'd come to Nashville with him. Ronnie had won a football scholarship at Eastern New Mexico State, but he'd had to forfeit it when he'd been injured.

"We met that night in Andrews, Texas," Ronnie Slaughter recalls. "I was working nights and got off at eleven p.m. Roy and I met at The El Rancho Cafe and talked until two or three a.m. Roy said, 'Hey, Ron, come go to Nashville with me. I'm going to make it. And you can't believe the young ladies that are attracted to me, as ugly as I am. It still amazes me that my music got me such a beautiful wife.'"

Ronnie considered Roy's offer. He'd been thinking about finishing college, resuming his football scholarship at Eastern New Mexico University. But now a recording star was inviting him to join a way of life that included Thunderbirds, rock 'n' roll and hot women. Ronnie remembers saying, "Roy, I don't have any talent.'

"'You can make it,' Roy said.

"'That's not my thing,' I said. 'My ambition is not to sing to a bunch of drunks.'"

Five years before, Slob Evans made the same decision when he dropped out of The Wink Westerners, feeling he'd spent enough time in honky tonks. Slob was now married, raising a family and selling insurance. Ronnie Slaughter watched Roy drive off to Nashville and he never regretted his decision to remain behind. In time, he finished college, settled in Wink with Barbara Wilson and raised a family of four children.

The next day, Roy, Claudette and R.D. came by Joe Melson's place in the T-Bird, pulling a U-Haul trailer loaded with all their belongings. Joe handed Roy a dub of "Blue Angel," they vowed to keep in touch, and Roy drove off with his little family. Joe returned to his job working in the mail room at Standard Oil and continued studying accounting at Odessa Junior College. The company was still paying his tuition and promising him a good job in accounting as soon as he completed his training.

Arriving in Nashville, Roy and Claudette settled in the suburb of Hendersonville. "They didn't have enough money to pay the damn rent, hardly," Chester Frady said. Chester and Gerry came from Texas to visit them, and Gerry said, "They didn't even have an icebox. They had Cokes and things in an Igloo cooler." Claudette had discovered frozen daiquiris and loved to sit with their new neighbors, drinking and gossiping while Roy feverishly pursued his career.

Chester and Gerry enjoyed going to the Grand Ole Opry on weekends in Nashville and also meeting Roy and Claudette's new friends, such as Margaret and Wesley Rose and Boudleaux and Felice Bryant, who wrote "Bye Bye Love," "Take a Message to Mary" and "All I Have to Do Is Dream" for The Everly Brothers. Felice and Roy had met in the lobby of Acuff-Rose Publishing Company. "He had his first wife, Claudette, with him," Felice recalled. "She was just this little girl with a tiny baby in her arms. He was so shy and quiet. He wouldn't even sing his songs. And he had the whitest skin I'd ever seen, almost like an albino. He just looked so fragile.

"Roy and Boudleaux would sit all night and philosophize about everything." After one all-night bull session, Roy dove into the Bryant's swimming pool and then fell asleep at poolside. "He burned himself real bad," Felice said. "He got as red as a beet; you know how pale his skin was. We tried to remove some of the heat from him with white vinegar, but he was hurting."

Felice and Boudleaux's son Del said, "My family and Roy all lived within a mile of each other in those days. We spent a lot of time together. We had the only swimming pool, so everyone sort of gathered at our house. Seeing Roy in a bathing suit is something you don't soon forget.

"My parents loved his voice. Mom always said he had the prettiest voice she ever heard. She would always get him to sing in the kitchen with just this gut-string guitar and his voice. We had an old log home, and the acoustics were great. He sounded like an angel. I think Dad was probably more proud of Roy's version of 'Love Hurts' than any other version of the song.

"Roy was such a gentle person. Never heard him get angry or loud.

His classic remark was 'Mercy!' That's all he would say when something happened. If something horrible occurred, he'd just say, 'Oh, mercy!' "

Other Hendersonville friends included architect Braxton Dixon and his wife Anna. Anna remembers running into Claudette and R.D. in the dentist's office. "Roy DeWayne looked like Claudette," Anna recalls. "At the dentist, Roy DeWayne saw our little girl, Barbara, and said, 'Mama, I want to go play with my little girl friend.' He was crazy about Barbara." Anna soon became "like a sister" to Claudette, though Claudette was seventeen years her junior, and Braxton and Roy became so friendly that later on, when Roy was rich from record royalties, he commissioned Braxton to build a lavish house for him on Old Hickory Lake, complete with an indoor swimming pool.

Soon after settling in Nashville, Roy started worrying about coming up with another hit. He knew he could never maintain his momentum as a recording star unless he had a steady flow of new songs. "If you want to be a big singer, you need a big song" was the oldest adage in Nashville. Joe Melson remembers getting a call from Roy. " 'Fred Foster thinks you should get on out here,' Roy said. 'He says my career is really looking good.' On a wing and a prayer I quit my job, loaded my family up and we drove to Nashville in my '55 Oldsmobile. Roy had a new T-Bird because he'd got his money first."

Joe and his family arrived in Hendersonville after dark. "We looked around and it was nothing but bushes and trees," Joe commented. "This area was not built up then at all." In a day or two Roy and Joe resumed working on "Blue Angel" and finished it within a week. Their country-oriented associates in Nashville were unenthusiastic. "If you'd a-played them some corn music," Roy said, "they'd all a-boogied and jumped.' "

Nevertheless, "Blue Angel" was recorded on August 8, 1960, and it was one of Roy's most moving performances. In this rapturous lullabye, he croons and yodels as he comforts a girl whose lover has left her. Then he assures her that she has nothing to fear, because he loves her himself and will never leave her. Though not one of Orbison–Melson's trademark crescendo songs, the public rewarded this pop jewel by sending it immediately into the Top 10, where it crested at #9, remaining in the Top 40 for eight weeks. Roy and Joe had had two Top 10 hits in four months—and 1960 was still young.

To take advantage of his new popularity as a recording star, Roy undertook a hectic tour schedule. Patsy Cline, his neighbor, was also a hopeless workaholic, and she and Roy appeared on the same bill. Patsy was a big spender and usually in debt. Since she couldn't make a living cutting records, hitting the road regularly was her only recourse, though it created serious problems in her marriage. Touring would also undermine Roy's marriage. Just as Patsy's husband Charlie Dick worried about his wife sleeping with musicians on the road, Claudette, according to her Aunt Patty, would eventually have reason to suspect Roy. But in the early '60s, the marriage was still sound, or so it appeared to Billy Pat Ellis when he came to Hendersonville to visit them. "They looked like a happy family to me," Billy Pat says.

Roy and Patsy Cline toured the South in Patsy's used Cadillac. Both Patsy and Roy were great Cadillac aficionados and loved nothing more than driving these "road barges" every chance they got. But Patsy was more than Roy's match when it came to reckless driving. After a show they did one night, he rode with Patsy to the next gig in her old white Cadillac, and she was like a madwoman at the wheel. The Caddy was rocketing down the highway, and Roy began to fear this might be his last ride. Dottie West was also in the car and said that Roy was in abject terror. "Oh, boy, could that Patsy drive that car," Dottie said. "Roy Orbison was holding on for dear life in the back seat. Patsy was a daredevil behind the wheel."

Patsy Cline once described her professional life as "singing in clubs and sleazy joints, traveling on dusty, rutted roads, and staying in motels that have seen better days. It's also signing autographs, doing the very best job you can, and meaning something special to a whole bunch of strangers who suddenly become like family to you." According to Claudette's mother, Claudette and Patsy became friends from the time they met. Patsy was undergoing a career slump; "Walkin' After Midnight" was a hit for her in 1957, but then, like Roy, she had lost her way. Having survived career doldrums with Roy, Claudette would have been able to offer Patsy Cline informed interest and sympathy.

Patsy was viewed as a bit of a tart by the Nashville establishment. Grand Ole Opry comic Grampa (Marshall Louis) Jones said, "You couldn't miss ole Patsy when she'd come in. She was a good-looking gal with a nice figure and used to really turn the guys' heads with the way she wiggled when she walked." Faron Young, who had a crossover hit with Willie Nelson's "Hello, Walls," put it even more bluntly. "She had quite an ass, and a figure like an hourglass." Through Patsy's experience on the road, Claudette was able to gain insights about musicians and singers that may have alarmed her. On lonely winter nights away from her husband and baby, it was not unusual for Patsy to seek comfort and pleasure in the arms of men touring with her, such as Porter Wagoner and Faron Young. Was Roy doing the same with female performers or fans on his tours? Some of the musicians he worked with say he was.

According to Kadon, Claudette's cousin, "Claudette was very unhappy, and I think Roy knew it. Very unhappy. She adored Roy and after they moved to Tennessee and he became so popular she was alone again, just as she'd been in childhood. He was always on tour and when he was at home their house was like a hotel—his producers, writers, managers, band, everybody was there, and although he was there, he wasn't there. He was still working and they had no time for themselves. I know she was very lonely and unhappy. She thought the children could help fill that gap, but she missed Roy. She wanted to spend her life with him and all of a sudden here's all this fame and money and she couldn't go anywhere and Roy wasn't there.

"Success went to Roy's head. He didn't know how to handle it and Claudette sure didn't. His advisors took over and being a country boy he said do whatever it takes. An unsophisticated young man suddenly in the world of high finance and fame, he let other people take control and he was utilized. Everyone got a piece of pie and the bigger the pie the better. Claudette had to go to Orbie Lee Orbison for money. Every penny she got she had to ask for. She was on an allowance."

Stardom was lethal for Roy Orbison because it made him feel invincible. Though Bobby Blackburn says, "I'd bet my right leg that Roy was true to Claudette," others say he took his wife's loyalty for granted while he played the field, assuming that he was above ordinary mortals and could have everything he wanted. He had taken on responsibilities that he was incapable of handling, such as a wife who was a teenage dropout and a child who was largely cared for by solicitous relatives. Infatuated with his own talent and career, surrounded by yes-men and hangers-on and befuddled by vanity and an increasing dependence on amphetamines, he was stumbling into a way of life that could consume him and most of his family.

The news of Joe Ray Hammer's death was a terrible blow to Roy. "Joe Ray had always been the superstar in the relationship," Bobby

Blackburn recalls, "and he'd just been named the youngest band director of a 5A school in Texas—Midland Lee High, a brand new school." On a trip to Wink, Roy showed up at Joe Ray's band class, flaunting his Cadillac and hit records. "All his students made out over Roy," Bobby said, "and that upset Joe Ray." In a month, he committed suicide. "I called Roy in Tennessee and told him and Roy said, 'I don't believe it.'" But it was so. Joe Ray Hammer had blown his head off with a 12-gauge shotgun.

Chapter 6

After "Only the Lonely," the hits came tumbling from Roy Orbison and Joe Melson. "Running Scared" followed "Only the Lonely" by only a few months and it became their first #1 hit in America. Most critics call "Running Scared" paranoid, but it was not. At this point in his life, Roy's fear of losing everything was well founded; as Roy himself said, "I was *worried* in that song." It describes the terror of a man who's afraid his girl is about to go off with another man. The last word of the song reveals that he has been able to hold onto her, at least for the present. The intensity of feeling Roy achieved in his performance was almost unparalleled in pop or rock. In this song, he seemed to take heartbreak beyond the point of nervous breakdown. Even after thirty years, "Running Scared" stands as the definitive expression of early rock's romantic agony.

"Running Scared" also represents an artistic turning point in Roy's singing career. In this song, he pushed his voice beyond what even he and Joe had thought was possible. "I didn't have a teacher to tell me what to do," Roy said, "so I didn't know I wasn't supposed to sing high and low or wherever I wanted to sing. In the recording session of 'Running Scared,' I was singing very softly at the end of the record. Someone flipped the switch and said, 'Look, we're going to lose the record if you don't really give us that note because we can't hear it.' That sort of embarrassed me so I said, 'Run it by one more time and you'll hear it this time.' So then when it got time to hit the note, I just hit it. All the musicians looked around. They could hear it as well. We got the record and it was sort of a flowering of my voice."

"Running Scared" went into the U.S. Top 40 on April 24, 1961. By the end of May, it was #3, right behind "Daddy's Home" and the chart-topper, Ricky Nelson's "Travelin' Man." On June 5, Roy Orbison captured the #1 spot. But even his greatest success was tinged with irony. For many years, "Running Scared" held *Billboard's* record as the #1 hit that had the *shortest* run in the Top 10—four weeks.

Roy and Joe soon returned to the charts with another smash hit. In

August, "Crying," Roy's own personal favorite, leapt into the Top 5. Opening with ominous beats on the tom-tom, "Crying" is another of Roy's hopeless love songs. Ending on a damning note, the song describes a rejected lover who will be crying for the rest of his life, who loves the woman who has left him more now than he did when they were together. The grain of hope contained in "Running Scared" is replaced by grief and doom. Explaining the song's enormous success, Joe Melson said, "People get release through these big, driving, stair-stepping songs, and they love it because they have expressed through Roy what they've been wanting to cry out." Roy was never more inspired nor in better voice.

Discussing the record with Greg Mitchell of *Crawdaddy* in 1974, Roy said that "Crying" was inspired by a girl he was "dating" around 1958–59, but since he married Claudette in 1957, either he was speaking euphemistically of his wife or running around on her or simply confused. "The story behind 'Crying' was, I was dating this girl and then we broke up—this must have been two or three years before I wrote the song. I went to the barbershop to get a hair cut and I looked across the street and there was this girl I had split up with. I wanted to go over and say, 'Let's forget about what happened and carry on.' But I was very stubborn. So I got in the car and drove on down the street and got about two blocks away and said, 'Boy you really made a mistake. You didn't play that right at all.' I would say that I had tears in my eyes—I'll go that far—but whether I was physically crying or just crying inside, is the same thing. This is what I saw: I was all right for a while, I could smile for a while, I was feeling pretty good until I saw you last night."

Roy was on a magnificent roll. Even the B-side of "Crying" was a hit. "Candy Man," a Beverly Ross–Fred Neil tune, went to #25 in October. As 1961 ended, Roy could look back on two years of fantastic success—six straight smash hit singles.

Roy now had enough songs for an album. "I remember when my first Monument album was ready to come out," he said. "I went and visited Sam Phillips in Memphis to let him listen to it and clear up a couple of points. Sam was sitting around with his brother, Jud. And Sam said, 'Shoot, I've got enough stuff on you to release an album myself, and I'm gonna do it and it will outsell your Monument album.' Jud just looked at him and said, 'Sam, are you crazy?'"

The Sun album was called *Roy Orbison at the Rockhouse*, and Roy's Monument album appeared under the title *Lonely and Blue*. Neither sold enough copies to make the charts. Though Roy's singles became familiar to the public through disk jockeys and massive radio exposure, there was nothing to promote the albums. As a personality, Roy was invisible. People knew what Elvis Presley and Ricky Nelson looked like, and feature stories described their lives and personalities, but Roy Orbison never emerged as a celebrity, at least not in the U.S. Perhaps the people around him did not find Roy promotable, and perhaps they were right. In his interviews he seemed bland. And his appearance was not the sort to sell records. On the picture sleeve for one of his singles, "Ride Away," Roy is shown on a motorcycle, but with his skinny arms and gawky Adam's apple he seems out of place, and the effect is unintentionally comical.

It was the kind of notoriety Elvis Presley aroused that Roy desperately wanted, but even a skillful sideshow hawker such as Colonel Tom Parker couldn't have sold Roy Orbison. Roy simply didn't possess the physical package to justify a major publicity blitz. His success represented a triumph of talent over hype and sex appeal. Many of his U.S. fans never saw him, not even a photograph, because the press shunned him. Though Roy was egotistical enough to think he was a household name, he never achieved that kind of celebrity status, certainly not in America. "When I became very popular—I think they call it a household name—everybody else, without exception, would hire a publicist to get their names published, to get their picture here and there. I didn't have a PR man until I hired someone in England in 1967. So from '59 to '66 never once did I pay anyone a penny to get my name spread around. I just didn't believe, and I still don't believe, in building talent through publicity." Most publicists would contend that Roy missed the point. Professional publicists and public-relations experts claim that they are able to help a performer achieve celebrity by constructing an image, carefully choosing what is said and done in front of the press and the public. Whether there is any validity to that claim is debatable. But Roy could never have had first-magnitude fame no matter what he paid. The handful of genuine rock superstars— Elvis, The Beatles, Michael Jackson—are sex objects who promote themselves as such, whether it's Elvis' bumps and grinds, The Beatles' tight pants and long hair, or Michael Jackson's surgically reconstructed face. Roy deluded himself to the end of his life, bragging, "I made enough money to buy a legend. We conceived a plan to do that, but I didn't buy it." Superstardom eluded Roy Orbison for the same reason he was never a class favorite at Wink—he didn't have the looks or the personality for it. It should have been enough for him to be a great singer, but it wasn't.

Roy went on a tour with Patsy Cline in the early '60s, and, though Orbie Lee Harris said Roy had done so previously, Roy claimed that his habit of performing in sunglasses began on this tour. "The image, like the voice, came in stages," Roy said. "I never sat down with anyone and said, 'Let's design an image.' I started using sunglasses in Alabama. I was going to do a show with Patsy Cline and Bobby Vee, and I left my clear glasses on the plane. I only had the sunshades, and I was quite embarrassed to go on stage with them, but I did it."

Bobby Vee, who'd replaced Buddy Holly on the Winter Tour after Buddy's fatal plane crash, was by now a teen idol, churning out slick, polished hits like "Run to Him." Patsy was #12 on the pop charts with "I Fall to Pieces." Neither Patsy Cline nor Roy Orbison had been able to survive the pressure of their lives without damage to their health. In June of 1961, Patsy was hospitalized after being involved in a head-on car collision; afterwards she suffered a nervous breakdown and had only recently returned to work for this tour. Roy was being treated for an ulcer by Dr. Charles Gillitt of Hendersonville. On the $50,000 life insurance policy Charles Evans wrote out for Roy on September 25, 1961, Roy listed April 1961 as the date of his first duodenal ulcer attack, and under "duration of the illness" he wrote "To present."

When Claudette's brother Bill arrived in Hendersonville for a visit in 1961, Roy gave him the key to his T-Bird. "We were waiting for 'Crying' to come out and Roy didn't have an abundant amount of money," Bill said. "He was still livin' on what royalties had come in— four months, maybe six months he'd been gettin' royalties. While I was up there, we didn't go any place, really. Joe Melson and I became friends, and I'd work with Joe in the basement or the studio. He was getting ready to do some songs of his own, and we worked on four or five songs, perfecting them for dubbing. I'm not a musician, but I could help Joe polish his performance by giving him feedback. 'Well, I think it might work better this way,' I'd say. I was giving Joe the younger people's point of view about what sounded good.

"Roy was waiting every day to see *Billboard* and the Top 10 to see if he was going to make it. 'Crying' finally hit the charts while I was up there, around eighth place. It was a fun time in my life. I was seventeen years old. Larry Parks, a drummer, was a real good friend of Roy's, and Larry, John, Roy and I went down to the recording studio, where Roy was taping a song, 'Blue Bayou,' I think. Our days would start at night when everybody else was going to bed. We'd go down to the recording studio and work on a song all night.

"When I was in Tennessee, Roy was the same way he'd been in Texas. He never did change. He was the friendliest person you would ever want to meet. I don't know anybody who had a bad word about him or he had a bad word about them. He was a jolly fellow back in the '50s, always joking, he'd laugh at the drop of a hat. He and I got along great from the very first.

"Claudette just seemed to be goin' with the flow up there. Roy had her on a pedestal. He thought the world of her. You could tell the way he felt from the way he talked to her and the way he looked at her when he talked to her, in regular conversation, from the very first all the way up to the time I left their house. Roy paid attention to anybody that had anything to say. He'd listen to anybody. He was a smart fellow, a genius. He could have succeeded in anything he went into that he was interested in, like architecture. You ought to see his drawings of houses.

"Grady Lee, Roy's brother, was there with his wife and little girl. We all went out on a picnic. Roy's older brother, Sammy, and I used to ride motorcycles together. Roy bought them all motorcycles.

"They were all good people up there around Roy and Claudette. Felice and Boudleaux Bryant gave me my goin' away party when I left to join the service. It was at their house, a nice place with a swimming pool. They had two or three sons, just a little bit older than I—a very nice family. They served barbecue, and then we all went in swimmin'."

Roy was receiving so many invitations to appear in England that he decided to go over and take a look. Chester and Gerry came to Hendersonville to keep the children while Roy and Claudette went overseas in 1961. Roy and Claudette ended up loving to travel together so much that they went all over the world—including India and Hawaii—and Chester and Gerry ended up staying nine months in Hendersonville.

In the spring of 1962 Roy made a whistle-stop tour of Australia, playing concerts in Melbourne, Sydney and Brisbane. Also on the bill was Australia's answer to Elvis Presley, a singer named Johnny O'Keefe. Roy appeared on the Australian TV show *Bandstand*, where

The Bee Gees were a regular attraction. Years later, Roy's cover version of The Bee Gees' song "Words," though a commercial disappointment, was a virtuoso performance.

While in London in June 1962, Roy gave a press conference in the Mount Vernon Room of London's Westbury Hotel. With the exception of "Only the Lonely" and "Dream Baby," his British sales were sluggish. "It's one of my ambitions within the next two or three months to really consolidate the world market for my records," he said. He took off his glasses to pose for the cameramen, something he wouldn't have considered doing years later. British reporters referred to his "Jodrell Bank ears" and plain face.

"I had a contract to sign," he said, "and decided that I might as well sign it in London, fix up a few details and take a look around the British market." The British reporters mistakenly categorized Roy as a country & western singer, and he went along with them, since country songs were currently in fashion in England, with Frank Ifield's "I Remember You" at the top of the charts. "I'll cut a record especially for the British market," he said. "It will be very near the C&W style, but will be tempered to your taste. The guitars of C&W could mean a lot here." Roy then made a prophetic statement about the direction of popular music. "You don't seem to have the kind of rhythm group that we have in the States. I'm sure that is what the kids want: strong, beaty rhythms that make them jump." Within a year, the British Empire would be in a frenzy over The Beatles.

After the press conference, Roy gave a free concert with a pick-up group in the Westbury's reception area, running through ten numbers for the assembled journalists and fans. He was shrewdly laying the groundwork for what would prove to be his most loyal constituency, the British public. One day, Roy was flipping through a British magazine and read an item saying, "The highlight of the evening was Del Shannon's version of Roy Orbison's 'Crying.'"

"I got to thinking that if he did that well with my songs," Roy said, "I might do as well if I came over." Negotiations began for a national tour in October 1962. Since Roy was not deemed strong enough to headline alone, and since England had no pop singers of Roy's calibre, Sam Cooke, whose "Chain Gang," "You Send Me" and "Everybody Likes to Cha Cha Cha" were soul classics, was lined up to share the bill. But Sam cancelled the tour when his personal life started falling to pieces. Within a year Sam would be dead, shot by the manager of

Los Angeles's Hacienda Motel, who accused him of attempting to rape the girl he'd checked in with. The coroner brought in a finding of justifiable homicide.

Carl Perkins was approached to substitute for Sam on Roy's U.K. tour, but negotiations bogged down once again, and Roy's plans for an English tour were shelved. Returning to the States, he looked in on the burgeoning folk scene in New York's Greenwich Village. On May 24, 1962, he attended Bob Dylan's twenty-first birthday party. To Bob, Roy was rock's grand opera singer. Their meetings over the years would be few but significant. Two of rock's best singer-songwriters, both Orbison and Dylan courted mystery, Roy behind his dark glasses and Bob behind a bogus identity as a social outcast. In reality Bob Dylan was a middle-class Jewish boy from Hibbing, Minnesota, named Robert Allen Zimmerman. Like Roy, he had grown up listening to Hank Williams and Slim Whitman, had formed his first band from Hibbing High's marching band, had been unable to hold his band together, and had flopped as a folksinger in Minneapolis, Aspen and Denver coffeehouses before hitting it big in Greenwich Village. Eventually, Roy and Bob would end up in the same band, The Traveling Wilburys, in 1989.

Claudette and Roy had their second son, Anthony King Orbison, in 1962. Like R.D., he grew into a handsome little boy, inheriting only one of his father's features—his large ears—and Claudette announced her intention to have them corrected surgically when he was a little older. Tony became the daredevil of the family, climbing trees, jumping off roofs and slamming his go-cart through the shrubbery. "Evel Knievel had nothing on Tony," said his grandfather, Chester Frady. As they grew up, Tony and R.D., left alone much of the time or with grandparents during Roy and Claudette's frequent absences, became extremely close. "Roy called Tony 'Superbear,'" Bobby Blackburn remembered. "At first he was 'Tony the Tiger,' named after the breakfast cereal's mascot, but Tony got fat as a child and was more like a bear than a tiger, so he became Superbear."

In 1962, Roy had his seventh hit single in Cindy Walker's "Dream Baby," which went to #4. Cindy Walker had written Bob Wills' "Dusty Skies" and was a veteran Nashville songwriter. Roy's next hit, also in 1962, was a ballad called "The Crowd," which went to #26. His record sales continued to decline in England, where "The Crowd" stopped at #40 in the summer of '62, but a former EMI secretary named Janet Martin helped found the Roy Orbison fan club to keep his name before the public. She apologized to the British press for Roy's recent flops, saying, "He was very disappointed about 'The Crowd' and 'Workin' for the Man' not making it, which ended his big run of chart success in Britain. He has some theories about why this was so. 'The Crowd' he thought too fussy while in 'Workin' for the Man' he reasoned that the lyric was too complicated."

In the U.S., Roy was touring in Florida when his band ran up a bar tab at the Jack Paar Hotel in Clearwater and he fired them all on the spot. He formed another group at his next engagement, a package show in Montgomery, Alabama, including two musicians who would become good friends, Bobby Goldsboro and Paul Garrison. "Roy and I were very close," Bobby said. "Not only was he an incredibly talented guy, which is obvious, but what a lot of people don't know about him was how funny he was. He was always joking around. We have a lot of inside jokes and we played a lot of pranks." Roy and Bobby co-wrote "Stand by Love" and "Baby's Gone," both recorded by Gene Thomas. Bill Dees later joined the band, and he and Roy started writing songs together in what would prove to be one of Roy's most fruitful collaborations.

The band was called The Candymen, and they appeared with Roy on *The Ed Sullivan Show* and ABC's *Shindig* and toured England, Scotland, Ireland and Canada, as well as Australia and New Zealand with him, playing The London Palladium, The Cow Palace and the Seattle World's Fair. "Orbie Lee Orbison, we called him O.L., traveled with us," drummer Paul Garrison said. "He wanted to become Roy's manager and eventually it worked out. He loved it, handling the money and whatever he could do.

"Roy liked to hang pretty close to the rest of the guys on tour. He knew he looked weird. In Idaho, some rednecks got threatening. We were in a restaurant and we'd been working and driving and were completely worn out, needing shaves and a shower and clean clothes. The rednecks said, 'Hey, look at them. Who do they think they are?' They were making fun of us, so I said, 'Let's get outta here!'—and we did. We played everywhere from Corpus Christi and Salem, Oregon, to Phoenix, Arizona, and Cedar Rapids, Iowa."

In September 1962, Roy at last had an album on the chart. *Roy Orbison's Greatest Hits* (Monument) went to #14. The same month he had a hit single with "Leah," which went to #25. According to Gerry, this exotic tropical island song was inspired by Claudette during one of their trips to the Hawaiian Islands. The B-side "Workin' for the

Man," went to #33. In January 1963, one of Roy's best-loved songs, "In Dreams," went into the Top 10, cresting at #7.

Roy said he literally dreamed his latest hit. When he awoke, he immediately set the lyrics of "In Dreams" to music. Some of his other songs had also come to him during sleep—they were usually announced as Elvis Presley's newest hits by a DJ in Roy's dreams.

"In Dreams" put Roy back in favor with the British, going higher on the charts than it did in America and remaining a hit in England for five months. When Duane Eddy was unable to fulfill a British tour commitment, Roy replaced him. Janet Martin called Roy from London and informed him that second act on the bill would be a new group called The Beatles. "I've never heard of them," Roy said.

His British promoters, Danny Betesh and Peter Walsh, nervously wondered if anyone as homely and staid as Roy could draw crowds, and they discouraged television exposure, fearing Roy's looks would cut into ticket sales. Impresario Tito Burns said, "I saw Roy's photo *after* agreeing to present him. This was the era of the good-looking boys like Cliff [Bennett of The Rebel Rousers], and here was, let's face it, an older person wearing tinted spectacles, singing slow, sad songs who, I understood, didn't move a muscle on stage."

In the spring of 1963, Roy left to commence his British tour, and Chester and Gerry Frady once again came to Hendersonville to help Claudette with the children. Gerry related that the only complaint Claudette voiced about her marriage at this time was Roy's use of diet pills. Claudette and her parents were sitting downstairs listening to the radio one night when Grant Turner announced on WSM that Patsy Cline had gone down in a Piper Comanche 250 somewhere between Dyersburg and Nashville. Gerry Frady said Claudette was devastated by this news. The only identifiable parts of Patsy's dismembered body were the back of her head, her upper shoulders and her right arm. To make matters worse, Jean Shepard's husband Hawkshaw Hawkins had also been killed in the crash. Jean and Hawk were neighbors of Roy and Claudette's and Jean was having her babies at the same time as Claudette. A Grand Ole Opry regular, Jean would become one of America's most durable country stars, and Hawkshaw, forty-one, was at the beginning of a promising career as a singer. Jean was pregnant with one baby and nursing another when she got the news of her husband's death. The memorial service was held at a Phillips-Robinson Funeral Home branch in Madison, and over 1,000 people jammed Gallatin Road, including Kitty Wells, Dottie West and Loretta Lynn. Claudette had to be sedated, and many of the mourners collapsed in hysterics when word went around that country star Jack Anglin had been killed in a car crash on his way to the funeral.

Roy was to begin his British tour in May. He found some of his old friends living in London, such as Gene Vincent, who was playing the club circuit and had a small following of Teddy boys. Like Roy, Gene complained of ulcers. Johnny Tillotson, who recorded a cover version of "Only the Lonely," was also in London, and Johnny's "Poetry in Motion" was a #2 smash. "Roy always goes down real great with audiences," Johnny told British reporters. Del Shannon, Chet Atkins and Floyd Cramer also praised Roy in the British press.

Roy liked Del Shannon very much. They were both spectacular falsetto singers, both hitting it big, and both beginning to lose their personal equilibrium in the disorienting glare of the limelight. Del found success difficult to survive, and the pressure to come up with hit after hit proved intolerable. He resorted to drinking and eventually committed suicide. Roy was also caught in the grip of this obsession, losing all sense of self and feeling he was only as good as his last hit.

He began his three-week tour with The Beatles, Gerry and The Pacemakers, MC Tony Marsh, comedian Erkey Grant, David Macbeth and Louise Cordet on Saturday, May 18, opening in Slough. "Someone had given me a tape of Paul McCartney singing 'Dream Baby,'" Roy said. "I hadn't heard of them, but I figured they must be fans."

Indeed they were, but Roy's relationship with them began inauspiciously. Though this was *The Roy Orbison/Beatles Tour* and The Beatles were set to open the show for Roy, who was the acknowledged headliner, he noticed that the theater was plastered with Beatles posters. Stalking inside and confronting his manager, he asked, "What is all this crap? What's a Beatle anyway?" He felt a tap on his shoulder and turned around. John Lennon was staring at him coolly. "I am," he said. John turned and walked away, and then Roy said to his manager, "Take those posters down!" He later admitted he felt "small" after this display of grandiosity.

At rehearsal, Roy met his backup group, The Terry Young Six. Barry Booth on keyboards and John Rostill on bass had both heard that Roy expected them assiduously to follow the Bill Justis arrangements used on his records. Nervous about the rumored incompetence of English rock musicians, Roy said he had "arrived about a week early to rehearse with my backing group until I'm satisfied." At the theater, Roy learned there was time for only one quick run-through before the performance. His drummer's equipment hadn't arrived yet, so Ringo Starr's unassembled percussion instruments were borrowed. In the darkness of the auditorium, John Lennon watched as Roy, the big star from America, tuned his guitar, aided by Barry Booth at the electric organ. The rehearsal proceeded without a hitch. "Roy was very easy-going," Barry recalled. "We'd made ourselves acquainted with some of his songs prior to his arrival and just dived into the rehearsal situation."

Later, in his dressing room, Roy received an unexpected visit from John Lennon and his manager Brian Epstein. They were an unstoppable juggernaut in business, and they proceeded to challenge Roy's top billing. Unfortunately, Roy did not have a manager to do battle for him when they barged in and John demanded, "How should we bill this? Who should close the show? Look, you're getting all the money, so why don't we close the show?"

Roy was nonplussed. How did these upstarts dare usurp his billing? He was an established recording star, the tour was built around him, and his new record, "Falling," was a U.K. Top 10 hit. In the years to come, he would give many contradictory versions of his reaction, no doubt trying to disguise his embarrassment and humiliation. "I didn't know whether I was getting that much more than they were," Roy said to Spencer Leigh on Radio Merseyside. "It wasn't that much—and the tour had sold out in one afternoon." But later Roy said, "I agreed because I was singing ballads and they were singing songs like 'Twist and Shout,' so it all made sense. Anyway, I was making four to five times as much money as they were, so I gave them a break. As you can see, it was the right move!"

Roy had no choice. History was on The Beatles' side. The rock boom was gaining momentum in England and The Beatles were creating hysteria at decibels not heard since the heyday of Elvis Presley. Big American stars like Roy were being demoted from the top of the bill in England, and a few months later The Ronettes would be toppled by The Rolling Stones during their joint tour. Roy accepted the situation with apparent equanimity, giving up his limo and riding in the bus with The Beatles. Ironically, the #1 record that was making superstars of The Beatles had been inspired by Roy. " 'Please Please

Me' was my attempt at writing a Roy Orbison song," John Lennon admitted. "I wrote it in the bedroom at my house at Menlove Avenue, which was my auntie's place. I'd heard Roy Orbison doing 'Only the Lonely.'"

On opening night, Roy stood backstage, dejected over lost billing and aware that he was about to go before an audience that had come to see The Beatles. But when he went on stage and sang "Only the Lonely," "Candy Man," "What'd I Say," "Crying," "Running Scared" and "In Dreams," he stirred the audience to frenzy. The cheering and screaming started with "Running Scared" and continued through the set. According to biographer Philip Norman, The Beatles were suddenly "deeply uneasy" about being top of the bill. "As Orbison performed, chinless and tragic, The Beatles stood in the wings, wondering how they would dare to follow him." At the conclusion of his act, Roy came backstage, but the crowd started yelling, "*We want Roy! We want Roy!*" When Roy started to go back on stage, Lennon and McCartney could restrain themselves no longer, grabbing Roy by the arms and refusing to let him take his curtain call. Roy struggled, but John said, "*Yankee, go home!*"

"I was held captive by The Beatles," Roy recalled. "It was an opening night to end all opening nights. I walked on stage with my sunglasses on, and all over Europe we were an instant success. Big time. I probably also wore something black that night, and that's how come the black outfits and dark sunglasses stuck."

The Beatles, of course, had nothing to worry about and could well have afforded to let Roy take his curtain call. When they finally went on stage that night, the screams ascended to an unnerving pitch and volume. They were without peers. Despite the rivalry of Roy and John Lennon, the group's titular leader, Roy said, "I felt that John was a kindred soul. He was more like me than the others were." Years later, however, when Roy's career was salvaged from ruin by one of The Beatles, his benefactor was not John Lennon but George Harrison.

George provided a tactful description of the 1963 tour and the conflict over the reversal in billing. "Beatlemania was starting to get big, but Roy was the big star from America. So how they dealt with that, they went through the show, then put Roy on, and then we had to close after him. The audience was just enthralled with him. It was a very frightening thing to be behind the curtain waiting to follow Roy Orbison. He just killed them. We were in awe of him."

Roy told a reporter from *Melody Maker* that both he and George Harrison were inclined to oversleep. "George and I missed the bus a lot," Roy said. "They left without us. We slept in."

Ringo Starr said, "Roy would slay them and they'd scream for more. In Glasgow, we were all backstage listening to the tremendous applause he was getting. He was just standing there, not moving or anything."

"We spent a lot of good time together that tour," Roy said. "Going to England to open for the Beatles was not like going into Pittsburgh and trying to find out where you're going to play, do the show, and leave. Everybody was in England—the record companies, the artists, the entrepreneurs, all the media." The world press was drawn to England by the Profumo scandal, which was about to bring down the government. While covering the sexual exploits of government officials, society figures and a Russian spy, all of whom had slept with a call girl named Christine Keeler, reporters noticed that an even greater upheaval was taking place in British life as The Beatles and Roy proceeded along their tour route. No one in British entertainment had ever made an impact like The Beatles. Roy was quick to predict that they would become an international sensation, and when The Beatles asked Roy to manage them in America, he sought advice from friends in Nashville. The sages of Nashville counseled him to decline this opportunity of a lifetime, and Roy told Joe Melson that his colleagues' miscalculation probably cost him $50 million.

Paul McCartney called Roy one of the greats of rock 'n' roll. "We toured with Roy in the early days and he was a really good guy," Paul said. Gerry Marsden, who soon hit the U.S. charts with "Don't Let the Sun Catch You Crying" and "Ferry Across the Mersey," agreed. "Roy, God bless him, said, 'No, I don't want a limo: I want to travel with the boys.' We'd have singsongs on the coach. Roy had this very, very extraordinary ability for doing three to five octaves with his voice which we all tried to do and it made us speak strange for days after singing his songs—but they were nice songs to do."

Like Roy, The Beatles always seemed to be penniless, expecting someone else to pay. One day, they told a reporter who had called for an appointment, "Here, pick up some food for us on the way, will you?" The Beatles also shared Roy's fondness for amphetamines, having discovered Preludin, which they called Prelleys, while playing at Reeperbahn dives in Hamburg.

Roy's guitarist Bobby Goldsboro told John he should wear contact lenses, and John took his advice. "I mean, I couldn't be seen in horn-rimmed specs on stage," John said. "That would never do for a Beatle, folks! But the contacts are not easy to control." John frequently lost them during the tour, and everyone would get down on the floor with him and search for the contacts. A few years later, John would have no compunction about wearing his hippy granny glasses on stage.

The souvenir program for the tour was full of information about Roy: "Roy Orbison's new home recently completed on the shores of Old Hickory Lake near Nashville gives him the leisure and relaxation needed in his busy schedule of world wide tours and songwriting chores. It was personally designed by Roy and his wife, Claudette, and follows the architectural lines of a Swiss chalet. His hobbies are cars—his favorite is a 1939 Mercedes Benz, his favorite books cover the history of WWII. Roy's favorite actors are George C. Scott and Laurence Olivier and his favorite actresses are Romy Schneider, Dorothy Malone and Angie Dickinson. Green is his preferred color, his 'best of all movies' is *Ben-Hur*, and his favorite TV program is *East Side West Side*. For food Roy eats anything but his strongest liking is for the Poly-Indian, Mexican and Italian varieties. Summer is his favorite season. Favorite school subject was history, and his favorite classical music is that recorded by Mantovani. 'Best of all country artists' in Roy's judgment are Ray Price, George Jones and Buck Owens. Favorite recipe: Carne-alla-Pizzavola. 1 lb. tender lean meat sliced paper thin. 2 ripe tomatoes. $\frac{1}{2}$ cup olive oil. Oregano. Garlic powder. Salt. Pepper. Chop tomatoes and sprinkle seasonings over them. (Season to your own taste.) Add olive oil and top with meat. Cover and cook VERY FAST, stirring to mix all ingredients. Do not overcook. (5-8 minutes.)"

The tour kept Roy so busy he didn't get to see as much of London as he wanted to. Like most Americans who grew up during WWII, Roy looked on London as the front line of battle, and the city appealed to his keen sense of history. He was an avid reader of Shakespeare and of Shirer's *Decline and Fall of the Third Reich*. John Lennon thought it was funny that Roy could get excited over something like a Spitfire buzzing their tour bus. "I would have loved to see Sir Laurence Olivier in a play," Roy said. "I intended to visit the Tower of London. I wanted to visit a big car factory. But most of all, I would have liked to meet Sir Winston Churchill—just for the pleasure of shaking that great man by the hand." When Marilyn Monroe voiced such desires in public, she soon found herself in The White House or at Princeton in Albert Einstein's bed. Perhaps Roy was dreaming of an invitation from Chequers. After all, nothing was too grand for a rock 'n' roll star.

After the tour, Roy flew home to Nashville for a two-day rest before taking up dates in Canada and California. "I shall definitely be back for another tour next May," Roy told his new British friends. As an international star, he would now have even less time for his family.

Roy made a remark to a *Melody Maker* reporter in 1963 that indicates a totally impoverished personal and spiritual life. "I have such a tight schedule," he said, "that if I take a vacation, I can feel the work going by." Work had become his god, and it was a god that would fail him miserably in the crises that were soon to befall him and his family. The first of them began when Claudette came across an intimate letter from one of Roy's girlfriends and, in retaliation, began an affair with Braxton Dixon, the builder of their new Hendersonville house. Billy Pat Ellis said, "Roy didn't know of it for a while. Claudette had the affair because Roy was gone a lot and she got lonely and wanted to prove she was attractive again—same as any married woman who has an affair."

Describing Claudette's lover, Roy's drummer Paul Garrison said, "'Brak' was an unorthodox builder. He would create the homes that he wanted to, whether he had a buyer for them or not. He built Johnny Cash's home assuming some musician would buy it and he was right. Brak would get in a truck and start driving down the road and he'd see something he liked and say, 'Hey, look at that unusual stone. I'll get that and use it.' If you look at Johnny Cash's wall, it has chunks of coal and smooth stones that come from Pigeon Ford River. Brak would use textures and shapes and configurations and go from one extreme to another. He used nature wherever he could, like bathroom lavatories made out of man-eating-size shells from the Australian reefs.

"Roy was friendly with Brak and ordered a house built to 'spec.' Roy was gone and Braxton was there every day, building the house. Claudette was a young, attractive and very personable woman. She'd been tagging along with Roy and enjoying things and Roy absolutely worshipped the ground she walked on. She had everything she needed, but when Roy was gone, she had nothing to do, time on her hands— 'Roy's gone, I'm bored'—and somebody began to pay her a little attention. Braxton was maybe that individual who began to warm up to her."

Bobby Blackburn felt, "Claudette had the affair because she's a woman. Roy ignored Claudette when he had one hit after another. He had his job to do, and she had her affair out of loneliness and boredom and a feeling of uncertainty. She had no interest in leaving Roy; it was a fling."

Braxton's wife, Anna, remembers this time of her life as the sheer torment it was. "Roy Orbison and I had something in common," she says. "Braxton Dixon was going with Claudette. Even though I was fond of Roy, after that I didn't have much to do with them. Roy was the finest man there ever was. He never hurt anyone.

"Braxton and I were married twenty years when it happened, and he was twenty years older than Claudette. She was a pretty girl but a weakling. I am blaming Braxton. And why did I put up with it? I had four children and Anna can't fight city hall!

"We were dear friends with the Orbisons. He started building the house in the early '60s and the affair started at that time. Claudette was a good-looking woman and she drew him to her bedroom. It was cruel of Braxton to have an affair with a woman he was building a house for.

"Felice Bryant said, 'Anna, kick this woman out of your house. Get rid of Claudette.' She knew Claudette was easy. Claudette didn't come from high-class people. She was lonely and young. When I found out, there was nothing I could do to let Roy know."

Either Roy remained unaware that his marriage had come apart or he pretended that he didn't know. If his masochistic song "She Cheats on Me" reflects his own state of mind, he not only was willing to let Claudette have her affair but actually went out of his way to conceal from her his knowledge of it, fearing that a confrontation would result in which she would leave him. In any case, when he returned to England in the fall of 1963 for his second national tour, he took Claudette with him. R.D. accompanied her on the plane but Tony, the baby, remained behind with the Orbison grandparents. In London, they leased a flat on the fashionable Victoria Embankment, and soon Claudette discovered the joys of shopping in Harrod's; Roy preferred sightseeing. At home, they relaxed and played in their indoor swimming pool with R.D. After awhile Claudette returned to the States to enroll R.D. in school.

Roy had become so popular in Britain after his first tour that his LP *Only the Lonely* went to #15 in June '63 and *Crying* went to #17. The British also embarced Roy's new single, "Blue Bayou," a Melson–Orbison collaboration that had only gone to #29 in the U.S. American resistance to the record was curious, because it would become one of the most popular of all Roy's songs, covered by the leading artists of succeeding generations of rockers.

Quick to recognize "Blue Bayou" as a timeless pop standard, the British made it a #3 hit. In America, "Blue Bayou" was only the B-side of "Mean Woman Blues," which went to #5.

Joe Melson explained what happened: "We had released so many ballads, and now they were looking for a rocker, so they put 'Blue Bayou' and 'Mean Woman Blues' side by side, which was a mistake if you were going to push 'Blue Bayou.'

"The public hadn't yet heard a rocker by Roy, so they were ready after all the ballads for a change. That was the strategy—the rock 'n' roller was a change among all those beautiful ballads, and the disk jockeys picked up on it.

"'Mean Woman Blues' hit big and 'Blue Bayou' didn't; the success of 'Mean Woman Blues' took away from 'Blue Bayou,' because it gave the American DJs something different to play at that time. If they hadn't had it, they would have made 'Blue Bayou' a Top 10."

When Roy began his next British tour on September 28, 1963, again opening in Slough, he called his show *The Big "O" Show With Roy Orbison*. Paul Garrison was along as his drummer, and they played Hanley, Nottingham, Glasgow, Sheffield, Liverpool, Manchester, Harrow and East Ham. Back in London Roy recorded a moving Willie Nelson Christmas song called "Pretty Paper," and it went to #15 in the U.S. This unusual tune tells about a sad, lonely figure sitting on the sidewalk as Christmas shoppers rush by, too busy to remember that it's the season for caring and giving. Willie had sung the song to Roy in his hotel room, and Roy had loved the idea of having a seasonal hit.

After playing Scarborough, Newcastle and Blackburn, Roy flew to Ireland for five days of one-nighters before going on to a tour of Canada. This time, Roy said goodbye to his loyal British fans by printing a letter in *Disc* Magazine. He sounded like a confirmed Anglophile, writing:

"I think the standard of your groups these days has improved tremendously. Once they copied us, but now they are creating their own sounds. I think The Beatles are great. Claudette thinks so, too. I dig 'Thank You, Girl'; she loves 'From Me to You.' Last Saturday I did a *Saturday Club*, and it was a real pleasure to find everyone so cooperative in the studio. Certainly, we have nothing back in the States like *Saturday Club*. You can say the same for *Pick of the Pops* and your *Two-Way Family Favourites*.... Right now I'm having a new home built in my hometown of Hendersonville, Tennessee. It's very modern. All redwood, glass and stone from the same locality. We shall have a heated stone floor, a swimming pool in the living room—with a kiddy pool right alongside. And the whole house overlooks a lake."

Roy flew to Canada in October, playing Winnipeg, Regina, Calgary, Lacombe, Edmonton, Hinton, Lethbridge, Vancouver, Quesnel, Dawson Creek, Prince George, Chilliwack, Albeni and Ladysmith. In an interview with *The Edmonton Journal* in October, Roy confessed he had seen very little of his wife and two sons over the past nine months. "I've been on the road all that time," he said. The photograph accompanying the story would not have pleased Claudette had she seen it. Roy was kissing a young woman named Judie Gundersen, who was celebrating her eighteenth birthday. Discussing his "ideal date" with the reporter, Roy said, "I like brunettes. I don't know why, I just do." A four-column headline screamed: "SINGER PRAISES CANADIAN GIRLS."

"On November 22, 1963," Roy's drummer Paul Garrison remembered, "we'd worked a show and we were all asleep and when we woke up it was three in the afternoon. We flipped the TV on and came across the news: 'The President's body is being removed from the plane in the nation's capital.' Of course we were shocked, and that night it was a very poor show. People just weren't in the spirit. We had to go ahead and perform. They were thinking about postponing it, but we had a pretty full house. We were playing in a gymnasium. Roy felt very sorry, but there wasn't much to say. The shock of it all was over everyone."

At Christmas, Roy's "Pretty Paper" rose to #15 on the charts. Without a break in his frantic work schedule, Roy took off for Australia for a tour with The Beach Boys, Paul and Paula and The Surfaris. He asked Claudette to meet him in Honolulu on his way home, and she happily agreed. "She was sorry she'd had the affair," Claudette's Aunt Patty said. "It just devastated her. 'I wish it had never happened,' she told me. 'I love Roy dearly. I really love him.'"

On Claudette's way to meet Roy in Honolulu, she stopped to see her brother Bill in Los Angeles. Bill was stationed in the Navy in San Diego, and he had just emerged from some trouble after striking an officer and two noncoms when they criticized his shoes at inspection. One afternoon Bill and Claudette strolled down Hollywood Boulevard and when they got to Frederick's of Hollywood, the sexy lingerie shop, Claudette wanted to go in. She glanced over the merchandise for a few minutes and then purchased two extraordinary negligees for $10,000. Bill remembers, "I said, 'Claudette! Roy is gonna kill you.'

" 'No, he won't,'" she said. 'He likes me in this kind of thing.'"

A few nights later, Claudette most likely modeled her Frederick's purchases for Roy in their Waikiki hotel suite. If he complained about her expenditures, no one ever heard of it.

After the Australian tour, Paul Garrison met his girl in Miami, Florida. Phylis was a beautiful Pan American stewardess, and as they danced in Bobby Dees' Peppermint Twist, Paul suddenly saw The Beatles. They had five simultaneous Top 10 U.S. hits, they'd recently done *The Ed Sullivan Show* and were relaxing in Florida. "None of us has quite grasped wharrit's all about yet," John said. Roy didn't see The Beatles during this tour, when they took America by storm. "I talked with them on the phone and invited them to my home where they would be guaranteed no publicity," Roy said, "but in their own humorous way, they replied that they weren't interested if there was no publicity. Anyway, I hope to catch up with them when I'm next in England."

In April, Roy left on another British tour, and The Beatles attended his twenty-eighth birthday party on April 26, 1964. Claudette flew over to London with Roy DeWayne, and the party was held at La Dolce Vita restaurant in Soho. A mob of nearly hysterical fans beseiged the restaurant's front entrance, and limousines deposited the celebrity guests at an emergency exit. In photographs of the party, the guests are in what looks like the cozy back room of a pub. Claudette looks every inch the rock star's wife, elegantly dressed and coiffed. In the center of the action, little Roy DeWayne smiles happily, standing amid The Beatles, the place every music fan in the world wanted to be at that time. Roy's birthday cake was shaped like a big white guitar, and Ringo and John both tried to feed Roy forkfuls of cake. Coming to his rescue, Claudette diverted The Beatles by feeding Ringo and John from her fork.

Roy became such a sensation overseas that when he played a series of dates in Irish ballrooms, many girls in the audience became hysterical and unmanageable. Ignoring security guards' warnings, they stormed the stage and attacked Roy. As sound equipment and instrument stands cascaded to the floor and the scent of pubescent colleens assailed his nostrils, Roy submitted to fondling, groping and mauling, a scene he'd probably never envisioned years earlier in Wink. The Irish shows were halted three times as police, guards and ushers pulled the girls off Roy and led them, flushed and deranged, back to their seats. Outside theaters, in hotel lobbies, on the street and in stores, Roy and Claudette were pursued by screaming fans. Though it pleased Roy at last to be considered a sex object like Elvis and The Beatles, Claudette was far from amused. Like any wife, she resented it when cute teenagers went backstage and into Roy's dressing room after a performance. The Thompson newspapers spread provocative photos of a girl named Molly Weston kneeling at Roy's feet and handling his black Chelsea boots as she removed them from his stockinged feet. Roy lolled in a chair at his dressing table, a lascivious gleam discernible behind his Ray Ban Wayfarer sunglasses.

On May 9, he appeared on the popular British TV show *Thank Your Lucky Stars*. "Janice," the show's teenage critic, had an authentic Birmingham accent and graded new releases by giving them points: "Oi'll give it foive." Roy had fun on the show, enjoying what he called the "busy production." Whole sets were constructed for each singer, who came on the show and proceeded to lip-synch his latest hit record.

Roy's popularity reached new heights in Britain when "Borne on the Wind," which wasn't even considered worth releasing in the U.S., went into the British Top 20 in 1964. This pulsating, exciting song had a strong Mexican flavor, and it was Roy's first breakout collaboration with Bill Dees.

Roy scored his sixteenth hit single with "It's Over," which went to #9 in the U.S. On June 25, "It's Over" became the #1 hit in England, toppling Cilla Black's "You're My World" from the top of the U.K. chart. "It's Over" remained in the #1 position the week of July 4th, an appropriate victory for a Yank in London. "At a time when British artists are all-powerful in their own country," Roy said, "I regard the attainment of number-one position in Britain as the high spot of my career." After two glorious weeks at the top, "It's Over" was finally overtaken in England by The Animals' "House of the Rising Sun."

Roy celebrated this peak moment in his recording career during a two-day London stopover by buying a 1939 Mercedes with "FXR 706" painted on a front fender. He saw the sedan on the street while riding in a cab with Paul Garrison. "Go!" he ordered Paul. "Get me that car! Pay him anything, but get it!" Paul approached the wary owner, who was reluctant until he realized he would be dealing with a rich rock star. Suddenly, anything was possible, and Roy got the car. When it was shipped to the U.S., Paul had to pick it up in New York and drive it to Nashville. "It looked like something Hitler would ride in," Paul said. "The steering was on the right, and imagine pulling up to the Holland Tunnel in that. I had to reach all the way across the seat to pay the tolls. Then it broke down in Orange, New Jersey, and I had to live in a motel while a gasket came from Germany. Roy had flown direct to Nashville."

The more successful Roy got, the less Claudette and the boys saw of him. It was not that he didn't adore them. In fact, he was overjoyed when Roy DeWayne began to demonstrate musical ability at eight years of age. Roy gave him piano and guitar instruction, using his hit songs as teaching tools. R.D. also displayed precocious songwriting ability, and he was beginning to sing. One day, he shocked Roy, Claudette and his little brother Tony by delivering a credible soprano recitation of "Crying."

Roy had never had any concept of a balanced life, in which work, play and spiritual or social pursuits share equal time. Given the opportunity to overachieve, he would choose work every chance he got. An inveterate night owl, he claimed that he was "compelled" to compose at odd hours. He said that he preferred "midnight" recording sessions, and his pre-session activities smacked of idiocyncrasy bordering on insanity. "I like at least six hours of movies," he said. "It freshens my mind. If there is nothing good on at the local movie houses, then I watch them on television. We have full-length color films on Fridays, Saturdays and Sundays, so I always try not to get booked on those nights." It was a stultifying, isolated existence. At home he liked to vegetate in his writing room, hunched over contracts, sheet music, tour schedules, bank accounts and the complete works of Winston Churchill. That Claudette sought solace in another man's arms was not surprising.

Claudette was about to inspire Roy's most successful song, but it took his partner, Bill Dees, to remind Roy of her magical beauty. Roy had been primarily responsible for their hit, "It's Over," but it was Bill Dees who sparked "Oh, Pretty Woman." "We'd just begun about six in the evening," Roy recalled. "You get started writing by playing anything that comes to mind, and about that time my wife came in and wanted to go to town to get something. I said, 'Do you have any money?'

"And Bill Dees said, 'Pretty woman never needs any money.'

"Then he said, 'Would that make a great song title?'

"I said, 'No, but "Pretty Woman" would.'

"So I started playing the guitar and he was slapping the table for drums. That was the conception, and by the time she got back, which was about forty minutes—we had the song."

In "Oh, Pretty Woman," Claudette inspired not only the biggest hit Roy would ever have; for years to come, "Pretty Woman" would occupy a special place in the hearts of all pop and rock fans. This virile, pile-driving male tribute to womankind expresses all that is healthy and happy in relations between the sexes, and it came directly from Roy's heartfelt adoration of women in general and of Claudette in particular. That he should have let ambition come between him and his wife when he obviously worshipped her made the steady, irreversible erosion of their marriage even more poignant.

"Oh, Pretty Woman" went into the #1 position on the U.S. chart in September 1964. It was Roy's first U.S. chart-topper since "Running Scared" three years before. Despite the current popularity of The Animals' "House of the Rising Sun," now an international hit, "Oh, Pretty Woman" held fast at the top, remaining the #1 choice of American record-buyers for three solid weeks. Roy's collaborator Bill Dees was so happy that he walked into the Hendersonville construction-and-supply company where he was employed and announced, "I quit."

"Oh, Pretty Woman" was a monster smash in England that fall, going in and out of the #1 position over a two-month period. In October, it toppled Herman's Hermits' "I'm Into Something Good" and held fast at #1 for two weeks. Sandi Shaw's "Always Something There to Remind Me" took over the top spot for the next two weeks, and "Oh, Pretty Woman" regained #1 for the week of November 14. When The Supremes' "Baby Love" went into #1, "Oh, Pretty Woman's" heady U.K. chart-topping performance was over.

According to *Billboard*, "In a 68-week period that began August 8, 1963, Roy Orbison was the *only* American artist to have a number-one single in Britain. He did it twice, with 'It's Over' on June 25, 1964, and 'Oh, Pretty Woman' on October 8, 1964. The latter song also went to number one in America, making Orbison impervious to the chart dominance of British artists on both sides of the Atlantic." The British Invasion had not yet caught up with Roy Orbison, but it would, all too soon.

Paul Garrison was one of the drummers who worked on the recording of "Oh, Pretty Woman." "In that session we used two drummers," he recalled. "Buddy Harman was also there. We were trying to get this lick together, and Boots Randolph was on that session. I think he played organ, a few things, he just filled in. We used Anita Kerr as the background group. We just couldn't get the lick, the offbeat or the upbeat. Downbeat, upbeat, rock and roll, was the biggest thing going then. [Two quick beats, pause, one beat.] And Roy—the opening (do-do-do-do-doom), I could hear him and I could hear something like a pulse in my head (wump-wump-wump). We kept playing with that and Buddy was trying to do something, and I said, 'Buddy let's try this, let's go to this.' I did bass drum and snare and *sock*! it at the same time. When we started that, it started a real drive on the very beginning of that thing. It really picked up. There were many spinoffs from that beat. It's nothing original. There have been many songs, including big bands, but big bands used a lot of rhythm guitar with the downbeat—WWII era. But this had a pulse to it that normal rock 'n' roll songs did not do a lot of. The Beatles and The Rolling Stones immediately picked up and used that lick."

Jerry Kennedy played guitar on both "It's Over" and "Oh, Pretty Woman." "Billy Sanford and myself played, and we can't remember who the third player was," Jerry noted. "About the most adamant Roy would get would be to say, 'Let's try it this way for a second.' And he was so unique. From a musician's standpoint, Roy went against the grain. The first time you'd hear something, it wouldn't sound right. But after a few playbacks, it would start to grow on you."

When Roy cut a song, he always left plenty of room for improvisation. "I was semi-known around the studio for saying 'Mercy,'" Roy said. "When we went into the studio to record 'Oh, Pretty Woman,' it was, as usual, without any formal arrangements. So when we got to a note that wasn't in my range, or anyone else's, I substituted the word and everyone just smiled. That's how we got the growls too. It was a matter of doing it and waiting to see if anyone said no. That time, they left them in. It had an interesting effect on foreign audiences. In France, 'Mercy' sounds like I'm saying 'Thank you.'

The worldwide sales of "Oh, Pretty Woman" totaled a staggering seven million. Chet Atkins told Roy it was "the best commercial record" he'd ever heard. "It goes through a lot of emotions," Roy said. "I didn't think of this as we were writing the song, but the guy's observing the girl, and he hits on her, real cool and macho, and then he gets worried and gets to pleading, and then he says, 'Okay, forget it, I'm still cool,' and then at the end she comes back to him, and he turns into the guy he really is. That range of emotion in a short piece of music I think is very important."

Though it was not a hit, the B-side of "Oh, Pretty Woman," a gaucho song called "Yo te amo Maria," also by Roy and Bill Dees, is just as beautiful as the A-side. The recording is actually a duet, with Roy and Bill singing harmony as perfect and sweet as Don and Phil Everly. "Oh, Pretty Woman" is also a duet through more than half its length, and again, Roy's singing partner sounds like Bill Dees. Roy permitted Bill to take the lead during the chorus of "Yo te amo Maria" but typically withheld any credit for Bill on the label. Both sides of this record display Roy's exquisite craftsmanship, not only in his singing but in every instrumental detail—the Spanish guitar and mellow trumpets on "Yo te amo Maria" and Paul Garrison's macho drums and Jerry Kennedy's cocky eight-note guitar riff on "Oh, Pretty Woman."

"I always felt each instrumental and vocal inflection had to be special," Roy said. "I'd spend almost as much time on those as I'd spend on the song itself. Looking back on it now, I felt I was blessed much like the masters, I guess—the guys who wrote the concertos. I'd just have it all in my head." Bob Moore was Roy's general supervisor in the studio. Besides playing double bass on Roy's records, he provided the musical scores required by the intricate Orbison creations, often assisted by Bill Justis. Since Roy was not a practiced sight reader, the scores were painstakingly devised as he hummed and improvised his intentions. The basic group behind Roy's great sound was drummer Murray "Buddy" Harman, pianist Floyd Cramer, guitarists Jerry Kennedy, Hank Garland, Gray Martin and Ray

Edenton, bassist Bob Moore, Harold Bradley (with his Framus electric) and Boots Randolph, who led the brass and woodwind sections.

The splendor and originality of Roy's musical vision, as expressed in "Oh, Pretty Woman" and "Yo te amo Maria," the recordings that represent the high point of his early '60s work, place him in the same league as rock 'n' roll's other '60s mastermind, Phil Spector.

In the autumn of 1964, Roy, Paul and the rest of his road band took off on their second Australian tour with The Beach Boys. "We left winter conditions in the U.S. and arrived in sunny Hobart, Tasmania," Paul said. "Hobart is the last stop before Antarctica, founded by prisoners but today a city of fountains, wildflowers and narrow streets. We stayed at King's Cross Hotel, and Roy and I met a nice lady in the restaurant there. Roy invited her to the show and afterwards she followed us to the airport. The fans set up a band at the airport and played all the songs of all the stars. More than rock 'n' rollers, we were missionaries from the outside world."

Girls were readily available to Roy and his band, according to Paul, and Roy occasionally treated himself to a groupie. The Beach Boys turned the tour into a sexual romp, and their drummer, Dennis Wilson, the only genuine surfer among the band and the best looking of the lot, had a theory that fellatio did not count as infidelity, and that he could remain true to his girl at home while having groupies administer oral sex.

When Roy's tour with The Beach Boys ended, he and his band played the U.S. and Canada, Roy flying and the band following in a cramped car. "Buddy Buie owed Roy some money," Paul said, "and Buddy told him, 'Roy take my car so I can pay you what I owe you.' It was a '55 Chevrolet two-door Bel-Aire. "Four of us went all the way across the West in that damn two-door car pulling a trailer. Roy never travelled with us. There were streaks all over the sides of the car where Cokes and coffee were thrown out while traveling. The car was filthy inside. One of the guys had a girlfriend traveling with us, three in the front seat, three in the back."

Eventually, Roy bought a big Dodge motor home, and Claudette began to go along on the tours. "I'd see her in her curlers," Paul said. "She was like one of the family. Claudette would come right up there in front and stay with us. This was a luxury motor home sleeping eight, and we put over 100,000 miles on that unit in about a year.

Claudette and Roy had a bed in the back, and then there were bunks on each side and tables and sofas that converted into beds." Bill Dees often drove the motor home, but most of the band took turns at the wheel. Paul got nervous one night when he saw Billy Sanford trying to watch Johnny Carson on TV and drive at the same time. "Bill, if you're going to do that," Paul said, "you let me do the driving." Bill remained at the wheel, but Paul stayed up to keep him awake. Sometimes Paul would borrow one of Roy's "diet pills" to fight drowsiness and exhaustion.

They passed through Las Vegas on their way to a gig, and everyone piled out for some rest and recreation. Claudette, Bobby Goldsboro and his wife Mary Alice, Roy, Bill Sanford, and Buddy Buie of The Atlanta Rhythm Section all posed happily as Paul Garrison photographed them. Roy was amused by a life-size statute of a camel, and Bobby Goldsboro and Claudette looked on as Roy enjoyed himself, crawling under it and clowning.

"Roy was always very suppressed, a very private guy," Paul recollected. "He enjoyed his privacy but he also wanted to be recognized. He was contradictory and torn." When Paul was asked why Roy's band, sometimes known as The Candymen, never became famous, like The Beatles and The Rolling Stones, he said, "I guess Roy didn't want that."

In October 1964, Roy had a busy TV schedule. He appeared with The Candymen on *The Ed Sullivan Show*, along with French heart-throb Jean Paul Vignon, The Harlem Globe Trotters, Juliet Prowse, Connie Francis, Allen & Rossi, George Kirby and Jeanne Carroll. In mid-October, they went to Hollywood to appear on ABC's *Shindig*, sharing the bill with Glen Campbell and Bobby Rydell. Later that month, Roy flew to London to star in two TV shows—Val Parnell's *Sunday Night at the London Palladium,* backed up by Erroll Garner and Beryl Reid, and *The Roy Orbison Show*, with Julie Rogers.

When Roy returned to the States, his odious domestic situation at last erupted. "I had a friend who was willing to do anything for me," Anna Dixon remembered. " 'Call Roy and tell him, because I have to stop it,' I said. When she got Roy on the phone, she said, 'Roy, I am one of your admirers. I feel you should know Claudette is stepping out on you. Ask her. A family is in jeopardy, in pain.'

" 'Who's speaking?' Roy asked.

" ' A fan. You don't deserve this. You can stop this.'

"Roy took his firearm and threw it in the lake. He said to Claudette, 'Who are you going with?' and she said, 'Braxton Dixon.'

"Roy called me and said, 'Hello, dear. How are you? Can I speak to Braxton?' I remember Braxton sat on a marble table we have and said, 'Oh, Roy, don't get excited. There's nothing to it. It's nothing serious.' But Roy said, 'You are ready to complete my house. I don't want to see your face around here anymore.'"

"Roy finished the house himself," Bobby Blackburn said. "He hired a carpenter and between the two of them they finished it. Then he divorced Claudette in Nashville. My wife left me at the same time and Roy said, 'Well, Bob, look at the bright side. With your wife, it could be anything—she's going for more money or fame. But in my case, it's gotta be I just ain't no good. She's just lookin' for a longer dick.'"

Suing on grounds of "cruelty," Roy was given a decree *nisi*. Later, in England for a tour and a TV appearance on *Sunday Night at the London Palladium*, he confirmed to a *Daily Mirror* reporter on March 7, 1965, that he and Claudette were no longer married. "Very few people were in on it," Roy said. "Divorce is something you don't rush out and shout to everyone."

"Claudette didn't want the divorce," Bobby Blackburn said. "Would *you* leave Roy Orbison for Braxton Dixon? Roy got off real light—fifty dollars a week child support. He got custody of the kids and let her move in with Nadine and raise them. Claudette went first to Pasadena [a suburb of Houston, Texas, where Roy's parents were then living] and was with Nadine and the boys. I was in Houston when Roy sent her twelve long-stem roses with a card that said, 'My Pretty woman.' I told her, 'Hang in there. Don't worry about it. Whatever he says you do it. Hell, he didn't want to get rid of you very bad or he wouldn't let you live with his mother!' Claudette was a level-headed girl."

The Frady family seems reluctant to address the divorce. Claudette's Aunt Patty acknowledges only that there was a separation, and she insists that it was Claudette herself who told Roy of her affair. "It kind of blew up then, and they were separated. Claudette was pregnant during the separation, and there was talk of divorce. She came to Houston with Roy DeWayne and Anthony King. She was really upset about Roy's drugs. Back in '64-65, I didn't know much about what drugs people were taking. She could have said drugs or diet pills. I never did see her take anything. I think I would have known if she'd been taking drugs. I know she didn't take drugs when she was pregnant. If she'd taken them she wouldn't have been so upset about Roy taking them. Anyway she came to Jacinto City [near Houston] and lived there in a house, and it was near to Orb and Nadine, who had moved to Galena Park."

Patty was also an attractive divorcee, about thirty-five years old, and she lived near Claudette. Raising two sons by herself, Patty was holding down two jobs, one at Coca-Cola and another at a lounge called The Sportsman's Club in Houston. Patty and Claudette spent some time together. The singer Roy Head lived in Patty's apartment complex, and B.J. Thomas, though only fifteen, was hanging around The Sportsman's Club, singing whenever the manager would let him. In a year or so, B.J. hit the charts at #8 with Hank Williams' "I'm So Lonesome I Could Cry," which Roy Orbison also cut in the '60s, and a little later, B.J. went to #5 with "Hooked on a Feeling" and to #1 with "Raindrops Keep Fallin' on My Head." He destroyed his career and almost his life with alcohol and drugs, had a spiritaul experience with the help of his wife in Fort Worth, Texas, and made a great comeback as an inspirational singer.

Patty remembers, "When Claudette was in The Sportsman's Club one night, a young singer got up and performed Roy's hit, 'Crying.' Later, he came to her table and asked, 'Well, how did I do?' 'Fine,' she said, 'but nobody's as good as Roy.'"

Roy was as far away from his broken home as he could get. Touring Australia with The Rolling Stones, Rolf Harris and Dionne Warwick, he accepted second billing to The Stones, since there was no longer any question about English supremacy on the rock scene. The British Invasion was crushing everything in its path, and it was now considered a privilege to appear anywhere on a bill with The Stones or The Beatles. Mick Jagger related, "The Stones did a tour with Roy Orbison, Australia and New Zealand. We always liked Roy Orbison. All those songs were huge hits in England when we were young. I remember sitting in these coffee bars when I was a teenager mooning over those ballads, making believe they were about the girl on the other side of the jukebox."

In Roy's interview in Australia with reporter Jeff Penberty in January 1965, he seemed somewhat addled, which was understandable in view of the collapse of his marriage. " 'Excuse me,' " Roy said, rubbing his sleepy eyes. 'Have to catch some shut-eye when I can—only had two hours since last night's show in Adelaide.' He padded across the carpet in black socks, toothbrush in hand, looking more like an abstract painter than a teenage idol...A thin young man burst through the door wanting to know the time. 'This is my drummer Paul Garrison,' Roy explained. 'Relax Paul, the show doesn't start for an hour. Paul's my only permanent musician—everywhere I go he goes.' Paul seemed unconvinced about there being plenty of time and fidgeted unhappily when he noticed Roy still had to put on his stage outfit and do a radio interview before going to Festival Hall. Unperturbed, Roy went on in his soft voice, reminiscing... 'My daddy was an oil man and although there was nothing around us but oil wells I was only interested in singing. I've never had a job.' The star waved his hand, flashing a huge gold ring set with four large diamonds. 'My success means I can buy anything that takes my fancy now.'" Such gross distortions of the truth suggest that Roy had either taken complete leave of his senses or had decided to create a grand new image of himself as a product of the idle rich, or perhaps he was just having a little fun at the expense of the press.

Reminiscing about Roy many years later, Mick Jagger said, "I remember he was a very shy person. Onstage, he didn't move hardly at all, but he sang very well. From watching Roy, I learned how to sing a dramatic ballad. And I remember we took him to the hot springs in New Zealand. I've got this snapshot of Roy Orbison, sitting in these hot springs, his glasses still on. A fine figure of a man in the hot springs, he was."

The Stones' "The Last Time" was a #1 hit in the U.K. and in the Top 10 in America. They were the first major group to drop theme costumes and wear anything they wanted to on stage. Usually looking like they were in the clothes they'd slept in the night before, they created a new style known as wrecked rock-star elegance. They were the bad boys of the British Invasion, getting busted for drugs, overdosing, scandalizing Ed Sullivan, driving Marianne Faithfull to despair, and, in the case of Keith Richards, letting teeth rot and fall out. Roy wasn't impressed with the Stones at first, but he began to appreciate them more when he recognized that they were using the sounds of black rhythm and blues.

The age of the orgiastic rock 'n' roll tour was in full swing, and The Stones made an unreleasable movie, *Cocksucker Blues*, about their experiences on the road. Australia was not always receptive to their hijinks. At a concert in Christchurch, New Zealand, Mick Jagger's remark, "Our hotel has too few bathrooms, so you can't blame us if we smell," did not please the audience. Keith Richards called Invercargill "the arsehole of the world," and their audience was so unresponsive they retreated into the wings in embarrassment. Ian Stewart said: "You could put your bed in the middle of the street at five o'clock in the afternoon and nothing would disturb you." Some hotels in New Zealand refused to book them, and in Auckland, a hostile crowd pelted them with eggs.

Mick's girl friend Marianne Faithfull was extremely attentive to Roy. Flirtatiously, she asked him to remove his dark glasses. Confronting him in a backstage corridor, she told him, "I've always wanted to see what you really look like." In the 1980s, Roy would refuse the same request from talk-show host Joan Rivers, but Marianne was a ravishing beauty and already a rock legend at eighteen and Roy found her as irresistible as The Stones had. When he consented to remove his dark glasses for her, Marianne took credit for what she termed his "unveiling," and a picture of the two of them appeared in *Melody Maker*. For the photographer, Roy permitted her to don his shades, and Marianne peered gaily over the frames. In the photo, Roy and Marianne both look touchingly young, innocent and carefree. Sadly, darker days were ahead for both of them. "I ended up on drugs," Marianne said. "All my traumas and all my unhappiness Mick changed into brilliant songs, and it made me sick to see these things which were destroying me making him greater and greater." Before her affair with Mick broke up, she suffered a miscarriage and a suicidal, near-fatal drug overdose in Australia.

The Australian tour was a triumph for Roy, paving the way for a #1 hit, "Penny Arcade," which Americans ignored on its release in the U.S. four years later. In performance, Roy more than held his own with The Stones. According to Roy, on their last night in New Zealand, Mick Jagger dared him to sing "the worst record you've ever made."

"I'll be happy to," Roy replied, 'if you'll do the worst record you've ever made."

Roy kept his end of the bargain, singing "Ooby Dooby" during the concert that night. When The Stones went on, Roy stood in the wings, wondering what song The Stones' would choose. Jagger reneged on the deal. "I watched the performance but they didn't do their worst record," Roy said. "There was a little gathering afterwards and, in lieu of their not doing their worst record, they gave me a silver cigarette case. 'From The Rolling Stones to Ooby Dooby,' it's inscribed."

Roy's influence on The Stones was obvious in the record they cut after the Australian tour. "(I Can't Get No) Satisfaction" owes a debt not only to Roy and Bill Dees' recording of "Oh, Pretty Woman" but to Paul Garrison's percussive work and Jerry Kennedy's eight-note guitar pyrotechnics as well.

At the conclusion of the Australian tour, Roy returned to his lonely home in Hendersonville, but the memory of Claudette was too painful. He leased the house and took an apartment in Nashville. Now over his initial bitterness and resentment, Roy realized he was still in love with Claudette, and both sorrow and passion can be heard in his voice in his 1965 record, "Goodnight." In this ballad he wrote with Bill Dees, Roy extols and mourns the woman-child who's left him. He says she's been untrue, she longs for another man's arms and she doesn't want to come back to him. As in many of Roy's songs, he touches on the humiliation he feels as a cuckold, saying that all the neighbors are aware of their troubles. He still thinks of her with great compassion and love, enumerating the qualities he misses most—her tenderness, her kisses, and most of all the way she used to tell him goodnight. But now he realizes it was all a lie, and he has lost her forever.

If Roy was indeed singing about Claudette and if he loved her so much, why didn't he go back to her? Paul Garrison figured that Claudette's affair "remained a burr under his saddle" for the rest of his life; he couldn't quite bring himself to forgive her. Claudette's Aunt Patty said, "He resented that someone had taken someone who belonged to him. Whatever he'd done with the girls overseas, he expected Claudette to remain faithful, barefoot and pregnant. I'll bet you Mr. Orbision, his daddy, kept it kind of raw. RAW. He was mean." And Bobby Blackburn observed, "He thought Kris Kristofferson wrote 'Darby's Castle' about him, about how it took hundreds of days for the house to be built and only minutes to be burned." Another parallel in the Kristofferson song is that Darby is so preoccupied with his profession that he fails to notice that his wife is sad and grieving and is surprised when she makes a fool of him. "She had no interest in leaving Roy," Bobby said. "It was a fling, but Roy took that kind of crap seriously. His attitude was 'those goddamned women.' We decided all girls were likely to do it again."

"Goodnight" deserved to be a hit, but it was one of Roy's greatest disappointments. Though in March 1965 it gave him his eighteenth hit single and entered the Top 40, Roy's standards after the world-beating triumph of "Oh, Pretty Woman" were impossibly high. He was disheartened when the recording failed to make the Top 20. It just missed, reaching #21 and remaining in the Top 40 for six weeks. It sold considerably better in the U.K., reaching #14. The B-side, "Only With You," is another first-rate song, but it did not even make the Top 40. Roy sang "Goodnight" during a 1965 concert at the London Palladium, and just before he left his dressing room to go on stage, he told his father that he had "hopes for a reconciliation." Evidently Claudette, in Houston, was feeling the same way. *The London Daily Express* quoted her as saying, "I never really wanted to leave him." But they remained apart. Roy's record sales were declining dramatically and he devoted himself during the remainder of 1965 to frantic efforts to revive his recording career. By the millions, American record-buyers were deserting their native singers and fleeing to the British camp, which boasted such novel new attractions as Petula Clark, Herman's Hermits and The Dave Clark Five.

In August 1965, Roy and Bill Dees' Latin-styled "(Say) You're My Girl" just barely scraped into the Top 40 at #39. This was Roy's first real turkey since 1962. "I'd had a record on Monument after 'Pretty Woman' that didn't sell any," Roy told *Rolling Stone's* Steve Pond. "It was called '(Say) You're My Girl,' and after doing upwards of five, six, seven million for 'Pretty Woman,' for the next record not to sell, I couldn't believe it. I was thinking it would probably *accidentally* sell some, you know? I was leaning toward leaving before then, and that convinced me."

Roy's contract with Monument was at an end, and he decided to seek a new record label. After great triumphs, Roy Orbison stood on a stark precipice, and below him was nothing but the darkness of failure.

Chapter 7

MGM Records, hungry for big names, wooed Roy with a lot of money, so Wesley Rose, his manager, was prepared to make sizable demands when he negotiated Roy's new contract at Monument. He invited Monument's president, Fred Foster, to make his bid. The auction had certain ground rules: Roy wanted an advance, a movie deal and guaranteed television appearances. Foster said he didn't have a movie studio and suggested that Wesley Rose get the television exposure for Roy himself. "That didn't go over too well," Foster said.

Wesley Rose knew that he could get whatever he wanted for his client, and waited. Meanwhile, Foster consulted with Sam Phillips of Sun Records. They ran into each other at a DJ convention in Nashville's Holiday Inn and went to Fred's luxurious Presidential suite to talk. According to Sam, "When Fred told me the asking price for Roy Orbison, I said, 'Man, that's a call that only you and your auditors and your backers can make. Lord, I wish I could tell you. Roy may keep on going and the chances are that he could. Y'all have had a hell of a good run.'

"'The kind of guarantee they're offering,' Fred said, 'I'm just afraid, man, that if I get obligated like that I can't develop other talent. I'm just going to be so limited.'

"'Fred, I know exactly what you're talking about. That was the same thing that happened to me with Elvis Presley. Of all the artists I had, nobody wanted a goddamned one except Presley. RCA owned NBC, radio and TV equipment, manufacturers, they owned every damn thing you could think of. So they could lose money here, and make it up there, whereas your sole dependence is on that product.'

"'I probably can develop two or three more for what I'd guarantee Roy,' Fred said.

"'Maybe you can, maybe you can't,' I said. In the record business, you talk about rollin' bones. Las Vegas is not much more of a gambling approach than the record business."

Years later, Sam remembered, "He wanted Roy, man, he wanted to keep Roy."

Foster did not submit a bid. "When I told Roy that I couldn't and wouldn't," Foster said, "Roy understood. It was an amicable parting."

Roy now joined the ranks of fading rock stars fleeing to MGM. As the British Invasion had decimated the ranks of U.S. singers, both Johnny Tillotson and The Righteous Brothers had gone to MGM, and Bob Dylan was considering a move there, if they could come up with the $1.5 million advance his agent demanded. Besides the financial inducement MGM offered Roy, he felt they might help him attain the stardom he dreamed of but had never achieved at Monument. Even *Life* Magazine, the celebrity Bible of the time, didn't know who Roy was. An appearance in *Life* meant not only stardom, but mainstream stardom. In its 1965 article "Who the Hell is Bobby Vinton?" the writer said that Vinton had mistakenly been named #1 vocalist of the year. Roy Orbison, *Life* pointed out, had more #1 records than Vinton. "So the question is, who the hell is Roy Orbison?"

"MGM was a big company," Roy said, "and they painted a rosy picture for me and gave me a lot of money. And the first few things for MGM were hit records, so I knew that everything wasn't terribly amiss. But the transition wasn't really that smooth. I think the records were okay, maybe, through '68 or so. MGM offered access to motion pictures and TV as well as records. It also meant financial security and that meant I'd have all the time I needed to create."

Roy was the first signee for Mort Nasitir, president of MGM Records in 1965. "I got to know Roy and really admire him in every respect," Nasitir said, "his artistic integrity, the deeply religious spirit that moved him and his superior musicianship. He was an extraordinary performer, with a style uniquely his own. He could walk out on stage and people in the audience would say, '*This* is Roy Orbison?' And then he would begin to sing 'Only the Lonely' or something and they would say, 'THIS is Roy Orbison!' We had a couple of quick hits with Roy at MGM, then came the typical record-industry low when he couldn't buy a place in the charts."

Though Roy's move to MGM was widely regarded as a career miscalculation, the magnificent records he cut there prove that, artistically if not commercially, it was not a total loss. Fred Foster said that he and Roy were a winning combination, and he was right. But there would be other winning combinations in Roy's life. At MGM, working with people like Jim Hall, Bill Elhiney and Emory Gordy Jr., Roy would achieve some of his best work. On July 8, 1965, Roy went into a recording session at MGM and cut a song he and Bill Dees wrote called "Crawling Back." Moving and unforgettable, this mesmerizing pop largo describes a relationship as hopeless as Roy and Claudette's had been. In the song, a couple is locked in a dance of death in which the woman is unfaithful and the man keeps crawling back to her because he knows she can't do any better than him. This was definitely not the sort of thing the upbeat, bouncy music of the mid-1960s was about, and "Crawling Back" stalled at #46 in the U.S. and #19 in the U.K.

Roy had three hit singles at MGM—"Ride Away," "Breakin' Up Is Breakin' My Heart" and "Twinkle Toes." All three deserve their place among Roy's twenty-two Top 40 singles in the years 1960-66, but the most interesting songs of this period did not sell. Besides "Crawling Back," the beautiful losers of the MGM years include "Too Soon to Know," "She," "Walk On," "Southbound Jerico Parkway," "God Love You," "Remember the Good," "Losing You," "You Fool You," and Roy's covers of classics such as "Danny Boy," "More," "The Three Bells," The Bee Gees' "Words," "I'm So Lonesome I Could Cry," "A Legend in My Time," "Why a Woman Cries," and, perhaps the most impressive performance Roy ever gave, "Unchained Melody." Though most observers blame MGM for the failure of Roy's great records there, the real reason is probably that these were the years—the latter half of the '60s and the early '70s—when record-buyers were exploring psychedelia, revolution, sex, drugs and evil with groups such as The Beatles, The Rolling Stones, The Moody Blues, Jefferson Airplane, The Doors, The Byrds and The Grateful Dead. True, big ballad singers like Tom Jones continued to arrive on the scene, but they were better looking than Roy and they weren't selling his kind of sadness.

MGM publicists tried to create a glamorous image for Roy, but their press releases unintentionally revealed the truth that there was little to envy in his life, which sounded hectic and scattered, "Roy has a frantic schedule," announced the MGM publicity director. "He works in a great rush; to make a record, Roy recently told an interviewer, 'We quickly get some ideas together, rush into a studio and usually finish writing the songs on the spot. It was that way with both "It's Over" and "Pretty Woman."'" When he's at home, Roy enjoys working with his hands. These include woodcraft, painting and pottery and molding things. During his time at home Roy likes wearing one-piece lounging suits, the kind, as he put it, 'that are nicely casual but kind of dressy too.' Roy spends as much as eight months a year away from home, a fact which for a time resulted in his leasing his lovely home and renting a small apartment in Nashville. When he is on the road in the U.S. and Canada Roy travels in a thirty-foot house-on-wheels which has TV, a shower, a parlor up front, a complete kitchen with refrigerator and stove and even a mobile radio-telephone. 'I just wanted to be a fellow who sold a few records,' Roy says. 'I think I was afraid to be really big but now I look into the future and hope for other things. I'd like to write a movie score and maybe produce a picture. Honestly I'd like to be more and more an all-around showbusiness personality.'"

The truth was that Roy was in trouble in just about every aspect of his life. "I couldn't eat," he said, "I couldn't sleep, I couldn't communicate, and I certainly couldn't write a song." In this condition, Roy signed a twenty-year exclusive writing and management deal with Wesley Rose in 1965. The deal called for Roy to assign all royalties to Acuff–Rose. The firm would then pay him a sum of $10,000 annually, plus any overage above $200,000. Later, Roy decided the deal was grossly unfair to him and went to court over it.

In Jacinto City, in 1965, Claudette Orbison gave birth to their third son, Wesley Kelton. "She like to have died with Wesley," her mother Gerry said. "It was coming breech. I had to leave, she was having such a hard time. They got it turned and delivered it all right." Roy came to see his children, and these visits upset both Claudette and him. Divorce hadn't changed the fact that their lives remained profoundly unsettled. Though Roy pretended not to care for Claudette any more, it worried him to see her at loose ends. She was no longer the lively little girl he had celebrated in "Claudette," but a disturbed young woman. When he said goodbye, she seemed close to tears. He began to return more often, and occasionally it was like old times. The nature of Roy's financial commitment, as described by Patty Maddux, was nominal. "When Claudette came to Houston, she didn't have anything but two kids with her. The only money she was getting was I suppose from Mr. Orbison. Orbie Lee Orbison would give her her allowance or whatever. I suppose it was him—it might have been another manager. One time she borrowed some money off me because she hadn't got her money from them."

February 13, 1966, was a joyous day for Roy and the entire Frady family. They came to hear him sing at the big Fifth Annual Go-Texas Hootenanny at Sam Houston Coliseum in Houston, Texas. The hootenanny went on all through the day and into night, and during the break between shows, Roy took his band and the Frady clan to dinner at Nifa's Restaurant. There were thirty in the party, all sitting at a long table. Roy and Claudette were smiling at each other happily. He had to leave the restaurant early to get ready to go onstage, and as he was running upstairs, he split his trousers. Claudette was wearing a black coat and immediately took it off and handed it to him, saying, according to her mother, "You look great in black! Wear it!" She departed with Roy while the others proceeded to Houston Coliseum to look for their seats. B.J. Thomas came on and sang his hits "I'm So Lonesome I Could Cry" and "Lazy Man." Then Marty Robbins took the stage and sang "El Paso" and "A White Sports Coat and a Pink Carnation." Gerry Frady recalls that when Roy came out and started singing "Breaking Up Is Breaking My Heart," a woman sitting in front of her said, "Aw, my gosh, if I'd have known he looked like that, I'd never have bought that record. I ought to go home and break it." At that moment, Claudette arrived and sat down next to Gerry, who punched the woman on the shoulder and said, "What record is that you have of Roy's?"

"I think it's 'Only the Lonely.'"

"Here's his wife right here. I imagine she'd just love to break that record for you." The woman slumped down and said, "Oh, my goodness! I think his voice is better than Elvis Presley's! I love his voice!" The woman belonged to the sponsoring group for the Hootenanny, radio station KILT.

After the show, the Fradys went backstage, then Roy and his family all climbed into Patty's Mustang and went to her house. "Roy had on this old flowered bathrobe of mine," Patty recalled. "He was lying around while Claudette sewed up his pants. Roy had also lost a button off one of his shirt sleeves, but the decided to take the other one off too. My son Chris was in awe of him. He loved Claudette so much, but he hadn't been around Roy until now. When Roy took that other button off, Chris asked him for it. He put it in a frame with a picture of Roy."

Roy said he was going to buy brand-new motorcycles for everybody in the family who wanted one. The next day, Claudette, Chester, Orb and Sammy, Roy's brother, accompanied him to a two-story Houston showroom, where Roy turned them loose to pick out their dream machines. Claudette and Roy chose new BMWs, the Rolls-Royce of 1960s motorcycles, while Chester settled on a used black-and-white Harley. Later, the men rode their motorcycles all the way up to Tennessee. As Roy, Chester and Orb rode along, enjoying their powerful new bikes, it began to grow chilly after sunset. They pulled up to a grocery store to see if they could buy some Wallerford work gloves, but the only pair in stock had two right-hand gloves. Roy took them anyway, jamming one on his left hand as best he could. Chester and Orb laughed when Roy held up his splay-fingered hands and waved them about.

Shortly afterwards, while Roy was on a tour in England, he had a serious motorcycle accident and broke his ankle. He told *Disc* Magazine, "This was a tour I remember more than any other." It marked the beginning of a tragic chain of events that would alter his life forever. After he was released from the hospital he proceeded to the Granada Theatre, where he overheard someone say, "He doesn't have to sing with his foot, does he?" It was Easter Monday, and though in pain, Roy went on. For the remainder of the tour, he had to sing his songs from a seated position, his foot in a plaster cast. Journalists referred to the "irony" of Roy's latest hit record, which was entitled "Twinkle Toes." In Houston, learning of Roy's accident, Claudette was mindful that he often went on even when he was sick, and now she began to fear that he could permanently damage his ankle. One of her father's motorcycle accidents had almost cost him his leg, and Claudette was aware of how difficult it could be for bones to heal. She decided to fly to London, and she caught up with the tour in Chester. He was on crutches and severely drugged, and Claudette was tired and haggard, but they flew into each other's arms. Roy told the *London Daily Express*, "We both suddenly realized we didn't want to be apart—and that was it. It was wonderful to see Claudette again."

They celebrated Roy's thirtieth birthday in a restaurant in London's Soho district. Claudette and Roy had reconciled too late to forestall the divorce, and they decided to remarry. Roy told *The Daily Sketch*, "It was all a hush-hush affair. Only the essential witnesses were there." Bill Dees was Roy's best man. After the ceremony, Roy and Claudette went to Florida to celebrate.

"The reconciliation occurred after Wesley was born," Patty Maddux said. "Roy came to Jacinto City to get Claudette and the boys and put their life back together. Everything was fine when they reconciled, and I was supposed to go and work for Roy in the office building he had bought in Nashville. They were happy again. Chester and Gerry moved into the house in Jacinto City Claudette had been living in."

After they settled back into the big house on Old Hickory Lake, Claudette called her Aunt Patty. "I want to tell you something," Claudette said. "Don't tell anybody, but I'm taking guitar lessons. I'm going to play and sing and surprise Roy!"

Claudette's sister Dinky, now in her early teens, came to Hendersonville for a visit, and Roy met her at the airport in his Excalibur. "The car didn't have any doors, or if it did, they weren't in use," Dinky said, "and I remember having to climb up and over to get in. Driving to the house was my only one-on-one with Roy. I never really got to know him, never felt close to him. He always stayed up in his room, writing almost constantly or playing his guitar. He very seldom came down and socialized, not even for meals. Mother used to always tell me that Roy was so witty but I never saw it. He had too much closeness as far as people were concerned when he was on tour and when he was home he wanted to remove himself from people. He spent a lot of time with those model airplanes. Claudette was sad over the situation. They'd been married even since she was a kid. She had everything she wanted but still there was something missing. That was probably one of the reasons she went into Catholicism. She was reaching out for something. Someone she was impressed with was a Catholic—I'm not sure who—and she went in that direction. Claudette went through two years of schooling to convert. She started looking at religion in a different light from what she'd grown up with. I know that she was spiritually oriented and trying to put down roots for herself and her children. Roy didn't join her in her conversion to Catholicism; he let her do whatever she wanted to do because he was away from home so much. I'm pretty sure Claudette finished her catechism and entered the church, though I don't think her sons had yet converted. Her Catholicism was something that was real important to her, and she was dedicated to it."

Claudette believed in reincarnation. "We are given many lifetimes," she told Gerry, "but in each one, we are expected to learn certain lessons and grow." Claudette had already come a long way. A child bride, she was at last beginning to explore her own talents and interests. She was becoming her own person, less dependent on Roy for her happiness and sense of purpose.

Gerry and Chester came to Hendersonville for a visit in 1966, delighting in the company of their three grandsons, Roy DeWayne, Tony and the baby, Wesley. R.D. and Tony were leading charmed lives, getting everything they wanted. After having grown up in the Depression, Roy and Claudette now rejoiced in being able to shower expensive toys on their children. R.D. and Tony were perfect play-mates, closer than any brothers their grandparents had ever seen. R.D. was seriously overweight due to a steady diet of junk food, a sure indication of derelict parents.

"Tony and Roy DeWayne were as different as Grady Lee and Roy," Gerry said. Tony was like Grady, the wild one, and Roy DeWayne took after Roy. "Roy DeWayne was quiet, sweet, loving and affectionate," she continued. "Tony didn't have time for any of that kind of stuff. He was always ready to go outside and play."

Though lovable, the kids were spoiled and unruly. "One time we were going over to Boots Randolph's," Gerry said. "Roy DeWayne jumped in the car and started backing it up. He was seven or eight years old." "God dawg," Chester said, recalling the frightening incident. "He said he was going to get the car ready for us—back it out."

Dealing with rich children was a new experience for Chester and Gerry. One day, Gerry took the children shopping with her, and at the supermarket checkout stand, R.D. announced he wanted some comic books. Gerry, who had just enough money for the groceries, recalled telling him, "No, we're just getting food today. We're not going to get any toys."

"Why?" R.D. demanded.

"Never mind why," Gerry said. "We can't afford it."

"What do you mean 'can't afford it?'" R.D. huffed. "I have my own money. I'm just asking for a loan until we get back to the house."

Gerry stuck to her guns. "They were used to walking in there and grabbing anything they wanted," she said. "That didn't go over so well with the old folks."

On the day before Chester and Gerry returned to Texas, Claudette and her mother went to lunch together in Hendersonville. It was a gloomy, rainy day, and as they sat in the restaurant, they looked out the window and saw a funeral procession pass by on Gallatin Road. For some reason, Claudette saw herself dead in the rain. "Mother," she said, "I hope I'm not buried in the rain." The remark would haunt

Geraldine Frady as long as she lived. Rain was one of the most familiar symbols in Roy's songs, and it was usually associated with goodbyes, as in "Here Comes the Rain, Baby." In that song, Roy was probably thinking of Claudette when he mentioned how much she hated the rain and how he'd stop it from falling for her if he could.

In 1966, The Rolling Stones returned to Australia for another tour, this time without Roy. By this time, The Stones were an international sensation, strong enough to draw big crowds without having to lean on name stars like Roy, and the Australian crowds greeted them warmly. Mick said their shows were better than on the last tour because they had appeared then with Roy Orbison and drawn "mixed crowds." The remark was self-serving, inaccurate and hypocritical, especially in view of Jagger's later praise of Roy. As one of the conquering heroes of the British Invasion that was knocking so many American singers off the charts, Mick may have resented Roy's reputation as the world's top male vocalist, which he was then being called in the British press. Though Roy was proud of this distinction, his fall from the charts had given him such a lesson in humility that he was careful not to let anything these days go to his head. "I never forgot that I was a working man's son from West Texas," Roy said. "When success came, I didn't go crazy and say, Oh, I'm above this or this. I tried to keep my perspective." Roy was beginning to realize that life is made up of highs and lows, and that if you keep your humility during the good times, it will serve you well during the bad. As he put it, "I knocked the tops off the mountains, and I also filled in the valleys."

At last Roy had his family back around him, and life seemed secure again. He was only thirty years old and had already known the extremes of poverty and great wealth, loneliness and the companionship of family, and now his life seemed to be on an even keel. According to Anna Dixon, Roy even managed to forgive Braxton and Claudette. "Roy told me, 'Anna, you love him and I love her and they done wrong but if you're willing to forgive, so will I.'"

But Anna had not forgotten what she and her family had been put through, and when she saw Claudette shopping in a store one afternoon, she confronted her. Anna remembered saying, "Claudette, I'm seventeen years older than you and I loved you like a sister. You've been cruel. The Lord will take care of you."

Anna's grim prophesy was soon realized. Claudette's time was quickly running out because of the dangerous toys she and Roy played with. Roy was addicted to fast cars, powerful motorcycles and danger, and Claudette always went along for the ride. Roy was so obsessed with his motorcycle that he parked it in the den of his house. Both he and Claudette doted on the fleet of gleaming automobiles that filled the garages and drive. Claudette herself had a Jaguar and a Thunderbird, and in 1966 she presented Roy with a gift that delighted him—a 1925 Studebaker. A service-station attendant in Hendersonville still talks about what an exhibitionist Roy was in his sport cars, how he would wait until everyone in the station area was looking at him and then gun his Ferrari, spinning the wheels as he pulled out onto Gallatin Road.

He was a show-off and perhaps a little dangerous with cars, but the deadliest vehicle on his property would prove to be the motorcycle he'd bought Claudette. She took it out on June 6, 1966, when they rode in tandem to the National Drag Races in Bristol, Tennessee, some two hundred miles away. After the races, they started back home, and by dusk they were roaring through the countryside near Gallatin. A few more miles and they would be in Hendersonville. At a Gallatin intersection, Roy told Claudette he was going to show her a short cut and pulled ahead of her. They were at Highway 109 South and Cole's Ferry Road. Roy took off so fast that he was already out of sight when Claudette pulled into the intersection and was struck by a pickup truck. Claudette was thrown in the air and came down on the hood, and was finally caught under the truck.

She lay on the pavement in front of York's Grocery. A man ran into the street, knelt beside her and tried to find her pulse. Someone called an ambulance and almost immediately the siren could be heard approaching. A Gallatin woman named Aline Hampton stopped her car and got out to see if she could help. Claudette's white pants suit was ripped open, and Ms. Hampton placed her sweater over Claudette's exposed body. "She was blue," Ms. Hampton said, "like a bad bruise, solid blue all over. I thought she was already dead."

Roy had gone only a few blocks when he heard the siren and sped back to the intersection, arriving at the same time as the ambulance. Remaining on his motorcycle, he looked at Claudette's inert body lying on the highway. He put his head down, and Ms. Hampton, who did not know who he was, noticed that "his fingers stiffened out." Claudette could not be moved, he was told, and he finally dismounted and went inside York's Grocery. Someone brought his motorcycle over to the store. "He sat there paralyzed," Ms. Hampton said, "and laid his head down." When he was informed that Claudette could at last be moved, Roy went outside and crawled into the ambulance after her.

They rushed her to Sumner Memorial Hospital on Hartsville Pike. Doctors worked on her for an hour, but her liver was badly damaged and it was hopeless. Claudette Orbison was dead at twenty five. Her body was taken to Phillips–Robinson Funeral Home in Hendersonville. "And then it was left to me to tell our three boys," Roy said to a *London Daily Sketch* reporter fifteen years later. "I explained to Roy DeWayne and he seemed to understand."

According to Anna Dixon, it was exactly six weeks since she'd told Claudette, "The Lord will take care of you." "When my brother heard she'd died in a motorcycle accident," Anna recalled, "he said, 'Anna, don't predict anything about me.'"

The truck driver who killed Claudette was Kenneth Herald, thirty, a ceramic tile contractor whose address was given as Lake Winds Motel. He was not injured. On June 7, he was charged with manslaughter and posted $750 bond. The hearing was set for June 15, but Roy did not prosecute, saying, "The guy will be suffering enough, knowing he killed somebody."

After telling his children, Roy called his father and mother in Galena Park and asked them to inform Claudette's parents, who lived nearby. Orb got Chester on the line and told him that Claudette had been in a highway accident. They talked a while, and finally Chester realized that his daughter was dead. He couldn't face telling Gerry and instead went to find his son Bill, who was in a karate class. All he could manage to tell Bill was that Claudette had been in a wreck. Later on, at the airport, as they waited for the plane with Gerry, Nadine, Orb and Dinky, Chester drew Bill aside and admitted that Claudette was dead. "I just went to pieces," Bill recalled. "He said she was killed instantly and almost decapitated. She didn't feel any pain, didn't suffer. I broke down."

When they arrived in Hendersonville, Gerry Frady, still unaware that her daughter was dead, expected to be taken to the hospital. She couldn't understand why she was being taken to Roy's house and was still insisting that she wanted to go to the hospital when they pulled up in the driveway. Finally given the facts, she broke down and had to be given a sedative. Later, they all went to the funeral home, and Roy was there waiting for them. Together they viewed the closed casket, and Gerry recalled, "I pitched a fit because I wasn't gonna be sure she was gone unless I saw her. They wouldn't open it. She was tore up too bad."

Requesting to be left alone in the room for a while, Bill went up to the casket and touched it. "I just fell to pieces again," he said. "She was taken too early. I kept thinkin', Why not me? I go out lookin' for adventure. In the service, I'd saved lives, jumped into icy water, scrambled after live ammunition on deck and got away with it. But for her to get killed and me still be here, I never could understand that. A lot of things I wished I was able to talk to her about. We understood each other, but now it was too late." When he came out of the room, Roy asked him to be a pallbearer for Claudette. "All right," Bill agreed. "It's the last thing I'll be able to do for her."

On the day of the funeral, Gerry remembered what Claudette had told her at lunch recently, that she hoped they wouldn't bury her in the rain. Nonetheless, it started to pour. The funeral services were held at Phillips–Robinson at ten a.m. Wednesday, and it was not a Catholic Mass. Bobby Blackburn was present but recalled little about the funeral except that he met Wesley Rose there for the first time and did not like him. "He was a little too smooth for me," Bobby said. "He said, 'I've lost The Everly Brothers. I put so much into them and then they run off and left us. You can't invest in talent—you have to invest in people.' I thought that strange, and I didn't think Roy should have named his kid Wes." The service over, Roy invited Bobby Blackburn to join him in his funeral-home limo. "He said, 'Come on with me and Mama to the cemetery,'" Bobby recalled, characterizing Roy's condition as "level-headed—shit happens. He was broken up but glad to see me. Roy had started smoking Gauloise cigarettes and as we drove from the chapel to the graveyard, he said, 'Try one of these son-of-a-bitches. It'll set you free.' We talked again about Joe Ray Hammer killing himself."

Roy hated every minute of the funeral. He despised funerals; while they honor the dead and provide an opportunity for the living to grieve, none of this was for Roy Orbison. "Life has to go on," Roy said later to Charles Evans. "I can't let this kill my life." Bobby Blackburn says, "Roy and I went out to Printers' Alley for a night on the town when Claudette died." Printers' Alley is Nashville's nightclub row, located in the center of the hilly downtown area. Bobby claims that on another occasion he saw Claudette's name scrawled on the inside wall of Tootsie's Orchid Lounge, a famous bar next to the Ryman Auditorium, original home of the Grand Ole Opry. "Roy was never in that place in his life," Bobby says, adding that Claudette was there with the wife of another singer, and the girls were obviously out cruising.

Early on the morning after the funeral, Gerry Frady was upstairs in the bedroom when she heard a song that sounded as if Roy had just written it. There were speakers all over the house, and it was an advance copy of Roy's latest record, "Too Soon to Know." It did indeed sound like a eulogy for Claudette, but in fact it had been recorded a few days before the accident. A Don Gibson song, this was one of Roy's MGM records, and though it was about the end of a love affair rather than the end of a life, it couldn't have come at a more appropriate time. Stately and dignified in its sorrow, "Too Soon to Know" could have served as Claudette Orbison's dirge. When the record was released in England it went to #3, but in the U.S. it stalled at #68.

Nadine told Gerry that she and Orb would be moving from Texas to live with Roy. Someone had to take care of the children while he was on the road working. "Roy came up to me," Gerry recalled, "and he said, 'We've got to carry on. We can't be selfish and want her back for our own purposes. We're going to miss her but y'all go on and do your life. If there's anything you ever need or want, just call me.'"

Music had been one of Roy's gods, and now he turned to his career for help in dealing with his grief. "It wasn't an effective therapy except to say it kept me occupied," Roy confessed, "so I didn't have much time to think. I was having to record a lot, and I'm a bit hazy, but I think the company [MGM] was sold. So on one hand you had a company that wasn't really viable, and then on the other you had me, with things happening around me and to me. I mean, it was a dark period. All I was doing was surviving. I was trying to work my way out of the turmoil. It takes time to get back on your feet. I just wasn't up to the demands of recording."

Roy started riding his motorcycle again only a few weeks after Claudette's death. "People have accidents in automobiles, in airplanes, just as much," he told *Disc* on June 25, 1966. "At least, I'd like to feel this way about it. I don't know yet that I really do. My thinking just isn't connected at the moment. I think it's a bit early to say how I feel." Roy also retained his passion for racing cars, and he began to spend even more time hanging out with the gang at Otis Deck's Garage. Roy had his cars worked on there, and he sponsored Otis Jr.'s race car.

Before the races at the Nashville Fair Grounds, Roy permitted two of his friends from the garage, Jerry Harrison and Buford "Boggie" Deck, to take his Excalibur around the track, ahead of the pace car, and lead the rest of the racers. "It was a big deal in Nashville," Jerry recalled. "The announcer said it was Roy Orbison's car, and we got a big thrill."

After Claudette's death, Roy turned to prostitutes, according to Bobby, who says they drove to Juarez in Roy's Jaguar XKE two-seater convertible and visited a cat house. As they sat in the bar buying their girls some drinks, someone played Roy's "Yo te amo Maria" on the jukebox. When Roy and Bobby took a trip to the men's room, Roy said, "For gosh sakes, don't tell them that that's me's singing that song. I want to be incognito." When they returned to the table, Roy's girl kept getting coins from him and playing "Yo te amo Maria." Since she obviously loved it so much, Roy finally couldn't resist telling her, "That's me singin' that song." She looked at him for a moment in silence. When the next song came on the jukebox, she said, "That's *me* singing *that* song." And when the next song came on she said, "And that's the bartender."

"They gave us a hard time," Bobby recalled. "But it was great fun, bein' single and singin' songs with Roy in Mexico."

Roy and Bobby were on their way to Hollywood in the Jag, because Roy had decided, one month after Claudette's death, to become a movie star. MGM tossed him an Elvis Presley reject called *The Fastest Guitar Alive,* a silly film about a man who had a rifle concealed in his guitar; it was impossibly inane even by B-movie standards. Roy's lapse of judgment in taking the role may have been attributable to the fact that he had always been an avid movie fan, and starring in his own film, however trite, was one of the prerogatives of a rock star that he did not intend to miss. "It was intended to be a serious film," Roy told Glenn A. Baker. "*Cat Balou* had just won an Oscar and so they changed it to comedy."

On September 7, Roy reported to MGM in Culver City to begin shooting. His co-stars were Sammy Jackson, Maggie Pierce, Joan Freeman, Lyle Bettger, Ben Cooper and Sam the Sham. Sam's real name was Domingo Samudio, he had a current #2 hit record called "Lil' Red Riding Hood" and his "Wooly Bully" had been the top-selling record of 1965. Lyle Bettger was a familiar villain from *Union*

Station and *The Lone Ranger,* and Ben Cooper had been a promising actor in the 1950s, appearing with Anna Magnani and Burt Lancaster in Tennessee Williams' *The Rose Tattoo,* but now, like Roy, he was down to B-movies.

When the film was released, John Mahoney wrote in *The Hollywood Reporter:* "Orbison appears unlikely to generate the same kind of celluloid excitement as Elvis Presley. Not only does he look quite different than he sounds, but he is clearly not cut out to carry conventional romantic leading roles . . . the film has in its favor brevity, the best production values a low budget can buy and seven original songs, likeably performed . . . . Orbison gives a good performance and generates a degree of natural charm . . . . Of the seven original songs by Orbison and Bill Dees, 'Pistolero,' 'River' and 'Medicine Man' impressed most, though all have potential."

Roy attended the premiere in New York on January 15, 1967, with a new girlfriend. Francine Herack was a twenty-three-year-old airline stewardess from Los Angeles, and reporters called her the "new pretty woman in Roy's lonely life." Roy told the New York *Daily Mirror* that he hoped Francine would visit him on his forthcoming tour but added, "It looks as though it's impossible—so we're thinking of spending a holiday in Jamaica instead when we can really get to know more about one another."

Some reporters noted the physical similarities between Francine and Claudette, mentioning that they were both attractive brunettes. But soon Roy was seeing other girls as well, and none of the relationships became permanent. He persisted in dating, whether he felt like it or not. In addition to his own needs, he had the boys to think of. "A father isn't enough," he said. "I can only take them part of the way." On Christmas 1966, Roy was with R.D., Tony and Wesley, showering them with expensive presents. He was also considering 2,000 applications for the highly remunerative job of nursemaid for his boys. In April, he selected a middle-aged British woman named Dorothy Cook. She had been the head typist for an insurance company and was therefore able to help Roy with secretarial tasks as well. Ms. Cook moved into the house with her husband Bob, who was hired to look after Roy's extensive car collection. On occasion, he also doubled as Roy's chauffeur.

Having provided for the children as best he knew how to, Roy went back to work, recording and touring. If the idea of rest and rehabilitation occurred to him, he failed to act on it. Roy was a man who chewed his fingernails to the quick, suffered from an ulcer and chain smoked, and instead of seeking help, he tried to numb his pain with addictive behavior, whether it was sitting through three movies in one day, drinking beer or taking speed and sleeping pills. As Roy told a *Punch* writer, "I'm not very good at just sitting around." Even if he were, Nashville was hardly the place to do it. "Nashville is full of people like me," he said. "They don't often see home. When they do, they like to stay in it. There isn't much social life, except among the wives." Sometimes Roy was home only two months out of twelve. "This business takes years off your life," he said. "I know, even though I keep myself fit, that I'm going to have to slow down in the next year." Roy never did slow down, nor did he realize that it was not the music business, but his choice to overwork, that subtracted years from his life.

The Fastest Guitar Alive was a failure at the box office and he starred in no more films. Doors were beginning to close for Roy Orbison, and it must have been painful. He cut a superb album in December 1966, *Roy Orbison Sings Don Gibson,* but it didn't sell. Roy and Don were both at MGM, and their teaming as singer and songwriter on this album was inspired. Don was from Shelby, North Carolina, and he was ten years Roy's senior. Around Nashville, people said if your career was in trouble and you desperately needed a hit record, dust off some old Don Gibson songs, such as "Sweet Dreams," "I Can't Stop Loving You" or "Oh Lonesome Me." Unfortunately, he wasn't able to help Roy, and this LP did nothing to stop the downward spiral of Roy's career.

Produced by Jim Vinneau, the album is a treasure-trove, with Roy giving beguiling performances of "Sweet Dreams" and "Lonesome Number One." The gem of the album is Roy's rendition of "I'll Be a Legend in My Time." Oddly, neither the public nor the Nashville recording community responded. In 1974, Ronnie Milsap had a #1 hit with the same song and won the Country Music Association Award as Best Male Vocalist of the year. That the CMA managed to overlook Roy's definitive cut a decade earlier is a gaffe of the same magnitude as Hollywood's failure to award an Oscar to Greta Garbo, one of its greatest actresses.

Roy's stimulating and innovative record, "Communication Break-down," written with Bill Dees, was also ignored, going no higher than

#60 on the chart. In this unusual song, Roy was working through his pain over Claudette. "I was probably lucky," he said, "because I could write songs about those experiences and get them out of my system." In the lyrics, he analyzed how their marriage went wrong. They didn't take enough time to be intimate, to take long walks or have leisurely conversations. Money became an obsession and then a worry. Their life was too busy, too full of distraction, temptation and worry.

Roy's choice of material to record did not find favor with Wesley Rose. "When his wife got killed in that accident in '66, naturally everything was at a standstill," Rose said. "He's one of the strongest people I know but it was hard to ask him to go into the studio or to get him involved in writing. All of a sudden his songs leaned that way—sick type of things." What Rose failed to realize was that Roy was drawing on his experience, moving away from the self-pity of his early work and beginning to grow as a person and as an artist.

A few years later, Roy's former record producer, Fred Foster, said that it was a mistake for Roy to do the album, *Hank Williams—The Roy Orbison Way*. "This was not a prudent thing to do to build his career," Foster said. "*Hank Williams* was an exercise in futility to me." Elaborating, Foster explained that so many recording stars had already done Hank Williams songs that by the time Roy got around to covering them, the public was sick of Hank Williams. Though the album didn't sell, it's a superb piece of work, and Roy's versions of Hank Williams classics are definitive. "I'm So Lonesome I Could Cry" gave Roy the chance to show off the full range and power of his voice.

Roy was back in his big house on the lake and his neighbor, Johnny Cash, was at last getting a grip on his life. With strong spiritual guidance from June Carter, Johnny kicked drugs, and soon he returned to the charts with "A Boy Named Sue," a #2 crossover smash. Unfortunately, Roy's career did not experience the same resurgence. Although Joe Melson and Donald Gant gave him an elegant song called "Cry Softly, Lonely One," the record didn't even make the Top 40. Roy had seventeen hits before 1965, when the British arrived, and only five thereafter. The Platters in the same period dropped from twenty to two, Johnny Mathis from eighteen to two, The Drifters from sixteen to none, Connie Francis from thirty-five to none and Brenda Lee from twenty-seven to two. Like these singers, Roy was finished as a top recording artist, another victim of the British Invasion.

In August 1967, with The Beatles' "All You Need Is Love" at the top of the chart, "Cry Softly, Lonely One" only made it to #52, and this was Roy's final U.S. solo hit single for over twenty years. From now on, he was written off as an anachronism by both the record-buying public and the rock press. However, the songs Roy Orbison continued to write and sing were probably as good as or better than anything on the charts. Though Roy was finished as a recording artist, he conceived during his darkest days his brightest dream—he would have a comeback if it killed him.

Chapter 8

"Roy and I had a good time being single in England," Bobby Blackburn said, recalling Roy's 1968 British tour. "We had girls in Upper Brook Street you wouldn't believe." Roy left his three motherless sons in the care of his aging parents back in Tennessee and came to England with the intention of making up for missed pleasures. Now that Claudette was dead and buried, he rolled through London and the north of England like a conquering hero, wowing the sellout crowds at his concerts and, according to Bobby Blackburn, sleeping with any girl he wanted to. Bobby accompanied Roy on this spree and describes the function he performed with relish: "I was Roy's official 'food-taster.' He didn't get to eat anything till I'd tasted it first and made sure it's all right. Got to be safe for 'The King.'" Bobby proved more effective at screening the women cycled through their Upper Brook Street digs than at protecting 'The King' from being swindled by crooked agents. "We subleased the Cunard flat, furniture and all," Bobby recalled. "Roy said, 'Looks like a nice place for two old boys from Wink to spend a month, huh?'" One of Roy's assistants got it for 160 pounds a week and then, according to Bobby, upped the price to 600 pounds a week for Roy.

"We had a calendar on the wall to keep track of the girls—when they'd be arriving and when they'd be leaving. Roy had been touring in the north of England—two months of one-night stands—before we came to London for him to play The Talk of the Town. The big thorn in our side was Barbara [his future wife], who he met in Leeds. She was sixteen, I think. She followed him to Stockton, and then the big thing was to keep track of her air flights and make sure we didn't have too many girls in the flat by the time Barbara got there. We had to make sure there was just one girl in the flat, and we could always pass her off as mine."

Roy's new fascination, Barbara Wellhonen, a German teenager, started their relationship by insulting him. "I was wearing a denim jacket at the time," Roy recalled, "and the first thing she said was what a terrible jacket it was." Barbara herself confirmed the story, admitting, "I wasn't impressed with his Levi jacket, and they're now very much in style." Some people are put off by Barbara's confrontational style, but at thirty-two, all that Roy saw was a girl half his age who was interested enough in him to critique his attire. "I told her it didn't belong to me," Roy said, "that I'd just borrowed it to stop catching cold. But I said that if she turned up at the show the next night, I would show her my best suit." Bobby recalls, "Roy had on my Levi jacket and Barbara said, 'That's the ugliest damn coat I've ever seen in my life.' 'That's okay,' Roy said, 'it's Bob's.'" Though Barbara was ignorant of Roy and his music, he liked her and saw her again when she attended his second show at Batley. When they parted, they exchanged addresses and agreed to keep in touch. But once Roy and Bobby got to London and started carrying on with all the girls they'd met on the tour Barbara became a problem.

"There were a couple of Texas sisters in London," Bobby continued, "and Roy fell in love with the sixteen-year-old and I dated the eighteen-year-old twice. Terry Widlake, a musician we worked with, came in and said, 'Her parents are on the phone and want to know where she is.' I said, 'I haven't seen her since last night, about 9:30.' About that time she walked out of Roy's room. Then Roy came out and hands me 100 pounds and says, 'Find her a room and take her. Barbara will be here all weekend. She's coming from Stockton-on-Tees.' So I leave with 100 pounds and a girl to meet at the train. When Barbara left, Roy had the girl.

"Then Sammy Davis, Jr., called from The Playboy Club to see if Roy would participate in the Biafra Aid fundraiser. Roy played it, and they didn't have any idea who Roy was except an American. Sammy got up to sing 'Oh, Pretty Woman' with Roy, who didn't care for singing a duet with Sammy—or anyone else. But to Sammy, we were two single boys living alone, and he was going to pay us back for helping charity. Every day for months, Playboy bunnies said, 'Sammy said call and see if we could come over and cook supper for you and Roy.' But we didn't want anything to do with the bunnies. We were eating at The Playboy Club and a bunny came up to the table. Roy said, 'Get your ass out of my face or cover it up, one.' A butt about an inch from your nose when you're trying to eat is too rich for my blood."

Leaving London to resume his tour, Roy kept in touch with Barbara, despite all the girls he was juggling. "We were carrying on a romance long-distance at the time of the fire," Roy said. The fire he referred to destroyed his home and much of his family in 1968, an unbelievably tragic blow coming so soon after Claudette's death in 1966. The deadly conflagration was started innocently by R.D. and Tony, on September 14, 1968, in his Hendersonville home. Roy was performing in Birmingham and scheduled to appear Saturday night in Brighton. At 6:30 that evening, in Hendersonville, Nadine and Orb were upstairs while R.D., Tony and Wesley were in a room downstairs. The boys were playing with fire, using a lighter and what Roy later described to Billy Pat Ellis as "model airplane dope." Suddenly, a corner of the bedding ignited and the flames quickly spread. They tried to put them out, but little hands just wouldn't do the job, and Wesley, who was three years old, ran upstairs to Orb and said, according to his great aunt Patty, *They made a fire.*

Orb quickly drew a panful of water and rushed downstairs. Smoke was pouring from the room, and Orb yelled, "Get outside!" The boys ran out, Orb threw the water into the bedroom and then started up the stairs with the boys. Because of the airtight construction of the house, smoke was already engulfing them. In a moment, the whole basement, full of thousands of dollars worth of model airplanes, glue, oil paint and crumbling comic books, went up in a flash.

Upstairs, Orb tried to force the door open but the vacuum held it shut. Nadine was clutching his arm and R.D. and Tony were standing just behind him and he was holding Wesley. Gasping for breath, Orb sank to the floor. There was less smoke down there and Orb breathed in enough fresh air to regain his strength and stand up and try the door one more time.

"I got it open about two inches," Orb told Chester Frady, "and that air sounded like a freight train coming in. We were blown out the door—me, Nadine and the baby—and it sucked the other two boys back in."

What the boys were sucked into was an engulfing flame, followed by the awful maw of an implosion. The house caved in on itself and then shot straight into the sky, raining down on Old Hickory Lake like a firestorm. "I remember seconds before and after the blast," Wesley said. "After the blast I wasn't able to look back and see the house. My grandparents kept my head turned away."

"I saw the fire," Johnny Cash recalled, "and I ran and got my hose and started trying to spray it." Johnny then phoned the police and the fire department.

Jerry Harrison had been hanging out at the police department when the call came in, and he rode his motorcycle out to Hendersonville with the firetrucks and patrol cars. He remembered that a small crowd had gathered on the street, watching the fire. An Associated Press dispatch dated September 16, 1968, quotes Chief George Thompson of the Gallatin Fire Department as saying Orb "was trying to get the three children out of the house when the fire broke out. He had gotten the kids almost to the front door when an explosion erupted in the basement. One of the youngsters got out, but we believe the other two are trapped inside." A later AP dispatch flashed the terrible news: "Two small sons of singer Roy Orbison were missing and presumed dead Saturday night after fire destroyed the country music star's lakeside home near Hendersonville."

Bobby Blackburn was with Roy in England at the time and recalled, "After Roy's performance that night, we took a limo from Birmingham to Brighton. Barbara was with us in Birmingham for a week, but she didn't go to Brighton with us. We weren't in the hotel fifteen minutes before the phone rang. It was Wesley [Rose]. 'I've got good news and bad news. Roy's house burned down. The boys are dead. Orb and Nadine are all right. The baby's okay. You need to go tell Roy about it. We need to make some arrangements. I have to talk to him.'

"'I'll do it in my own time.'

"'There's too many arrangements to be made. I have to talk to Roy right now.'

"I thought, The bastard probably would. [I said] 'Then call him and talk to him. I'll tell him in a few minutes.'

"Wesley Rose called up again. 'Have you told him?' I called the desk at the hotel and asked for the house doctor. I didn't know what Roy's reaction was going to be. Someone at the desk said, 'We'll get a doctor.' In fifteen minutes, a doctor was up in my room and I said, 'I've got to go tell this guy his kids burned up.' Roy was down the hall, and the doctor walked down to his room with me. I said, 'Give me a few minutes to talk to Roy.'"

Inside the room, Bobby found Roy reading Winston Churchill's *History of the English Speaking Peoples*. Bobby delivered his gruesome message, which Roy later recounted in a *Daily Sketch* article on April 17, 1970: "I can remember the exact words. Bob said, 'Your house has burned down. Roy and Tony are gone.'"

According to Bobby Blackburn, "Roy was pretty upset. The doctor gave him something to 'numb the mind.' Then we loaded the limo and drove to Heathrow Airport."

"I was totally shattered," Roy told *The Daily Sketch*, "probably because I was not close to them. I was here. They were there. I didn't know about my mother, my father or my youngest son until my road manager put me at ease about them an hour later." Bobby Blackburn said that he remembered telling Roy everything at the same time—"the good news and the bad news." In any case, Bobby noted, "At Heathrow Airport, I told him I'd go with him, but he said, 'There ain't no use both of us going through this shit again.' I'd been with him at Claudette's funeral too. We both had a thing about funerals, didn't see any sense in them."

Despite Roy's contempt for funerals, arrangements were made for his dead sons at Phillips–Robinson Funeral Home in Hendersonville. Even before Roy's plane touched down, relatives began to arrive, including the maternal grandparents, Chester and Gerry Frady, their children Dinky and Bill, and cousins Ronnie and Kadon. The night of the fire, Chester and Gerry had gone to a dance in Highlands, a Houston suburb, and Gerry had felt a premonition. "I wasn't exactly sick," she recalled, "but something was bothering me. I used to have them about Claudette a lot, but I didn't when she got killed." Gerry asked Chester to take her home, and as soon as they arrived, they received a phone call from their nephew, Ronnie, telling them that their grandsons were dead. "Bill had to call a doctor or a pharmacist," Gerry remembered. "He told them what had happened and said, 'I need some medicine for my mother, to calm her down.' Bill went and got me some pretty strong medicine from the doctor and I got so sick I tried to get up during the night to get me some water and I had to crawl to the sink."

They drove from Texas to Tennessee through violent storms, and when they arrived they found their three-year-old grandson, Wesley, staying with Nadine and Orb at the house of a friend who had taken them in. Wesley's hair was singed and he had some big blisters on his body but the burns were not serious; Orb had skinned his knee and elbow when he'd been blown out the front door, and Nadine was unhurt.

"Ms. Orbison was doped up," Gerry recalled. "She still hadn't got over Claudette." When Roy finally arrived, he too was on sedatives and, according to his British biographer, Alan Clayson, in the weeks and months ahead, "sleep wouldn't come, no matter how many medicines were prescribed." A remark Roy made to *The Daily Sketch* indicates that he did not possess the kind of internal life that would provide help in a crisis: "If you weren't religious before, then I think it would be hypocritical to start praying." He was still too proud to ask for help, so he turned to sleeping pills. "Daddy never was an alcoholic," his son Wesley said, "but he had a dependency on sleeping pills on the road and had treatment for something of that nature."

"Roy was in shock," Gerry felt. "After Claudette's death, Nadine and I would be talkin' on the phone and I'd ask her how Roy was doin'. A year or two afterwards, she said, 'Well, where he used to cry ever' day, it's about once a week now.'" Roy probably had his mother in mind when he cut his 1962 record, "Mama," a song about a brokenhearted man calling his mother on the telephone to share his torment. "Ms. Orbison heard 'Mama' one time," according to Gerry, "and said, 'I'll never listen to that again.' It just tore her up. He'd let go around his mother, but not anyone else."

When Roy went to look at the scorched rubble where the house had stood, he was accompanied by his father Orb, his brother Sammy, his father-in-law Chester, and his brother-in-law Bill Frady. A Coke bottle and a stick marked the places where R.D.'s and Tony's bodies had been found. According to Chester, as he stood gazing at the spot, "Roy came over and said, 'There'll never be another house built here.'" And there wasn't—Roy sold the property to Johnny Cash, who said he'd plant an orchard there. On the visit that day, Roy's major concern, according to Chester, was to retrieve some jewelry that had been kept in a drawer in the basement. Making their way through the debris, Roy and his relatives disappeared into the stairwell and in a few minutes Roy emerged carrying rings and bracelets.

The guests at the crowded funeral included Roy Acuff, Wesley Rose and his wife Margaret, Joe Melson and Paul Garrison. The two caskets were decorated with white doves, and a children's choir sang. After the service, the mourners, by now familiar with the long drive from the Phillips–Robinson Funeral Home to the graveyard, set out to bury their dead for the second time in two years. The procession of limos inched along Gallatin Road in a cold, drizzling rain. At Woodlawn Memorial Cemetery, Bill, Sammy and Ronnie were among the six pallbearers for R.D. and Tony. "We was standin' there," Bill said, "and Ronnie, my cousin, I don't know if he was on the same casket I was or on the other one. I remember standin' there and he hit me with his elbow. I turned to see what he was nudgin' me for and that's when I saw Claudette's grave, right there beside them. That almost made me break down, seein' her grave again."

"They had a tent set up for the family to sit under," Kadon recalled. "The boys were buried at Claudette's feet on either side of her. Afterwards, we went to somebody's house, a friend of Roy's. Roy was very calm. He greeted everyone at the door, and he talked to everybody. *This isn't happening*—that's what he looked like. It wasn't real yet. Later, when everyone left, he had a real hard time. He had some counseling after the boys died."

R.D. and Tony had attended the Goodpasture School and after their deaths a small memorial was made to them in the hallway. Photographs of the boys were displayed side by side, with the caption, "This is what Heaven is made up of."

Roy once described how he survived these darkest hours. He was being interviewed on *CBS Morning News* in the 1980s, two decades later, and retrospect may have lent more spirituality to his remarks than he possessed at the time of his trials. "Through the grace of a loving God, and Jesus Christ, and my faith, and good friends and kindred souls, people who had been through the things I had just gone through—through their love and understanding—and through the career, I worked my way through that and tried to make it not the earth-shattering thing that it was, just like I tried not to if a record sells a million, I try not to make it any more important than it is, too."

Moving as they are, those words bear little relation to Roy's actual condition directly after the tragedy. Harold Bradley, who was a guitarist on many of Roy's hits and who saw him at the time, said, "He asked if I could come by this hotel. He didn't have a home. I went over there, knocked on the door, and he opened it. Inside, it was absolutely dark, food wrappers scattered all over the room. He evidently hadn't been out of that place in a week. He already knew he had lost his kids, but he wanted to talk about getting some guitars. I think that was kind of a way of regaining his sanity. What is nice is that his life didn't end in that hotel room. He came back."

In the midst of these horrendous blows, Roy decided not only to undertake a tour but to get married again. Bobby Blackburn recalled, "A month later, I got a telegram from Roy telling me to meet him in

Leeds. He had Barbara with him then and said they were going to get married." Roy announced his nuptials at a press conference called at the Westbury in London to publicize his three-week stint of British cabaret dates. According to an Associated Press dispatch:

> Roy Orbison showed off his new bride to the press yesterday, revealing one of the year's best kept show business secrets. Orbison married an attractive German teenager, Barbara Anne Wellhonen Jakobs, March 25, 1969, in Nashville. Since coming to Nashville to record several years ago, he has remained something of a mystery. The couple had been in Germany last Wednesday visiting the bride's parents. The new Ms. Orbison, 19, comes from Bielfeld near Dusseldorf. Her father is a wealthy industrialist and German consul to Panama. Barbara is tall and dark haired. Before she met Orbison she was studying medicine. "Now I am giving that up," she said. "I am going to travel around with Roy."

The reference to Barbara's age as nineteen is curious considering that Barbara, in a 1985 telephone interview with Australian school children, said that she was seventeen when she left Germany and came to America to marry Roy. In either case, at thirty-three Roy was twice her age, so once again he had taken a young wife.

The question of what to do with Wesley, one year old when he lost his mother and three when he lost his brothers, was not simple for Roy. Incredibly, he managed to lose his only surviving son when he married Barbara. Wesley himself explains how this occurred, taking up the story at the time of the fire. "We went to a friend's house and then lived in a motel two or three months in Nashville. I was raised by my grandparents. I saw my dad three to five times a year. I felt left out by his new family but actually wasn't. My dad never disowned me and always treated me with respect as being his boy. I always felt I was part of him. So how come our separation? It was left up to me to decide whether to stay with my grandparents or Roy and his new wife. I finally chose my grandparents."

As he grew up and entered school, Wesley became an outcast. "Dad was a star and everyone thought we had money," he explained. "I wouldn't socialize and share the wealth—that's what they thought. I didn't have it. They'd say, 'Bullshit, he's one of the biggest.'" He left public school and voluntarily enrolled in Castle Heights Military

School, but he couldn't fit in there either. By the ninth grade he wanted back in public school, where he could wear his hair long. "I went for that, then discovered there was not the same class of rapport there at all. Fend for yourself. Teachers give you something to do and you do it. If not you're fighting the system. Other kids understood that, I didn't."

Wesley's maternal grandparents, Chester and Gerry Frady, were distressed when they learned of the bizarre living arrangements in Hendersonville. Roy designed and built two new houses in the neighborhood where the destroyed house had been, one for himself and Barbara and another for his parents. According to the Fradys, Wesley told them that he wasn't living with his father and sometimes had difficulty even gaining access to him.

If Roy's personal life was once again out of control, his career was headed for total eclipse. Some time after his fall from the charts, he was seen by New York literary agent Jay Acton in a sleazy Times Square country & western bar, singing to a handful of night owls. "Maybe there were fifty people inside," Acton said, "but Roy was great, singing his hits in perfect voice. We went up to meet him after the show, and though he was nice, he was pathologically shy." But at least he was alive, which was more than could be said of many of the people he'd toured with during rock's magnificent, harrowing decade. Gene Vincent, a friend from Roy's rockabilly days, died in California at the age of thirty-six, burned out and broke. The original Rolling Stone, Brian Jones, an alcoholic and drug addict, was fired from the band in 1969 and found dead the following month in his swimming pool.

Pat Boone, the teen idol of Roy's college years, hadn't had a Top 40 hit since 1962 and was having alcohol problems; he would never attempt a musical comeback. The Beach Boys were also falling apart, their string of twenty-six hit singles cut short by the British Invasion. Brian Wilson had expressed his fear of The Beatles to Roy as far back as their mid-'60s Australian concerts together. "I told Brian that The Beatles would be the biggest group in the world," Roy said. "I had to do it very tender and very nicely because The Beach Boys were #1 then." Brian was so upset that he stopped performing, was replaced by Glen Campbell, blew up to 240 pounds and became a cocaine and heroin addict, refusing to shower or shave. Another Beach Boy, Dennis Wilson, fell under the spell of mass-murderer Charles Manson and had an affair with Patti Davis, daughter of future President Ronald Reagan, before suffering alcoholic seizures and drowning in Marina del Rey at the age of thirty-seven.

Roy's old friends Don and Phil Everly were no longer popular in America but, like Roy, they retained some of their former lustre in England. Both brothers' lives had been disrupted by drugs, and they were bitter and angry at each other. Don suffered a nervous breakdown and was hospitalized, and a few years later one of the great singing partnerships in rock 'n' roll came to an explosive end in the middle of a concert.

In their heyday, Roy had toured Australia with Paul and Paula, and then, after a few hits, Paul and Paula quickly dropped from the charts, becoming curiosities of the decade's early optimism, before President Kennedy's death. Paul went to Kansas City and raised a family and Paula tried to make it as a solo act in Texas before moving to Southern California and getting married. Though they would reunite a dozen years later for a country single, "Any Way You Want Me," the public ignored them. The Surfaris, who'd also toured Australia with Roy, tried folk rock and then disappeared from the recording scene altogether. Friends from Roy's early Beatles tour, Gerry and The Pacemakers, split, unable to adjust to changes in the rock world.

The Beatles were headed for disbandment and litigation in 1969, largely because their drug use had wrecked their lives. George Harrison was at a party with Britain's Princess Margaret when he learned that his apartment had been raided by the police and his wife Patti busted, and when he appealed to Her Royal Highness for help, she declined. John Lennon and Yoko Ono were in an equally unlikely predicament, their peace campaign degenerating into a brawl when their promoter knocked five teeth out of a photographer's mouth and broke his jaw. Roy spent some time with Paul McCartney after the breakup of The Beatles and said, "We talked about the early days of The Beatles and our tour. He commented on the 'Big Voice' and how they were sort of frightened, which was a compliment."

Ronnie Hawkins had ended up in Canada. According to Hawkins, Roy was alcoholic. "In later years," he said, "when his career was up and down, it was rumored he was drinking way too much. But if you're in show business, with all the ups and downs, sometimes you will take a drink!" The Hawk was having ups and downs of his own. His protégés deserted him in Canada and went to live with Bob Dylan in Woodstock. As The Band, they became the hottest act in rock in 1969, creating masterworks such as "Up on Cripple Creek" and "The Night They Drove Old Dixie Down," which gave Joan Baez a #3 hit in America and a #6 in England. Meanwhile, according to *Billboard,* "Ronnie Hawkins spent most of his time in the Canadian club circuit, reminiscing about his sexual excesses and sitting out his ten-year contract with Roulette."

Roy was not invited to participate in the 1969 Woodstock Festival, which turned out to be the culmination of a whole era of rock 'n' roll. After Woodstock, it was no longer possible for anyone to deny that rock 'n' roll, now fifteen years old, was the most popular music of the century, and Roy began to think of himself as a living legend. He had always disdained his rockabilly roots but now he began to advertise them.

Though Roy was no longer a star attraction in America, he could still pull down about $2,000 a night in England. In the British cabaret business he was in the same league with Ms. Mills, a pianist, Les Dawson, Del Shannon, and Freddie and The Dreamers, roughly equivalent to a Vegas lounge act. A British magazine rock popularity poll relegated Roy to twenty-seventh place, well below Brenda Lee and Adam Faith. He was losing respect in the U.K. nightclub business, and occasionally Roy or Acuff–Rose had to serve High Courts writs on agents or tavern keepers who'd failed to honor their contracts. *The Evening News* reported that Roy claimed "substantial loss of reputation" as a result of The Sands cancellation of a four-night run in Brighton. The engagement had already been advertised, and Roy complained that he suffered embarrassment. He received a settlement when his ten-day tour of American military bases in Germany was cancelled due to Army maneuvers.

He was also losing his status as a recording artist in the U.K. "Heartache," which hadn't even charted in America, stalled at #44 in Britain. "Dad had qualms about releasing 'Heartache,'" Wesley Orbison recalled. "It was after the fire and he was afraid people would associate it with the tragedies. He was sensitive about it and so he put it out later." Not much later, however; it was released in 1968, the same year his sons died. The following year, Roy's single, "My Friend," was a #35 hit in the U.K., and in October, his "Penny Arcade" rose to #27. Neither made it into the U.S. Top 40. Though American critics dismissed it as a gimmicky uptempo song, "Penny Arcade" is an imaginative work that stands up well after twenty years.

Roy's glory days were at an end and darkness now fell over his career, but his influence on the new generation of rockers was profound, and many of the songs he had written and made famous would lead to the advancement of other major careers. John Fogerty, for instance, reintroduced "Ooby Dooby" when he was with Creedence Clearwater Revival.

Bob Dylan tried to reach Roy around this time, and if he had succeeded, the miracle of *The Traveling Wilburys* and Roy's 1988 comeback might have occurred twenty years earlier. Bob had come to Nashville to cut *Nashville Skyline,* which would bring about a great flowering of country music in America, and though he managed to round up Johnny Cash for a duet on the album, he didn't find Roy at home. "I was in Canada in late '68 or '69," Roy said, "and there was a knock on my door back in Nashville. And my wife went to the door and it was Bob Dylan coming to say hello. Unfortunately, as I said, I was in Canada. So that was a compliment—anytime anyone takes the time to come to your home and knock on the door, it's marvelous."

Most of the excitement in rock emanated from the West Coast in the 1970s, and the young California artists were quick to acknowledge the rich legacy of the solitary figure in black known as the Big O. California embraced Roy as Nashville never had, though it would take years for their appreciation to get Roy himself back on the charts. In the 1960s, the "LA Sound" had been the light and bright rock of The Beach Boys and The Mamas and The Papas. Early Hollywood country rock was pioneered by Ricky Nelson, but the LA scene found its resident genius in Gram Parsons of The Flying Burrito Brothers. With the advent of The Byrds, Gram Parsons, and Dylan's Nashville album, country and rock began a fusion that inspired major '70s artists such as Emmylou Harris, Linda Ronstadt and The Eagles, all of whom would figure prominently in Roy's life for the next ten years. Gram loved Roy's old recording of a Felice and Boudleaux Bryant song called "Love Hurts," and Gram and Emmylou Harris recorded it and brought it back into circulation. Gram fell in love with Emmylou, but unfortunately, Gram's life was cut short by his alcoholism and drug addiction. He overdosed on a mixture of tequila, morphine and cocaine, dying in a Joshua Tree motel in the Mojave desert. In the macabre aftermath, his body was stolen from a baggage ramp at Los

Angeles International and returned to the desert, where it was burned on Cap Rock. Despite the brevity of his life, Gram's vision of fusing rock and country music firmly established the California myth of the rock star as cowboy and outlaw. No one was more central to that ethos than Roy Orbison, who had grown up a few miles from Pecos, Texas, and whose music would always be enriched by a country & western flavor.

Describing her meeting with Roy, Emmylou Harris said, "My then husband Brian Ahern and I met Roy a couple of years before we did 'That Lovin' You Feelin' Again.' Roy came over to our house. It was just one of those picking parties that happens sometimes. Everybody was passing the guitar, and he sang. I remember commenting that I'd probably never sell that house because Roy Orbison had sung in it."

A former backup musician of Roy's, Bobby Goldsboro, was hitting his stride in the late '60s with an international mega-hit called "Honey," which captured the #1 position on the U.S. chart and held it for five weeks. The song was about the death of a young bride. Bobby was now an important star, a regular on TV talk shows and a headliner in supper clubs. With Top 20 hits like "Autumn of My Life" and "Watching Scotty Grow," Bobby scored eleven hit singles in the years between '64 and '73, and "Honey" made *Billboard's* all-time Top 100 Records 1955-86, placing 82nd. Not one of Roy's hits had sold enough to make it onto this elite list of domestic best-sellers.

Another career Roy helped launch was that of Sonny James, who revived "Only the Lonely" and took it to #1 on the country chart. Sonny scored sixteen consecutive #1 country singles in the next few years, including "Since I Met You, Baby," "It's Just a Matter of Time" and the unforgettable "Only Love Can Break a Heart." For Roy Orbison, this marked the beginning of a long, slow comeback. The light at the end of the tunnel was a long way off, but at least it was shining.

Chapter 9

Roy and Barbara started building their new family in 1970. Their first son, Roy Kelton Jr., was born that year, followed by Alexander four years later. "Johnny Cash was in the waiting room when I had my first boy by natural childbirth," Roy said. "I walked into the room after it was over and Johnny said, 'Well, what is it?' And I said, 'It's a baby!'" Wesley was still consigned to his unofficial guardians, Nadine and Orb, and he was facing plenty of trouble ahead.

Though Roy's career went nowhere in the '70s, his influence was evident in the significant new performers who came on the rock scene in the U.S. and abroad. In England, Jeff Lynne and The Electric Light Orchestra's "classic rock" was inspired by Roy. "First thing I ever heard of Roy's was 'Only the Lonely,'" Jeff told *Rolling Stone*. "I was probably thirteen or fourteen. I remember it giving me goose bumps, it was so different. I finally got a tape of all his songs and played it for like five years nonstop." One of Elton John's early hits owed its emotional opulence to Roy. The composer Bernie Taupin said, "Everyone at one time or another tries to write a Roy Orbison song. Mine was 'Don't Let the Sun Go Down On Me.'"

In America, a new group called The Eagles came to see Roy when he was performing in San Francisco in the 1970s. Terry Widlake, Roy's personal representative and bass player from 1968-78, almost cancelled the show because of problems he was having with a band member as well as club management. "There was no sound and lighting personnel at band call," Terry said, "and I was ready to pull Roy out of the show. In hindsight, of course, I am glad that I didn't. The manager came to our dressing room prior to the early show fairly drooling. He was amazed to discover that there were so many celebrities in that audience. It was reported to us that The Eagles were out there, Boz Scaggs and even Bette Midler."

The Eagles had started as Linda Ronstadt's backup band, and when their gigs with her were over, they decided to stay together. The Eagles' string of hits, including "One of These Nights" and "Take It to

the Limit," epitomized the California outlaw-rock sound of the '70s—
country with a rock flavor, which was essentially pure Roy Orbison.
Terry Widlake says The Eagles came backstage to meet Roy after the
show. This led to Roy's tours with The Eagles, which brought him to
the attention of a new generation of rock fans.

Bruce Springsteen would also play an important role in Roy's life.
Bruce was still an unknown in 1970 when he made a long trip down
South to be the opening act for one of Roy's shows. Though he was a
Jersey boy, Bruce considered Roy to be his role model as a singer. He'd
started playing guitar at thirteen, joined a band called The Castiles at
fourteen and was playing The Cafe Wha in Greenwich Village by
1967. Later on, he would climax his great rock concerts with driving
renditions of golden oldies, including songs by Roy and Buddy Holly.

Glen Campbell was another popular singer of the '70s who revived
early Orbison songs. In April 1971, Glen recorded Roy's old Cindy
Walker hit, "Dream Baby," and the record went to #31 in the U.S. and
#39 in the U.K. Glen had been on a winning streak since 1967's "By
the Time I Get to Phoenix" and in the '70s he was well on his way to
his first #1 smash, "Rhinestone Cowboy." However, his notorious
affair with Tanya Tucker in the '70s seemed to drain him, and his
career never recovered its early glory.

Roy continued making records, but he couldn't seem to come up
with a sound that Americans would buy. His *Memphis* LP reflected a
measure of personal and artistic growth, but it went unnoticed. The
best new songs on the album are "Why a Woman Cries" and "Take
Care of Your Woman," both written by Jerry McBee. They tell a man
everything he needs to know about women and how to keep them
happy. For once, Roy left morbidity behind, and his performances of
these wise songs are sensitive and intelligent. "The Three Bells" and
"Danny Boy" are also on this LP and are among the best versions of
these standards ever cut.

Roy was so bewildered by his disappointing record sales that he
continued to question and doubt his artistry. "As MGM got pro-
gressively worse," he said, "I made less effort unconsciously, so it was
a downhill ride. The company wasn't selling the product and I
possibly wasn't delivering product good enough to sell. I got out of my
contract in 1973 and oddly enough, since then the company has done
very well. But I did the right thing in joining them and then in leaving.
I've had a lot of time to think about it. Even though I had the personal
problems and the record company problems, I still was basically happy

because practically every record I released was a hit somewhere in the world. I got five gold records overseas on one song that didn't sell 20,000 here. In fact, right now [1974] I'm a bigger draw than when 'Pretty Woman' was #1 all over the world. I do more work, I make at least twice the money. I'm in a good mood, I'm happy, content. I've been in a situation of little money and in a position of a lot of money. I've had few friends and a lot of friends. One causes about as many problems as the other."

Americans flocked to the discos in the 1970s, and the new interest in dancing created a demand for fresh and exciting music. The Hues Corporation, Barry White, Giorgio Moroder, Gloria Gaynor and Donna Summer knew exactly how to get people out on the dance floor, and though Roy tried, his attempts at writing and singing disco music were dismal. Angry and defensive over his failure to adapt to changing times, he bragged, "I can't say that I have any regrets. I don't think I could single out anything that I would have changed. I like the fact that as far as principles go that I was true to them. I never tried to write a 'folk song' or 'protest song' or drug-oriented song or any type of thing that was happening. I still record, I still write, I still sing with the same feeling. What I'm doing now, and what I've always done, and what is right, and what I know, is what I love to hear, and when this coincides with what the public likes, then I will have a hit record. And it will be one of my very, very many." Roy made this boast in 1974, but he was not to have another hit record until 1988, when his success would result from his dependence on virtually the entire rock community.

In the '70s, Roy began to show up on the soundtracks of motion pictures, which ultimately would prove to be an important factor in his comeback. The first was Antonioni's counterculture epic, *Zabriskie Point,* in which Roy sang "So Young." It's one of Roy's supercharged, bravura performances, but the song's seriousness is diminished by the sentimental notion that love is the exclusive province of the young, the wild and the free. Roy then contributed to a film of David Bowie, one of the most gifted of the new '70s rockers. Bowie used Roy and Joe Melson's beautiful "Blue Bayou" on the sound track of his intellectual sci-fi thriller *The Man Who Fell to Earth.*

In the same year, Roy appeared in a concert with Johnny Cash. As for his other professional activities, Roy said, "I tended to fulfill commitments around the world, then come home and rest." After playing 125 gigs on 105 consecutive nights in 1974, Roy said, "In the

'70s, I got to the point where I just didn't want to go on. You'd begin another tour; you'd get a bit ill and a bit confused and, finally, you can't see the point in either touring or not touring. It was only around '75, after I'd called a halt to the whole thing and reassessed the point of it all, that it started getting to be fun again." Sometimes only a handful of people showed up for his shows, and Roy started cutting corners by using only three musicians—guitar, bass and drums— which was a smaller backup group than the one he'd started with, The Wink Westerners.

In the winter of 1973, Roy's older brother, Grady Lee Orbison, came to Hendersonville for a visit. It was an icy, snowy day, and on one of the sharp turns on the twisting road to Roy's house, Grady's car went out of control and crashed. He was killed instantly. Grady was only forty years old. After his days as a high school football hero in Wink, his life had gone downhill. Work in the oil fields was as hazardous as it was hard, and Grady suffered two serious accidents, one injuring his back and the other severing his left thumb. His marital life hadn't gone much better. He and his wife Merlene had had two children, Ronnie and Orbie Kelton, but the marriage had deteriorated after the discovery that Grady had been visiting Mexican whorehouses. Merlene then went to live in the Northwest. Grady married again and he and his second wife also had a baby. At the time of his death, he was living in Tennessee and working in petrochemical plants as a gunniter.

According to Bobby Blackburn, neither Roy nor his father attended Grady's funeral. "Roy didn't like illness and sick people," Bobby Blackburn says. "He and Orbie Lee had a pact not to go to each other's funerals." The funeral was held at Phillips–Robinson—Bobby says that Barbara asked, "We're doing so much business with you people, do we get a discount yet?"—and Grady was buried with Claudette, R.D. and Tony in the section of Woodlawn known as The Sermon on the Mount.

Although Roy Orbison had escaped the hard life his brother and father led in the oil fields, sometimes he seemed to work as strenuously as any roustabout. He toiled on the stages of Europe for seven months straight, including dates in Crete and Taiwan, with only nine days off. As a result, he was only a few years away from a major medical setback.

In 1974, Roy left MGM and signed with a new label, Mercury. Greg Mitchell of *Crawdaddy* magazine talked to him on the eve of his '74 comeback attempt and found Roy "more of a curiosity than a legend." Roy was not taking his obscurity gracefully. He sounded stuck in the past, defensive and bitter. He was deluding himself into thinking his latest record "Sweet Mamma Blue" might have a chance on the charts when it was already clear to everyone else that it was a flop. Wesley Rose said a fall tour was now in jeopardy because "we had thought we could ride the single."

Roy's voice had lost much of its power and richness. *Crawdaddy* reported, "'Sweet Mamma Blue' is more croon than Caruso." The album also proved disappointing. Called *I'm Still in Love With You*, it represented a sharp decline from his MGM records and sank without a trace. It was mostly a country album, and Roy sang a Johnny Ace '50s song called "Pledging My Love" in addition to some of his own compositions, like "Crying Time" and a new version of "Heartache." The only promising moment on the LP came when Roy hit a big note at the end of "All I Need Is Time."

Though success now eluded him, Roy was gamely making his second attempt at family life. Barbara told the *London Daily Sketch* how she explained Roy's celebrity to her young sons. "It is a job just like other dads have, like doctors, lawyers, train drivers or anything else," she said. "If they think their father is something special, something different, too soon in life, it can destroy their sense of values."

Roy persisted in his dangerous hobby of motorcycle riding, saying "It clears the air." He enjoyed a rich man's pleasures, doting over a stable of luxury cars and hanging out at Joe Towe's Classic Car Restorations, the garage in Hendersonville where Roy began to build his second car collection. Joe restored a TR6 and TR3 for him. "Roy would come by the garage and sit and visit," Joe said, "or I'd go up to the house. When we were up there, he'd usually get out a model airplane kit and go to work with the glue and paper. When he came to the garage, he usually wore cutoffs and sandals. He loved it here because he could just be himself." During one of his tours, he called Joe from the road and told him, "I see a '36 Ford. Should I buy it?" Another time he called and said, "They've got a '52 Mercury here, and the guy wants $30,000 for it. What should I do?" Joe always told him whether the car was a good investment. Joe's son and Roy's sons played soccer together at the Hendersonville school, and the families always showed up to root for their youngsters.

Roy and his second family were now living in the luxurious new home he'd built in Hendersonville. It included three kitchens, three bathrooms, master bedrooms lined with rosewood, a leather-padded writing room and a swimming pool. "Yes," Roy said, "I suppose I have a feeling for the aristocratic way of life, and to have been in Berlin and Paris in the '20s would have been my cup of tea." Down the road a piece, where Wesley lived with his grandparents, there was little sign of Weimar glitter or any other kind of luxury.

Bruce Springsteen became the new white hope of rock 'n' roll in 1975. Bruce fully acknowledged Roy's influence. His album *Born to Run* was an instant Top 10 sensation in '75, and on the opening cut, "Thunder Road," Bruce saluted Roy by name, saying that Roy sang for lonely people. Though Bruce and the LP were both subjected to microscopic scrutiny by the media, including simultaneous cover stories in *Time* and *Newsweek,* no one remarked on Bruce's extraordinary reference to Roy in the opening bars of the most celebrated album of the decade.

Though he was neglected in America, Roy's popularity in Australia was on the rise again. During the 1975 tour, the Sydney concert was sold out two weeks in advance. A second show was scheduled and sold out in two days. Arrangements were made for a matinee as his third show, and it sold out in two hours on the strength of radio advertising. The next year, 1976, he had another Australian tour, receiving fifteen gold records and one platinum, plus gold plaques from New Zealand.

In America, Roy had sunk to performing to houses that were ninty-nine percent empty, such as Cincinnati Gardens, where he played on his fortieth birthday in April 1976. The occasion was a Van-a-Rama, with a stage set up at one end of the Gardens and a sort of flea market at the other, where merchants could park their vans and hawk their wares. Photographer David Shoenfelt was present that night and said that as Roy sang, people continued to walk up and down the aisles, talking and inspecting displays where the vans were parked. Roy did two shows that night, and according to Shoenfelt, he sang as if he were in Carnegie Hall.

In 1976, a heavy-metal band called Nazareth covered "Love Hurts," the durable Boudleaux Bryant song that Roy made famous. Roy was also pleased to hear that his LP *The Very Best of Roy Orbison,* heavily promoted on British TV, had gone to #1 in the U.K. And on March 14, 1977, Roy opened a show for The Eagles, whose LP *Hotel California* was the current #1 hit album in America.

In 1977, Roy's old Sun touring partner Barbara Pittman talked to Elvis Presley in Memphis three months before he died. "I knew he was ill," Barbara said. "He had a bad heart and bad hypertension."

"I'm bored," Elvis told Barbara. "The only time I feel alive is when I'm in front of an audience, in front of my people. That's the only time I really feel like I'm human." Roy's and Elvis' personal lives had followed the same disastrous pattern. Both married young girls, neglected them and lost them to lovers. Elvis had at last wearied of teenagers and complained, "I'm tired of raising kids. I don't have the patience to go through it all over again."

Roy could be biting and sarcastic about Elvis Presley, but he changed his tune after Elvis paid him a fulsome compliment from the stage of the Hilton Hotel in Las Vegas in 1976. Several years before, during an interview with *Crawdaddy's* Greg Mitchell, Roy said, "I bought twelve tickets for my family and friends for an Elvis concert not long ago in Murfreesboro, Tennessee, and it was *terrible.*" Later, when Roy attended Elvis' Vegas show, Elvis had Roy spotlighted at his table, told him to take a bow and informed the audience that Roy was "the greatest singer in the world." When Elvis completed his set, 2,000 fans mobbed Roy, asking for the autograph of the world's greatest singer. Roy managed to extricate himself and slip backstage to visit Elvis. "We hadn't seen each other in years," Roy said. "He hugged me. We talked about everything—Jerry Lee Lewis, touring. He was a little overweight but looked really good." Elvis was in fact obese and would be dead eight months later, but after his compliment that night, Elvis could do no wrong in Roy's eyes. "I know Elvis had a strong faith," Roy said, "but it was just that there was no one close enough to him, that loved him enough, to tell him what he was doing to himself."

Despite deteriorating health and worn-out hearts, both Roy and Elvis were touring frantically. Though middle-aged, they were still acting like Sun Records hell-raisers. Sometimes, Elvis collapsed on stage, babbled incoherently, and split his pants (he had gained so much weight). He was addicted to both speed and barbiturates. On August 16, 1977, Ginger Allen discovered Elvis dead in his bathroom at

Graceland. He reportedly died of congestive heart failure, but later, his drug abuse was disclosed. Terry Widlake broke the news to Roy, who was in Los Angeles to play the Santa Monica Civic Auditorium. "Roy cried like a baby," Terry said.

Roy returned to Monument in 1977 to record an LP called *Regeneration*. Like everything else about this unfortunate album, the title was ill-advised, for this LP was far from regenerative for Roy's fortunes. If, as Fred Foster claimed, he and Roy were such a winning combination, why was their reunion album a failure? The material Roy was given to cut was deplorable. "Southern Man" is about an extremely unappealing bumpkin who brags about making love to fat women and drinking hard liquor. In "No Chain at All," he boasts of sleeping with a different woman in every port. Another cut, "Old Love Song," can be excused as inoffensive—subtle and sexy, it celebrates the harmony of lovemaking. "Can't Wait" is Roy's attempt at disco, but it lacked the flair of '70s disco wizards. Though "Born to Love Me," "Blues on My Mind" and "Something They Can't Take Away" are pretty songs, they were out of step with the times. Dennis Linde's "Belinda" is a soaring crescendo song, the best cut on an otherwise undistinguished album, but even in this tune, the ideas are twisted. The man is in love with a tart, and he has so little self respect that he seems to be telling her, You can have me if you can't do any better. Such groveling was long out of style, but Roy was stuck in the past, singing the same old songs. And nobody was listening.

Roy and Fred Foster tried to blame each other for the album's failure. Roy said, "In '77, I made a record that I wasn't pleased with, really, for Fred Foster. I didn't write any of the songs, and I only had a few days to do the album." Foster claimed Roy was ill, that he "actually got sick as we were doing the album. While he was in the hospital recovering from that, I think he re-evaluated where he was, and his life, and what he wanted. He said, 'I don't think I want to do any more records for a while. Will you release me from my contract?' I did."

Referring to his illness, Roy said, "I had no idea it was coming." One day he felt a tight, sharp pain in the middle of his chest. Though Roy did not know it, the blood to his heart was blocked by clogged arteries, and he wasn't getting enough oxygen. He went to a doctor and had a thorough heart examination, but no irregularities were found. Roy felt free to accept an invitation from the Presley family to sing at a tribute to Elvis. The event was staged at The Liberty Bowl in Memphis, and at one point in the proceedings, Roy made the mistake of running up a long flight of stairs. Suddenly, the pain stabbed at his chest again and he grew dizzy and collapsed. "I figured I'd better go to Hawaii and lay around in the sun," Roy said. "I got the pain again on the way home." He rang the doctor, who told him to come on in. Another heart check was done, and afterwards the doctor looked at Roy and said, "You can go home and watch the Super Bowl."

Then the woman who was Roy's specialist came in the room, talked to him a few minutes, and said, "We're going to put a camera inside you and take a look at your heart." His arteries were full of plaque, and one of them was closed ninty-five percent, one seventy-five percent and another sixty-five percent. He was barely alive. "You have to have open-heart surgery," she said. "Okay," Roy replied. "Let's just get it on."

Roy's operation was performed at Nashville's St. Thomas Hospital. "I was lucky," Roy said. "Without immediate attention I could have had a massive coronary." In the operating room, just before going under anesthesia, Roy said, "Leave me a nice scar up top. I wear open-necked things. Make sure it's a clean, pretty incision. I perform with my shirts open pretty far down." The doctors looked at him as if he'd gone crazy. "Look, son," the thoracic surgeon said. "We're trying to save your life. We're not worried about scars."

"Well, I am," Roy said. "Make sure it's right."

The coronary by-pass took four hours to perform. "The second day after the surgery," Roy said, "I thought I was going to die. The next day I wish I had of died. On the third day, I took a nap and woke up and I can't tell you the difference. It was like instantly going back to being seventeen years old. Instantly, it increased the blood flow by sixty percent. My hearing, sight and perceptions were magnificent. Luckily, after the surgery they had about thirty minutes to stitch it from the inside, and in therapy afterwards, all the women and the men were very jealous about the scar, because it was so nice.

"My perception about everything—about who my friends were, about what the music business was all about, songs, everything—was all totally repaired instantly." Roy praised his "fine doctors," and he listened attentively to the advice they gave him. "What you need to do is exercise a bit," his doctor said. "You need to not smoke. The one thing that will put you in the grave is to worry about things and carry the stress that has brought you to this point. Let me give you some advice. If there's anything bothering you or upsetting you, disturbing you, either move it or go around it."

Roy did not follow this advice to the letter. About a year later, while promoting his new LP *Laminar Flow,* he told a London interviewer, "I have a beer occasionally now and smoke occasionally. I'm really rockin' now." He said he "didn't do much" the first year after surgery, "just enough to make sure I could still do it, and then last year I spent a great deal of time negotiating, which takes a lot of stamina and is not my forte. I don't like to do business. I started in January and haven't stopped. I'm working in Europe for four weeks."

Roy made *Laminar Flow* for Elektra Records, and the contents were as unappetizing as the title, an obscure aeronautics term. "It was like a half-finished project to me," Roy said. "That was less than a year after the surgery." With this album, Roy was again trying to find his way into the disco sound of the '70s. *Laminar Flow* is less bumptious than *Regeneration,* but there is not a memorable cut in the album. "Lay It Down" tries to be sexy but succeeds only in being vulgar, and "Love Is a Cold Wind" is replete with the despondency and self-pity of a typical Orbison song without any of the conviction or drama. *Rolling Stone* wrote Roy off, dismissing the album as "an embarrassing travesty . . . maybe the most soul-less album ever recorded at Muscles Shoals."

A much more significant event for Roy was Linda Ronstadt's 1977 rediscovery of an old tune he'd written with Joe Melson called "Blue Bayou." Released in September, it was the prime track from Linda's Grammy-winning platinum album *Simple Dreams.* Her single of "Blue Bayou" went to #3 for two weeks and remained on the chart for twenty-four weeks. Unquestionably, the renewed recognition as a result of Linda's album was the biggest thing that had happened in Roy's career in over a decade. "I think the renaissance started with Linda Ronstadt recording 'Blue Bayou,' which wasn't even the A side in America," he said. "It sold seven to ten million for her, and I guess I felt validated or something. That was in '77." By the end of the decade, Roy could talk about "going for the top" again musically. According to Barbara, he became interested once more in writing, and he felt his best music was still ahead of him.

Barbara needed Roy at this time, however, and he put aside his career to help her. Barbara suffered from agoraphobia, a morbid fear of open places that held her captive at home all the time. "It was a hard time for Roy," Barbara said. "My mother was also gravely ill at the time. Our family was left pretty immobile. Roy was very patient and loving. He sort of set aside his plans to take care of me."

Wesley's young life, always difficult, reached its nadir in high school. He had felt uncomfortable in both public and private schools, bouncing from one to the other, but in adolescence he had finally chosen public school, where long hair was permitted. Now his tribulations began in earnest. "The tragedies and Dad being a star troubled me in high school. It was also the time of Barbara's problems and Papaw being sick and I was needed at home, or I felt like that was what I should do. I experimented with speed and Quaaludes and got busted for marijuana. I had it in two or three different sacks for myself because I could get it cheaper that way. But it looked like resale if you had it in several sacks instead of one sack, and I couldn't prove the difference. Because I was a minor I got off. It was not a felony. There was not a bunch of cash on hand, no proof I was dealing. The teachers and the whole community seemed to be against me. They all wanted to get at Daddy. 'We'll call your father and see if he can't take time off the road and come talk about his son.' I told them to talk to my grandparents. 'They're old softies,' they said, 'not right for a kid growing up.' I told them I was instructed not to give out my father's number to anyone, and they thought I was being cocky.

"I didn't finish school. Eleven years—I almost finished, but didn't finish the eleventh grade. I split before the exams, figured I'd get my GED and be a musician. I got my high-school equivalency within a year. I didn't want any more of school."

Roy's chief advice to his son at this time was that he should go out on his own at sixteen. Wesley understandably found that strange since he was well aware that Orb continued giving Roy money all the way through college. But these were not Roy's most rational years. He had a cocaine habit and, according to Bobby Blackburn, "a condo in Malibu for some of his wilder escapades. Roy did cocaine in the '80s. He was playing in Vancouver and I was living in Portland, Oregon, and this happened in Portland. He did a whole bunch. Later I asked, 'How much did you just take?' 'About $700 worth,' Roy said. 'Well,' I said, 'it's back to the beer for me!'"

The fate of a has-been is particularly harsh in America, where the highs and lows are extreme. Washed-up celebrities usually retain sufficient clout to command TV commercials and charity telethons, but Roy was discarded as suddenly and finally as the hoola hoop, and a singing comeback seemed impossible. Only a determination for visibility at any cost could have led him into as trashy a venture as the 1980 film *Roadie*. Hard as it is to believe, *Roadie* was every bit as bad as Roy's first movie, *The Fastest Guitar Alive*, but at least that one was from a major studio. The film is about a groupie named Lola Boullaibaise, whose ambition is to screw Alice Cooper. Lola considers herself a "Sister of Mercy of Rock 'n' Roll." A groupie, she says, is the spark plug of rock, and she's what keeps the band going.

If a good film could be done about groupies, *Roadie* wasn't it. Nor had Roy's acting improved since his first film fifteen years before. He still looked like he'd stumbled onto the set and was patiently waiting for directions. Mercifully, he only had a cameo role. He is seen hanging out in a low-life dive, and when a brawl erupts, he and Hank Williams Jr. quell it by going onstage and singing "The Eyes of Texas." Roy was used for comic relief when he could have sung "Kaw-Liga." He certainly had the background as a Wink Westerner to create a barroom scene of unique authenticity, but *Roadie* was a total waste of his talent.

But *Roadie* was not entirely purposeless for Roy Orbison. He and Emmylou Harris sang a duet on the soundtrack called "That Lovin' You Feeling Again," which went to the top of the country chart and won the 1980 Grammy Award for Best Country Performance by a Duo or Group. The same year, he toured California with The Eagles, who were doing their old benefactor, Linda Ronstadt, a big favor by campaigning for her boyfriend, California Governor Jerry Brown, then seeking the Democractic nomination for President. Roy won an army of new fans from The Eagles' largely teenage following. "It was a modern-day thing," he said, "and a lot of fun." He began to have new hopes for reviving his career as a performer. "Things are moving at a very good pace. I got this feeling around '54, I got this feeling around '59, and I get this feeling now that what I want to do is going to happen."

In the summer of 1980, Roy played The Lone Star Cafe in New York, a country-music joint on lower Fifth Avenue. The modest room was packed with old fans and recent admirers of Linda Ronstadt's "Blue Bayou," including Miss Ronstadt, who dropped in to catch Roy's act. Her recording of "Blue Bayou" was Roy's favorite cover of one of his songs, and Linda once said, "I fell in love with 'Blue Bayou' the first time I ever heard it, long before I recorded it."

Roy told an AP reporter who interviewed him backstage at The

Lone Star that 1980 was going to be his big year, that within the next few months shooting would commence on *The Living Legend,* an authorized film of his life story. "I want to avoid people having a wrong account of my life," he told *The Daily Sketch* on April 27, 1980. Martin Sheen was set to play the lead, though it seemed like odd casting, considering Sheen's good looks. Roy was so confident that the backers could get his film biography off the ground that he was already planning to re-record ten of his songs for the sound track and to write two new tunes with his "Lovin' You Feeling Again" collaborator Chris Price. Eventually, Roy withdrew from the project, distressed over delays and budget cuts. While his backers regretted Roy's decision, they barreled ahead with the project, changing it to a fictitious story about a singer resembling Elvis Presley. It was filmed in North Carolina by local entrepreneur and would-be actor Earl Owensky, who also starred.

Though he liked to be known as humble and mild, Roy's ego was very touchy. He even found Ronstadt's "Blue Bayou" a mixed blessing. "For the longest time I was wondering when I went on tour and did 'Blue Bayou,' would the younger generation think I was copying Linda Ronstadt?"

Though Roy said "I feel I'm contemporary" and disdained rock revivals, he did one on September 5, 1980. He appeared at the second annual Buddy Holly memorial concert at the Civic Center exhibition hall in Lubbock, Texas, which was clearly billed as "The Legends of Rock 'n' Roll." He played to a big hall that was half empty. Bo Diddley opened for him, singing "Bo Diddley" and "I'm a Man." Then, heralded by wildly inappropriate theme music for *Star Trek,* Roy came on at 9:15 p.m., dedicating his portion of the show to Buddy Holly. "He sang 'Crying' from the heart with such enthusiasm, conviction and style that one has to wonder why he's not touring more these days," wrote William D. Kerns, entertainment editor of *The Lubbock Avalanche-Journal.*

The MC, Jerry Coleman, introduced Buddy Holly's family, who received a standing ovation, and then The Crickets—Sonny Curtis, Joe B. Mauldin, Jerry Allison and Waylon Jennings—played "Oh Boy," "Maybe Baby" and "Rave On." Funds raised from the concert would help pay for a statue of Buddy, Lubbock's most famous citizen.

On July 19, 1981, Odessa, Texas, announced "Roy Orbison Day," and Roy played there for the first time in fifteen years. Before the concert he was given the key to the city. "It's such a shame," said his

old friend Annette Bailey Spiers. "There wasn't a huge crowd there."
A reception at The Holiday Inn was hosted by Charles Evans and Billy
Pat Ellis of The Wink Westerners. "We got a couple of cases of beer
and two or three cases of Cokes and after the concert we had a reunion
in Roy's room at the hotel," Charlie said. For Roy, it was virtually *This
Is Your Life*. At the end of the party, Roy went over to Claudette's
parents and sat talking with them long after everyone else had left. "I
should take more time with Wesley," Roy said. "I should play ball with
him or *do something*." They agreed wholeheartedly.

After Texas, Roy was off to Santa Ana, California, for a one-night
stand at The Crazy Horse Saloon. Playing second-rate venues in the
era of stadium rock concerts, Roy sometimes despaired of ever
achieving a comeback. To make matters worse, much of his best work
was unavailable for airplay, even if the DJs had wanted him. "Since
Monument Records went into bankruptcy in 1981," he said, "my
masters have been tied up in court. There weren't copies available for
radio to play or for fans to buy."

When Don McLean's cover of "Crying" topped the U.K. chart for
three weeks in 1980, Roy was ecstatic. Don's record company had at
first rejected it as being "too slow," but when Don sang it on Dutch
television, "Crying" began an amazing new life. In America, it
charted at #5 and remained in the Top 40 for fifteen weeks. In
England, it held the #1 spot the weeks of June 21 and 28 and July 5.
"After Linda Ronstadt in 1977," Roy said, ticking off the key factors
in his career resurgence, "Don McLean did 'Crying,' and it was a
hit." Don McLean was famous for his #1 smash "American Pie," a
saga of the death of Buddy Holly that went on for eight and one half
minutes and was the biggest-selling single of 1972.

When Roy tired of his native land treating him like a lounge act, he
went overseas and was accorded a reception more befitting a rock
deity. Roy made a triumphant appearance behind the Iron Curtain in
1980, arranged by an Oklahoma promoter named Jim Hall. A
complete symphony orchestra was promised, and Roy loved the idea of
at last singing with the big backup band of his dreams. The occasion
was a Communist bloc music fest called The Golden Orpheus
International Festival for Bulgarian Pop Songs, Slunchey Brjag,
Bulgaria. Roy was the first American ever to appear there. The
concert was filmed in Bulgaria and shown throughout Eastern Europe.
When Roy started looking for someone to conduct the symphony
orchestra, his regular band members, Jim Johnson and Terry Elam,
suggested Tim Goodwin, a brilliant young Memphis musician.

"What was involved," Tim remembered, "was taking the old arrangements that Anita Kerr had done and lifting them off the record on a couple of songs and re-scoring them, not changing anything but just picking them out by ear and re-scoring them for the orchestra, as well as to compose some new orchestral arrangements to accompany songs that didn't have an orchestra on the original records. 'Pretty Woman,' for instance, didn't have an orchestra, but Roy wanted to see how it would sound with a full symphony backing him up. It was a whirlwind couple of weeks where I was scoring like crazy and copying like crazy. In fact, we were doing some of the parts and going over them on the airplane flying to Sofia."

Roy was expecting a grim sight when he landed in his first Communist country, but instead he saw a city that reminded him of Las Vegas. Sofia was the playground of the Warsaw Pact nations and a favorite seaside resort for high-level East German officials.

Roy knew he was a star in Western Europe, but he had no idea that people behind the Iron Curtain were familiar with him. He tried walking down the streets, but hordes of fans immediately surrounded him. "Everybody knew who he was," Tim said. "Rather than being able to move around in the city, as he wanted to, he ended up spending most of his time in his hotel room. We had girls who were offering to marry us just to get them out of their own country.

"Roy got to where he was staying in his room the whole time, and we'd take food to him. He'd only open the door if you did a specific knock, and the knock was the rhythm to 'Running Scared.' If you did that bolero rhythm, da-da-da-da, he'd open the door. Every time we went out to eat, somebody in the band ordered a dish to go for Roy."

Roy's regular band, mostly from Nashville, consisted of Jim Johnson, Bucky Barrett, Barbara South (vocals), Richard Law, Terry Elam and Marshall Pearson.

At the concert, according to Tim, "Roy would start a song like 'Crying' and these people were throwing babies in the air. He'd start the first couple of measures and they knew what he was going to do. He was Top Ten in Bulgaria right then and there. When his records originally came out they weren't letting anybody hear decadent American music over there, so a lot of the stuff was relatively new to them. But they knew it all. They didn't know the language or even the alphabet but they sang along in certain parts of every standard."

Tim Goodwin had never heard Roy sing live before this tour. "Jim Johnson told me, 'When he sings, it's going to make the hair stand up on the back of your neck.'" During the show, Roy had his songs laid out in an order that built to a pitch. "I was standing on his left," Tim said, "and he was facing the audience. My back was to the audience, because I was conducting. We had a monitor system so everybody in the symphony orchestra could hear the singing clearly and know where we were in the music. Roy was farther away from me than the monitor speaker was, and yet I could hear him, just the natural acoustics of him singing, his voice was so strong, louder than I could hear the monitor system. He was doing 'Crying,' and he got to that real high note, and he just zinged right in on the pitch, it was just perfect, and there was no vibrato to help him cheat on the pitch. It was clear as a bell. The strings were playing and the band had built up and he hit that note and sure enough, the hair on the back of my neck just all started standing up. It was an incredible physical sensation.

"Being around Roy was one of those musical experiences that was why I went into this business in the first place. He was always a gentlemen. Everybody else on that tour got good and sloshed at least a couple of the nights that we were there, but he was low key. He'd eat his food and we'd sit down and have these quiet little conversations. He'd strum his acoustic. He didn't cuss, I never saw him get mad at anybody. I saw him when he was mad but I never saw him get mad at anybody. He was angry when we got back to London, waiting for some transportation to show up. Everybody was real put out, pissed off, tired, wanting to get to the hotel—and there'd been a screw up. Roy was the only one who didn't sit around and bitch and moan. He was just cool about the whole thing. Everybody I know who knew him in this period—his comeback—a lot of younger guys that were working for him, none of them knew him as wild or temperamental."

"He had two heart attacks during the time that I knew him," Tim Goodwin added. "One was before Bulgaria, and one of them was some little while after that. He had to go off the road. They had almost six months booked and they ended up cancelling the first couple of months of it.

"Barbara was awfully important to him. She took care of so much for him. Actually, what Terry didn't take care of, Barbara did. She handled everything while Roy was away for six months out of the year. From everything I picked up from Terry and from Roy when I was around him, Barbara was his contact with reality. Being on the road is a hard, brutal life—living in hotels, eating hotel food, trying to find something decent on television. At his age, he wasn't catting around and drinking or carousing, so he didn't wear himself down too much

London, 1964: John Lennon (far left) and Ringo Starr (fourth from right) feed Roy pieces of a guitar-shaped cake at a party for Roy's twenty-eighth birthday. Claudette (right) looks on, while Roy DeWayne Orbison smiles below. (UPI/Bettman Newsphotos)

Roy DeWayne Orbison standing between paintings of his parents by artist Wayne Ingram. (Courtesy Chester and Geraldine Frady)

This snapshot was taken by Claudette's parents the last time they saw her before she was killed in a motorcycle accident in 1966. (Courtesy Chester and Geraldine Frady)

Roy, outside his Hendersonville, Tennessee, home, with his and Claudette's three sons: Roy DeWayne, Tony and Wesley. The two older boys were killed when the Orbison's house went up in flames on September 14, 1968. (Courtesy Chester and Geraldine Frady)

In 1969, Roy married a German-born seventeen-year-old, Barbara Anne Wellhonen Jakobs. Here they are in 1971 with their six-month-old son, Roy Kelton, Jr. (UPI/Bettman Newsphotos)

Record producer Jack Clement with Barbara and Roy Orbison. (Country Music Foundation)

Roy with an expensive new toy and his friend and mechanic, Joe Towe. (Courtesy Joe Towe)

April 23, 1976: Roy walks on stage to perform during a Van-a-Rama auto exposition in Cincinnati, Ohio. Fewer than one hundred fans attended, and there was no mention that it was his fortieth birthday.
(© 1990 David A. Shoenfelt)

Wesley Orbison, Claudette's only surviving son, with all his grandparents, Nadine and Orb Orbison and Chester and Geraldine Frady. (Courtesy Chester and Geraldine Frady)

Roy accepting his Rock 'n' Roll Hall of Fame Award on January 21, 1987. (Gary Gershoff/Retna)

Roy, Bo Diddley and Carl Perkins celebrate their induction into the Rock 'n' Roll Hall of Fame at the Waldorf-Astoria in New York. (UPI/Bettman Newsphotos)

Enjoying some camaraderie with his band, Roy in performance, May 15, 1987. (© 1990 David A. Shoenfelt)

The Traveling Wilburys in 1988. Left to right are Bob Dylan, Jeff Lynn, Tom Petty, George Harrison and Roy Orbison. (Neal Preston/Outline)

Roy waving goodbye after his last concert on December 4, 1988, at the Front Row Theatre in Highland Heights, Ohio. Roy died two days later in Hendersonville, Tennessee. (© 1990 David A. Shoenfelt)

like a lot of people, especially younger guys, but still, it meant a lot to him that Barbara was there, taking care of things."

Roy was still at the very beginning of his comeback, but in March 1982, there was another important milestone. Van Halen made a cut of "Oh, Pretty Woman," and it went to #12, becoming the popular group's first Top 10 hit. Over dinner at Terry Elam's house in Bartlett, with Tim Goodwin and other friends, Roy spoke of the "little bitty clubs and fairs" he was playing, not unlike the beer joints in Monahans and Ft. Stockton where The Wink Westerns had started out. "I've tried doing new music," Roy said, "but it wasn't successful. At this point, my age is against my doing new music. Van Halen and Linda Ronstadt prove my old stuff is good enough. The old material is what's gonna get me going. I only throw in only two new tunes out of the whole evening and everything else is the old stuff."

In September 1982, Roy filed a $50 million suit charging his manager-publisher of twenty-four years, Wesley Rose, with mismanagement and fraud. As Bobby put it, "Roy liked him till the day he filed a suit against him. Roy wanted control over his music. He called Wes and ran into a hassle. Then he hired a Los Angeles attorney to get the rights to his music. The lawyer sent in a team of investigators to Acuff–Rose and then built a $50 million lawsuit." Appearing in Nashville Chancery Court, Roy asked for the return of "Blue Bayou," "Running Scared," "Only the Lonely," "Crying" and "Oh, Pretty Woman." Shocked and hurt, Wesley Rose claimed Roy had allowed himself to be influenced by others. Roy was angry at himself for his own lack of aggressiveness and poor direction. He was sick to death of his low profile.

When questioned by a reporter about the outcome of the suit, Roy responded, "We came to a nice arrangement. Seven figures!" According to Bobby, "Roy said, 'I'll end up with $2 or $3 million.' 'Well,' I said, 'that's not a bad days' work. Let's go to the courthouse and petition a name change for your kid, Wesley.'"

In an ironic sequel to the lawsuit, the Nashville law firm representing Roy turned the tables and sued him for unpaid fees amounting to $153,975.

In May of that same year, 1982, Roy and Jerry Lee Lewis appeared together at the Country Music Festival in London. They were the major attractions, and it was the first time Roy and Jerry Lee had shared a bill in almost thirty years.

Also in May, Roy played The Club Bene in Sayreville, New Jersey, and a fan named Robert Burroughs was in the audience. It was a small-town dinner theatre seating 750, and it was about ninty percent full. "Roy didn't look good that night," Burroughs recalled. "His double chin was heavier than usual." When the applause died down after "Crying," Roy gave the audience a sample of his famous dry wit. "Thank you very much," he said. "I've had a lot of requests this evening, but I'm going to sing anyway."

Roy kept up a full schedule—perhaps too full—because on February 2, 1984, *The Ft. Wayne Journal-Gazette* reported:

> Roy Orbison is undergoing treatment in Canada for an undisclosed ailment, a hospital administrator said Wednesday. Orbison, forty-seven, was admitted to the Charles Camsell Hospital in Edmonton, Alberta, on Tuesday. He was in Edmonton for a series of nightclub performances.

Two days later, he was

> recovering from a respiratory ailment in a hospital in Edmonton, Alberta. The country singer had attracted more than 3,000 fans during his ten-day engagement at an Edmonton nightclub. He had bronchitis and sinusitis and with the change in climate and a ten-night run, he just never had a chance to shake it, Terry Elam, his road manager, said.

In the 1980s, both Roy and Barbara Pittman, his old Sun Records colleague, began to play Rockefeller's, an old bank building in downtown Houston that was converted into a nightclub. "We followed each other in and out of Rockefeller's all the time," said Barbara, by now an internationally celebrated rockabilly legend. "Roy and I both did live videos at Rockefeller's, and I did an album. It's a great place. He was working little clubs like this. Rockefeller's I know for a fact didn't pay much money, and he was coming back there quite often." One night, Orbie Lee and Billie Harris caught Roy's show at Rockefeller's. "I took along a photo of Roy as a young boy," Billie related. "I showed a member of his band that picture and said, 'Take it to him and tell him I'm here.' In a little while they came out and got me and took us backstage. Roy signed the picture 'with love.'" When Roy introduced Orbie Lee Harris to his band in the dressing room, he said, "I have known this man since I was about four years old, probably longer but that's as far back as I can remember." Orbie Lee Harris remembered seeing Roy's brother Sammy "handling the concession—the T-shirts and the buttons. Roy was handling the money himself."

Bob Claypool of *The Houston Chronicle* asked Roy how he'd kept his voice as strong as it was twenty-five years ago. "I don't know why that is," Roy told him. "But I haven't lost any of the top end that I can tell. I don't do anything special for it, and I don't baby it. It's just there, I guess. It's a gift, and I've been lucky."

Barbara Orbison called Chester and Gerry Frady and told them Roy was singing at Rockefeller's and that she was producing a video of his performance. "We were shocked," Gerry said. "It was the first time Barbara had ever called and invited us." Roy and Barbara entertained the Fradys in his big touring bus, which was parked out back.

Roy also played Billy Bob's Texas in Fort Worth. Gerry and Chester saw him there, as did Claudette's Aunt Patty. Roy always gave his audiences a good show in the 1980s, but he didn't stay on stage one minute longer than he had to. On November 17, 1984, his audience in Colorado Springs, Colorado, gave him a standing ovation but their cheers turned to jeers when they realized he wasn't going to sing another song for them. According to *The Colorado Springs Gazette-Telegraph's* reviewer, "Orbison's abrupt departure overshadowed a lot of what he had done in the sixty-minute concert. Central Station owner Sam Guadagnoli said, 'Their contract called for a ninty-minute concert. But what can I do? You have to pay half the deposit before they get here, then you pay the rest before they go on stage. So you have nothing over them after that."

The reviews of Roy's March 1985 shows in Maine indicate that he was incorporating a memorial to Elvis Presley in his act these days. A hush invariably fell over the crowd when he sang his poignant song "Hound Dog Man." One reviewer wrote, "The song took on a sincerity rarely achieved when sung by a touring performer night after night . . . . Only his professionalism kept his voice from breaking." Critics were beginning to compare Roy's performance of "Oh, Pretty Woman" to Van Halen's. "Though his leads weren't as fast as Eddie Van Halen's," wrote one, "they had more soul." Another reviewer felt, "Linda Ronstadt's 'Blue Bayou' paled in comparison to Orbison's version last night. His drawl and range combined to make it one of the highlights of the set. 'Crying' got a standing ovation that started before the song was over. Orbison accepted roses from the audience, and as if to prove that his voice was not a fluke, reprised 'Crying' hitting the same note even stronger." Critic Ariel Lipner wrote in *The Worcester (Maine) Gazette*, "His voice is a tad bit more modest than in his glory days but really not a whole lot. When he hits his classic high note on 'Crying,' earning a spontaneous ovation, he replayed the last verse and did it again, even better. His sustain is just as strong as ever, a most impressive accomplishment considering he's almost fifty. To prove it was no fluke he repeated the feat four songs later on, 'It's Over,' and another standing ovation once again showed the Orbison voice is timeless."

Chapter 10

Roy moved to the West Coast in 1986. He and Barbara took R.K. and Alex to live in Malibu, leaving Wesley and his elderly, widowed grandmother behind in Tennessee, thus precipitating yet another crisis in his divided family. When Roy and Barbara left Hendersonville, they sold not only their house but the house that Wesley and Nadine were living in. "We were dumbfounded," Wesley said. "It was a jolt and a half and still is. We'd lived there ever since we'd left the motel after the fire. The house was provided for Mamaw and Papaw to live their years out. But Papaw died in 1984. He was the life-force of the family, and it didn't take long after that before the house was sold. We moved to a two-bedroom apartment. Dad promised, 'We'll do a lot of things when the situation improves in Malibu.'" Roy said he had to sell the houses and move to Malibu or he would lose everything, and he was determined not to lose his second family. Roy, and later his estate, probably handled expenses for Nadine's Hendersonville home. Nadine Orbison declined to comment on the situation, and when Barbara's name came up, she said, simply and touchingly, "She's mine, too."

In their new Malibu home, Roy, Barbara, R.K. and Alex appeared on *Life Styles of the Rich and Famous,* flaunting their swimming pool and tennis courts and the usual driveway full of exotic cars. Back in Hendersonville, Claudette's Aunt Patty Maddux paid a visit in October 1987 and found Nadine and Wesley living at the other end of the spectrum. "Roy had the money to see that his mother was well taken care of. I felt guilty that I hadn't done something about Wesley because Claudette asked me if anything ever happened to her if we'd take care of Wesley. He wasn't treated right. Ms. Orbison is an invalid with nobody but Wesley to take care of her. She can't sit up except for fifteen or twenty minutes at a time. And yet your father is on *Life Styles of the Rich and Famous!* And that's his son! And his mother! That's why I say the man had no control."

"Money was generated in the mid-1980s," Wesley said, referring to Roy's suit against Acuff–Rose, "but before it came they got to Malibu and we never knew how much or what happened. Dad said 'seven figures,' but it probably was more like eight figures if you include the payout over a number of years. Daddy didn't talk business with us very much. That was unusual, I thought."

Roy made a rare public reference to Wesley in an interview with Chris O'Neill. At the time, Wesley was twenty years old, and the interviewer asked, "What's he doing with himself?" Roy said, "He just... he plays the guitar mostly. He's been with a band. They don't play professionally, but they get together most of the time."

Since Roy had been making money in Texas honky tonks for years and already had a hit record by the time he was Wesley's age, his impatience with his oldest son would be understandable if it weren't for the fact that his actions—seeing his son only a few times a year since childhood—clearly indicate parental negligence.

When Orb had died in '84, true to the pact made with his father, Roy did not attend the funeral.

Increasingly frustrated over his moribund career, Roy found sympathy from a reporter from *The Houston Post* as they sat in Roy's touring bus in 1986. "Rock 'n' roll styles and tastes changed," the reporter wrote, "and Roy's hits stopped coming. No one has ever figured out why, really—after all, lots of old rockers have made it back to the charts through country music. But no producer has yet had the good sense to sit down with Orbison and make a prolonged run at the charts. It's crazy, especially in light of the fact that Roy is still a powerful live-show draw, and, second, that he retains, at forty-nine (he'll be fifty next month), all of his youthful vocal power. He hasn't even lost the top off his phenomenal range."

The reporter wrote it was clear that Roy was obviously wondering when the Rock 'n' Roll Hall of Fame would get around to him. Sam Phillips had already been inducted. "I must be around twelve or thirteen on that list," Roy estimated.

The move to Malibu was good for Roy. The West Coast has always held a magical allure, and in the late '80s, a positive attitude and an emphasis on recovery from destructive personal behavior and substance abuse characterized the California scene. At first in the thousands and then in the millions, people were seeking a spiritual connection with what Roy, using the language of AA, called "a power greater than ourselves. You set out to whip the world, and then you get beat up a little bit. In my case, you say, 'Father, I'm gonna let you have it. I've done what I can do, I'm turning my life and my will over to God.'" He'd obviously familiarized himself with the tools of spiritual growth—prayer and meditation. He also learned what to pray for—not money, fame or women, as he once had, but simply to be in touch with God's will. When Roy's life and career around this time took an inexplicable turn for the better, he became so enthusiastic that he began to discuss his spiritual awakening with journalists, although Barbara urged discretion.

With the insular parochialism of Nashville far behind him, and in the more salubrious atmosphere of Southern California and its enthusiastic recovery programs, Roy's fortunes continued to improve. He resumed participation in idiosyncratic movie ventures, hoping one day to connect with a winner. For Nicholas Roeg's 1985 film *Insignificance,* Roy and Will Jennings wrote a song called "Wild Hearts." While the movie was not a great success, the cast had a couple of well-known names, including Gary Busey, who starred in *The Buddy Holly Story,* and Tony Curtis.

In the latter half of the 1980s, Barbara Orbison became Roy's manager. "Barbara and I felt we had to put everything in order in my career," Roy said. "We never had the right management, the right agency, the right record company all at once." About this marriage/business partnership, Barbara reminisced, "Roy respected me as a partner in life, in music and in our personal life . . . We kept it real clean each day. We learned to separate our relationships . . . Lots of times what he asked me to do as a manager I wouldn't have done as a wife or as a lover. And lots of times, what I had to tell him as the artist he wouldn't have listened to as a husband and a breadwinner. So we really matured to live this life that we lived, and to really have magic in it."

With all these improvements in management, it's surprising to learn that the most decisive factor in the resurrection of his career came about against his will. He refused to let his song "In Dreams" be used in the film *Blue Velvet,* but the director defied him and used the song anyway. The dismal *Roadie* and *Fastest Guitar Alive* were good enough for Roy, but not *Blue Velvet,* which ended up on many critics' lists among the best movies of the '80s.

Roy Orbison had flirted with the movie industry long enough to know that the medium had incredible power to create hit records. The most obvious example of the rock era was Bill Haley's "(We're Gonna) Rock Around the Clock," which was a turkey until MGM used it under the title credits of the 1955 film *The Blackboard Jungle*. After that, the tune shot to the #1 position, where it remained for eight weeks and, more significantly, helped launch the rock era. *Blue Velvet* would play an equally potent role in Roy's career, thanks less to Roy's judgment than to David Lynch's nerve.

In the film, the recording of Roy's "In Dreams" was a stunning tour-de-force, and *BAM* Magazine called Roy "the emotional epicenter of the film." After the movie became a hit, Roy appeared on a television show with David Lynch and addressed him affectionately throughout the interview. "Everyone was starting up my career without me," he said, referring to David, Linda Ronstadt, Don McLean and Van Halen. "In *Blue Velvet*, we had notoriety from the film, which used 'In Dreams' bizarrely. When I first saw the film, I was shocked and taken aback that that sweet little song could be used that way. I'm glad he did use it."

"In Dreams" is a deceptively simple song. A man goes to sleep, dreams that his girl will always belong to him, wakes up to discover she's deserted him, cries and praises dreams as being the only place good things happen. Though Roy had always considered it "a sweet little song," the lyrics betray an abnormal psychology. The song's morbidity made it exactly what Lynch needed for *Blue Velvet*, one of the more disturbing mainstream movies ever made. The song says dreams are better than reality, states a preference for delusion over truth, and proposes that in the ideal relationship the man should own the woman. It's a concept of human relationships that has nothing to do with love and everything to do with power and control. The song is so appealing because everyone wants security and someone to love—as did Roy before he met Claudette Frady. But on close inspection the relationship is horrible.

It was that utter if unintentional depravity of Roy's vision of life in "In Dreams" that made it an appropriate theme song for *Blue Velvet*. The film's villain is a sadistic psychopath who takes a woman hostage and makes her his sexual slave. Lynch used "In Dreams" in a scene between Frank Booth, played by Dennis Hopper, and his friend Ben, a painted, effeminate brothel-keeper who specializes in fat prostitutes. As the whores look on, Ben, played by Dean Stockwell, lip-synchs "In

Dreams," and Frank gets so excited that he goes out and beats up an innocent young man.

Lynch sat his cast down every few hours during shooting and asked them to listen to the song. On the movie's release, "In Dreams" became an instant cult favorite. Now, at last, there was a demand for Roy Orbison.

Blue Velvet led to one of the most important relationships of Roy's life, Bono of U2, who would be instrumental in the triumph of Roy's final album *Mystery Girl.* "I was introduced to Roy Orbison's music at a very late stage," Bono said. "I was given the soundtrack to *Blue Velvet* by The Edge's wife. I was in London in the summer, and it was kind of hot and humid. It was one of those nights where I couldn't sleep, and I just listened to 'In Dreams' over and over all night. It's the most extraordinary pop song. I think it's five or six completely different melodic sections tied together. It breaks all the rules of pop music. I hadn't realized he was such an innovator. And I'd never heard a voice quite like it. There seemed to be this Pandora's box that he opened up, and there seemed to be all the dreams and nightmares in there, all mixed up."

"Bono," Roy's new admirer, was Dublin-born Paul Hewson. Just as Roy had formed The Wink Westerners three decades previously, Paul organized U2 in the late 1970s while he was still a schoolboy. The one called "The Edge" was David Evans, and the others were Adam Clayton, Larry Mullen Jr. and Dick Evans. The band was originally called Feedback, then The Hype, and Paul Hewson found his name on a hearing-aid, Bono Vox. U2 topped the Irish charts in '79 and '80, conquering America in 1981 with a national tour and LPs called *War* and *The Joshua Tree.* When Roy became associated with them later on, Bono and The Edge wrote "She's a Mystery to Me" for Roy, and Bono was Roy's producer when he cut the song for *Mystery Girl.*

Roy's fans in Ireland, England and throughout the U.K. remained his most loyal support group over the years, and he frequently let them know how much he appreciated them. One of them, Michelle Booth, a fifteen-year-old English girl from Reading, near London, he came to know quite well. When he heard that she was in a coma after having been hurled from a speeding train by a maniac, he sent her a tape saying, "Michelle, the next time I come to England you're invited to come to the concert, free of course, and come back stage. I very much want to wish you the very best for the future—health, wealth and happiness." Michelle regained consciousness, and she was convinced that Roy's voice helped "pull me around." Her parents had also played "Oh, Pretty Woman" over and over, and both she and her folks said Roy's song raised her morale as she lay in the hospital.

About two years later, when Michelle was seventeen, Roy came to England on a concert tour and fulfilled his promise to her.

Roy thought of England as his "second home." He started his tour of one-nighters Saturday in Manchester. "We may do two or three nights in a club," he said, "but we'll consider them one-nighters." During the tour, a reporter quizzed Roy about an engagement he'd supposedly cancelled and Roy promptly corrected him. "No, I didn't cancel. I don't remember ever cancelling a show."

"I thought the Palladium thing perhaps didn't happen," the interviewer said.

"On a couple of occasions I've been announced to appear, but I didn't agree to appear. They announce that you'll appear, and then they sell tickets and make a lot of money, and then they offer you a lot of money, hoping you'll come and hoping you're not committed. And I wind up looking like a real bad old man, or mean man. But I don't ever remember cancelling any date, ever."

Roy was still performing "Hound Dog Man" as a permanent feature of his show. "It's sort of a dedication to my good buddy Elvis," Roy said. "We were very close for almost twenty years. It was just for him. It really wasn't meant to be heard. Naturally, it's a commercial thing to be sold, but what I mean is I don't mind if no one buys it. It's for Elvis. I saw Elvis in December before he died in August. We gave each other a big hug. He was solid as a rock and he looked good. His weight was down and we talked for two hours until he went on again. He was in fantastic shape."

Asked about what destroyed Elvis, Roy responded, "I think he was trapped and couldn't get out. Bad times happened later in his life than it did in mine. Plus, you have to be on your own in a way, even though you have others around you. You have to have some sort of inner strength. He was not being given good advice at all, toward the end, from what I hear."

Contrasting his obscurity in America with his British popularity, Roy said, "Everybody in the States says, 'You're real big in England, aren't you?'

"'Well,' I say, 'more or less.'

"I don't know what they mean by that, but one of the things they mean by that is I'm not very big in America. It just so happens that I'm currently as popular in America as I am in England. I've just done a humongous tour with a group called The Eagles, and that was terrific. We've got great plans for the future, for this summer, after the English trip."

The interviewer observed that Roy, Neil Sedaka and Gene Pitney were among the British people's favorite singers. "I don't try to analyze things too much because it will put you out of business, but it's due in part to the fact that I take the time and effort to come over to England and appear," Roy said. "A lot of artists don't. The few that do come will only come to London for two or three days and maybe some of the other larger cities. I've been coming steadily since '62, so that's eighteen years right there. So that's part of it too, and the writing aspect too, being a writer-singer, you can somehow sing a song that you write better than someone else can."

Back in the U.S., Roy learned that he was to be inducted into the Rock 'n' Roll Hall of Fame. To make it into the Hall of Fame, a singer must have cut his hit records twenty-five years before. The organization was founded by Ahmet Ertegun, who has been president of Atlantic Records and other companies. Members are selected by 300 voters in the music industry, and in 1986, the Hall of Fame's first year, Elvis Presley, Sam Phillips and Jerry Lee Lewis were honored. Roy was inducted at the organization's second annual dinner at the Waldorf-Astoria Hotel in New York on January 21, 1987.

Though Roy had yearned for this recognition from his peers, he had his doubts about the new foundation. "I didn't know if they were serious," Roy said. "I looked around, looked up in this big room at huge pictures of all the guys who were coming in. And I remember seeing some pictures of guys who weren't there, who couldn't be there because they were gone." Roy felt the pictures of Eddie Cochran and Jackie Wilson suddenly made the evening "dramatic and over-whelming" to him. He had toured with Eddie Cochran in the '50s, and Jackie Wilson's bel canto high notes in "Lonely Teardrops" and "(Your Love Keeps Lifting Me) Higher and Higher" had rivaled Roy's.

Bruce Springsteen stood at the podium, looking dapper in a tan suit and bolo tie. Bruce was at the peak of his fame. Like Roy, he was a survivor of the suicide machine; a '79 motorcycle accident had injured his leg and he'd been laid up for three months. Then came the '80s, the days of *Born in the USA,* "We Are the World," Julianne Phillips and all seven Springsteen LPs on the U.K. charts simultaneously.

Now, Roy was on the dais with Springsteen. Roy, though he was carrying too much weight, was elegantly dressed all in black but for a silver vest and a diamond Maltese cross at his throat. Bruce spoke words that would help cinch Roy's comeback, winding up his speech by saying, "I carry his records with me when I go on tour today . . . In '75, when I went into the studio to make *Born to Run,* I wanted to make a record with words like Bob Dylan that sounded like Phil Spector, but most of all I wanted to sing like Roy Orbison. Now everybody knows that nobody sings like Roy Orbison. Congratulations and thanks for the inspiration."

As Roy recalled later, "I got into the spirit of the thing. I was really cool until I had to stand on the side of the stage during Bruce's speech. He said so many nice things, I didn't know what in the world to say. But I took the speech from him. He had it written down, and I said, 'Can I take this speech.'"

Roy accepted his trophy, stood at the podium, smiled and lifted a nervous finger to his chin. "Thank you very much," he said. "I've spent thirty years trying to be cool and now I'm nervous and I have to go back to the restroom again. What a wonderful thing to honor people in rock 'n' roll. I'm really impressed. I think it's fantastic. All of us in the business sing for many reasons. One of them is to belong. I also want to thank Bruce—you can't follow that guy. I feel I truly belong."

Roy stepped away from the podium and shook hands with Bruce. Then he stood, beaming and savoring the honor. Although his first love and muse lay far away, buried in Nashville, she seemed present that night as the band began to play "Oh, Pretty Woman," the song that Claudette Frady had inspired.

Roy threw his arm around Bruce Springsteen in a warm embrace, then held his trophy high over his head and shook hands with Ahmet Ertegun. "If you're out on the road touring," Roy said later, "or in a case like after the Hall of Fame—it validated my career. It was a super night and it was a sort of coming together of past career and what we were doing at the time. It also brought me together with all these people and I actually saw Bruce and said hello to all the other people and they say well that's great, I'd like to have him and there are a lot of guys around who say, 'Let's get together and write a song.'"

Roy's voice had never left him, but what he'd needed ever since the end of the great MGM years in the '70s was material, *songs*. Soon, the biggest stars in the business, guys like Bono, The Edge, George Harrison, Tom Petty, Jeff Lynne and Elvis Costello, would offer their best to Roy.

Roy was suddenly in demand as a guest on television network talk shows. Host Joan Rivers annoyed him when she asked him to remove his sun glasses on camera. He gave her a flat no, flubbed his next few lines and scolded her for making him nervous. Chastened, she reversed her strategy and flattered Roy with cloying and inaccurate compliments, saying "You're so cute, so warm, so adorable." Roy said nothing, waiting for her to compose herself. Finally she chirped, "Do you know your music was in the movie *Blue Velvet?* Did you like it?"

"They're beating people up to this pretty song," Roy said. "I didn't quite understand it."

When Roy went on *The Tonight Show,* guest host Jay Leno asked him about the many rumors that had been floating around. "I heard you were killed with Beaver in 'Nam, that you were blind, that you're a recluse and never go out, wear black—"

Roy cut in and said, "Yeah, and I beat my wife."

He appeared on the show with Canadian country singer k.d. lang. She and Roy contributed a song, "Crying," to the soundtrack of an otherwise undistinguished film called *Hiding Out,* and they repeated it for Jay Leno. Roy had done some beautiful duets in his time, like the one with Emmylou Harris, but the Orbison/lang "Crying" stands out as the best. Two powerful, emotion-packed voices soaring together, Orbison and lang could raise goosebumps on a stone. If Roy was the Caruso of rock, as he was often called, then k.d. lang was the Maria Callas of country music. "They asked me if I wanted to do a duet of 'Crying,'" Roy told Jay Leno. "I was trying to work it out in my mind. I wasn't doing too well until I heard the tape. k.d. and I met at the recording session, and worked in Boston and Toronto."

Reporter Malcolm Boyes stood in for host Robin Leach in January 1987 when Roy appeared on a segment for *Life Styles of the Rich and Famous* at his new home in Malibu. Boyes said Roy could now "retire in luxury from his hits," and Roy was shown next to one of his guitars that had been enshrined at The Hard Rock Cafe. "His new home is decorated with priceless antiques," Boyes said. "The driveway is filled with the finest exotic cars from Europe and America. The

California lifestyle suits them perfectly." Coming on camera, Barbara said, "When you drive up to this place you feel like you live in the country. It's real peaceful. You're away from everything and the air is wonderful."

As R.K. and Alex played tennis, Roy and Barbara strolled through a flower garden, with the blue Pacific in the distance, and then sat down together and watched their healthy kids at play. While many segments of *Life Styles* are brassy displays of excess that invoke feelings of loathing or envy in the viewer, the segment on Roy and his family stirred other emotions. They appeared to be loving people who knew how to treat each other well.

"I was in the business before it was fashionable to be rowdy," Roy said. "I wasn't much of a drinker but pretty much of a rabble-rouser. A triple bypass came out of that and I was working ninety days after that to prove that I could work."

As usual when he spoke of alcohol or drugs, Roy contradicted himself, in one breath saying he was so much of a rabble-rouser that he drove himself to a triple bypass and in the next claiming he'd avoided addictions.

The scene shifted from Malibu to downtown Beverly Hills, where Roy looked chic, strolling along Rodeo Drive in his black leather jacket with fashionably padded shoulders. As a middle-aged man in dark glasses and dyed hair, obviously trying to appear younger than his years, he blended in perfectly with the compulsive youth-seekers of Beverly Hills. The only mystery was that it had taken him so long to get to California.

In concluding the show, Malcolm Boyes said, "Roy is looking forward to rocking into a ripe old age."

Roy's most engaging TV appearance was on *Portrait of a Legend,* a show co-produced by Maria Shriver and hosted by James Darren, a '60s teen idol who was born the same year as Roy, 1936. As a wistful string instrumental version of "Blue Bayou" played in the background, Roy told the story of his life.

James Darren said Roy had found "quick and early success in Nashville," and Roy corrected him. "To be perfectly honest, when I came to Nashville I didn't do very well after the success of 'Claudette' by the Everlys. I was writing songs and not doing very well. I moved back to Texas and kept writing songs and started recording and not much happened until 1959, which coincided with some kind of payola scandal with the government. All of a sudden there were a lot of new people heard on the air for some unknown reason and I was one of them. 'Uptown' went to about #40 or #30 and 'Only the Lonely' went to #1 in the spring of '60. That began twenty-seven or twenty-eight hits in a row."

Roy was revising history rather drastically. "Only the Lonely" never went to #1 in the U.S. and 'Uptown' never made the Top 40. Though Roy was in the process of a slow comeback in the 1980s, he was still looking behind him, embroidering his legend, or looking forward to grandiose dreams. He revealed that in his fifties he was just as ambitious as he'd been when he'd first started out as a young singer.

James Darren closed the show by saying, "While the musical world changed and passed Roy Orbison by, after two decades music caught up with him again, renewing his status as a legend."

True, but Roy lacked the vitality of someone living his life fully in the present. It took success to make him feel alive, but, ironically, he had never been able to handle success well. For him and for everyone around him, the limelight was lethal. That had been true in the past and it would prove to be true in the future. He liked extremes, whether it was an audience cheering him, speeding on a motorcycle or doing $700 worth of cocaine in one night.

Chapter 11

Roy Orbison's life had little continuity—it was a series of intense involvements and abrupt terminations. Though he said he felt Wink was his home from the moment he set foot there, he was so ashamed of it when he got famous that he said he came from Odessa. The friends of his youth were dropped as soon as they were no longer useful to him. Starved for love, he won Claudette, but promptly left her for a life on the road. When Claudette died, he virtually ignored her family, and they were deeply hurt by his silence. He left three small children with their grandparents and went carousing in London; two of the children died.

In 1987, Roy gradually began to put all the scattered pieces of his life back together again. Some instinct seemed to tell him to go back through is past and make amends, it was time for Roy to go home to Texas. As late as the 1980s, he was still speaking bitterly of the macho boneheads who's called him degrading names and made his adolescence miserable, but in 1987 he felt an urge to set matters straight between him and his native state. When Texans, depressed from the oil crunch, appealed to Roy forhelp, he came home to perform in the Oil-Aid Concert/Midland/Odessa, a benefit for the economically depressed Permian Basin. Though both cities had been devastated by the oil slump, Roy charged them a fee of $12,500 for his services. He was understandably wary of returning to the state where he had suffered emotional injuries, and several days before the concert, he took a dismissing tone in a telephone interview from his studio in Los Angeles. "Actually, it was good for me to have grown up in West Texas, because I wasn't caught up in any musical influence," he said. "Except for Bob Wills' western swing, there wasn't any musical influence. So when rock came along, I was ready for it."

Arriving in Texas on April 24, Roy continued to make disparaging remarks about Texas, telling *The Odessa American* that the state was "a little out of the way." The promoter, Dennis Grubb, and his five partners had closed their drilling company in 1986 because business had dried up. The concert was organized to raise money for the unemployed white-collar class. "Everybody talks about the poor oil-field workers, the roughneck," said Grubb, "but what about the geologists who are mowing lawns and sacking groceries?" Keith Briscoe wrote in *The Odessa American:*

> Rock legend Roy Orbison had a small but enthusiastic crowd on its feet for most of his hour-long oil-aid concert Saturday night at the Chaparral Center in a rare return to West Texas. The Rock 'n' Roll Hall of Famer from Wink won standing ovations for his hallmark hits "Only the Lonely," "Ooby Dooby," "Crying," "Pretty Woman" and "Running Scared." He stuck to his classics, backed up by synthesizer, hard percussion and female vocals.

After the concert, some of Roy's friends from Wink wanted to visit with him. Bill and Margaret Beckham had driven over with Barbara and Ronnie Slaughter, Kathryn Crawford and her mother Mary Mangrum. "We went backstage," Bill Beckham said, "and a guy's standing there guarding the door. I went up to him and said, 'We'd like to visit old Roy. We went to school with him.'

"And the guy said, 'Yeah, you and 10,000 more.' And I said, 'Well, you go back there and tell him my name and see what he says.'

"So he did, and here come old Roy, saying, 'Well, hello. It's good to see you.'"

Keith Briscoe observed the reunion and wrote, "Belying his superstar status Orbison was modest and mild-mannered backstage as he greeted the entourage from Wink. He autographed the 1954 Wink High School annual toted by Olivia Sturdivant of Midland, gave a big grabbing hug to former school chum Ron Slaughter of Wink and traded faded memories with Shirley Hill of Monahans. After posing for a group picture with the faithful from Wink, he seemed genuinely humble."

"It's good to be back in West Texas," Roy said to Ronnie. "You need to be reminded of your roots." Then he posed for a photo with Ronnie, Mary Mangrum, Kathryn Crowford, Barbara Slaughter and Margaret and Bill Beckham. Briscoe wrote, "Local fans were delighted to find that, despite fame, fortune and tragedy, the rock star was 'the same old Roy' many of them had known as classmates at Wink High School in the Fabulous Fifties."

Mary Mangrum of Kermit said, "He kissed us, remembered us by name." Kat Crawford recalled, "I was standing next to Roy and said, 'Do you know that Bobby D., my husband, passed away?'

"'Yes,' he said, 'Caddie Heasley told me in Houston.'

"'That's Bobby D.'s old girl friend, Roy,' I said, and I gave him a pinch and said, 'What was she doin' tellin' you?'"

To the people of Wink, Roy Orbison was still Facetus. Mildred Howard, Roy's seventh-grade music teacher, admitted, "I never dreamed he would do anything." Ed Costello of KOSA said, "I don't think anybody thought he was that big at the time." J.L. Dodd, Roy's high school teacher, now principal of Wink High, related, "To us, Roy is just a hometown boy who made it big. Around here, we only care about the person, not whether he's rich or poor or famous."

After returning to California, Roy said, "That's the way the people are out there. I'm sure they think of me as just a good ol' boy. But I always thought the best thing to come out of Wink was me and the 1952 state championship football team." Though Roy *professed* humility, modesty was never one of his virtues.

After eight years without a label, Roy at last landed a new recording contract. *Blue Velvet* convinced Jeff Ayeroff and Jordan Harris, co-managing directors of Virgin Records, to sign Roy. Virgin was a Beverly Hills outfit specializing in young stars like Paula Abdul, and both Ayeroff and Harris had wanted Roy when they'd been at A&M Records in 1981 but their bosses had said Roy was passe´ and would never score a comeback. "Roy was unique," Ayeroff said, "and I thought he could be part of this era, too. There is something timeless about his voice and his music. When I saw *Blue Velvet* at the Paramount in Hollywood, I started thinking the movie made Roy's music current again. I have absolute respect for David Lynch and if he sees the same thing in Roy's music, I knew I was on the right track." Ayeroff and Harris put Roy together with T Bone Burnett, who had worked with Los Lobos, Elvis Costello and the BoDeans, and on April 23, 1987, Roy's fifty-first birthday, he re-recorded "In Dreams" at Oceanways Studios in Los Angeles. The two-record album, *In Dreams: The Greatest Hits,* was issued May 18, 1987. The original master tapes were unobtainable from Monument Records.

"We did all the songs in one take, concert style, with no overdubs," Roy said. "Virgin heard them and wanted to put them out. It was like playing the songs one more time, after touring all this time, which I'm always happy to do. As much as I was tempted to do more polished versions of the songs, we tried to get the same sound and feeling as best we could. I didn't want people to be confused about the two versions, but I didn't want them to hear something that wasn't on the original."

Though the album's title song was produced by Roy, David Lynch and T Bone Burnett, Barbara Orbison took top billing as executive producer of the LP. Roy's producer credit appeared underneath Barbara's and was set in smaller type, but Roy got his crack at grandiosity on the album cover. The photographic collage by Dean Chamberlain shows a sexy man in a black leather jacket standing on a bluff overlooking the lights of L.A. A beautiful woman lies at his feet, like an adoring, willing slave. In front of them is a red convertible with big tailfins, and a record player is perched on the trunk, with discs scattered around it. Beside the car is a home movie screen showing Roy in front of a mirror, and a songbird is perched on his finger. Ironically, it is Roy the singer/poet, the real Roy, who is on the screen while the cool-cat fantasy figures are represented as being in the real world. Clouds swirl around the entire collage, mixing dream and reality, just as they were mixed in Roy's consciousness.

When Roy went to Nashville to promote the album before a convention group, Ayeroff said, "People were so excited that they were standing on their chairs. Who else ever had a voice like his?" A reporter covering the event wrote that Roy "revealed a still supple voice, capable of hitting in full-voice every operatic note he did twenty-five years ago. As odd as it sounds, last week's private show was Roy Orbison's first Nashville concert. 'It's not that I have any bitterness or anything about Nashville,' Roy said. 'For years I didn't pay as much attention to anyplace in the U.S. as maybe I should have. I didn't play Chicago until 1979, didn't play Los Angeles until the '80s.'"

Roy sounded small and constricted on the album, though, and *In Dreams* proved not to be the comeback record he'd hoped for. Nor did his next movie soundtrack assignment, for *Less Than Zero,* bring him any attention. Though a critical and box-office disappointment, it was an elegantly shot film, based on Brett Easton Ellis' novel about a group of affluent young people destroying themselves with drugs in 1980s L.A. In the movie's final scene, as Robert Downey Jr. lays his head on Andrew McCarthy's shoulder and dies of an overdose, Roy sings "Life Fades Away" with poignant, chilling eloquence. He wrote this new song with George Danzig, a man in his early thirties who looked like a Hell's Angel. "He told us a lot of cool Elvis and Beatles stories," Danzig said in *Pulse* magazine in 1988. With this one song, Danzig joined the pantheon of distinguished Orbison collaborators, on the same level with Bill Dees and Joe Melson.

Roy had a shrewd publicist at Virgin Records named Sarah McMullen, and her efforts to focus media attention on Roy began to pay off. "There was a lot of interest in Roy," she said, "but also a lot of misconceptions. A lot of people thought he was blind because of the dark glasses. They thought his first wife had just died. It was as if time had stood still. So we got writers out to his shows to meet him. More than anything, they came away talking about his voice. They didn't think of him as a '60s act anymore."

When people asked if Roy was blind, as thousands frequently did, Sarah answered, "No, he's not blind, he just wears glasses. As a matter of fact, in a *Rich and Famous* TV show, he was seen tossing the ball back and forth with his sons. He said, 'Maybe if people see me catching the ball, they'll stop thinking I'm blind.'"

On May 22, 1987, Roy appeared on *Saturday Night Live,* and the host that night was Dennis Hopper, star of *Blue Velvet.* Producer Lorne Michaels liked Roy so much he asked him to sing three songs instead of the show's usual two. "Roy still has the three octaves he always had," said *SNL* publicist Jeb Baird. "He just knocked Lorne Michaels out."

On August 14, 1987, Roy began to tour the U.S. at a breakneck pace. In a little over two weeks, August 14–September 4, he played the Paul Masson Winery in Saratoga, California; the Landmark Theatre in Syracuse, New York; the Melody Fair in North Tonawanda, New York; the Coliseum Theatre in Latham, New York; the South Shore Music Circus in Cohasset, Massachusetts; the Oakdale Music Theatre in Wallingford, Connecticut; the Temple Civic Center in Rochester, New York; the Music Theatre in Warwick, Rhode Island; the Club Casino in Hampton, New Hampshire; the Cape Cod Melody Tent in Hyannis, Massachusetts; and the Hilton Ballroom in Eugene, Oregon.

"The audience sang along with every song," wrote critic Lucy Shepherd. "Some people were moved to tears as he hit a high note and sustained it for longer than singers half his age ever could. It's a too short set which began after 9:00 p.m. with 'Only the Lonely.' His stage presence is haunting."

Roy's opening act was two country singers named Foster and Lloyd. Joking with a reporter after the show, Radney Foster said, "We were called to open for this man—I can't recall his name, but he's certainly going places." Bill Lloyd told Michael McCall of *The Nashville Banner*, "Opening for him was really our first road gig as a band. We were too nervous to try to talk to him, at first, but we approached him after the third show. He was as nice as he could be."

Lloyd asked Roy to autograph an old single that had "Crying" and "Candy Man" on its two sides. As Roy signed he told the young singer that he was in a fine tradition of people who'd opened for Roy Orbison, mentioning The Beatles. "He told us, 'Now don't you do what The Beatles did to me,'" Lloyd said. "That's the sort of kind thing he would say. He was very gracious."

David Zimmerman wrote in *USA Today*, "The three-octave voice endures, tingling and re-tingling new and middle-aged spines. He still has 'all the high notes,' which means on a good night he can nail high C in full voice, 'and I don't know how high I can go in the falsetto. When the voice is there and right and I don't have to think about it, it's wonderful—like playing a fine instrument.'"

In September, Roy taped an all-star tribute for Cinemax at The Coconut Grove in Los Angeles' Ambassador Hotel. "We were planning on doing a cable special for a long, long time," Roy said. "Barbara was the driving force in making the Cinemax special a reality. T Bone Burnett was also involved."

As a video, it was released by Virgin Records under the title *Roy Orbison and Friends: A Black and White Night*, so named for its moody black-and-white cinematography. Issued in May 1988, the HBO videocassette sold a healthy 50,000 copies. The musical director and presiding genius of the star-studded event was T Bone Burnett. He had figured importantly in Bob Dylan's life and now he would contribute significantly to an artistic high point in Roy Orbison's. J. Henry Burnett was born in St. Louis and came to Fort Worth when he was five. In his teens, he worked in the Fort Worth studio where "greaser hits" like "Hey Paula" were recorded. He was involved with Bob Dylan's Rolling Thunder Revenue in 1975 and was instrumental in Dylan's conversion to Christianity. Later, he recorded albums that were so good *Rolling Stone* called T Bone the best songwriter in America. T Bone assisted David Lynch on Roy's *In Dreams* LP, and thanks to this unusual, gifted and spiritually supercharged man, Roy's Cinemax special had a look and sound that inspired and enriched everyone who saw it.

How Bruce Springsteen happened to show up on the program was typical of the miraculous event *Black and White Night* turned out to be. The staff of Home Box Office, the cable network that owned Cinemax, had no idea Springsteen was going to be on the show until he strolled into rehearsals on September 29, 1987, for the following night's live taping. Bruce performed "Dream Baby" with Roy, and co-producer Betty Bitterman said, "You should have seen the look on Bruce's face when he watched Roy sing."

"We had a rehearsal and Bruce had obviously taken the chord sheets home and practiced," Roy recalled. "As we went on stage Bruce said, 'Should I be nervous?' I said, 'No. I'll take care of that.' It was terrific to look around and see Bruce playing guitar and Elvis Costello doing his bit. I really loved every moment of it."

The only country singer Roy asked to participate was k.d. lang. She sang background vocals with Jennifer Warnes and Bonnie Raitt, and the backup male vocalists were Jackson Browne, J.D. Souther and Steven Soles. Few who saw the show would ever forget the sweet sound that came out of this sextet when they sailed into the opening strains of "Only the Lonely." Among the session men were Bruce Springsteen, Elvis Costello, Tom Waits and Glen D. Hardin. With this lineup, Roy's special turned into one of rock's finest hours, as uniquely exciting as Elvis' Singer Special or the "We Are the World" video.

Roy had to push Tom Waits on stage because Tom felt he wasn't as big a star as the others on the special. "Tom's a wonderful character," Roy said, "an absolutely magical child and personality. You kinda have to say, 'Come on, Tom!' and he'll smile and say, 'Okay.' It wasn't that he wasn't of the same calibre because he was. Bruce Springsteen and I were going to do a duet and he said, 'You'll have to invite me up. I'm not going to get up on stage and sing with you without being invited.' So I had to motion for him to come up. I think it's respect." "Ooby Dooby" was the evening's surprise, with most of the virtuoso musicians on stage taking a solo turn, and eventually Roy looking at Tom, who was on keyboards, and saying, "Your turn!" Tom went wild at the organ, and though his moment was brief, it was electrifying. After playing a few notes he stopped, and Roy looked at him, puzzled and a little shocked. "There again," Roy recalled, "a magical personality like that will do what he wants to and that's great. Everybody should. What Tom was doing fitted but I think everyone was a little startled. He is quite a startling person."

With Elvis Costello's spectacular keyboard work on "Down the Line," James Burton and Bruce Springsteen's virtuoso guitar duet in "Oh, Pretty Woman," Springsteen's flawless harmonizing with Roy in "Uptown," and k.d. lang's "sha-la-la's" on "Mean Woman Blues," the evening became a jam session of superstars.

Looking around the audience, which included Leonard Cohen, Rebecca DeMornay, Dennis Quaid, Harry Dean Stanton, Patrick Swayze and Billy Idol, Roy said, according to *People* magazine, "There was a time in the '70s when I wondered if people still cared about my music at all."

After the show, Roy asked his musical guests to join him in a room backstage. Crammed in the small space were lang, Springsteen, Costello, Browne, Waits, Burnett, Raitt, Souther and Warnes. Roy thanked them for taking time from their busy careers to help him. k.d. lang recalled, "Roy looked at all of us and said, 'If there is anything I can ever do for you, please call on me.' He was very serious. It was his way of thanking us. It was very emotional."

Discussing this special, Roy said, "The thing was to see these guys working so hard as musicians, as opposed to being frontmen. Bruce Springsteen is a solo type of singer. He's a wonderful person to work with. I was expecting someone like him to be a little difficult, but he was great. Some artists that I have worked with who are lesser-known have been much more difficult to work with. Anyway, nobody brought any attitude problems with them. They left their egos at the door. When everyone got settled in you could see how much energy was drawn from each other. Real professionalism. They've all got road experience and I'm just grateful we captured this moment on film. And would you believe we did it all in one take! We just prayed that there'd be no mistakes. The idea was to just do it and get it right the first time. Bottom line is we got lucky!"

A freak accident almost destroyed the original Cinemax print before anyone had a chance to see it. One of California's big earthquakes struck just as the show was completed, and a chandelier fell on the tape. "With all the mess from the earthquake," Roy said, "we couldn't find the tape for more than 24 hours. If that tape had been destroyed, I would have been singing an extended version of 'Crying.' We could never have gotten all those guys together again."

Glowing reviews began to appear. In December 1987, *The Houston Chronicle's* Bruce Westbrook wrote, "Orbison anchors the band like a seasoned veteran with strong and steady professionalism." *The Boston Globe's* reviewer didn't care for Bruce Springsteen's attempt to harmonize with Roy on "Dream Baby" and "Uptown." "Springsteen was tripped up by his shyness and sounds gruff and clumsy, trying to mesh with Orbison's glassy smooth voice," he wrote. "He would hardly seem the stadium superstar that he is but his ordinariness is actually endearing in this context...Who wouldn't be petrified to harmonize with Roy Orbison? The man has the voice of an angel...Roy's boyish roly-poly face dominates the camera...amid a new soft focus, soft fade lighting he looks almost like a floating spirit. The effect is to put the viewer in a trance which further heightens the romantic suggestion of such tear-stained ballads as 'Crying' and 'In Dreams.'" *The Nashville Tennessean's* critic wrote, "His songs are melodically and rhythmically advanced and lyrically sophisticated, majestically arranged...Just one of his tunes, 'Oh, Pretty Woman,' anticipates the guitar figure of The Beatles's 'Day Tripper.'"

Some of the people who'd worked with Roy on the special discussed the show with reporters, and for all of them it had been a memorable experience. Bruce Springsteen said, "When he sings it is happening in the present. He's not doing an oldies tune. Totally modern. It's happening *now* because emotionally it's happening for him now. Whenever he sings that stuff, he closes his eyes and wherever he goes that's where it's at." J.D. Souther said, "The first single I ever bought was 'Ooby Dooby' and I've been trying to sing like that guy ever since. He's got this unbelievable operatic rock 'n' roll voice."

Now that his career was in high gear again, he relished getting all the work he could handle. On October 15, he played the Valley Forge Music Fair with Carl Perkins. Also in October he was inducted into The Nashville Songwriters Hall of Fame and soon afterwards went to New Orleans to open a new franchise for the Hard Rock Cafe. For a survivor of triple bypass surgery such hyperactivity was suicidal, but

Roy's thirst for attention was insatiable. "I'm feeling accepted and loved," he told David Hinckley of the New York *Daily News*.

He continued to patch up old relationships, calling Joe Melson in Hendersonville and suggesting they write some songs together. Roy was calling from Malibu, and Joe told him to come visit him and his family the next time he was in Tennessee. "He wanted to write," Joe recalled in 1989. "I started thinking what would be good, knowing we would be back together. I started some that had the markings of the way we wrote and possibly one could have been the magic number. We were corresponding and I was sending tapes to California and working with him. Then he came here in '87 and visited my home." Joe says he and Roy started working on several songs, and it was just like old times again.

Bobby Blackburn was another old friend Roy kept in touch with, and Roy's thoughtfulness during Bobby's health crisis demonstrates that Roy was capable of deep and abiding friendship. In January 1988, Bobby suffered a severe stroke that left him permanently disabled and confined to a wheelchair. After his stroke, Bobby called him from his hospital bed in Bakersfield, California. "Roy was magnificent," Bobby said. "He called me three or four times a day for the next three weeks. He was in New York City, and he and I had a thing about the news sign on the Times Tower in Times Square. We'd seen it as kids in World War II newsreels and were real impressed when the news would come rolling around that building in flashing lights. 'Well,' Roy said, 'I'm here in the hotel room reading the ticker on the Times building. It says "HARD ROCK CAFE TRIBUTE TO ROY ORBISON SOLD OUT."'

" 'Well,' I said, 'that can't be bad.'

" 'I'm having lunch today with Billy Joel and Christie Brinkley.'

" 'Well, enough about me, Roy! How are you doin'?' Later, Roy came to Englewood, California, where I was at a rehabilitation center for stroke victims. I remember he smoked all my cigarettes, and you can't get cigarettes in the hospital any more. When we went to the cafeteria, I said, 'Smoking or nonsmoking?'

" 'Smoking if they got one,' Roy replied. 'You got some cigarettes, haven't you?' I had four or five, and that son-of-a-bitch sat there and smoked every one of my Camels!" Bobby remembers that he and Roy talked that day about the deadpeckers, the old men who'd sat on the benches in Wink when Roy and Bobby had been kids. "Our goal had been to be deadpeckers together and talk about the good old days,"

Bobby said. Now, that goal had been reached, except that they weren't sitting on benches in Wink but in a stroke rehabilitation center, and Bobby was in a wheelchair and Roy was a triple bypass survivor. Despite this tenuous hold on life, they sat enjoying the last of Bobby's Camel Straights. Over the years, besides Lucky Strike Greens and Camels, Roy had also smoked Gauloise and Sherman. "Shermans impressed Roy," Bobby recalled. "They're from The Sherman Smoke Shop on Fifth Avenue, and you put them down and they go out. They were three dollars for ten back in the '60s. They were mild unfiltered with no additives and no chemicals." It was truly amazing that neither Roy nor Bobby had ever graduated to filtered cigarettes, but at this late date, after the strokes and the heart attacks, perhaps it no longer mattered.

In February 1988, Roy was in New York to play at the Beacon Theatre on Upper Broadway but had to cancel due to illness. A week later, he and Bob Seger were presenters on the Grammy Awards and he still sounded and looked as if he had the flu. He finally played The Beacon in March. "He was great," said fan Robert Burroughs. "As usual, the highlight was 'Crying,' which brought the audience to its feet. He reprised the last half but wouldn't do it a third time despite continuing applause." Roy also filmed a walk-on performance in the movie *She's Having a Baby*. At the conclusion of the film Roy and other celebrities came on screen and suggested names for the couple's first baby. The soft and caressing way he uttered "Orbie Lee" made it sound like the most desirable thing any baby could be called. As Roy emerged from the film studio on February 21, he was interviewed by David Hinckley from the *Daily News*. Ironically referring to his tiny walk-on performance, Roy said, "I wonder if this movie will make me a star?" In Roy's estimation, he had never stopped being a star, and he resented it every time a reporter referred to his "comeback." "I never left," Roy said. "I've done my roadwork all along. I've seen with other artists that if you take off for even a year or two, it shows. To me, that's the difference between performers who just do it for a while and the ones who picked up guitars as teenagers and never put 'em down." Roy wanted it clearly understood that he belonged to the latter group. It was true that he had probably spent more of his life on the road than with his family, but for years he'd been perceived as a has-been. He hadn't been a recording star for decades and still wasn't. In the 1970s, he didn't have any significant gigs in America, where his name wouldn't draw enough people to fill up a lounge. Yet he persisted in denying the calamities that had brought about his downfall in late '60s, and he regularly informed reporters that he didn't need a comeback. Roy's pride blinded him to the truth, and soon it was evident to the press that he was kidding himself.

Visiting with Roy that day, Hinckley found him "frustrated but philosophical." Roy was already working on his comeback LP *Mystery Girl,* and he explained that he was so busy he'd had to delay the release date. "Actually," Roy admitted, "it's good that all the rest has happened, because when it comes out, it will just be my new record, not a 'comeback.'" Nothing, of course could have been farther from the truth.

Roy's Beacon Theatre performance capitivated critic Matthew Auerback, who wrote in the *Daily News,* "Roy Orbison's talents are more than intact. He proved it at The Beacon Saturday. But before we go any further, let's talk about that voice. I tell you, folks, it's better than ever. I mean, he had no right hitting some of those notes twenty-five years ago, but on songs like 'Crying,' 'Running Scared' and 'Leah,' he shook the place....By the opening notes of 'Oh, Pretty Woman,' the crowd was on its feet, letting this incredible singer know how good he sounded and made us feel."

Returning to Malibu after a tour in Colorado, Roy went back to work on *Mystery Girl.* On April 9 he confided to a reporter from *The Tennessean* about some difficulties he was having with his collaborators. "With some people," Roy said, "because of who they are, I expect that we'll be writing a rock 'n' roll tune and it turns out that they have more of a Roy Orbison-type ballad in mind. Lately though we're just writing *songs,* which I prefer—not trying to imitate anything in particular from the past. And nobody dominates the writing session, just whichever of us has the hot idea at the moment."

Roy's distinguished collaborators for *Mystery Girl* included Bono of U2, whom Roy met at a concert in London. After the concert, Roy went backstage to compliment the performance, and when Bono saw him he jumped up and said, "I can't believe that you are here. I listened last night all night long for the first time in my life to 'In Dreams' over and over and over again." Picking up his guitar, Bono continued, "I'm writing a song for you. It's called 'She's a Mystery to Me.'"

Bono and Roy were enchanted with one another. "He was a bit of a magician," Bono said. "He was as gentle and wise and as mysterious as his voice. I felt completely out of my depth in writing a song for him."

Barbara Orbison, who was with Roy and Bono that night, later recalled, "They worked that night and then they got together again and again."

"We got together at the Grammy Awards in January in New York," Roy said. "And then when he came out to do *Rattle and Hum* in Los Angeles, he would come to the house and we'd work a little bit. Then Bono found enough time between records to come out and play guitar on the session and also produce it. He came down and sang the song for the musicians and then went in and started playing and it was all done like we were in concert. He played guitar and then came in for the mixing too."

Describing the same session, Bono said, "When Roy went to sing the song in the studio, I stood beside him and sang with him. He didn't seem to be singing. So I thought, 'He'll sing it the next take. He's just reading the words.' And then we went in to listen to the take, and there was this voice, which was the loudest whisper I've ever heard. He had been singing it. But he hardly moved his lips. And the voice was louder than the band in its own way. I don't know how he did that. It was like sleight of hand."

"She's a Mystery to Me" brought a new relevance and depth to the art of Roy Orbison. Written by Paul Hewson (Bono) and David Evans (The Edge), the song took Roy beyond the heartbreak and self-pity of "In Dreams" into exciting new territory. Like "In Dreams," it is about a man who falls asleep and encounters a beautiful woman who puts a spell on him. He is blinded by love, helpless and confused. The song presents obsessive romantic love as the nightmare it is. Blood, enslavement, violence, hauntings, visitations—the language of "She's a Mystery to Me" had never before appeared in an Orbison song.

Though Roy would revert to people-pleasing in "You Got It," promising his girl anything she wanted, "She's a Mystery to Me" lays bare the true nature of destructive relationships and eschews Roy's customary sentimentality. Thanks to Bono and The Edge, at last Roy achieved a contemporaneous sound and was steered clear of self-pity.

Just as Roy had refused David Lynch permission to use "In Dreams" in *Blue Velvet,* by his own admission he tried to prevent his *Mystery Girl* songwriters from turning out "Roy Orbison-type songs" for him, so his growth on this album was accomplished against his will. But at last, encouraged and even pressured by artists like Bono and Elvis Costello, Roy explored new territory, gaining deeper musical and psychological insights. "Elvis Costello and I were doing the same thing that Bono and I were doing," Roy said. "He's sending me a tape and I'm sending it back to him. It was a big undertaking, just to get everything together. Then, Bono would come in and say, 'Here's what we do.' 'I'm in the process of relearning,' Bono said. 'I'm a better singer for having heard you sing.'

"'I'm a better producer for watching you produce,' I said. And we both meant it. I've learned a lot from working and writing with these guys."

Besides Bono and Elvis Costello, "these guys" were Tom Petty, Jeff Lynne, Mike Campbell, Steve Cropper, Steve Jones, Will Jennings and T Bone Burnett. "These days you don't just go for the big names," Roy said, "but you go for the talent. Bob Dylan and I have started writing a song that I want to finish and Bruce Springsteen and I have worked on a song and Bono has written and produced a song for me on the new album. Steve Cropper is playing on the new album too. I just called him up and asked him and he was happy to do it. These days it's a delight. You just call a guy up for his talent and the love you have for him as opposed to the name and they'll say sure I'll play. They claim that I was some kind of inspiration to them, which was great. I really appreciated that. I could say the same thing about them because I enjoy their work too. It's like a feeling that musicians are a family and like a family institution we can fuss a little bit between us but not to anybody outside. Jeff claims I'm his favorite singer which doesn't hurt because he's a fabulous producer if not my favorite."

Jeff Lynne was the mastermind behind the innovative sounds The Electric Light Orchestra made on mysterious and lushly orchestrated hit records such as "Evil Woman," "Can't Get It Out of My Head," "Turn to Stone," "Telephone Line" and "Strange Magic." Referring to Roy and Jeff, Barbara Orbison said, "They had a bond that went beyond bonds."

In the mid-1980s, Jeff, who lived in his native England, made a telephone call to Roy, then still living in Tennessee. They met in Hendersonville later and began to write songs. "I left and came back to L.A.," Jeff said. "Then I heard nothing from him for a year. And then he phoned me and said, 'Oh, I've just moved to Malibu. Can we get together again and finish up those bits, or try some new bits?' We never actually got together and wrote anything just then, but about six months after that, we started to think about *The Traveling Wilburys*.

And that was going on at the same time as I was producing what would become the three tracks I did on Roy's album *[Mystery Girl]*."

In the middle of making *Mystery Girl*, the opportunity came up to work with Jeff, Tom Petty, George Harrison and Bob Dylan on *The Traveling Wilburys, Vol. I*. With these two great albums in the offing, Roy stood at the threshhold of the most exciting phase of his career. After a long, dry period that extended over three decades, he was about to spring not one, but two smash LPs on the world, as well as two hit singles. Getting out of Nashville, the scene of his protracted fallow period, and into the creative rock community around L.A. and Malibu proved to be the most important action of his life. A visit Roy made to Joe Towe's garage in Hendersonville just before moving to California sheds light on the changes that were taking place in Roy in the '80s, changes that led to the renewal of his career and his life.

"I'm tired right now," he told Joe. "I'll get to trying' something soon. I'll get motivated in Malibu."

Interviewed in 1989, Joe said, "He was burnt out. He told me he was going to 'go fishing for a while, go to a car show and get wound up again, get out there with some songwriters and entertainers.'"

Roy found the motivation and the energy he was looking for in California, and he wrote a serene, nostalgic salute to his new home state called "California Blue." His collaborators on this *Mystery Girl* cut were Jeff Lynne and Tom Petty. Praising these new friends he found in California, Roy said, "It has increased my enthusiasm and taught me a lot. When you get busy as a professional, a lot of things you already know can fall away somehow. If you haven't written for a good while there are certain things that you must do for the song to be given to you because I believe that songs are gifts and you have to be prepared and work a few days and get ready for it. I am an intuitive sort of fellow and when I start recording I go in and say, 'Okay, what do we want to do now?'"

Elvis Costello contributed a song on *Mystery Girl* called "The Comedians," and it was Elvis' effort to create a stunningly contemporary version of a Roy Orbison song. "The Comedians" is to Roy's "Running Scared" what Bono's "She's a Mystery to Me" is to "In Dreams." In "the Comedians," Costello takes the kind of romantic love Roy used to weep over and satirizes it mercilessly. Rarely has a pop songwriter so powerfully exposed the romantic fallacy of surrendering control of one's life and feelings to another human being. The song gives Roy his best vocal workout on the album.

Discussing Elvis Costello and "The Comedians," Roy said, "He's a terrifically hard worker. Just all business. We had some fun too but he's very serious about it. If he was going to play rhythm guitar then he would play it correctly. Elvis had written this song before and then he spoke to Bruce Springsteen and they discussed me and how and what I would sing and then he rewrote it for me and the song's about a guy who's running the machine—ferris wheel—stops it at the top and runs off with the girl. It's about a relationship in general."

Surprised by Roy's choice of material, an interviewer asked him, "Does this story appeal to you?"

"Sure," Roy replied, "and Elvis wrote it with great care and a lot of love and you can tell that. As a performer I write most of my songs but not always. I did not write 'Dream Baby,' 'Mean Woman Blues' and 'Candy Man.' But when they're right you can tell." Roy's reply to the reporter's question appears both evasive and rambling, hinting that he was incapable of grasping or expounding on the subtleties in the Costello text. It was a long way from the simplistic self-pity of his old songs, like "Only the Lonely," to the sophisticated self-awareness of "The Comedians."

"The Only One," another of the album's subtle, original songs, was written by Wesley Orbison, in collaboration with Craig Wiseman. It's an acerbic view of romance and the intense self-involvement of a brokenhearted man. Perhaps Wesley had heard enough self-pity in his father's songs over the years and decided to make this rueful commentary on love. The songwriting team of Wesley Orbison and Craig Wiseman was a success on their first cut.

The only song on the album that remained resolutely stuck in the past was "You Got It." In the lyrics, co-authored by Jeff Lynne and Tom Petty, Roy assumes his customary posture of supplication in front of his beloved. He will give her anything in the world if she'll only be his girl. When Sam Phillips heard "You Got It," he recognized the old Roy. "He's defensive in that song," Sam said. "It's like he's afraid he's going to lose her any minute." Ironically, this was the biggest single on the album, zooming into the Top 10 when it was released in 1989.

Roy received so much help from so many people on this album that the extensive acknowledgements on the liner notes had to be set in minute type. Everyone from session musicians to family and friends receives a mention. While most record covers mention only the star, the title and the songs, *Mystery Girl* inexpicably included not one but two liner-note acknowledgements to a *publicist,* and Barbara Orbison received no less than *five* mentions.

Roy was walking a tightrope on this album, trying to absorb new lessons from his young, hip collaborators and yet please his old fans with sentimental retro hits like "You Got It." A great comeback album was the happy result. "I hope the new album sounds new enough to be fresh," Roy said, "but not so new and so different that it would be much different from what I've been doing." With the killing work schedule songwriter David Briggs described—"seven days a week, and he held up well after midnight"—and the worry and apprehension expressed in Roy's public statements, Roy was beginning to sound like he could die over this album. Working late with weary guitarist Mike Campbell, Roy looked haggard and sounded obsessed and unreasonable. "Any time you play an instrumental," he told Mike, "you have to be brilliant if something's going to hold up for twenty or thirty years." A strange look came over Mike Campbell's face. He was probably just trying to enjoy himself, making music and having fun, but Roy was behaving like a grim workaholic, driven by grandiose expectations and fretting over a distant future he would not live to see.

Chapter 12

When a reporter asked Roy who he'd like to sing "Happy Birthday" to him on his fifty-second birthday, he replied, "Bruce Springsteen, Bob Seger, Whitney Houston and Bruce Hornsby." His friendship with Bruce Springsteen was the great joy of Roy's middle years, and the love of this devoted admirer had already been demonstrated at Roy's Rock 'n' Roll Hall of Fame induction and the Cinemax special. After Bruce's endorsement of Roy, the entire rock world followed suit, and soon the reigning superstars of the day were willing to do Roy any favor he asked. No wonder Roy mentioned Bruce first among his favorite singers. Next came Bob Seger, the Michigan rocker who hit it big with "Night Moves" and "Against the Wind." Whitney Houston, daughter of Cissy Houston and cousin of Dionne Warwick, was the most interesting recording star of the mid-1980s, scoring #1 hit singles with "Saving All My Love for You," "How Will I Know," "Greatest Love of All" and "I Wanna Dance With Somebody (Who Loves Me)" while still in her early twenties. Bruce Hornsby scored a #1 hit in 1986 with "The Way It Is."

For his fifty-second birthday present, Roy said he wanted "a Ford convertible with a great stereo," because he was considering an extended summer tour in 1988. "If those four would come and sing 'Happy Birthday' it would be great." Roy's wish came true. At a concert in L.A. Bruce Springsteen serenaded him in front of an audience of 20,000.

Though Roy was engaged in work on *Mystery Girl,* his ambitious solo album, *The Traveling Wilburys* project began to take shape in Los Angeles in 1988. What started out as a lark ended up becoming a grand synthesis of rock 'n' roll. Drawing on the talents of three founding fathers of rock, Roy, George Harrison and Bob Dylan, with crucial contributions from two younger artists, Tom Petty and Jeff Lynne, *The Traveling Wilburys* encompasses almost half a century of rock achievement—Roy's rockabilly and inspired balladry, George Harrison and the British Invasion, and Bob Dylan and folk/country rock. It is one of the great albums in the history of the genre, and many of the songs reflected the positive transformations in the personal lives of the artists. *The Traveling Wilburys, Vol. I* summed up rock's past while defining new artistic and moral directions for popular music.

Roy Orbison was not alone in his need for a comeback album. *Wilburys* would be the first significant LP in years for Dylan, who'd fallen into a rut. His August 1986 concert in Paso Robles, California, was a disaster, with Dylan laboring through torturous, distorted renditions of his famous hits, evidently trying to make them sound new. George Harrison also needed a hit. After the breakup of The Beatles in 1970, he had emerged as the most talented individual Beatle. His three-record set *All Things Must Pass,* produced by Phil Spector, included the unforgettable "My Sweet Lord," but his triumph was marred by a lawsuit which successfully established that he had unwittingly plagiarized The Chiffons' "He's So Fine." In his personal affairs he seemed to sink into a mid-life crisis. After losing his wife Patti to Eric Clapton, he began seducing women almost randomly, including Ringo Starr's wife Maureen. He remarried, acquired an English estate called Friar Park and turned to movie production, but he was cursed with a $15.5 million bomb called *Shanghai Surprise,* starring Sean Penn and Madonna at their worst. Returning to the record business with a sigh of relief, he was recording a new album when he and Roy Orbison saw each other for the first time since their 1963 tour.

As Roy told interviewer Martin Ashton, "When Jeff Lynne, Tom Petty and I were writing songs at Jeff's house and George came in, we went out for dinner and George said he needed to write and record a third song for a European single and we all agreed to do it. George said, 'Okay, let's call Bob Dylan and see if we can use his studio.' He answered on the first ring which was unusual and said, 'Come on over.'

"And then George went to Tom Petty's house to pick up his guitar and Tom said he didn't have anything else better to do so he came along too. We sat in the garden and had a little barbecue and wrote a song called 'Handle With Care' and went into the garage to record it and finished it the next night. George took the song to the record company who told him it was much too good for a B side so he didn't know what to do with the song.

"Then George suggested we make an album, so we looked at each other and said, 'Okay.' But we didn't ask any of the record companies or managers or attorneys or anybody. We just went ahead and did it and no one knew about it. It was right in the middle of my album with five songs recorded and five to go. We just kept it a secret until the writing and singing was done and then we mentioned it to the record companies, to CBS, Warner, Virgin and MCA, who all said no problem, which was great. I think if we had tried to get together and told everyone that we were forming a little group they would have told us that there were too many problems. I remember one executive said, 'Well, I'm not going to stand in the way of history,' and just hung up the phone."

According to Bobby Blackburn, the most exciting thing about *The Traveling Wilburys* for Roy was that "he felt like he was getting a second chance with Bob Dylan." Bobby was referring to Roy's miscalculation in turning down "Don't Think Twice" when Dylan had offered it to him to record years before.

When Roy's *Traveling Wilburys* colleagues were interviewed by *Rolling Stone,* they spoke fondly and admiringly of him. Bob Dylan called Roy an opera star and George Harrison felt, "One of the things that really clinched the thing with the Wilburys with respect to me and Roy was when I found that Roy knew every word to every Monty Python song and the dialogue to all the movies and the TV series."

Tom Petty said, "When we cut 'Handle With Care' and Roy started singing that little break he sings, we all just couldn't believe it. No one could ever make a sound like that. We went leaping around the control room. And we've all seen a few records made.

"I think it was the next day, George [Harrison] and Jeff [Lynne] came driving up to my house and said, 'We want to start a band. Will you join us?' I said yeah. We called Bob [Dylan] from my house, and he said okay. Roy was playing a show in Anaheim. So Jeff and George and myself and our wives drove to Anaheim, and I remember running into his dressing room. And we said, 'Roy, we want you to be in our band.' And he said okay. And we just went crazy. And he was so calm: 'Sure, sounds like a lot of fun.' Then we went out and watched the show. And it was incredible. All the way home, we were going, 'Roy Orbison's in our band.' I don't think we ever got over it."

Nine days after they began, in the summer of 1988, they had ten new songs, many of them composed at the Los Angeles home of Dave Stewart of The Eurythmics, who was Bob Dylan's producer. "We would arrive about twelve or one o'clock and have some coffee," Jeff Lynne said. "Somebody would say, 'What about this?' and start on a riff. Then we'd all join in, and it'd turn into something. We'd finish around midnight and just sit for a bit while Roy would tell us fabulous stories about Sun Records or hanging out with Elvis. Then we'd come back the next day to work on another one. That's why the songs are so good and fresh—because they haven't been second-guessed and dissected and replaced. It's so tempting to add stuff to a song when you've got unlimited time."

Tom Petty said, "We definitely didn't want to treat this like a supergroup. I don't even like the term all that much. But we were aware that it would be viewed as such. We look at the Wilburys as a completely other persona as ourselves. Roy was the nicest human being you could ever meet. He was always happy. He had a great laugh—I loved his laugh. It was just a thrill. We were all in awe of Roy, and we told him so every ten minutes. That's the one thing I feel great about, that we loved him and hugged him all the time. There was nothing like that sound. Even when he was sitting next to you, quietly, or showing you a part, it could just give you chills."

Roy said, "I sound basically the same. When I was making my older records, I had more control over my vibrato—now, if I don't want to have the vibrato in the studio, I have to do a session earlier in the day, because by the evening it'll be there whether I want it or not."

The Wilburys' name was born when George Harrison and Jeff Lynne performed at the Prince's Trust concert in 1987. Britain's Prince Charles complimented the singers after the concert and told them that they should form a band. When they asked what they should call it, the Prince of Wales said, according to Petty, "The Traveling Wilburys." Harrison became Nelson Wilbury, Petty was Charlie T., Jr., Lynne was Otis Wilbury, Dylan was Lucky and Roy was Lefty. "My name came from Lefty Frizzell, the country singer of the '50s who was a great inspiration to me and still is a favorite singer," Roy said. Lefty's greatest success, like Roy's, had come early in his career, and Lefty was without a recording contract at the end and most of his twenty albums were out of print. Every time it appeared that Lefty was about to become a has-been, he came up with a hit from out of left field, like the 1973 classic, "I Can't Get Over You to Save My Life." He was the prototypical hard-drinking, hard-living, hard-singing country star. On July 19, 1975, he suffered a massive stroke at his Nashville home and was rushed to Memorial Hospital but died at 11:20 the same night. In his final years he looked a full decade older than his forty-seven years.

Roy and his friends in The Traveling Wilburys evolved a biography for the group as they worked on the album. They were half-brothers who had different mothers but the same, carefree father. "We wanted a lighthearted name as opposed to anything serious," Roy said. "We were thinking of The Beatles in *A Hard Day's Night*—something along those lines." Roy was the elder statesman among the brothers, and when the other guys got to kicking too much, Roy spoke up for the family's honor, saying, "Some people said Daddy was a cad and a bounder. I remember him as a Baptist minister."

George Harrison considered making a full-length movie based on the liner notes, which were attributed to Michael Palin. A lyricist for Barry Booth, a musician who had worked with Roy in England, Palin had helped create Monty Pyton's *Life of Brian,* a feature film made possible by a loan from George Harrison. The Traveling Wilburys are described as an ancient people who were destroyed by agents, managers, nightclub owners, tour operators, recording executives, wives, roadies and drummers.

The songs represent a progression from the darkness of heartbreak, loneliness and self pity to the light of self-acceptance, service to others and serenity. "Handle With Care" is the confession of an aging rocker who feels uptight and has made a mess of his life. Roy Orbison's voice soars onto the record in this song wailing that he's sick and tired of being sick and tired. To cure himself the rocker in the song goes to meetings and becomes hypnotized. It is a sarcastic reference to alcohol and drug recovery programs, where reluctant patients often complain about "brain-washing" until they spend some time in recovery and finally realize that their brains needed washing.

Referring to his solo lines about loneliness in "Handle With Care," Roy said if there was one line for him to sing, "that's gotta be it. I felt it was pretty typical of what I should be singing." Was Roy "the lonely guy's Lonely Guy?" reporter Jim Sullivan asked. "It's just the kind of guy that comes out sometimes when I write," Roy replied. "Probably, it's one side of my personality coming through. I read a lot into what I write and it's mostly feelings. There's some happy ones, too. On the new album [*Mystery Girl*], there are a couple of occasions where I'm in good shape."

Roy's solo, "Not Alone Anymore," is a variation on the theme of his old songs, such as "Blue Angel." A sensitive lover offers a woman sympathy for her heartbreak and suffering, thinking this will make her love him. She, however, has found herself another man, and she's no longer alone and in need of a shoulder to cry on. It's a thrilling blues number, awash with cascading strings, and, like so many of Roy's songs, it is saved from being maudlin by the nobility of his voice.

In "Headed for the Light," the LP takes a welcome turn toward spiritual strength. By the end of the album, in "End of the Line," the boys sound like old-timers in AA, singing about helping others, giving up worrying over the future, renouncing enslavement to diamond rings and all material things, trying to live one day at a time, expecting the best instead of the worst, being grateful just to be alive, being happy even if they're alone and not in love with anyone, being contented even if they're old, beginning to live and let live, practicing forgiveness on a daily basis, and, finally, embracing death—the end of the line—as the entryway to eternal life. These beliefs are recognizable as those learned in recovery programs for alcohol and drug addiction. That these artists shared their beautiful songs and their hard-earned wisdom anonymously, none of them permitting their real names to be used in connection with the album, was an act of unprecedented humility in the history of popular music. The only key Roy offered to those wanting to know who wrote the songs on *Vol. I* was his statement that the lead singer on each cut wrote that particular song. While Bob Dylan had four songs, Roy had only one, because his solo, "Winged Victory," based on William Blake's "The Sick Rose," was thrown out.

When *The Traveling Wilburys Vol. I* was released, *Rolling Stone* singled out Roy's solo turn, "Not Alone Anymore," saying Roy "hurts as good as he ever has. It proves [he] has lost none of his tremendous vocal prowess." The following year, when *Rolling Stone* included *The Wilburys* among "The 100 Greatest Albums of the Decade," the editors again stressed Roy's contribution, writing, "Orbison's haunting, dynamic vocals are enshrined on the operatic 'Not Alone Any More.' He reclaims his former glory." Critic Mike Daly referred to Roy's inimitable vocals on the album's first single, 'Handle With Care,'" and found that Roy's solo, "Not Alone Anymore," "harkened back to his classic dramatic tearjerkers of the '60s: 'Crying,' 'It's Over,' 'In Dreams.' 'Not Alone' whetted the appetite for the singer's first album of new songs in years, due from Virgin Records in February 1989...The Wilburys were the talk of the industry, and old Lefty [Orbison] was the major reason." AP called him "a legend with ballads about lost love." David Zimmerman in *USA Today* referred to the album as Roy's "new triumph," and said "Not Alone Anymore" "ranks with his best work."

The album shot into *Billboard's* Top 10 within three weeks, and the single, "Handle With Care," went into the Hot 100 at #46. Back on the charts for the first time in a quarter of a century, Roy was no longer a has-been. Overnight, he was accepted as a relevant figure on the contemporary music scene. Roy could fill big venues on his own now, and some observers noticed tears in his eyes as he made his bows. "I've been taken aback by the way things are going," Roy confessed. "It's very nice to be wanted again but I still can't quite believe it."

Roy's old friends in Wink were delighted. Ronnie Slaughter and Susie Gray said that, after all Roy's years in the shadows, it was wonderful to see him become a rock 'n' roll star again. Almost a year after its release, as far into the future as July of 1989, *The Traveling Wilburys* would still be on the national bestseller charts.

Once again a recording star with a hit record, Roy wanted a new body to go with his new status, and he started working out and losing weight. Flattering photography was commissioned for his next album, *Mystery Girl,* on which he now frantically resumed work. Roy seemed to lose all rational judgment, assuming that drastic measures and frenetic activity could restore a quarter century of lost stardom and insure his new eminence on the pop scene. He had already survived a decade longer than many triple by-pass heart patients, and the strain he now subjected himself to would cost him dearly.

Roy put himself under impossible pressures while recording *Mystery Girl.* "At the moment," he said, "it's like the devil chasing me around." The first day he walked into the studio, he said, "What kind of song can I write that will equal 'Crying'?" Setting such unnecessary challenges for himself may well have helped shorten Roy's life. There was something gluttonous in the year he laid out for himself— cutting two strenuous albums, promoting them, touring, doing one-night stands, making videos, granting numerous interviews, running to Europe for prizes. Fame can be unhealthy for anyone, but for Roy it was poison. It happened in the 1960s, and now, at the end of the '80s, he was again being consumed by the very things he wanted. Though he was fifty-two, he was still the Depression kid going for the brass ring, whatever the cost. But this time he was running on borrowed time, precariously sustained by a surgically repaired heart.

Roy didn't ever appear to consider slowing down. "The will to go on is fairly relentless," he said in 1988. "I just accept that and go on with it. I *could* alter my life style and stay home for a few years but I've never been tempted to do it. Whatever drove me to do it in the first place is still burning away in there somewhere. Sometimes it does scare me that the process is likely to go on and on and on. A lot of artists I meet are thinking, 'It's OK for Roy, he's got it made,' but I only feel like I've got it made for the moment, at any moment. For me it's like a quest."

Word began to spread in the record industry and the music press that Roy Orbison had another monster hit in *Mystery Girl*. "People have been anticipating this record for a long time," Roy said. "It's taken a lot longer than I originally thought it would, but the end result should make it all worth while. Bono, Jeff Lynne, Diane Warren, Albert Hammond and Elvis Costello all co-wrote songs with me for the album."

Besides the two major LPs, Roy kept up a breakneck pace of performing in 1988. In January, he participated in "Elvis: A National Tribute" at The Showboat in Atlantic City. In June, he sang at a concert in California, and Jeff Lynne was in the audience. "I've never seen anything like it," Jeff said. "He had standing ovations halfway through his songs. There were about 5,000 people, and they were up and screaming, chanting and hollering, and then they sat down again. He basked in it, but he gave the love back just in his performance."

Roy appeared at Great Adventure on Saturday, June 4, and on July 27, he performed with rockers half his age—Southside Johnny and The Asbury Jukes—before 2,500 fans gathered at Manhattan's Pier 84, next to the aircraft carrier *USS Intrepid*. The Jersey band opened for Roy, and then we went before a crowd made up predominantly of younger people, all loyal followers of Southside Johnny. "They were crazy about Roy," said twenty-five-year-old fan Robert Burroughs, who was in the audience.

Roy then undertook a rigorous tour with his old friend Carl Perkins, who said they performed fifteen concerts over the summer months. Roy and Carl had been sharing the same stages now for thirty-two years, going all the way back to The Malco Theater, where Carl bloodied up the drunken Burnette Brothers. "I never saw the face of a paying customer that would have taken his money back after a Roy Orbison show," Carl remembered. "He was a picker. He was what I call a sly fox with that guitar. He didn't give you any movement, but he dug those things out of his guitar neck. He was a fabulous musician as was evident with the chord progressions within his songs."

Roy remained busy throughout the autumn. On September 23, he flew to San Francisco to wish a happy thirty-ninth birthday to Bruce Springsteen, who was supporting the Amnesty International Tour in behalf of political prisoners. In October, Roy was the featured attraction at the Arizona State Fair in Phoenix, playing the Veterans Memorial Coliseum. The band laughed when he told his bass player, "Cover for me on any notes I don't hit." They knew he never missed notes. In the limo on the way back to his hotel, he discussed his favorite subject, *Mystery Girl,* with Steve Pond. "There was some fear involved, because there was a legend in the background haunting me, and no way would I be able to live up to it. And then I realized it didn't matter. What mattered was jumping in with both feet and being committed and working hard and honestly . . . I was working as if I was doing it myself, completely alone, and felt the weight of that whole thing. But then I stopped long enough to be grateful, and I realized that everybody who was doing their thing on this album was doing it with a lot of love and care."

As a result of his heavy workload, Roy was rapidly losing weight and looking increasingly fragile. Roy was still smoking, and at this point he was gambling with his life every time he lit up. In the fall of 1988, *Rolling Stone* conducted a series of interviews with Roy, and Steve Pond noticed that he was smoking from a pack of Camels.

In the interviews Roy gave in 1988, his reflections on his years as a first-generation rocker amounted to a summing up of his career. Writer Martin Ashton asked, "Because of where you came from musically, did all the changes that were taking place through the '60s and '70s with The Beatles and punk rock seem very far away from what you were doing?"

"Yeah," Roy replied, "it did. It was pretty far removed from how I was operating. You can even say that you were going ahead this way or standing like a tree instead and then the wind comes along, the autumn comes, winter and springtime. I've always had a dream or a vision of myself making music that I personally want to express. 'Crying' was written at a time when people were mostly macho. Not only do guys not talk about it but you were not supposed to cry, so there was I coming out with 'Crying' and 'Running Scared' and 'Only the Lonely' and talking about feelings when the whole age was macho. I have always gone against the grain."

To the end of his life, Roy could never conquer his pride and face the truth about his fall from grace in the late '60s. He argued that people stopped buying his records because "it was the era of the album as opposed to the single. I function best when I am writing, and I was touring so much during the '70s, it was difficult to talk to someone about a record contract, but I was looking for a company like Virgin that would be a home base for me rather than just another record company."

Asked how he felt about his new audience of young people, Roy said, "My son goes from one thing to another but I was amazed that he had *Buddy Holly's Greatest Hits* and that he loved it and wanted to know about him. You now have a history of rock 'n' roll, but I think an artist must produce and give himself and what he's feeling right now. Being a legend is a great thing but it doesn't tune your guitar or change your tire. Having current product is very important for someone in this business."

As they completed *Mystery Girl* in November, they all watched *Wilburys* head for the Top 10. David Hinckley of the New York *Daily News* called *Wilburys* "a terrific album—thanks in large measure to Roy's harmonies, one-liners and the featured track, 'Not Alone Anymore.'" The Wilburys cut a video, and it began playing virtually nonstop on MTV. Elated, the band began to talk about a world tour. "It's exciting just to think about at least one show together, if not a tour," George Harrison said. "I'd like to be in the audience to watch it." Rarely happier, Roy said, "We're all fans of each other anyway."

Roy complained to Johnny Cash of experiencing heart pains around this time. "He told me he had to have something done," Johnny recalled, "but he didn't." Instead, Roy went off to Europe with Barbara. He had a full calendar overseas, promoting *The Traveling Wilburys* in London, accepting awards on the continent, and talking with reporters everywhere. On November 19, he performed at the Diamond Awards Festival in Antwerp, Belgium, where he was presented with the Diamond Career Award for "over twenty-five years at the top of the bill." As he took the stage, carrying a silver guitar and sporting a trendy pony tail, he had never looked better. His '60s sideburns had been tamed and his face was unnaturally smooth. Where were the jowls, wrinkles and pouches of only a few months ago? Gone was the nearly geriatric look of recent years; it had been replaced by a diminutive, almost elfin demeanor.

At his huge Antwerp concert, he stood in the center of a multi-leveled stage, a vast space glowing in blue and rose lights, with a huge "O" looming in the background. Spotlights strafed the audience, who were swaying and waving their arms and holding thousands of lighted candles, matches and cigarette lighters. White clouds drifted across the stage, and the whole place began to look like heaven. Roy sang his classics with some of the best backup singers and musicians he'd ever worked with. He lip-synched 'You Got It,' and a video of that performance soon showed up on MTV.

He joined Barbara in Paris for what she later described as a second honeymoon. "We were in Paris before she went back to America, and I went to Germany to work on the record. And in Paris we were the lovers. A whole week we had set apart where we didn't do business, we didn't check on the kids hardly. Because I needed a break, and we were to renew our relationship. Because we had just come out of the studio."

According to Martin Ashton of *BAM* Magazine, for Roy it was not all champagne and moonlight in Paris. "It was a long week," Ashton wrote. "He'd also been to France for interviews. Everyone wanted to know again about The Big O, the Man in Black, one of rock 'n' roll's most mythical and charming characters." Roy was enjoying himself but Barbara was concerned about Roy getting some antibiotics before he flew home the next day. Roy looked well, dressed from head to toe in black except for white socks, his hair tied in a pony tail.

Boston Globe reporter Jim Sullivan conducted a telephone interview with Roy in Paris. Sullivan asked him if he was excited about all the praise being heaped on him by young rock stars. Did he like being "hip"?

"It's very pleasing, as you might well understand," Roy said. "It's a nice thing that people say good things about you. I think it means more to me that they are in the business and a few of the people I've met said, 'I got in the business because of you' or 'You inspired me.' That makes me feel really good... it also tells you where you are. If you ever wondered if you're reaching anyone or touching anyone."

Sullivan mentioned that Roy's forthcoming album, *Mystery Girl,* would be his first release with original songs since 1979 and asked him what they were about. "It's still matters of the heart," Roy replied. At the end of their telephone call, they fell into a discussion on the subject of faith. "Born again is an overused phrase," Roy said, "and for some people it turns 'em off. But Jesus said, 'Lest you be born again—' It's exactly that kind of thing—but I'm not fond of the phrase. I've been developing a personal relationship with myself and with Jesus Christ, and it just kind of smooths everything out, puts everything in perspective."

By the time Roy was interviewed by Swedish journalist Kristina Adolfson in London, he was looking "drained." Kristina's original interview was scheduled for 5:00 p.m., but Roy's people called her to say he wasn't feeling well. They asked if she could reschedule the interview for noon, because Roy needed to take the afternoon off. "Sadly, I could not make it," she said, "but Roy, being a true professional, agreed to carry on at the original time."

During the interview, Roy became ill. "I've got a blinding headache," he said. "I don't understand it, it just won't go away. I have taken a couple of pills, but they haven't helped. It just keeps throbbing away." At the end of the session, he was preparing to return to America. "My life is a never-ending dream," he said. "I take one day at a time and never look too far into the future."

On November 30, at London's Heathrow Airport, Roy was still at work, busily promoting *The Traveling Wilburys* during a press interview. He bragged that the album took only twelve days to finish, still failing to see how his compulsive work habits were deteriorating his health. "I've been taken aback by the way things are going," he said. "I've been rediscovered by young kids who had never heard of me before *The Wilburys*. They are getting into my original songs and apparently the old stuff is selling at the rate of 20,000 copies a day. It's very nice to be wanted again though I still can't quite believe it."

Roy returned to America, and Barbara told the press she was going to Frankfurt to arrange a promotional tour. Roy undertook a strenuous U.S. tour that left him exhausted. One of the stops was The Channel club in Boston, and Brian Washburn, the manager, said Roy looked bad after his performance. "He obviously had to know that his heart wasn't very strong," Washburn said. "But he was adamant about giving the crowd its money's worth and he played all-out. By the end of the evening, he was really wiped out."

On December 3, Jim Sullivan wrote in *The Boston Globe,* "There had been rumors of a guest shot by Keith Richards or Robert Palmer, but it didn't pan out." Though Roy sang to a near sellout house, Sullivan criticized him for doing no Wilburys music or anything from *Mystery Girl,* but reported "awestruck smiles among the crowd" as

Roy maneuvered through his "mountain-climbing ballads." While Sullivan appreciated Roy's "unswerving commitment to his classics, what we all want is a glimpse into the future, and that Orbison did not provide Saturday night."

Sullivan later reported that Roy told him he'd wanted to play some of his new songs at The Channel, but he and his band hadn't rehearsed them yet. He promised to play new songs on "a major blitz" he was planning for early 1989. "This is the first time in a long time that I feel the old phasing into the new," Roy said. "I think everybody's going to like this album *[Mystery Girl]*; it's really got a lot of heart and soul."

After Boston, Roy went on to play small club gigs around Cleveland. Why one-night stands were necessary for a man with heart disease, who didn't need the money, who'd already secured his comeback with one hit album and had another one ready for release, can only be understood in light of Roy's insecurity, consuming ambition and compulsive work ethic. "My doctors tell me I could be killing myself," he said, and Barbara later told reporters, "He had heart problems for some time. We had all expressed our concern that he was working too hard. But Roy was a strong-willed person. He loved the fact that he'd been given a second chance for success, and told us several times he wasn't going to let it slip away from him. For Roy, that meant working harder and longer than anyone had a right to expect of him. He was driven."

On December 4, he arrived in Highland Heights, Ohio, to play The Front Row Theater. Photographer David Shoenfelt, who was present that night, said, "My wife Kathie and I were late getting to the theatre, but on the way in we passed Roy's gray limo on the highway. He was obviously late too, so we relaxed, knowing we wouldn't miss the show. We arrived when Patrick Sullivan, a local Irish comedian, was doing his act. Then Roy came on, wearing his black Gibson guitar and backed up by the same two guitarists he'd had in Belgium. Roy looked healthy and still had his pony tail. He'd lost thirty-five or forty pounds. He sang great, opening with 'Only the Lonely,' and received a standing ovation when he finished with 'Running Scared.' He took off his guitar and did the last stanza again as his encore. He was surprised by the length of the ovation, looking as if he weren't accustomed to this kind of reception."

Approximately 2,000 were in the audience at The Front Row. Before the performance, Roy had been scheduled for an interview with Bill

Hall on the radio program, "The Vinyl Word," aired on Akron's WONE. Since Roy was running late, his representative asked Hall to release him from the commitment, promising Roy would give him an interview when he returned to the area in February 1989. They said they were trying to get some, if not all, of The Traveling Wilburys to accompany Roy on the 1989 tour.

Roy rode his tour bus all the way from Cleveland, Ohio, to Nashville. As the bus crossed the state line into Tennessee late Sunday night, he turned to the band and said, "All right, I'm going home. I'm ready to be there." He proceeded to Hendersonville to visit Nadine, Wesley and Sammy. "Dad was wanting to spend time with us," Wesley recalled. "He wanted to share his new livelihood with us. He came to his senses at the end. There were times when Daddy wasn't himself. At the end it was his old self back. It was really weird to lose him at that time." Roy decided to stay in Nashville for a few days and then fly to London December 12 to shoot two more videos for The Traveling Wilburys. Ominously, one of them was called "End of the Line."

On Tuesday, December 6, Roy spent the day shopping for parts for model airplanes with his bus driver and all-around aide Benny Birchfield. Roy and Benny were both crazy about remote-controlled models. "Everything is fitting together so nicely of late," Roy had said in one of his final interviews. "Life is going real good for me now. I've got a lot of songs in me that I haven't written yet, and a lot of tours I haven't done. I'm just looking forward to each day knowing that Roy Orbison is making music again."

Benny was married to country singer Jean Shepard, who fixed them dinner that night. Roy and Benny were "having a great time," Jean said. Jean and Roy went back so many years, to the time when both young couples, Roy and Claudette and Jean and her husband Hawkshaw Hawkins, were just beginning their families. After Hawk died in the plane crash with Patsy Cline, Jean married Benny, and they had lived near Roy in Hendersonville since the 1970s. "Roy was so thrilled to be back in Nashville," Jean said. "he had been up there to College Heights Baptist Church with us several times and he was looking forward to going there again with us. He had rededicated his life three or four years back. He thought an awful lot of Brother Larry." Larry Gilmore was the minister at the College Heights church.

"We ate supper about 5:30," Jean said, "and he was going to spend the night with his mother. He went on over there." Roy's son Wesley described the last few hours of his father's life: "He had relaxed and had on a night shirt and jeans. He had a pony tail and when he took it down and fluffed it he looked like a horse with a mane. He kidded me. I was a rock 'n' roller as a youth—Levis and long hair—and Dad said, 'I see you got your hair cut. I'm the one with long hair now.' He took his hand and moved it down to my ears. 'Yeah, you got short hair now. My hair's like yours used to be.'

"I had a bone I wanted to pick. I was quizzing him about selling the houses and why that came down like it did. I wanted to give him a critique of the new album and show him my new song. We sat down to go over my songs a bit. An hour later, we were getting into talking about it. I went to the store for Cokes and popcorn. I returned, and he went to the bathroom for half an hour. I figured something was wrong. I knocked. No answer. I knocked again. Again no answer. I knew he was gone, and I was afraid to open the door. I told Sammy, 'We'll have to open the door somehow.' I got a screwdriver and opened the lock. He was leaning on the door so I couldn't open it. I forced it open and got in. I knew instantly what it was—he was on the floor, leaning on the door. Lifeless. I was in the bathroom alone with him. Then I called 911 and gave my name and address. They came in and put him in an ambulance and sat there 20 minutes trying to revive him."

Claudette's son, Wesley Kelton Orbison, was with Roy at the end. Roy was rushed to the Hendersonville hospital by ambulance but a spokeswoman there, Melanie Lamb, announced that efforts to revive him were unsuccessful. He was pronounced dead of a massive heart attack at 11:54 p.m., December 6, 1988. Roy was fifty-two years old.

Garland Briley, a funeral director at Phillips–Robinson in Hendersonville, remembered that Roy's body was taken to their Nashville facility. "I received a call at 5:00 a.m. at home. 'You'd better get down here. They're bringing Roy Orbison in.' We'd had recording stars before. Hundreds came through this little facility when Red Foley died.

"From Roy's death until he was delivered to the plane, it was a madhouse here. The widow had been abroad, and when she got back to California, twenty-four hours passed when she was totally unreachable. We didn't know what to do with the body. She simply couldn't deal with anything. Bright and early in the morning, Johnny and June Cash came to the funeral home and stayed two hours. Carl Perkins called. Two reporters from the London press camped out on our doorstep, and numerous people wanted to view the body. We had no instructions whatsoever from Ms. Orbison and could not reach her. When we did receive instructions finally, it was through Sammy Orbison."

Wesley Orbison confirmed that there were "days of confusion." But finally, he said, once Barbara had made the decision to have the funeral in California, "We saw to it that Roy was sent out to L.A. in a black casket, properly." Roy's body was flown to Santa Monica Friday, December 9, after lying at Phillips–Robinson for two days. According to Wesley, "Barbara wanted to cremate him, but I didn't want cremation. After thought and talking with other people, she decided. Roy was buried."

On December 7, 1988, Roy dominated *The Nashville Banner's* front page. His death was the lead story under a bold six-column banner headline, ROY ORBISON DIES AT 52, and a subhead which said, HEART ATTACK KILLS SINGER-SONGWRITER IN HENDERSONVILLE. Reporter Michael McCall wrote, "Singer-songwriter Roy Orbison, enjoying his greatest fame in twenty-five years, died of a massive heart attack at age fifty-two in Hendersonville late Tuesday . . . *The Traveling Wilburys Vol. I* is currently #8 on the *Billboard* pop chart, and "Handle With Care" is #45 on the pop singles chart . . . It is the first time Orbison has reached the Top 10 since 1964." McCall pointed out that Roy was a "heavy smoker."

Roy's death made the front page of *The New York Times,* which ran a teaser photo and caption on page one but relegated the obituary itself to the usual page deep inside the paper. The *Times*'s headline read, A SINGER FAMED FOR PLAINTIVE POP ANTHEMS, with the subhead, HIS BEST WORK EXPRESSED A LONGING, A FEELING OF ISOLATION. Predictably, the music magazines spread Roy all over their covers, including that of *Rolling Stone.*

The sensationalist tabloid press reported that Roy had committed suicide. On December 27, *National Enquirer* headlined ROY ORBISON KNEW GRUELING COMEBACK TRY COULD KILL HIM, and their story claimed "Roy Orbison worked himself to death—he knew he had heart trouble, that his relentless grind of one-night concert stands and ocean-hopping tours could kill him . . . 'My doctors tell me I could be

killing myself, but if I'm going to die, let me go out singing!'"
Somehow, it didn't sound like Roy.

In Nashville, the delay in announcing funeral plans left his old
friends frustrated and angry, and they began to clamor for some place
to mourn him. On December 9, *The Nashville Banner* headlined NO
WORD YET ON SERVICE FOR ORBISON. The reporter wrote that the
funeral was "expected to be announced later today by Orbison's
widow, according to a spokeswoman in the singer's L.A. office.
Though there is talk of a Celebration of Life in L.A., no details have
been announced and no decision has been made whether a Nashville
memorial service will be held."

Finally, Jean Shepard took matters into her own hands. "We just felt
the need to get together and pray for him," Jean said. "Good friends
are hard to come by and Roy was a good friend." The memorial prayer
service Jean organized took place at College Heights Baptist Church at
3:00 p.m. on Sunday, December 11, on Gallatin Road between
Hendersonville and Gallatin. The crowd was variously reported at
100–200. "It was pretty much just family and friends, including
Orbison's brother Sam and son Wesley," Larry Martin, the church's
music director, noted. Paul Garrison, who was among the mourners,
said, "The preacher told me Roy had been attending there." Although
Jean intended the event to be for the Nashville musicians who'd
worked with Roy, she welcomed all fans to attend. "It would be OK,
I'm sure," she said. "Roy belonged to the people." Nadine, who was
seventy-five and unable to attend because of the bitterly cold weather,
requested that in lieu of flowers, donations be made to the American
Heart Association.

Some of the mourners in Gallatin said they could not attend the
Celebration of Life, which they had heard was being planned for an
L.A. nightclub. Roy's band attended the Gallatin memorial and
brought his tour bus. Also in the congregation were many of the
session musicians who helped Roy when he recorded his early '60s
Nashville hits. "I didn't want to have a memorial per se," Roy's
brother Sammy told Robert K. Oermann of *The Tennessean*. "I wanted
to have a fellowship. Everyone has been just wonderful to us. The
media has treated everything so well. Do you know we have had
between 2,000 and 4,000 calls at the house? And that's with a private,
unlisted number." Wesley told Oermann that he was beginning to
follow in his father's footsteps as a songwriter and that his song "The

Only One" would appear on Roy's posthumous album *Mystery Girl* next February.

The warmth of the Nashville memorial contrasted sharply with the exclusive-sounding event planned by Barbara Orbison in Los Angeles. On December 10, Robert K. Oermann and Thomas Goldsmith wrote in *The Tennessean* that Roy's L.A. service was planned for Tuesday, December 13, and "a spokesperson for the family said the burial will be completely private." It was "scheduled for a prominent nightspot" and "the occasion will likely be attended by many of the late singer/songwriter's West Coast star friends."

Greg Thompson of Sarah McMullen Public Relations, Roy's publicist in Los Angeles, announced, "The memorial is private for family and friends; if fans were to show up they would not be admitted." Thompson added, "There's a possibility of a public memorial to be announced at a later date." Barbara was reported to be setting up a fund in Roy's name in Los Angeles as well; donations were to be sent to Crossroads School in Santa Monica. His personal belongings were to go to Barbara, who was named executor and was authorized to appoint a consultant to watch over royalties and consider publishing his biography. Joe Melson, however, estimated Roy's estate at around $10–15 million.

Bobby Blackburn was not impressed by the "Celebration of Life," held at The Wiltern Theatre. "Barbara talked," Bobby said, "and Joe Melson talked. I couldn't figure out why Joe was chosen, unless it was that Susie Melson is friends with Barbara. George Harrison and Tom Petty were there, and J.D. Souther talked, told about how he was eleven years old when he first heard Roy and spent his whole life trying to emulate him. David Lynch was there, and Kris Kristofferson. I didn't see many of Roy's friends there, only Barbara's. The Stray Cats played some of Roy's songs."

Wesley says he didn't attend the Los Angeles service because "I didn't care." Wesley's grandparents, Chester and Gerry Frady, said they were not invited nor even informed of the L.A. service. Nadine Orbison and Jean Shepard made sure, however, that the Fradys were aware of the Nashville memorial, though they were unable to attend.

The December 14, 1988, issue of *The Nashville Banner* carried an account of the "Celebration of Life." "Kris Kristofferson and Graham

Nash attended the funeral...Celebrities arrived Tuesday night by limousine, many of then shunning reporters and slipping through a back entrance at The Wiltern Theatre...Graham Nash said, 'He was an unbelievable vocalist. I'm here to pay tribute, to feel his presence, and to say goodbye'...There were performances by Bonnie Raitt, J.D. Souther and Brian Setzer playing with his band The Stray Cats. Other stars in attendance: Johnny Rivers, Tom Waits, Rita Coolidge, Dwight Yoakam and T Bone Burnett.

"But a reunion of the remaining members of Orbison's last band, The Traveling Wilburys, did not materialize. Tom Petty and Jeff Lynne, two of The Wilburys, watched the evening's performances but did not take the stage.

"Barbara delivered an emotional recollection of the performer's life, saying Orbison was very happy at the time of his death and appreciated the popularity of his music."

Roy Orbison was buried after a graveside service at Pierce Brothers Westwood Memorial Park on December 15. A year later, he still lay in an unmarked grave, not very far from Marilyn Monroe, Natalie Wood and Truman Capote.

On January 18, 1989, at the fourth annual Rock and Roll Hall of Fame induction dinner at The Waldorf–Astoria, Jann Wenner, publisher of *Rolling Stone* Magazine, dedicated the event to Roy Orbison. "We're very proud of the role we played in reestablishing Roy's career," Wenner said. Barbara was sitting at Bruce Springsteen's table along with his new girl friend and backup singer Patti Scialfa. When the audience enthusiastically applauded the dedication, Barbara rose and bowed. Then the inductees were announced—The Ink Spots, Rolling Stones, Otis Redding, The Temptations, Bessie Smith, The Soul Stirrers, Dion, Phil Spector and Stevie Wonder. In receiving his trophy, Stevie praised Roy, John Lennon, Redding and Marvin Gaye. Though all were dead, Roy was the first Hall of Fame member to die since being inducted. "In the final jam session," reported *Rolling Stone*, "Springsteen's performance of Roy Orbison's pop-opera classic 'Crying,' in tribute to the late singer, was one of the few jam numbers actually planned in advance. Well, sort of. 'I asked him about it beforehand, at the dinner,' Paul Shaffer [the band leader] said. 'He

wasn't sure whether he'd do it. But it seemed like a good idea to him.'
Once Springsteen got on stage, all it took was a brief review of the
song's chord changes before he turned on that deep, tremulous tenor.
He made up in emotive resonance what he missed in high notes."

Roy's death was the talk of the handful of regulars who show up for
coffee before dawn at The Wildcat Den Cafe. On December 9, 1988,
Wink Mayor Maxie Watts proclaimed Roy Orbison Memorial Day and
ordered the town's three flags flown at half mast. Charles Finnell, a
Texas state representative from Roy's home town, Vernon, managed to
get House Resolution 49 passed in the Legislature, making April 23
Roy Orbison Day in Texas. "All Texans," he said, "are honored to
claim him as a native son." Soon, Wink and Vernon would be in a
battle over credit for being Roy's home town. In April, Vernon held a
Roy Orbison Day, and the local bank had a flashing electric sign
saying ROY ORBISON DAY AT THE RODEO GROUNDS FEATURING BARBARA
ORBISON. A local band called The Baby Boomers played at the rodeo
grounds, and the crowd of approximately 3,500 seemed to have a good
time. In August, Wink staged a far more entertaining Roy Orbison
Day, and although Barbara didn't attend this time, Wesley and Sammy
Orbison did, Wesley making his debut as a singer.

Though *The Traveling Wilburys Vol. I* had been on the charts before
Roy's death, it sailed into *Billboard's* Top 5 in January 1989, peaking
at #3 for two weeks. When *Mystery Girl* was released the same
month, it joined *The Wilburys* on the charts, and on April 8, 1989, Roy
became the first singer since Elvis Presley to have two Top 5 albums on
the chart simultaneously—*Wilburys* was #4 and *Mystery Girl* #5. But
that was not the full extent of Roy's posthumous triumph. His single
from *Mystery Girl,* "You Got It," went into the Top 10, peaked at #9,
and remained on the chart for eighteen weeks, and his *Wilburys*
single, "Handle With Care," was on the chart for fourteen weeks,
peaking at #45. When the Grammys were handed out in 1990, *The
Traveling Wilburys* took top honors as the best album of the year. Roy
had once said in deceptively humble words, "I'd just like to be
remembered." What he had hoped for was nothing less than immor-
tality, and in a sense, his wish came true.

Notes

I conducted all my interviews for *Dark Star* in 1989-90. Complete information about the secondary sources referred to in the Notes will be found in the Bibliography followinng this section.

Code: I refer to the major sources for this book by their initials, alphabetized by last name, and I use RO for Roy Orbison and EA for myself.

MA—Martin Ashton
GAB—Glenn A. Baker
BB—Bobby Blackburn
RB—Robert Burroughs
KB—Keith Briscoe
AC—Alan Clayson
SD—Simon Dee
AD—Anna Dixon
BPE—Billy Pat Ellis
CE—Charles Evans
FF—Fred Foster
BF—Bill Frady
CF—ChesterFrady
C&GF—Chester & Geraldine Frady
GF—Geraldine Frady
PG—Paul Garrison
TG—Thomas Goldsmith
SNG—Susie Newbert Gray
BRH—Billie Rash Harris
OLH—Orbie Lee Harris
DH—David Hinckley
JH—James Hunter
JK—Jackson Kane/Jack Kennelly
PM—Patty Maddux
KM—Kadon Mahan
JM—Joe Melson
GM—Greg Mitchell
MM—Michael McCall

JN—Jesse Nash
EN—Ellis Nassour
BO—Barbara Orbison
CO—Claudette Orbison
WO—Wesley Orbison
CO'N—Chris O'Neill
SP—Sam Phillips
BP—Barbara Pittman
RS—Ronnie Slaughter
ABS—Annette Bailey Spiers
JS—Jim Sullivan
RT—Roy Trakin
PV—Paulette Viator
BW—Bryan Woolley

Chapter 1

RO at Finsbury Park—AC. Motorcycle accident—RB to EA; Colin Escott, *Roy Orbison: The Singles Collection* LP liner notes; AC. "If my story is ever to be really told" RO quoted by Peter Goddard. RO's early years—BB, RS, CE, OLH, Dan Evans, Frances Russell, Edith McKinney, J.L. Dodd, Buddy Gray, SNG, Lil Horner, Viola "Teach" Bayless, Patsy (Bailey) Dixon, Bobby Dale Smith, Kathryn Crawford, BPE, Frederico Gonzales, ABS and Frances (Payne) Long to EA. RO's maternal grandfather's alcoholism—WO to EA. Bowie Street duplex—Joyce Ann Ashby; Edith McKinney, Frances Russell to EA. "You Are My Sunshine"—*Billboard,* August 23, 1941, "My first music was country" RO quoted on double LP liner notes, *Roy Orbison: The Sun Years.* Consolidated Vultee—Bill Amburn. "I was influenced by country" RO quoted by RT. WW II experience—program notes, U.K. tour; Monument press release; Steve Pond. "I had a big drink" RO quoted by AC. Childhood love of movies—OLH to EA. Vernon radio debut—OLH to EA. "A Vow of Love" RO on TV show, "Portrait of a Legend." Vernon medicine show—RO to Jay Leno, *The Tonight Show;* AC. Country music—Bill Malone, Joseph Murrells, James Rice, Irwin Stambler, Grelun Landon. Hank Williams— Chet Flippo. Attitudes toward Wink—Sammy Orbison and BPE to EA. "We'd like for you" RO to Steve Pond.

Chapter 2

The Wink Westerners—CE, BPE, James Morrow, Henry Morrow, Bill Beckham to EA. Teen years—Kathryn Crawford, Bobby Dale Smith, RS, BPE to EA. Troy Parker quoted by BW. RO and Frankie Laine—BB to EA. Joe Ray Hammer—ABS, Patsy Bailey Dixon, BB to EA. Harvey Russell— BRH to EA. Early musical influences—RS to EA. "I would go to see Buddy

Holly's" RO quoted by GM, "The History of Rock 'n' Roll." "I met Buddy Holly in Lubbock" Waylon Jennings quoted by Chet Flippo, "Penthouse Interview: Waylon Jennings." "But Buddy Holly" OLH to EA. Early Texas TV—KB, Laura Ludewell. "The best thing" RO quoted by KB. RO's hair— SNG, ABS to EA. Junior prom date—CE to EA. Senior prom—ABS, BPE, BB, OLH, BRH to EA. "When the Wink" Helen Morton quoted by BW. Elvis Presley influence on RO—MA, GAB. College major in geology— "About the Sensational RO," souvenir program, Hastings Printing Company. College years, Teen Kings, "Ooby Dooby"—BPE to EA; RO quoted by GAB, MA. Teen Kings—James Morrow, Henry Morrow, JK, CE to EA. Pat Boone—RO quoted by J.N. Claudette Frady—JK, BPE, CE, BB, RS to EA. RO's drinking and sex life—Ronnie Hawkins quoted by Kerry Doole. "You won't get much money" Ronnie Hawkins quoted in film *The Last Waltz*. RO's use of diet pills—GF, PM, PG to EA. RO's cocaine use—BB to EA. RO's use of sleeping pills and treatment for drug dependency—WO to EA. "The road has taken"—Robbie Robertson in *The Last Waltz*. "The boys and I went"— RO quoted by Colin Escott, *The Sun Years* double LP liner notes. Je-Wel— BPE, James Morrow, Henry Morrow to EA. C&GF's motorcycle accidents— C&GF to EA. Legal problems "Ooby Dooby"—Attorney John R. Lee to EA. How RO was signed by Sun Records—SP, BPE, JK to EA. "The boys and I" RO quoted in *Sun Years* LP liner notes. "James was" Henry Morrow to EA. "There were some" RO to GAB. "She showed up" BB to EA. CO and RO— PV, KM, CE, CF, GF, BF to EA. RO and Columbia—Barry Bream. "We never met" BPE to EA. "In late '55 or early"—Johnny Cash, "The Roy Orbison Tribute Concert to Benefit the Homeless," February 24, 1990, Los Angeles. A record-store owner" BPE to EA. "It was 'Pop'"—James Morrow to EA. "I got a call" SP to EA.

Chapter 3

Sun Records—SP, Knox Phillips, JK, BPE, Marion Keisker to EA. Carl Perkins and "Ooby Dooby"—Perkins quoted by TG. Malcolm Yelvington quoted in *Los Angeles Times*. "Go Go Go"—BPE to EA. Claridge Hotel—JK to EA. "We all went to Beale" RO on TV show "Lifestyles of the Rich and Famous." "*Ballads?*" SP to EA. "I was working late"—Marion Keisker to EA. "Air fare" JK to EA. "Rockhouse" GF to EA. "The first artist" Jack Clement quoted by Peter Guralnick, *Lost Highway*. RO's dissatisfaction with SP and Sun—RO to GAB. "I knew his voice" SP quoted by Ken Tucker. Overton Park Shell—BPE, Michael Hanrahan to EA. RO and Elvis's double date, mutual interest in motorcycles—RO on Radio Merseyside's "On the Beat," quoted by AC. RO and CO's visit to Wink—Buddy Gray, SNG, Bill Bechkam to EA. RO and CO at Eagle Club—CF, GF, BF, KM to EA. RO's visits to Texas—OLH, RS, Bill Beckham to EA. RO's visit to Frady home— GF to EA. Teen Kings' gig at North Side Coliseum—SNG. Bill Dees—AC.

RO, Buddy Holly, Buddy Knox—Fred Bronson. Rivalry with Buddy Holly—
RO on Veronica Television (Dutch) quoted by AC. Slim Willet—RO quoted by
Joe Smith. Patsy Cline and Bill McCall—EN. RO and Jack Clement—*The
Sun Years* LP liner notes. "Roy had probably the best" SP. Teen Kings
conflict—SP, CE, BB, JK to EA.

Chapter 4

Teen Kings breakup—BPE, SP, JK to EA. RO and CO in SP's home—
Knox Phillips, SP to EA. Teen Kings and RO meet after breakup in Texas—
BPE, JK, OLH, BRH, RS to EA. Early Sun days—BP to EA. CO's
personality—PV to EA. What RO wanted in a woman—WO to EA. Origins
of RO's rock-ballad style—JM to EA. RO, Everly Brothers, Wesley Rose—SP
to EA. RO proposes marriage to CO—CF to EA. ROs effect on women—SP,
BP, CE to EA. Working with RO—Roland Janes to EA. RO meets The
Everlys—*The Sun Years* liner notes, and RO on Veronica Television (Dutch),
quoted by AC. RO, Eddie Cochran, Gene Vincent—RT, Joe Smith. "I
turned" RO to Steve Pond. Warren Smith as "Mr. Organizer"—*The Houston
Post,* March 19, 1986. Chuck Berry sentenced—*Chuck Berry,* p. 209. Carl
Perkins's alcoholism—Carl Perkins quoted in *Nashville Babylon.* The Everly
Brothers on Buddy Holly's drinking, as well as their own liquor and drug
use—Don and Phil Everly quoted by Kurt Loder, *Rolling Stone,* 1986. Little
Richard's girl friend, Lee Angel, and Buddy Holly—*Rock Wives.* Johnny
Cash's drug use—Johnny Cash, *Man in Black.* RO leaves Sun Records—*The
Sun Years* LP liner notes; GAB. "He floundered under the misdirection of
Chet Atkins" David Frieke. Phil Spector—*He's a Rebel.* FF signs Roy—FF to
SD; RO quoted by RT. Willie Nelson ("I always thought") quoted by Al
Reinert.

Chapter 5

RO and JM's arrival in Nashville—Boots Randolph to EA. "Raindrops,"
"Uptown"—JM to EA. "Only the Lonely"—JM to EA; GAB; FF to SD.
"We both compose" RO quoted in Monument biographical press release,
1976. "Joe wrote a good bit of it" RO on Veronica Television (Dutch) quoted
by AC. "I sensed what people needed" RO quoted by RT. "I never did get"
RO quoted by John Pitts "There's a lot of ways to be lonely" RO on *VH1
Tribute.* "The next session" FF to SD.

"Only the Lonely," Elvis Presley, Everly Brothers—JM to EA; RO to
GAB. "Only the Lonely" recording session—JM to EA; FF to SD, RO to
GAB. "I have to say *I* was the one" RO quoted by Robert K. Oermann, May
17, 1986. "Monument was not" RO quoted by DH, February 21, 1988. RO
and CO in metal house—1976 Monument press release. Disagreements re
credit "Only the Lonely," PA system—JM to EA. Duane Eddy to SD. Bruce

Springsteen—Rock 'n' Roll Hall of Fame induction. "There is no limit" RO quoted in Monument press release, 1976. "Blue Angel"—JM to EA. RO in Andrews, Texas—RS to EA. RO and CO's early Hendersonville years— C&GF, AD, Boots Randolph to EA; Felice Bryant and Del Bryant quoted by MM in "Remembering Roy." Dottie West on RO and Patsy Cline—Dottie West quoted by EN. Grampa Jones, Faron Young, Porter Wagoner on Patsy Cline—EN. Girls easily available to Roy's band on tour—BPE, PG to EA. Damaging effects of fame on RO and marriage to CO—KM to EA. RO's use of diet pills—GF, PM, PG to EA. RO and Joe Ray Hammer suicide—BB to EA.

Chapter 6

"Running Scared"—Steve Pond; recording session, *VH1 Tribute*; shortest run in Top 10, Joel Whitburn. RO's big emotional songs—JM to EA. "I went and visited Sam Phillips" RO quoted in a Monument concert program. Views on publicity—RO quoted by GM, "The History of Rock 'n' Roll." Patsy Cline's accident—EN—and Claudette's reaction—GF to EA. Sunglasses—RO quoted by Joe Smith. BF—GF, PV to EA. BF visits RO and CO—BF to EA. RO and CO's travels—C&GF to EA. 1962 Australian, British visits—AC. Sam Cooke—Barry Lazell. Bob Dylan—Bob Spitz. Tony Orbison—BB, C&GF to EA. Janet Martin—AC. RO fires band—PG to EA. Bobby Goldsboro's statement ("Roy and I")—Bobby Goldsboro quoted by MM.

RO replaces Duane Eddy—AC. "I've never heard of them" RO on Veronica Television (Dutch), quoted by AC. "I saw Roy's photo" Tito Burns to SD. CO re Patsy Cline's death—GF to EA. Patsy's marital problems—EN Patsy's death, funeral—Gerald Henry, Phil Sullivan. Johnny Tillotson, Chet Atkins, Floyd Cramer on Roy—unidentified British press clippings in PG collection. "Someone had given" RO quoted by DH, December 8, 1988. "What is all this crap?" and "I agreed because" RO quoted by JN. Roy's confrontation with The Beatles: AC, RO on TV show, "Portrait of a Legend." RO's relationship with his backup group—AC. "Roy was very easy-going"— Barry Booth quoted by AC. "arrive about a week" RO quoted by AC and *New Musical Express*, April 12, 1983. Roy's influence on Lennon and "Please Please Me"—Ray Coleman, *Lennon*; John Lennon quoted in *The Playboy Interviews*, Playboy Press, 1981; Lennon quoted by Bob Shannon and John Javna and AC. "As Orbison performed" —Philip Norman. "Yankee, go home!" RO quoting The Beatles in "Portrait of a Legend"; also quoted in almost the same form in AC, who quotes RO's interview with Spencer Leigh on *Radio Merseyside* . "I was held captive" RO to Leigh, quoted by Clayson. "It was an opening" RO quoted by Joe Smith. "I felt that John" RO on TV's *Life Styles of the Rich and Famous*. "Beatlemania was" George Harrison quoted by Goldberg, Ressner, Pond. "George and I" RO, March 26, 1977, quoted by AC. "Roy would slay them" Ringo Starr quoted by AC, Hunter

Davies, *The Beatles.* "You'll do just fantastic!" RO on "Portrait of a Legend" and in an unidentified clipping of a newspaper story by Chris Hutchins in Sheffield when RO first met The Beatles (PG collection). The Beatles ask RO to represent them—JM to EA. Paul McCartney calls RO "great"—quoted by DH, December 8, 1988. "Roy, God bless him" Gerry Marsden to SD. Beatles's Preludin use—Ray Coleman, *Lennon.* "Here, pick up" *ibid.* "I mean, I couldn't" John Lennon quoted by Coleman, *ibid.* "RO's new home"—souvenir program (PG collection).

Lennon's Spitfire story—AC. "I would have loved" RO quoted by *Disc,* May 23, 1964, and AC. Marilyn Monroe and Einstein—Shelley Winters to EA. "I have such a" RO, May 23, 1963. CO finds letter—PM to EA. CO's affair—AD, WO, BB, BPE, PG, Boots Randolph, PM, KM to EA. RO takes CO to London—AC. "Blue Bayou"—JM to EA. RO's letter ("You know those")—*Disc,* October 5, 1963. RO's nine-month separation from family—*The Edmonton Journal.* RO and JFK's death—PG to EA. CO regrets affair—PM to EA. CO in Frederick's of Hollywood—BF to EA. Beatles in Miami—PG to EA. "I talked with them over the phone" RO quoted by AC and *Punch,* December 23, 1988. RO's birthday party—caption, Bettmann Archive photo; AC; PG to EA. Irish concert—AC. Molly Weston—AC. Janice, "Thank Your Lucky Stars"—Philip Norman. "Busy production" RO quoted in unidentified clipping, PG collection. "At a time when" RO quoted by AC and *New Musical Express,* September 18, 1964. 1939 Mercedes—PG to EA. Roy DeWayne Orbison's "Crying"—AC. "I like at least" RO quoted by AC and *New Musical Express,* May 31, 1963.

CO inspires "Oh, Pretty Woman"—RO, "On the Beat," *Radio Merseyside,* quoted by AC; GF, PM to EA; Bill Dees quoted by Fred Bronson. "In a 68-week period that began August 8, 1963, Roy Orbison was the *only* American artist to have a #1 single in Britain. He did it twice, with "It's Over" on June 25, 1964, and 'Oh, Pretty Woman' on October 8, 1964"—p. 157, Bronson. "I quit" Bill Dees quoted by Joe Towe to EA. "Oh, Pretty Woman" recording session—PG to EA. "It goes through a lot" RO quoted by Steve Pond. Bill Dees's voice heard on "Yo te amo Maria"—AC. Jerry Kennedy's guitar riff—AC. "I always felt each instrumental" AC, quoting *The Face,* February 1989. RO and sex on tour—PG to EA. The Beach Boys in Australia—Steven Gaines, *Heroes & Villains.* Tour, *The Ed Sullivan Show, Shindig*—PG to EA. RO learns of CO's affair—AD to EA. RO divoces CO—BB to EA. RO and CO separate, CO's concern RO's drug use—PM to EA. B.J. Thomas's drug use—Fred Bronson, p. 402; Thomas's autobiography *Home Is Where I Belong.* "The Stones did a tour" and "I remember" Mick Jagger quoted by Goldberg, Ressner, Pond. Jeff Penberty interview, Australian periodical called *Young Sun* in PG collection. The Stones scandalize Ed Sullivan—Nicholas Schaffner. The Stones and drugs—Tony Sanchez to EA. Marianne Faithfull, Anita Pallenberg—Sanchez to EA. "I ended up on drugs"—Marianne Faithfull quoted by Nicholas Schaffner, p. 64. "Amazing number" (Richards); "Our hotel" (Jagger); "the arsehole" (Richards); "You could put" (Stewart) all quoted by Stanley Booth. Marianne and RO's glasses ("I've always")—AC and *The Daily Mirror.* The Stones' dare re worst songs— RO on Radio Merseyside's "On the Beat," quoted by AC. RO's resentment of CO's affair—PG, PM, BB to EA. "I never really" CO, March 30, 1966, quoted by AC. RO's reconciliation hopes—AC.

Chapter 7

RO leaves Monument, signs MGM—FF to SD; SP to EA. Bob Dylan, MGM—Spitz. "MGM was a big company" RO quoted by Steve Pond. "I got to know" RO quoted by MM. "Roy has a frantic"—Saul Handwerger, MGM press release. I couldn't eat" RO quoted in *New Musical Express,* December 20, 1980, quoted by AC. WO's difficult birth—GF to EA. CO in Houston— PM to EA. CO disturbed—AC. Houston Hootenanny—C&GF, PM, Frances Gatlin, PV to EA. RO's motorcycle shopping spree—CF to EA. "This was a tour" June 25, 1966, quoted by AC. "We both suddenly" March 30, 1966, quoted by AC. "It was all" June 8, 1966, quoted by AC. RO and COs reconciliation and CO's guitar lessons—PM to EA. CO's sadness, RO's isolation—PV to EA. CO and reincarnation—GF to EA. RO's children— C&GF to EA. Mick Jagger's "mixed crowds" insult—*Disc,* February 21, 1966, courtesy PG collection.

"Roy told me, 'Anna'" and "Claudette, I'm seventeen" AD to EA. CO's death—Aline Hampton to EA. "And then it was" April 17, 1970, quoted by AC. "The Lord will take" AD to EA. Kenneth Herald—*Nashville Banner.* "The guy will be suffering enough" RO quoted by BF to EA. CO's funeral— C&GF, BF, PM and BB to EA. "Life has to go on" RO quoted by CE to EA. "Roy and I went out" BB to EA. "It wasn't an effective" RO quoted by RT. Otis Deck's garage—Jerry Harrison to EA. RO and the prostitute—BB to EA. *Cat Ballou*—RO to GAB. "Orbison appears unlikely"—May 11, 1967.

Francine Herack—AC. "It looks as though" and "A father isn't enough"—March 9, 1967. Christmas 1966 and Dorothy Cook—AC. "I'm not very good"—December 23, 1988, quoted by AC. "Nashville is full of people" and "This business takes years"—*Melody Maker,* February 20, 1965, quoted by AC. "I was probably lucky" RO quoted by Erisch Menschler. "When his wife got killed" Wesley Rose to GM, "Roy Orbison Rides Again." "This was not a prudent thing" FF to SD. "We ran around" BB to EA.

Chapter 8

"Roy and I had a good time" BB to EA. "I was wearing" and "I told her it didn't" RO quoted in *Melody Maker,* August 24, 1974, and by AC. "I wasn't

impressed" BO to CO'N and Australian school children (RB collection).
"Roy had on my Levi" BB to EA. "We were carrying on" RO to Steve Pond.
"Fireproof" and "I remember seconds" WO to EA. "Get outside!" quoted by
C&GF to EA. "I saw the fire" quoted by BF to EA. "After Roy's
performance" BB to EA. "I was totally shattered" April 27, 1970, quoted by
AC. "I wasn't exactly sick" GF to EA. "Ms. Orbison was doped up" GF to
EA. "sleep wouldn't come"—AC. "If you weren't religious" April 27, 1970.
"Daddy never was" WO to EA.

"Roy came over" CF to EA. "We was standin'" BF to EA. "They had a
tent" KM to EA. "This is what Heaven" PM to EA. "He asked if I could
come" *Rolling Stone,* January 26, 1989. "A month later I got" BB to
EA."Roy Orbison showed off" Associated Press, "Secret's Out: Orbison
Weds," April 1969. "We went to a friend's" WO to EA. "Maybe there were
fifty" Jay Acton to EA. Pat Boone's drinking—Penny Stallings, Irwin
Stambler and Grelun Landon. "I told Brian that The Beatles" RO quoted by
GM, "The History of Rock 'n' Roll."

Dennis and Brian Wilson's drug problems: Penny Stallings; Steven Gaines,
Heroes and Villians. The Everly Brothers' drug problems: Don and Phil
Everly quoted by Kurt Loder in *The Rolling Stone Interviews: The 1980s.* "We
talked about the early" RO quoted by GM, "Roy Orbison Rides Again." "In
later years when his career" Kerry Doole, "Only the Best." "Ronnie
Hawkins spent" Barry Lazell. John and Yoko's promoter attacks photo-
grapher—Albert Goldman. Roy was 27th in popularity—*New Rockpile #5,*
May 1977, quoted by AC. "substantial loss" October 7, 1972, quoted by AC.
"Dad had qualms" WO to EA. "I was in Canada" RO quoted by GM, "Roy
Orbison Rides Again." Gram Parsons—John Rockwell in *The Rolling Stone
Illustrated History of Rock & Roll;* Penny Stallings, Irwin Stambler and
Grelun Landon, Barry Lazell, Stanley Booth. Gram's love for Emmylou
Harris—Randall Riese. "My then husband Brian" Emmylou Harris in
Rolling Stone, January 26, 1989.

Chapter 9

"Johnny Cash was in the waiting room" RO to GM, "Roy Orbison Rides
Again." RO to GM "The History of Rock 'n' Roll." "everyone at one time"
Bernie Taupin at the Roy Orbison Concert Tribute to Benefit the Homeless.
RO and The Eagles—Terry Widlake to Burt Kaufman, *In Dreams: Roy
Orbison Newsletter,* Fall 1989. Bruce wanted to sing like Roy—Bruce
Springsteen quoted by *USA Today,* December 14, 1988. "In the seventies I
got" RO in *Melody Maker,* September 1982, quoted by AC. Grady Lee
Orbison—OLH, BB, CE, Faye Kingston, Ruth Godwin to EA. "It's a job"
April 28, 1970. "It clears the air" RO to GM, "Roy Orbison Rides Again."
"Roy would come by" Joe Towe to EA. "Yes, I suppose I" *Daily Sketch,*
April 28, 1970. "It clears the air" RO to GM, "Roy Orbison Rides Again."

"Roy would come by" Joe Towe to EA. "Yes, I suppose I" *Daily Sketch,* April 28, 1970, quoted by AC. Van-a-Rama—David Shoenfelt to EA. "I knew he was ill" BP to EA. "I'm tired of raising"—quoted by Priscilla Presley to EA. "I bought twelve tickets" RO to GM. "Roy Orbison Rides Again." "the greatest singer in the world" CE and BPE to EA; DH, December 8, 1988. FF's claim that he and RO were a winning combination— FF to SD. "I know Elvis had a strong" RO in *Melody Maker,* August 27, 1977, quoted by AC. "Roy cried like a baby—Terry Widlake, *Ibid.* "In '77 I made a record" RO to Steve Pond, "Actually got sick as" FF to SD. "I had no idea it was" RO to Brian Matthew. "I have a beer occasionally" *ibid.* "A half-finished project" RO to Steve Pond. "an embarrassing travesty" *Rolling Stone,* August 23, 1979, quoted by AC. "It was a hard time" BO to Robert Hilburn, *Los Angeles Times* News Service, undated February 1989 clipping (RB collection). "Roy said Barbara was" BB to EA. "Barbara was in" WO to EA. "The tragedies and Dad" *Ibid.* "a condo in" BB to EA. "Roy and I did cocaine" *Ibid.* "I want to avoid" quoted by Clayson. "I fell in love with 'Blue Bayou'" Linda Ronstadt quoted by David Zimmerman. Odessa—CE, ABS, Buddy Gray, SNG, BPE, C&GF to EA. "Since Monument Records went into bankruptcy in 1981" RO to RT. Golden Orpheus—Tim Goodwin to EA. "I've tried doing new" *Ibid.* "Everyone stole" BB to EA. "Roy liked him" *Ibid.* Roy Orbison's lawsuit against Wesley Rose—Robert Hilburn, *The Los Angeles Times,* 1980. "We came to a nice arrangement" RO to JN, p. 11. Nashville law firm sues RO—*The Nashville Tennessean,* May 25, 1985, and Randall Riese, p. 219. London Country Music Festival—*Nashville Banner,* December 7, 1988.

"Roy didn't look good" RB to EA. "We followed each other" BP to EA. "I took along a photo" BRH to EA. Sammy "handling the concession" OLH to EA. "We were shocked" GF to EA. "Linda Rondstadt's 'Blue Bayou' paled" Peter S. Smith, Worcester, Mass. (clipping in Country Music Foundation library, masthead missing).

Chapter 10

Betty Ford Clinic—WO to EA. "We were dumbfounded" WO to EA. "She's mine, too" Nadine Orbison to EA. "Roy had the money" PM to EA. "Money was generated WO to EA. "All Nadine and Wes" CF to EA. "What's he doing with" CO'N to RO. "He just...he" RO to CO'N. "Rock 'n' roll styles" *The Houston Post,* March 19, 1986. "You set out to whip the world" RO quoted by MM. BO urged discretion—BO and RO quoted by JS. "Barbara and I felt we had" RO quoted by Steve Pond. "Roy respeted me" BO quoted by JH. "the emotional epicenter" MA, "Everyone was starting up" RO quoted by MA. "I was introduced to Roy" Paul Hewson quoted by Michael Goldberg, Jeffrey Ressner and Steve Pond, "Tributes." "Michelle, the next time" RO on "Nationwide," BBC-TV. "No, I didn't cancel" RO to Brian Matthew. The Elvis recollection is also from "The Brian Matthew

Show." Eddie Cochran, Jackie Wilson—RO, *VH1 Tribute*. $700 worth of cocaine—BB to EA.

Chapter 11

RO's $12,500 fee for Oil Aid—"Little Orbie Coming Home," *Midland Reporter-Telegram,* April 21, 1987. "Actually, it was good" RO quoted by KB, "Roy Orbison: A Homecoming." "a little out of the way" *Ibid.* "Everybody talks about" *Midland Reporter-Telegram,* April 21, 1987. "We went backstage" Bill Beckham to EA. "It's good to be" RO quoted by RS to EA. "He kissed us" Mary Mangrum to EA. "I was standing next" Kathryn Crawford to EA. "I never dreamed" quoted by KB, "Not a Love Affair, but Wink Flirts With Fame." "I don't think anybody" *Ibid.* "To us, Roy is" *Ibid.* "That's the way the" RO quoted by KB in "Roy Orbison: A Homecoming." "Roy was unique" Jeff Ayeroff quoted by Robert Hilburn, "Orbison's Music Proves Timeless." "People were so excited" Hilburn *Ibid.* "revealed a still supple" Robert K. Oermann, *The Tenessean,* May 17, 1986. "There was a lot of interest" quoted by Robert Hilburn *Ibid.* "No, he's not blind" quoted in *USA Weekend,* May 17, 1987. "The audience sang" August 25, 1987. "We were called to" quoted by MM in "Remembering Roy." "The three-octave" August 1987.

"We were planning" RO quoted by JN. "You should have seen" quoted by MM, *Nashville Banner,* October 9, 1987. "We had a rehearsal" RO quoted by MA. "Tom's a wonderful character" *Ibid.* "The thing was to see" and "With all the mess" RO quoted by JN. "Orbison anchors the" Bruce Westbrook. "I'm feeling accepted" December 8, 1988. "The first single I" J.D. Souther, *Ibid.* "These were just gifts" RO, *VH1 Tribute.* "He wanted to" JM to EA. "Roy was magnificent" BB to EA. "I wonder if this" February 21, 1988. "Roy Orbison's talents are more than" Matthew Auerback. "Roy Orbison plays Denver" David Menconi. "With some people" RO quoted in "Imitation Not Flattering to Orbison," *The Tennessean.* "I can't believe that you are" quoted by BO to JH. "I'm writing a song" quoted by RO to MA. "We got together at the Grammy Awards" quoted by MA. "When Roy went to sing the song" quoted by Michael Goldberg, Jeffrey Ressner, Steve Pond. "Bono would come in and say, 'Here's" RO quoted by MA. "These days you don't" RO to MA. "They had a bond" BO quoted by JH. "I left and" quoted by JH. "I'm tired right now" RO quoted by Joe Towe to EA. "He was burnt out" Joe Towe to EA. "It has increased my" RO quoted by MA. "He's defensive" SP to EA. "Seven days a week" MM, *Nashville Banner,* December 1988. "Any time you play an instrumental" RO to Mike Campbell in *VH1 Tribute.*

Chapter 12

"Happy Birthday" *USA Weekend,* April 23, 1988. George Harrison's lawsuit over "My Sweet Lord," Barry Lazell, p. 221; Peter Brown and Steven

Gaines, *The Love You Make,* p. 355. George Harrison seducing Ringo Starr's wife—*The Love You Make,* p. 353. "When Jeff Lynne" RO to MA. "He felt like he was" BB to EA. "One of the things that" George Harrison to Michael Goldberg, Jeffrey Ressner, Steve Pond. "When we cut" Tom Petty, *ibid.* "I sound basically the same" RO quoted by Steve Pond. "hurts as good" David Wild. "I'm feeling accepted and loved" RO quoted by DH, "Roy Orbison: A Rock 'n' Roll Original." *Mystery Girl:* JN; Steve Sholes; Steve Pond. Final appearances: RB, Jeff Lynne ("I've never seen anything like it" quoted by JH); Steve Pond; JS. "He told me he" Johnny Cash quoted by John Latta and Jerome George. "My son" RO quoted by MA. Diamond Awards Festival, November 1988, videotape (RB collection). "We were in Paris" BO quoted by JH. RO in Paris—MA. "Sadly, I could" Kristina Adolfson quoted by John Stratford, "Orbison's Last Words to His Loved Ones," name of publication obscured (RB collection). Peformance at The Channel: Lee Kornfeld, *Rolling Stone,* February 9, 1989; JS. "He obviously had to know" Brian Washburn quoted by Dave Thomas and Agnes Grehan, undated article in newspaper clipping (RB collection). "My doctors tell me I could be killing myself" RO quoted by Joe Mullins, David Wright, Roger Capettini. "He had heart problems for some time" BO quoted by Mullins, Wright, Capettini. Final performance, Front Row Theatre—David Shoenfelt to EA. "All right, I'm going home" RO quoted by MM, *Nashville Banner,* December 8, 1988. "Dad was wanting" WO to EA. "His idea and words were all controlled from the first by Barbara" WO to EA. "Everything is fitting" RO to JN. Jean Shepard interview—*Nashville Banner,* December 8, 1988. Last few hours of Roy's life—WO to EA. Roy's body at Phillips Robinson—Garland Briley to EA. "NO WORD YET"—*The Nashville Banner,* December 9, 1988. Roy's memorial in Gallatin: *USA Today,* David Zimmerman, December 12, 1988; *The Tennessean,* December 10, 1988. Memorial in Los Angeles: BB, PG, JM, C&GF to EA; Robert K. Oermann and TG, *The Tennessean,* December 10, 1988; *The Nashville Banner,* December 14, 1988; Robert K. Oermann, *The Tennessean,* December 9, 1988; Robert K. Oermann, December 12, 1988; Clark Parsons, December 13, 1988, *The Nashville Banner.* "Patrimony?" WO to EA. "Barbara talked" BB to EA.

RO Day, Vernon: C&GF to EA. RO Day, Wink: WO, CE, JK to EA. "Roy's Son Performs at Concert," Jamie Winn. Chart history of *Wilburys* and *Mystery Girl,* courtesy *Billboard* Magazine. RO and Elvis only singers to have two albums in the Top 5 posthumously, *Billboard* columnist Paul Grein, reported in *Lifeline* column, *USA Today,* April 5, 1989.

Bibliography

Books

Baez, Joan: *And a Voice to Sing With: A Memoir.* NAL. New York. 1987.

Balfour, Victoria: *Rock Wives: The Hard Lives & Good Times of the Wives, Girlfriends and Groupies of Rock and Roll.* Beech Tree/William Morrow. New York. 1986.

Berry, Chuck: *The Autobiography.* Simon & Schuster. New York, 1987.

Booth, Stanley: *The True Adventures of the Rolling Stones.* Vintage. New York. 1984.

Bronson, Fred: *The Billboard Book of #1 Hits.* Billboard. New York. 1988.

Brown, Peter and Steven Gaines: *The Love You Make: An Insider's Story of The Beatles.* NAL. New York. 1983.

Cash, Johnny: *Man in Black.* Zondervan. Grand Rapids. 1975.

Clayson, Alan: *Only the Lonely: Roy Orbison's Life and Legacy.* St. Martin's Press, New York, 1989.

Coleman, Ray: *The Man Who Made The Beatles: An Intimate Biography of Brian Epstein.* McGraw Hill. New York 1989.

————: *Lennon.* McGraw Hill. New York. 1984

Denisoff, R. Serge: *Waylon: A Biography.* St. Martin's Press, New York. 1983.

Des Barres, Pamela: *I'm With the Band: Confessions of a Groupie.* Jove. New York. 1987, 1988.

Di Mucci, Dion with David Seay: *The Wanderer.* Beech Tree Books/William Morrow. New York. 1988.

Dunphy, Eamon: *Unforgettable Fire: The Definitive Biography of U2.* Warner. 1987.

Eremo, Judie, ed. and the editors of *Guitar Player, Keyboard* and *Frets* Magazines: *Country Musicians.* GPI. Cupertino, California. 1987.

Escott, Colin and Martin Hawkins: *Sun Records: The Brief History of the Legendary Record Label.* Quick Fox Books. New York. 1975, 1980.

Flanagan, Bill: *Written on My Soul: Conversations With Rock's Great Songwriters.* Contemporary Books Inc. Chicago. 1987, 1986.

Flippo, Chet: *Your Cheatin' Heart: A Biography of Hank Williams.* Doubleday. Garden City. 1981, 1985.

Gaines, Steven: *Heroes and Villains: The True Story of The Beach Boys.* NAL. New York. 1986.

Goldman, Albert: *The Lives of John Lennon.* Morrow. New York. 1988.

Goldrosen, John: *Buddy Holly: His Life and Music.* Popular Press. Bowling Green, Ohio. 1975.

Guralnick, Peter: *Lost Highway: Journeys and Arrivals of American Musicians.* Harper & Row. New York. 1979, 1989.

_____: *Sweet Soul Music: Rhythm and Blues and the Southern Dream of Freedom.* Harper & Row. New York. 1986.

Helander, Brock: *The Rock Who's Who.* Schirmer. New York. 1982.

Hendler, Herb: *Year by Year in the Rock Era.* Praeger. New York. 1983, 1987.

Lazell, Barry, with Dafydd Rees and Luke Crampton: *Rock Movers & Shakers.* Billboard Publications, Inc. New York. 1989.

Lewis, Myra with Murray Silver: *Great Balls of Fire!* St. Martin's Press. New York. 1982.

Malone, Bill C.: *Country Music, U.S.A.* University of Texas Press, Austin, 1968, 1985.

Miller, Jim (ed.): *The Rolling Stone Illustrated History of Rock & Roll.* (Rev. ed.) Random House/Rolling Stone Press. 1976, 1980.

Murrells, Joseph: *Million Selling Records.* Arco. New York. 1984.

McNutt, Randy: *We Want to Boogie: An Illustrated History of the American Rockabilly Movement.* HHP Books. Hamilton, Ohio. 1988.

Nassour, Ellis: *Patsy Cline.* Leisure Books. New York. 1989.

Nite, Norm N.: *Rock On: The Illustrated Encyclopedia of Rock 'n' Roll.* Vol. I. 1974, 1982.

Norman, Philip: *Shout! The Beatles in Their Generation.* Fireside. New York. 1981.

Ochs, Michael: *Rock Archives*. Dolphin. New York. 1984.

Pareles, Jon and Patricia Romanowski: *The Rolling Stone Encyclopedia of Rock & Roll*. Rolling Stone Press/Summit Books. New York. 1983.

Ribowsky, Mark: *He's a Rebel: The Truth About Phil Spector, Rock and Roll's Legendary Madman*. E.P. Dutton. New York. 1989.

Rice, James: *Texas Honky-Tonk Music*. Eakin Press. Austin. 1985.

Riese, Randall: *Nashville Babylon*. Congdon & Weed, Inc., New York. 1988.

Rodriguez, Elena: *Dennis Hopper*. St. Martin's. New York. 1988.

Rolling Stone editors: *The Rolling Stone Interviews: The 1980s*. Sid Holt, ed. St. Martin's Press/Rolling Stone Press. New York. 1989.

Sanchez, Tony: *Up and Down With the Rolling Stones*. William Morrow. New York. 1979.

Schaffner, Nicholas: *The British Invasion*. McGraw-Hill Book Company. New York. 1983.

Shannon, Bob and John Javna: *Behind the Hits: Inside Stories of Classic Pop & Rock and Roll*. Warner. New York. 1986.

Smith, Joe, edited by Mitchell Fink: *Off the Record: An Oral History of Popular Music*. Warner Books, New York, 1988.

Smith, Steve and The Diagram Group: *Rock Day by Day*. Guinness Books. 1987.

Spitz, Bob: *Dylan: A Biography*. McGraw Hill. New York. 1989.

Stallings, Penny: *Rock 'n' Roll Confidential*. Little, Brown and Company. Boston. 1984.

Stambler, Irwin and Grelun Landon: *The Encyclopedia of Folk, Country & Western Music*. St. Martin's Press. New York. 1969, 1982, 1984.

Ward, Ed, Geoffrey Stokes and Ken Tucker: *Rock of Ages: The Rolling Stone History of Rock & Roll*. Rolling Stone/Summit Books. 1986.

Whitburn, Joel: *The Billboard Book of Top 40 Hits*. Billboard Publications, Inc. New York. 1987.

————: *The Billboard Book of Top 40 Albums*. Billboard Publications, Inc. New York. 1987.

Articles

Ashley, Joyce Ann: "Residents Cherish Special Memories of Roy Orbison." *The Vernon Record*. April 23, 1989.

Ashton, Martin: "Last Testament, Blue Angel." *BAM*. February 24, 1989.

Associated Press: "Orbison 'a legend in his own time,'" The *Palm Beach Post,* December 12, 1988.

————: "Secret's Out: Orbison Weds," April 1969. (London dateline.)

————: "Singer's Sons Lost in Flames," September 16, 1968.

Auerback, Matthew: New York *Daily News,* March 14, 1988.

Beckham, Bill: *The Winkler County News.* December 8, 1988.

Billboard 53, #34, August 23, 1941: 13.

Bream, Barry: "Roy Orbison: The Early Years." *Goldmine.* 1988.

Briscoe, Keith: "Roy Orbison: A Homecoming," *The Odessa* (Texas) *American.* April 24, 1987.

————: "Not a Love Affair, but Wink Flirts With Fame," *Odessa American,* April 24, 1987.

Brodnax, Ken: "Recalling a Legend." *The Odessa* (Texas) *American,* December 10, 1986.

Bryant, Boudleaux: *Lonely and Blue.* LP liner notes.

————: *Roy Orbison Crying. Ibid.*

————: *Orbison. Ibid.*

Claypool, Bob: *Houston Chronicle.* December 8, 1988.

De Santis, Solange: The Associated Press, *The Atlanta Journal-Constitution,* September 20, 1980.

Dickerson, Jim: *Mid-South Magazine, The Commercial Appeal,* October 20, 1985.

Doole, Kerry: "Only the Best," *Music Express,* #133, February 1989.

The Edmonton Journal: "Singer Praises Canadian Girls," October 26, 1963.

Escott, Colin: *Roy Orbison: The Singles Collection 1965-73.* Polydor/Polygram LP #839-234 liner notes.

Flint, Michigan, Journal, October 11, 1985.

Flippo, Chet: "Penthouse Interview: Waylon Jennings," *Penthouse,* September 1981.

Fricke, David: "Roy Orbison Remembered," *Rolling Stone,* January 26, 1989.

Ft. Wayne Journal-Gazette, February 2, 1984.

Goddard, Peter: "Only the lonely understand what Roy was cryin' about," *Toronto Star* (Robert Burroughs collection).

Goldberg, Michael, Jeffrey Ressner and Steve Pond: "Tributes," *Rolling Stone.* January 26, 1989.

Goldsmith, Thomas: *The (Nashville) Tennessean.* December 11, 1988.

Grizzard, Lewis: *Savannah Morning News,* September 11, 1989.

Hawkins, Martin and Colin Escott: *Roy Orbison: The Sun Years,* Charly (Sun) #CDX4 liner notes.

Henry, Gerald: *The (Nashville) Tennessean.* March 6, 1963.

Hilburn, Robert: "Orbison's Music Proves Timeless: Popularity of LP Is More Than Reaction to Rock Star's Death," *Los Angeles Times* News Service, 1989 (RB collection).

Hinckley, David: The New York *Daily News,* January 21, 1988.

————: February 21, 1988.

————: "Roy Orbison: A Rock 'n' Roll Original, 1936-1988, Elvis Called Him the 'Greatest Singer.'" The New York *Daily News,* December 8, 1988.

Hunter, James: "Roy Orbison's Finale: For the Lonely He Left Behind, the Passion of the Man Lives on in Song," The *Atlanta Journal-Constitution,* February 19, 1989.

Kaufman, Burt: "Interview: Terry Widlake," *In Dreams: Roy Orbison Newsletter,* Fall 1989.

Kerns, William D.: *The Lubbock Avalanche-Journal,* September 2, 1980.

Kornfeld, Lee: *Rolling Stone,* February 9, 1989.

Lane, Wendy E.: The Associated Press, *The Austin American Statesman,* December 8, 1988.

Latta, John, and Jerome George: "Johnny Cash: Roy Orbison's Tragic Death Saved My Life," *National Enquirer* (RB collection).

Lipner, Ariel: *Worcester (Mass.) Gazette,* March 9, 1985.

Los Angeles Times, January 12, 1989.

Ludewell, Laura: "Roy Orbison: A West Texas Legend," *The Odessa, Texas, American,* December 8, 1988.

Mahoney, John: *The Hollywood Reporter.* May 11, 1967.

Martin, Gavin: *Spin* Magazine, June 1989.

Menconi, David: *Boulder, Colorado, Camera,* March 4, 1988.

Menschler, Erisch: "Roy Orbison: Could He Shatter the Image?" *Juke,* March 18, 1989.

Midland Reporter-Telegram, "Little Orbie coming home," April 21, 1987.

Mitchell, Greg: "Orbison Rides Again," *Crawdaddy.* December 1974.

————: "The History of Rock 'n' Roll by Roy Orbison (as told to Greg Mitchell)," *Crawdaddy,* December 1974.

Morris, Edward: "Roy Orbison Estate Sued: Acuff-Rose Claims Contract Not Met." *Billboard.* June 10, 1989.

McCall, Michael: "Remembering Roy." *The Nashville Banner.* December 7, 1988.

————: *Nashville Banner,* October 9, 1987.

Mullins, Joe, David Wright and Roger Capettini, "Roy Orbison Knew Grueling comeback Try Could Kill Him," *National Enquirer,* December 27, 1988.

Nash, Jesse: *Music Express.* February 1989.

Nashville Banner, "No word Yet on Services for Orbison," December 9, 1988.

————: Claudette Orbison obituary, June 7, 1966.

New York Daily Mirror. March 9, 1967.

Northnagel, Larry: *Country Scene. Clarence (Missouri) Courier.* December 9, 1987.

Oermann, Robert K.: *The Tennessean,* May 17, 1986.

Page, Steve: "Premature Exit Taints Orbison Show," *Colorado Springs Gazette-Telegraph,* November 17, 1984.

Pareles, Jan: "Roy Orbison, 52, a Singer Famed for Plaintive Pop Anthems," *The New York Times,* December 8, 1988.

People. June 18, 1979.

Pitts, John Paul: *Midland* (Texas) *Reporter-Telegram,* April 24, 1987.

Pond, Steve: "Roy Orbison 1936-1988," *Rolling Stone,* January 26, 1989.

Pulse! Tower Records. April 1989.

"Recording Artist's Wife Crash Victim." *The Nashville Banner.* June 7, 1966.

Reinert, Al: *The New York Times Magazine*. March 26, 1978.

Ressner, Jeffrey: "Publisher Sues Orbison Estate." *Rolling Stone*. Summer 1989.

Rolling Stone, January 1, 1989.

Shepherd, Lucy: *Brockton (Mass.) Enterprise*, August 25, 1987.

Smith, Hazel: "Waylon Never Loses His Sense of Humor," People Section, *Country Music* Magazine, March/April 1989.

Sullivan, Jim: *The Boston Globe*, December 8, 1988.

Sullivan, Phil: *Tennessean*, March 6, 1963.

Tennessean, December 10, 1988.

————: March 7, 1963.

————: "Imitation Not Flattering to Orbison," April 9, 1988.

————: "Law Firm Sues Roy Orbison for Fees in Wesley Rose Suit," May 25, 1985.

Trakin, Roy: *Hits*. July 20, 1987.

Tucker, Ken: *Atlanta Journal-Constitution*, May 25, 1985.

————: *Philadelphia Inquirer*, May 19, 1985.

USA Today. April 5, 1989.

USA Weekend, April 23, 1988.

Variety. May 17, 1967.

Westbrook, Bruce: *The Houston Chronicle*, December 31, 1987.

Wild, David: "Here Comes the Fun," *Rolling Stone*, December 1, 1988.

Wilde, John: "Interview: The Big O." *Blitz*. 1989.

Winn, Jamie: "Roy's Son Performs at Concert," *The Wink Bulletin*, August 31, 1989.

Woolley, Bryan: "Remembering Roy," *The Dallas Morning News, Dallas Life Magazine*, April 23, 1989.

Wolcott, James: "Not Only the Lonely." *Vanity Fair*. March 1989.

Wynn, Ron: Memphis newspaper article, undated clipping in Country Music Foundation file .

Zimmerman, David: "His Voice Haunted a Generation," *USA Today*, undated Roy Orbison obituary in Robert Burroughs collection.

Documents

Monument Records press release 1976—a biography of Roy Orbison.

MGM Records press release by Saul Handwerger.

Gregler Amusement. June 1967.

Letter from Peter Walsh, managing director, Starlite Artistes Ltd., London, to Jim McConnell, Acuff-Rose, Nashville. April 24, 1964.

Souvenir program, Roy Orbison Day, August 26, 1989. *The Wink Bulletin.*

Souvenir program, Hastings Printing Company, Portland Place, Hastings, Sussex, England (Paul Garrison collection).

Souvenir program, *The Roy Orbison Concert Tribute to Benefit the Homeless*, February 24, 1990.

Roy Orbison's life insurance policy, written by Charles Evans: Amicable Life Insurance Company of Waco, Texas.

Audio Tapes (courtesy Robert Burroughs)

Chris O'Neill and fifteen Australian schoolchildren interviewing Roy, Barbara and their son Roy Kelton Jr., 1985

"Roy Orbison Tribute," Simon Dee, host, BBC Radio, 1989

"The Brian Matthew Show," BBC Radio, 1980

"Nation Wide," BBC TV, 1980

"The John Dunn Show," BBC Radio, 1980

Roy Orbison interview with Glenn A. Baker, Sydney, Australia, 1980, on LP *Roy Orbison: The Life of a Legend*, Baktabak Records, VBAK3002, "Interview Picture Disk."

Video (courtesy Robert Burroughs)

Roy Orbison "Live in Texas" (1986)

"CBS Morning Show" Interview (June 1986)

Lifestyles of the Rich and Famous (January 1987)

The Late Show Starring Joan Rivers (February 1987)

The Tonight Show, Jay Leno, guest host (Roy Orbison, k.d. lang—December 1987)

Diamond Awards Festival (November 1988)

VH1: A Tribute to Roy Orbison (1988)

The Last Waltz, The Band

DISCOGRAPHY

45 R.P.M. SINGLES

1956

"Ooby Dooby"/ "Tryin' To Get To You"	Je-Wel JE 101
"Ooby Dooby"/ "Go Go Go"	Sun 242
"Rockhouse"/ "You're My Baby"	Sun 251

1957

"Sweet And Easy To Love"/ "Devil Doll"	Sun 265
"Chicken Hearted"/ "I Like Love"	Sun 284

1958

"Seems To Me"/ Sweet And Innocent"	RCA 47-7381
"Almost Eighteen"/ "Jolie"	RCA 47-7447

1959

"Paper Boy"/ "With The Bug"	Monument 409

1960

"Sweet And Easy To Love"/ "Devil Doll"	Sun 353
(Re-issue of Sun 265 with overdubs)	
"Uptown"/ "Pretty One"	Monument 412
"Only The Lonely (Know The Way I Feel)"/	
"Here Comes That Song Again"	Monument 421
"Blue Angel"/ "Today's Teardrops"	Monument 425

1961

"I'm Hurtin'"/ "I Can't Stop Loving You"	Monument 433
"Running Scared"/ "Love Hurts"	Monument 438
"Crying"/ "Candy Man"	Monument 447

1962

"Dream Baby (How Long Must I Dream)"/ "The Actress"	Monument 456
"The Crowd"/ "Mama"	Monument 461
"Working For The Man"/ "Leah"	Monument 467

1963

"In Dreams"/ "Shahdoroba"	Monument 806
"Falling"/ "Distant Drums"	Monument 815
"Blue Bayou"/ "Mean Woman Blues"	Monument 824
"Pretty Paper"/ "Beautiful Dreamer"	Monument 830

1964

"It's Over"/ "Indian Wedding"	Monument 837
"Oh, Pretty Woman"/ "Yo Te Amo Maria"	Monument 851

1965

"Goodnight"/ "Only With You"	Monument 873
"(Say) You're My Girl"/ "Sleepy Hollow"	Monument 891
"Ride Away"/ "Wondering"	MGM K-13386
"Crawling Back"/ "If You Can't Say Something Nice"	MGM K-13410

1966

"Let The Good Times Roll"/ "Distant Drums"	Monument 906
"Lana"/ "Summersong"	Monument 939
"Breakin' Up Is Breakin' My Heart"/ "Wait"	MGM K-13446
"Twinkle Toes"/ "Where Is Tomorrow"	MGM K-13498
"Too Soon To Know"/ "You'll Never Be Sixteen Again"	MGM K-13549
"Communication Breakdown"/ "Going Back To Gloria"	MGM K-13634

1967

"So Good"/ "Memories"	MGM K-13685
"Cry Softly, Lonely One"/ "Pistolero"	MGM K-13764
"She"/ "Here Comes The Rain, Baby"	MGM K-13817

1968

"Born To Be Loved By You"/ "Shy Away"	MGM K-13889
"Walk On"/ "Flowers"	MGM K-13950
"Heartache"/ "Sugar Man"	MGM K-13991

1969

"Southbound Jericho Parkway"/ "My Friend"	MGM K-14039
"Penny Arcade"/ "Tennessee Owns My Soul"	MGM K-14079

1970

"She Cheats On Me"/ "How Do You Start Over"	MGM K-14105
"So Young""/ "If I Had A Woman Like You"	MGM K-14121

1971

"(Love Me Like You Did) Last Night"/ "Close Again"	MGM K-14293

1972

"God Love You"/ "Changes"	MGM K-14358

"Remember The Good"/ "Harlem Woman"	MGM K-14413
"Remember The Good"/ "If Only For Awhile"	MGM K-14413
"Memphis, Tennessee"/ "I Can Read Between The Lines"	MGM K-14441

1973

"Blue Rain (Coming Down)"/ "Sooner Or Later"	MGM K-14552
"I Wanna Live"/ "You Lay So Easy On My Mind"	MGM K-14626

1974

"Sweet Mama Blue"/ "Heartache"	Mercury 73610

1975

"Hung Up On You"/ "Spanish Nights"	Mercury 73652
"It's Lonely"/ "Still"	Mercury 73705

1976

"Belinda"/ "No Chain At All"	Monument ZS8 8690
"(I'm A) Southern Man"/ "Born To Love Me"	Monument 45-200

1977

"Drifting Away"/ "Under Suspicion"	Monument 45-215

1979

"Easy Way Out"/ "Tears"	Asylum F46048
"Poor Baby"/ "Lay It Down"	Asylum E46541

1980

"That Lovin' You Feelin' Again" Duet with Emmylou Harris)/ "Lola" (Craig Hundley)	Warner Brothers WBS 49262

1985

"Wild Hearts"/ "Wild Hearts" (instrumental)	ZTT ZTAS9*
"Ooby Dooby"/ "Crying" (live)	ZTT ZTAS9*

1986

"Rock and Roll (Fais Do Do)"/ "Birth of Rock And Roll" (from *Class Of '55*)	884 760 America-Smash
"Rock And Roll (Fais Do Do)"/ "Sixteen Candles" (from *Class of '55*)	America-Smash 884 934

1987

"In Dreams"/ "Leah"	Virgin 7-99388

1988

"Crying" (Duet with k.d. lang)/ "Falling"	Virgin 7-99434
"Handle With Care"/ "Margarita"	Wilbury 7-27732
(Traveling Wilburys)	

1989

"End of the Line"/ "Congratulations"	Wilbury 7-27637
(Traveling Wilburys)	
"You Got It"/ "The Only One"	Virgin 7-99245
"You Got It"/ "Crying" (Duet with k.d. lang)	Virgin 7-99245
"She's A Mystery To Me"/ "Dream Baby" (live)	Virgin 7-99227
"California Blue"/ "In Dreams"	Virign 7-99202
"Oh, Pretty Woman" (live)/ "Claudette"	Virgin 7-99159

33¹/₃ R.P.M. ALBUMS

1961

"Roy Orbison At The Rockhouse"   Sun LP 1260

   Tracks: "This Kind of Love"/ "Devil Doll"/ "You're My Baby"/ "Rock-house"/ "You're Gonna Cry"/ "I Never Knew"/ "Sweet and Easy To Love"/ "Mean Little Mama"/ "Ooby Dooby"/ "Problem Child"

"Lonely and Blue"   Monument M 4002
                                                 SM 14002

   Tracks: "Only The Lonely"/ "Bye Bye Love"/ "Cry"/ "Blue Avenue"/ "I Can't Stop Loving You"/ "Come Back To Me (My Love)"/ "Blue Angel"/ "Raindrops"/ "(I'd Be) A Legend In My Time"/ "I'm Hurtin'"/ "22 Days"/ "I'll Say It's My Fault"

1962

"Crying"   Monument M 4007
                                                 SM 14007

   Tracks: "Crying"/ "The Great Pretender"/ "Love Hurts"/ "She Wears My Ring"/ "Wedding Day"/ "Sumersong"/ "Dance"/ "Lana"/ "Loneliness"/ "Let's Make A Memory"/ "Nightlife"/ "Running Scared"

"Roy Orbison's Greatest Hits"   Monument M 4009
                                                 SM 14009

   Tracks: "The Crowd"/ "Love Star"/ "Crying"/ "Evergreen"/ "Running Scared"/ "Mama"/ "Candy Man"/ "Only The Lonely"/ "Dream Baby"/ "Blue Angel"/ "Uptown"/ "I'm Hurtin'"

1963

"Roy Orbison's Greatest Hits   Monument MLP 8000
SLP 18000

   Reissue of "Roy Orbison's Greatest Hits" (Monument M/SM 4009/14009)

"In Dreams"   Monument MLP 8003
                                            SLP18003

   Tracks: "In Dreams"/"Lonely Wine"/"Shahdaroba"/"No One Will Ever Know"/"Sunset"/"House Without Windows"/"Dream"/"Blue Bayou"/"(They Call You) Gigolette"/"All I Have To Do Is Dream"/"Beautiful Dreamer"/"My Prayer"

1964

"Early Orbison"   Monument MLP 8023
                                            SLP 18023

   Tracks: "The Great Pretender"/"Cry"/"I Can't Stop Loving You"/"I'll Say It's My Fault"/"She Wears My Ring"/"Love Hurts"/"Bye Bye Love"/"Blue Avenue"/"Raindrops"/"Come Back To Me (My Love)"/"Summersong"/"Pretty One"

"More Of Roy Orbison's Greatest Hits"   Monument MLP 8024
                                            SLP 18024

   Tracks: "It's Over"/"Blue Bayou"/"Indian Wedding"/"Falling"/"Working For The Man"/"Pretty Paper"/"Mean Woman Blues"/"Lana"/"In Dreams"/"Leah"/"Borne On The Wind"/"What'd I Say"

1965

"Orbisongs"   Monument MLP 8035
                                            SLP 18035

   Tracks: "Oh, Pretty Woman"/"(Say) You're My Girl"/"Goodnight"/"Nightlife"/"Let The Good Times Roll"/"(I Get So) Sentimental"/"Yo Te Amo Maria"/"Wedding Day"/"Sleepy Hollow"/"22 Days"/"(I'd Be) A Legend In My Time"

"There Is Only One Roy Orbison"   MGM E 4308
                                            SE 4308

   Tracks: "Ride Away"/"You Fool You"/"Two Of A Kind"/"This Is Your Song"/"I'm In A Blue, Blue Mood"/"If You Can't Say Something Nice"/"Claudette"/"Afraid To Sleep"/"Sugar And Honey"/"Summer Love"/"Big As I Can Dream"/"Wondering"

1966

"The Very Best Of Roy Orbison"   Monument MLP 8045
                                            SLP 18045

   Tracks: "Only The Lonely"/"Crying"/"Running Scared"/"It's Over"/"Candy Man"/"Oh, Pretty Woman"/"Blue Angel"/"In Dreams"/"Dream Baby"/"Mean Woman Blues"

"The Orbison Way" MGM E 4322
SE 4322

Tracks: "Crawling Back"/ "It Ain't No Big Thing"/ "Time Changed Everything"/ "This Is My Land"/ "The Loner"/ "Maybe"/ "Breakin' Up Is Breakin' My Heart"/ "Go Away"/ "A New Star"/ "Never"/ "It Wasn't Very Long Ago"/ "Why Hurt The One Who Loves You"

"The Classic Roy Orbison" MGM E 4379
SE 4379

Tracks: "You'll Never Be Sixteen Again"/ "Pantomine"/ "Twinkle Toes"/ "Losing You"/ "City Life"/ "Wait"/ "Growing Up"/ "Where Is Tomorrow"/ "(No) I'll Never Get Over You"/ "Going Back To Gloria"/ "Just Another Name For Rock and Roll"/ "Never Love Again"

1967

"Roy Orbison Sings Don Gibson" MGM E 4424
SE 4424

Tracks: "(I'd Be) A Legend In My Time"/ "(Yes) I'm Hurting"/ "The Same Street"/ "Far Far Away"/ "Big Hearted Me"/ "Sweet Dreams"/ "Oh, Such A Stranger"/ "Blue, Blue Day"/ "What About Me"/ "Give Myself A Party"/ "Too Soon To Know"/ "Lonesome Number One"

"The Fastest Guitar Alive" (MGM Film
Soundtrack) MGM E 4475
SE 4475

Tracks: "Whirlwind"/ "Medicine Man"/ "River"/ "The Fastest Guitar Alive"/ "Rollin' On"/ "Pistolero"/ "Good Time Party"/ "Heading South"/ "Best Friend"/ "There Won't Be Many Coming Home"

"Cry Softly, Lonely One" MGM E 4514
SE 4514

Tracks: "She"/ "Communication Breakdown"/ "Cry Softly, Lonely One"/ "Girl Like Mine"/ "Just Let Me Make Believe"/ "Here Comes The Rain, Baby"/ "That's A No-No"/ "Memories"/ "Time To Cry"/ "Only Alive"

1969

"Roy Orbison's Many Moods" MGM SE 4636

Tracks: "Truly Truly True"/ "Unchained Melody"/ "I Recommend Her"/ "More"/ "Heartache"/ "Amy"/ "Good Morning Dear"/ "What Now My Love"/ "Walk On"/ "Yesterday's Child"/ "Try To Remember"

1970

"The Big O" (*) London HAU 8406
(with the Art Movement) SHU 8406

Tracks: "Break My Mind"/ "Help Me Rhonda"/ "Only You"/ "Down The Line"/ "Money"/ "When I Stop Dreaming"/ "Loving Touch"/ "Land Of A Thousand Dances"/ "Scarlet Ribbons"/ "She Won't Hang Her Love Out (On The Line)"/ "Casting My Spell On You"/ "Penny Arcade"

"The Great Songs Of Roy Orbison" MGM SE 4659
Tracks: "Breakin' Up Is Breakin' My Heart"/ "Cry Softly, Lonely One"/ "Penny Arcade"/ "Ride Away"/ "Southbound Jericho Parkway"/ "Crawling Back"/ "Heartache"/ "Too Soon To Know"/ "My Friend"/ "Here Comes The Rain, Baby"

"Hank Williams The Roy Orbison Way" MGM SE 4683
Tracks: "Kaw-liga"/ "Hey Good Lookin' "/ "Jambalaya"/ "I Heard You Crying In Your Sleep"/ "You Win Again"/ "Your Cheatin' Heart"/ "Cold, Cold Heart"/ "A Mansion On The Hill"/ "I Can't Help It (If I'm Still In Love With You)"/ "There'll Be No Teardrops Tonight"/ "I'm So Lonesome I Could Cry"

1972

"Roy Orbison Sings" MGM SE 4835
Tracks: "God Love You"/ "Beaujolais"/ "If Only For Awhile"/ "Rings of Gold"/ "Help Me"/ "Plain Jane Country (Come To Town)"/ "Harlem Woman"/ "Cheyenne"/ "Changes"/ "It Takes All Kinds Of People"/ "Remember The Good"

"Memphis" MGM SE 4867
Tracks: "Memphis, Tennessee"/"Why A Woman Cries"/"Run, Baby, Run (Back Into My Arms)"/"Take Care Of Your Woman"/ "I'm The Man On Susie's Mind"/ "I Can't Stop Loving You"/"Run The Engines Up High"/ "It Ain't No Big Thing (But It's Growing)"/ "I Fought The Law"/ "The Three Bells"/"Danny Boy"

"The All-Time Greatest Hits Of Roy Orbison" Monument MP 8600
Tracks: "Only The Lonely"/"Leah"/"In Dreams"/"Uptown"/"It's Over"/ "Crying"/ "Dream Baby"/ "Blue Angel"/ "Working For The Man"/ "Candy Man"/ "Running Scared"/ "Falling"/ "Love Hurts"/ "Shahadaroba"/ "I'm Hurtin' "/ "Mean Woman Blues"/ "Pretty Paper"/ "The Crowd"/ "Blue Bayou"/ "Oh, Pretty Woman"

1973

"Milestones" MGM SE 4934
Tracks: "I Wanna Live"/ "You Don't Know Me"/ "California Sunshine Girl"/"Words"/"Blue Rain (Coming Down)"/"Drift Away"/"You Lay So Easy On My Mind"/ "The World You Live In"/ "Sweet Caroline"/ "I've Been Loving You Too Long (To Stop Now)"/ "The Morning After"

1975

"I'm Still In Love With You" Mercury SRM1-1045
Tracks: "Pledging My Love"/ "Spanish Nights"/ "Rainbow Love"/ "It's Lonely"/ "Heartache"/ "Crying Time"/ "Still"/ "Hung Up On You"/ "Circle"/ "Sweet Mama Blue"/ "All I Need Is Time"

1977

"Regeneration"   Monument MG 7600
   Tracks: "(I'm A) Southern Man"/ "No Chain At All"/ "Old Love Song"/
   "Can't Wait"/ "Born To Love Me"/ "Blues In My Mind"/ "Something
   They Can't Take Away"/ "Under Suspicion"/ "I Don't Really Want You"/
   "Belinda"

1979

"Laminar Flow"   Asylum 6E 198
   Tracks: Easy Way Out"/ "Love Is A Cold Wind"/ "Lay It Down"/ "I Care"/
   "We're Into Something Good"/ "Movin'"/ "Poor Baby"/ "Warm Spot
   Hot"/ "Tears"/ "Friday Night"/ "Hound Dog Man"

1986

"Class of '55   America/Smash
"(with Johnny Cash, Carl Perkins, and Jerry Lee
   Lewis)   830 002-1 M-1
   Tracks: "Birth Of Rock And Roll"/ "Sixteen Candles"/ "Class Of '55"/
   "Waymore's Blues"/ "We Remember The King"/ "Coming Home"/ "Rock
   And Roll (Fais Do Do)"/ "Keep My Motor Running"/ "I Will Rock And
   Roll For You"/ "Big Train (From Memphis)".

"Interviews From The Class Of '55 Recording
   Sessions (September 16-21, 1985)"   America AR-LP-1001
Interviews with Sam Phillips, Carl Perkins, Johnny
   Cash, Roy Orbison, Jerry Lee Lewis, Rick
   Nelson, and Chips Moman.
Available through mail-order only.

1987

"In Dreams: The Greatest Hits"   Virgin 90604-1
   Tracks: "Only The Lonely"/ "Leah"/ "In Dreams"/ "Uptown"/ "It's Over"/
   "Crying"/ "Dream Baby"/ "Blue Angel"/ "Working For The Man"/
   "Candy Man"/ "Running Scared"/ "Falling"/ "I'm Hurtin'"/ "Claudette"/
   "Oh, Pretty Woman"/ "Mean Woman Blues"/ "Ooby Dooby"/ "Lana"/
   "Blue Bayou"
   NOTE: These are 1985 re-recordings of the original versions, with the
   exception of "In Dreams" (recorded 1987).

1988

"For The Lonely: A Roy Orbison Anthology,
   1956-1965"   Rhino R1 71493
   Tracks: "Ooby Dooby"/ "Go! Go! Go!"/ "Rockhouse"/ "Devil Doll"/
   "Uptown"/ "I'm Hurtin'"/ "Only The Lonely"/ "Blue Angel"/ "Crying"/

"Candy Man"/"The Crowd"/"Dream Baby"/"Running Scared"/"Leah"/ "Working For The Man"/"In Dreams"/"Falling"/"Mean Woman Blues"/ "Oh, Pretty Woman"/"Blue Bayou"/"Pretty Paper"/"It's Over"/"(Say) You're My Girl"/"Goodnight"

"Traveling Wilburys, Volume One"   Wilbury 9 25796-1
(with George Harrison, Jeff Lynne, Tom Petty, and
  Bob Dylan)
    Tracks: "Handle With Care"/"Dirty World"/"Rattled"/"Last Night"/ "Not Alone Any More"/"Congratulations"/"Heading For The Light"/ "Margarita"/"Tweeter And The Monkey Man"/"End Of The Line"

1989

"Mystery Girl"   Virgin 7 91058-1
    Tracks: "You Got It"/"In The Real World"/"(All I Can Do Is) Dream You"/"A Love So Beautiful"/"California Blue"/"She's A Mystery To Me"/"The Comedians"/"The Only One"/"Windsurfer"/"Careless Heart"

"Our Love Song"   CBS AK 45113
    Tracks: "Born To Love Me"/"(I Get So) Sentimental"/"Evergreen"/ "Mama"/"Indian Wedding"/"Yo Te Amo Maria"/"Sleepy Hollow"/ "Love Star"/"Borne On The Wind"/"Old Love Song"/"Goodnight"/ "(Say) You're My Girl"

"Best-Loved Standards"   CBS AK 45114
    Tracks: "I Can't Stop Loving You"/"Distant Drums"/"No One Will Ever Know"/"Beautiful Dreamer"/"The Great Pretender"/"Let The Good Times Roll"/"Bye Bye Love"/"Dream"/"(I'd Be) A Legend In My Time"/"All I Have To Do Is Dream"/"Cry"/"What'd I Say"
"Rare Orbison"   CBS AK 45115
    Tracks: "The Actress"/"Paper Boy"/"With The Bug"/"Today's Tear-drops"/"Here Comes That Song Again"/"Only With you"/"Pretty One"/ "No Chain At All"/"Blues In My Mind"/"Drifting Away"/"Wings Of Glory" (unreleased)/"Belinda"

"The Singles Collection 1965-1973"   Polydor 839-234-1
    Tracks: "Ride Away"/"Crawling Back"/"Breakin' Up Is Breakin' My Heart"/"Twinkle Toes"/"Too Soon To Know"/"Communication Break-down"/"So Good"/"Cry Softly, Lonely One"/"She"/"Born To Be Loved By You"/"Walk On"/"Heartache"/"Southbound Jericho Parkway"/ "Penny Arcade"/"She Cheats On Me"/"So Young"/"(Love Me Like You Did) Last Night"/"God Love You"/"Remember The Good"/"Memphis, Tennessee"/"Blue Rain (Coming Down)"/"I Wanna Live"

"The Classic Roy Orbison (1965-1968)   Rhino R1 70711
 Tracks: "Ride Away"/ "Crawling Back"/ "Breakin' Up Is Breakin' My
 Heart"/ "Twinkle Toes"/ "Too Soon To Know"/ "Communication Break-
 down"/ "Cry Softly, Lonely One"/ "Claudette"/ "I'm In a Blue, Blue
 Mood"/ "Losing You"/ "Big As I Can Dream"/ "Pantomime"/ "You Fool
 You"(#)/ "It Takes One (To Know One)"/ "A New Star"(#)/ "Here Comes
 The Rain Baby"(#)/ "She"(#)/ "Walk On"
(#)—Included on CD only.

"Rare Orbison II"   CBS AK 45404
 Tracks: "Party Heart" (unreleased)/ "How Are Things In Paradise"
 (unreleased)/ "Darkness" (unreleased)/ "Yes" (unreleased)/ "Double Date"
 (unreleased)/ "Mama" (in German)/ "San Fernando" (in German)/
 "Zigzag"/ "Tired Old Country Song" (unreleased)/ "Mother"
 (unreleased)/ "Boogie Baby" (unreleased)/ "Indian Summer" (with Larry
 Gatlin and the Gatlin Brothers)

"The Sun Years"   Rhino R1 70916
 Tracks: "Ooby Dooby"/ "Claudette"/ "This Kind Of Love"/ "You're
 Gonna Cry"/ "Sweet And Easy To Love"/ "Mean Little Mama"/ "Trying
 To Get To You"/ "Go! Go! Go!"/ "Domino"/ "Devil Doll"/ "Fools Hall Of
 Fame"/ "Chicken Hearted"/ "You're My Baby"/ "Rock House"/ "It's Too
 Late"(#)/ "The Cause Of It All"(#)/ "I Give Up"(#)/ "I Never Knew"(#)/
 "I Like Love"(#)/ "A True Love Goodbye"(#)
(#)—Included on CD only.

"A Black And White Night Live"   Virgin 91295-2
 Tracks: "Only The Lonely"/ "In Dreams"/ "Dream Baby"/ "Leah"/ "Move
 On Down The Line"/ "Crying"/ "Mean Woman Blues"/ "Running
 Scared"/ "Blue Bayou"(%)/ "Candy Man"/ "Uptown"/ "Ooby Dooby"/
 "The Comedians"/ "(All I Can Do Is) Dream You"/ "It's Over"/ "Oh,
 Pretty Woman"
(%)—Not included in telecast.

(*)—This was released in the U.K. only.

MISCELLANEOUS RECORDINGS:

33¹/₃ R.P.M.

"Special Delivery From Bobby Bare, Joey Powers,
 and Roy Orbison"   RCA Camden CAL
                                              820
 Roy tracks: "Almost Eighteen"/ "Seems To Me"/ "Jolie"

"Demand Performances" (Various Artists)   Monument MLP 8010
                                            SLP 8010
  Roy tracks: "Love Hurts" (alternate take)/ "Uptown"/ "I Can't Stop
  Loving You"

"Zigzag" (Film Soundtrack; Various Artists)   MGM 1SE-21ST
Roy track: "Zigzag"

"Roadie" (Film Soundtrack; Various Artists)   Warner Brothers 2HS
                                                3441
  Roy track: "That Lovin' You Feelin' Again" (Duet with Emmylou Harris)

"Hiding Out" (Film Soundtrack; Various Artists)   Virgin 7 90661-1
  Roy track: "Crying" (Duet with k.d. lang)

"Less Than Zero" (Film Soundtrack; Various
  Artists   Def Jam/Columbia
                                                SC 44042
  Roy track: "Life Fades Away"

"My Spell On You"   WAA 8211
  Reissue of "The Big O" (London HAU/SHU 8406) LP, without "She
  Won't Hang Her Love Out On The Line" and "Penny Arcade"

"The Big O—The World's Best Singer" (Import)   Do it 002
  Various live recordings and rare singles

"The Big O Live In Birmingham, Alabama"
  (Import)   Do it 003
  Live 1980 concert recording

The following albums are 1970's fan-club releases:
"Roy Orbison Returns"   Big O 001
"The Connoisseur's Roy Orbison, Vol. 1"   Texan Star 001
"The Other Side Of Roy Orbison"   Texan Star 002
"The Connoisseur's Roy Orbison, Vol. 2"   Texan Star 003
"Big O Live at the SNCO"   SLP 001

45 R.P.M.
"MGM Celebrity Scene"   MGM CS 9-5
  Box set containing five promotional singles:
  "Ride Away"/ "Crawling Back"   MGM K 13756
  "Breakin' Up Is Breakin' My Heart"/"Too Soon
    To Know"   MGM K 13757
  "Communication Breakdown"/ "Twinkle Toes"   MGM K 13758
  "Going Back To Gloria"/ "Sweet Dreams"   MGM K 13759

"You'll Never Be Sixteen Again"/"There Won't Be
    Many Coming Home"   MGM K 13760
Also included: Cue Sheet/Biography/Jukebox Title Strips.

Roy also provided backing vocals for the following songs:

"So Long, Good Luck and Goodbye" (Weldon Rogers; Imperial 5451)
"You've Got Love" (Johnny "Peanuts" Wilson; U.S. Brunswick 9-55039)
"I Was A Fool" (Ken Cook; Phillips Int'l 3534)
"Find My Baby For Me" (Sonny Burgess; Sun Records)
"I'm In A Blue, Blue Mood" (Conway Twitty; MGM K 13011)
"I Belong To Him" (Jessi Colter; Capitol 4472)
"Leah" (Bertie Higgins; Columbia FZ 38587)
"Beyond The End" (Jimmy Buffett; MCA 5600)
"Zombie Zoo" (Tom Petty; MCA 6253)

ROY-RELATED PROJECTS:

LP's:

"The Sunset Strings Play The Roy Orbison
    Songbook"   Liberty LRP-3395
"Goodtime Party" (Bob Moore and his Orchestra)   Hickory LP 140

Index